Systemic Functional Linguistics and Translation Studies

Bloomsbury Advances in Translation Series

Series Editor
Jeremy Munday, Centre for Translation Studies, University of Leeds, UK

Bloomsbury Advances in Translation publishes cutting-edge research in the field of translation studies. This field has grown in importance in the modern, globalized world, with international translation between languages a daily occurrence. Research into the practices, processes and theory of translation is essential, and this series aims to showcase the best in international academic and professional output.

A full list of titles in the series can be found at:
www.bloomsbury.com/series/bloomsbury-advances-in-translation

Recent titles in the series include

Celebrity Translation in British Theatre
Robert Stock
Collaborative Translation
Edited by Anthony Cordingley and Céline Frigau Manning
Genetic Translation Studies
Edited by Ariadne Nunes, Joana Moura and Marta Pacheco Pinto
Institutional Translation for International Governance
Fernando Prieto Ramos
Intercultural Crisis Communication
Edited by Federico M. Federici and Christophe Declercq
Sociologies of Poetry Translation
Edited by Jacob Blakesley
Telling the Story of Translation
Judith Woodsworth
The Pragmatic Translator
Massimiliano Morini
Translating Holocaust Lives
Edited by Jean Boase-Beier, Peter Davies, Andrea Hammel and Marion Winters
Translating in Town
Edited by Lieven D'hulst and Kaisa Koskinen
Translation Solutions for Many Languages
Anthony Pym

Systemic Functional Linguistics and Translation Studies

Edited by
Mira Kim, Jeremy Munday,
Zhenhua Wang and Pin Wang

BLOOMSBURY ACADEMIC
LONDON • NEW YORK • OXFORD • NEW DELHI • SYDNEY

BLOOMSBURY ACADEMIC
Bloomsbury Publishing Plc
50 Bedford Square, London, WC1B 3DP, UK
1385 Broadway, New York, NY 10018, USA
29 Earlsfort Terrace, Dublin 2, Ireland

BLOOMSBURY, BLOOMSBURY ACADEMIC and the Diana logo are trademarks of
Bloomsbury Publishing Plc

First published in Great Britain 2021

Cover design: Ben Anslow

A catalogue record for this book is available from the British Library.

Library of Congress Cataloging-in-Publication Data
Names: Kim, Mira, (Professor of translation studies) editor. | Munday, Jeremy, editor. | Wang,
Zhenhua (Linguistics teacher) editor. | Wang, Pin (Lecturer in languages) editor.
Title: Systemic functional linguistics and translation studies / edited by
Mira Kim, Jeremy Munday, Zhenhua Wang, and Pin Wang.
Description: London ; New York : Bloomsbury Academic, 2021. |
Series: Bloomsbury advances in translation | Based on a symposium and workshop held at
the University of New South Wales, Sydney, Australia, in November 2016, and at a subsequent
conference in 2017 at the Martin Centre for Appliable Linguistics at Shanghai Jiao Tong
University in China. | Includes bibliographical references and index. |
Identifiers: LCCN 2020054779 (print) | LCCN 2020054780 (ebook) |
ISBN 9781350091863 (hardback) | ISBN 9781350091870 (ebook) |
ISBN 9781350091887 (epub)
Subjects: LCSH: Functionalism (Linguistics)–Congresses. | Translating and
interpreting–Congresses. | Translating and interpreting–Evaluation–Congresses. |
Systemic grammar–Congresses.
Classification: LCC P306.97.F86 S97 2021 (print) | LCC P306.97.F86 (ebook) |
DDC 415.01/81–dc23
LC record available at https://lccn.loc.gov/2020054779
LC ebook record available at https://lccn.loc.gov/2020054780

ISBN: HB: 978-1-3500-9186-3
ePDF: 978-1-3500-9187-0
eBook: 978-1-3500-9188-7

Series: Bloomsbury Advances in Translation

Typeset by Newgen KnowledgeWorks Pvt. Ltd., Chennai, India

To find out more about our authors and books visit www.bloomsbury.com
and sign up for our newsletters.

Contents

Figures

Tables

Contributors

Komail Al Herz is an Assistant Professor of Translation Studies at King Faisal University, Saudi Arabia. His research interests focus on literary translation, multimodality, functional linguistics and narratology. He has published a number of literary translations into Arabic and critical articles in literary magazines.

Sami Jameel Althumali is an Assistant Professor of Translation Studies and Systemic Functional Linguistics at the Department of English of Taif University, Turabah Campus, Saudi Arabia. He is the chairperson since 2017. He is a fellow of the UK Higher Education Academy. He earned his PhD in Translation Studies from Centre for Translation Studies, University of Leeds, in 2016. Since then, he has been teaching translation theories, translation technologies, consecutive and simultaneous interpreting and discourse analysis for undergraduate and postgraduate students. His research spans several areas including descriptive and applied TS, SFL, social semiotics, discourse analysis and corpus linguistics.

Giacomo Figueredo is a Senior Lecturer in Translation and Linguistics at Federal University of Ouro Preto, Brazil. His research interests include systemic theory, language description, multilingual studies, language typology and translation. His research has been on language description and multilingual text production, focusing on exact descriptions of systemic probability and dynamics across text types in different languages.

Mira Kim is an Associate Professor in the School of Humanities and Languages at UNSW Sydney. Her research interests focus on translator education, text analysis for translation, systemic functional typology, personalized learning, learner autonomy and international students in higher education. Currently she is working on *Korean Grammar: A Systemic Functional Approach* together with three co-authors.

Ekaterina Lapshinova-Koltunski is a Senior Lecturer at the Department of Language Science and Technology of Saarland University, where she has been involved in translator training and has worked in various projects involving English German translation. She has contributed to the collection, compilation, annotation and analyses of various (translation) corpora, including a corpus of student translations. Her main research interests lie in linguistic phenomena in multilingual texts, including translation (both human and machine), and she has published numerous studies in this area. Her most recent contribution in this area is the chapter entitled 'Exploring Linguistic Differences between Novice and Professional Translators with Text Classification Methods' in the volume *New Empirical Perspectives on Translation and Interpreting* (2020) edited by L. Vandevoorde, J. Daems and B. Defrancq.

Long Li is a Lecturer in Translation Studies at the University of New South Wales (UNSW Sydney). His research interests include Systemic Functional Linguistics (SFL), multimodality, typological differences between English and Chinese, the influence of political ideology in the translations of politically controversial English works by Chinese migrant writers and, more recently, English language proficiency amongst international students. His most recent publication is 'Who "Let All This Happen"? – Shifts of Responsibilities in Representing the Cultural Revolution in Jung Chang's *Wild Swans*' (2020).

Xueying Li is a Lecturer at the School of Foreign Languages and Literature, Hangzhou Dianzi University, China. She earned her PhD from the Faculty of Arts and Social Sciences, University of New South Wales, Australia in 2019. Her research interests focus on translation studies (TS), Systemic Functional Linguistics (SFL) and Legitimation Code Theory (LCT).

J. R. Martin is a Professor of Linguistics at the University of Sydney, where he is also the Deputy Director of the LCT Centre for Knowledge-Building. His research interests include systemic theory, functional grammar, discourse semantics, register, genre, multimodality and critical discourse analysis, focusing on English, Tagálog, Korean and Spanish – with special reference to the transdisciplinary fields of clinical linguistics, educational linguistics, forensic linguistics and social semiotics. Recent publications include a book on Youth Justice Conferencing (*Discourse and Diversionary Justice*, 2018) with Michele Zappavigna and a special issue of *Functions of Language* (2018) focusing on interpersonal grammar.

Jeremy Munday is a Professor of Translation Studies at the University of Leeds. His specialisms are linguistic translation theories, discourse analysis (including Systemic Functional Linguistics), ideology and translation and Latin American literature in translation. He is the author of *Introducing Translation Studies* (4th edition, 2016) and *Evaluation in Translation* (2012).

Stella Neumann is a Professor of English Linguistics at RWTH Aachen University, Germany. Her research interests focus on how variation shapes language, in particular, register variation across languages and varieties and the empirical modelling of translation through corpus-linguistic and experimental methods, drawing on functional language theory. Her publications include a book on corpus-based translation research (*Cross-Linguistic Corpora for the Study of Translations*, 2012) together with Silvia Hansen-Schirra and Erich Steiner and a monograph on register (*Contrastive Register Variation*, 2013). Most recently, she contributed a paper on translation research to the Abralin ao Vivo – Linguists Online series (https://aovivo. abralin.org/en/lives/stella-neumann-2/).

Beatriz Quiroz is an Associate Professor in Language Sciences at the Faculty of Letters of the Pontificia Universidad Católica de Chile, where she teaches and supervises undergraduate and postgraduate students in linguistics. Her research interests include systemic functional language description, with a special focus on Spanish grammar, and the various interactions between grammar and discourse. She is co-editor of the book *Interpersonal Grammar: Systemic Functional Linguistic Theory and Description* (2021) and co-author of the book *Systemic Functional Grammar: Another Step into the Theory – Grammatical Description* (2021).

Erich Steiner is a Chair Professor (now in retirement) at Department of Language Science and Technology Saarland University. His research interests focus on functional empirical linguistics and translation, where he has been involved in a number of research projects. Book publications include *A Functional Perspective on Language, Action and Interpretation* (1991), *Exploring Translation and Multilingual Text Production* (co-edited, 2001), *Translated Texts: Properties, Variants, Evaluations* (2004) and *Cross-linguistic Corpora for the Study of Translations. Insights from the Language Pair English–German* (2012, jointly with colleagues). He is currently involved in a book project on *Cohesion in English and German*.

Pin Wang is a lecturer at the Martin Centre for Appliable Linguistics, Shanghai Jiao Tong University, China. His chief research interests are: Systemic Functional Grammar and Functional Language Typology, with particular focus on Mandarin and minority languages of China. His recent publications include: *Complementarity Between Lexis and Grammar in the System of Person: A Systemic Typological Approach* (2017), 'Verbal groups in Manchu' (*WORD*, 2018), and 'Axial argumentation and cryptogrammar in interpersonal grammar: a case study of Classical Tibetan mood' (In J. R. Martin, Y. J. Doran and G. Figueredo (eds), *Systemic Functional Language Description: Making Meaning Matter*, 2020).

Zhenhua Wang is a full professor of linguistics at Shanghai Jiao Tong University, China, and the founder of the Martin Centre for Appliable Linguistics. His research interests focus on systemic functional linguistics, appraisal, discourse semantics, language and the law, and Chinese courtroom discourse. Recently he has published two books: *Discourse as System: Discourse Semantic Perspective* (2019), and *On Lagal Language: Discourse Semantic Perspective* (2020).

Introduction

Mira Kim
UNSW Sydney
Jeremy Munday
University of Leeds
Zhenhua Wang
Shanghai Jiao Tong University
and
Pin Wang
Shanghai Jiao Tong University

The idea for this volume originated in the third Roundtable on Translation and Discourse Analysis, a symposium and workshop held at the University of New South Wales, Sydney, Australia, in November 2016, and was thereafter consolidated at a subsequent conference in July 2017 at the Martin Centre for Appliable Linguistics at Shanghai Jiao Tong University in China. Both events fitted into a series of international round-tables and conference panels on 'Discourse Analysis and Translation' over the past ten years which have supported a growing body of researchers in Systemic Functional Linguistics (SFL) and Translation Studies (TS) as they opened space for dialogue and collaboration in the building of knowledge and new research agendas. This edited volume celebrates these endeavours. It brings together leading and emerging scholars in SFL and TS whose contributions foreground key issues and challenges and collectively address both general and specific ways in which the interests of both fields intersect.

SFL theory offers an appliable model for text analysis which has informed the work of TS scholars in a diversity of contexts as evidenced in this volume. The contributions vary with respect to foci. They may work from SFL theory to model applications in TS, or from TS concerns and concepts to seek relevant insights from SFL theory. Variations in SFL modelling of language are discussed and deployed. For example, some chapters attend primarily to the stratum of lexicogrammar while others incorporate attention to the stratum of discourse semantics and beyond to register variables of field, tenor and mode. In some cases specific linguistic systems are explored, for example, the grammatical system of TENSE, or the discourse semantic systems of APPRAISAL or CONNEXION. Studies are also informed by a range of methodologies and a diversity of data and source and target languages.

While the volume foregrounds the value of working in the intersecting spaces of SFL and TS, the challenges of doing so are also acknowledged. Although the importing of models from other disciplines and moulding them to new purposes is not new to TS, the technicality of SFL theory may present challenges at times, challenges that need to be weighed against the potential insights offered in the analysis of meanings in source texts.

A second critical issue is that of the languages in focus in given TS and the availability of systemic functional models of those languages, including systems at both the lexicogrammatical (e.g. Halliday 1994) and discourse semantic levels (e.g. Martin 1992; Martin and Rose 2007). It is of course essential that the SFL modelling of English is not assumed in the exploration of texts in other languages. Fortunately, this is currently an active front in SFL language typology studies (e.g. Caffarel, Martin and Matthiessen 2004; Martin and Doran 2015; Mwinlaaru and Xuan 2016; Martin 2018; Martin, Doran and Figueredo 2020; Martin, Quiroz and Figueredo 2021; Martin et al. 2021).

The first and last chapters (Chapter 1 and Chapter 10) bookend the volume with current and evolving SFL theoretical accounts of the modelling of relations between languages – a fundamental issue in the fields of language typology and TS. Within this framing the chapters move from primarily addressing theoretical concepts in both SFL and TS to a stronger focus on practical applications.

Chapter 1 by J. R. Martin and Beatriz Quiroz explains and illustrates SFL modelling of multilingual similarity and difference as outlined in Matthiessen (2018) and discusses its relevance to the fundamental concern with *equivalence* in TS. Similarity and difference are modelled as a cline that operates along multiple dimensions of hierarchy and delicacy in the theoretical architecture of SFL. Ascendancy along these dimensions (e.g. stratally from lexicogrammar to discourse semantics; axially from structural realizations to their systems and in rank from smaller to larger message units) maps a trajectory from more different to more similar. Translation or interpretation from source to target text tracks this ascendency to access source language systems with increasing similarity to target language systems – a process that the authors refer to as *distantiation*. After de Souza (2010), the translated target text is a *re-instantiation*. The authors model this activity by focussing on the systems of TENSE in Chilean Spanish and English and through a detailed comparative analysis of a set of bidirectionally translated short texts.

In Chapter 2, Erich Steiner examines the concept of 'reading' in SFL, as it is modelled in Martin and White (2005: 206), and explores its relevance to the activity of translation. The author elaborates on the key concept of instantiation introduced in Chapter 1. This is modelled as a cline of the meaning potential of a language from its most generalized level (the system as a whole) through progressive constraints with respect to genres, registers and text types to specific instances of text, and then finally readings of that text – what the author refers to as the ultimate instance of text. The author then engages in a detailed consideration of the relevance of the concept of reading in TS; in particular, in terms of the role of the translator and the concept of translator agency. He explores the readings of a specific English language text in its pre-translation phase and incorporates analysis of the role of the translator and of 'translational agency'. The process gives rise to questions directed both at aspects of the linguistic theory and the conceptualization of the concepts of equivalence in TS.

In Chapter 3, Stella Neumann foregrounds Halliday's conceptualization of register in SFL and its relevance to the consideration of text types in TS. The author notes that in contrast to earlier work on types of text, the SFL construct of register offers a stronger theoretical foundation that has informed analyses of context in source texts and in the comparison of source and target texts (e.g. House 1997, 2015). The core concern of the chapter is how registers vary cross-linguistically and cross-culturally and how corpus-based methodologies in TS are deployed to identify lexicogrammatical shifts in translation equivalents that point to cross-cultural register variation.

In Chapter 4, Jeremy Munday critically discusses opportunities for a dialogue between theories in SFL and TS. The author attends specifically to a shared interest in interpersonal meaning related to questions of subjectivity and stance and how the SFL system of APPRAISAL which models this in discourse has been taken up within TS. The author looks to ways in which the elaborated linguistic system might be refined to foreground dimensions most relevant to the practice of translation. Particular attention is paid to the appraisal system of graduation and the potential to adjust the intensity of evaluative meanings in translation. Throughout the chapter the discussion in grounded in illustrative instances.

The interplay between corpus-based TS and SFL informs Chapter 5 by Ekaterina Lapshinova-Koltunski. Corpus-based methodologies have greatly influenced both SFL and TS by providing access to, and permitting analysis of, large databases of texts. In this chapter the author interrogates the theoretical underpinnings and practical implementations of these empirical methodologies. The chapter constitutes an instance of the integration of the theoretical and practical interests that characterize the book as a whole.

From this point a series of chapters focuses on applications of SFL systems in different translation scenarios towards a systematic understanding of source texts and comparison with and between target texts. These include analyses of existing translations within a Descriptive Translation Studies framework (e.g. Toury 2012) and applications in translator training.

In Chapter 6, Xueying Li and Mira Kim explore the nature of translation as a decision-making process in a comparative study of four different English translations of Cao Xueqin's Chinese novel *Hong Lou Meng* (*Dream of the Red Chamber*). The study focuses on the ideational metafunction of language and more specifically on expressions of logical meaning through which experiences are linked to one another. The authors take a discourse semantics perspective deploying the system of CONNEXION (Hao 2020) in analysing translation shifts. They attend in particular to the two subsystems: EXPLICITNESS (i.e. explicit or implicit realization) and TYPE (i.e. addition, comparison, time, consequence). A grounded approach based on the close analysis of translated texts enables the authors to build a system network of translation choices and a basis for comparative claims, all of which are exemplified for the reader.

Komail Al Herz, in Chapter 7, draws on SFL to evaluate shifts in translation in interpersonal meaning expressed through modality and the effect this has on narrative point of view, that is, the angle from which the story is relayed. The data constitute the Arabic translation of J. M. Coetzee's *Waiting for the Barbarians*. The approach adopted in the chapter builds on the seminal work of Simpson (1993), whose model of analysis links lexicogrammatical choices to the impact these have on the macro-level narration. Given that such shifts in translation may not be systematic, the author speaks of a 'blurring' of psychological point of view rather than wholesale upheaval or distortion. The chapter offers a descriptive study of existing translated products and a model for trainee translators in using tools of SFL to analyse source texts and identify marked or problematic features.

In Chapter, 8 Sami Jameel Althumali focuses on the potential contribution that knowledge of SFL concepts and metalanguage might make to tertiary-level translator training, a field of practice that is under-researched. The chapter reports on an experimental study conducted with a class of translation students in which a control group and an experimental group both take an existing module in English-to-Arabic translation, while the experimental group additionally takes a 20-hr SFL-based training course. The author provides a detailed account of the research design, assessment processes including pre- and post-exams and results and reports on findings that suggest greater improvement in the experimental group, with cautionary notes on the limitations of the study, and suggestions for a continuing research agenda.

Chapter 9 by Long Li identifies an innovative front of work in SFL and TS which takes account of paratextual features in translations. The author takes a social-semiotic multimodal approach to multimodality to analyse and compare both verbal and visual elements in a descriptive study of book covers in translations of *Wild Swans* by Jung Chang. The analysis of visual elements draws on Kress and van Leeuwen's visual grammar (2006). The chapter will doubtless encourage ongoing work in this field.

In the final chapter (10), Giacomo Figueredo re-sharpens the focus on SFL theory and its relevance to multilingual studies in language comparison, typology and translation studies. The chapter tackles issues of the impossibility of direct comparisons of languages and the intrinsic complexity of language translation. The SFL model proposed here for addressing the issue in multilingual studies centres on the Saussurean concept of valeur which underpins the fundamental principle that 'all languages are meaning-making resources organized as a system'. As the author explains in detail, the amount of valeur in any system (in any language) can be quantified and this can constitute a basis for comparison. The model is exemplified in a case study of interpersonal language relations in Brazilian Portuguese and English.

Note

The co-editors wish to thank all authors for their valuable contributions towards a multifaceted picture of the potential in working at the interface of systemic functional linguistics and translation studies, and for pointing to directions for future collaboration and research.

References

Caffarel, A., Martin, J. R. and Matthiessen, C. M. I. M. (eds) (2004), *Language Typology: A Functional Perspective*, Amsterdam: John Benjamins.

de Souza, L. M. F. (2010), *Interlingual Re-instantiation: A Model for a New and More Comprehensive Systemic Functional Perspective on Translation*, PhD Thesis, Federal University of Santa Catarina, Florianopolis.

Halliday, M. A. K. (1994), *Introduction to Functional Grammar*, 2nd edn, London: Arnold.

Hao, J. (2020), *Analysing Scientific Discourse from a Systemic Functional Linguistic Perspective: A Framework for Exploring Knowledge Building in Biology*, London: Routledge.

House, J. (1997), *Translation Quality Assessment: A Model Revisited*, Tübingen: G. Narr.

House, J. (2015), *Translation Quality Assessment: Past and Present*, Abingdon: Routledge.

Kress, G., and van Leeuwen, T. (2006), *Reading Images: The Grammar of Visual Design,* 2nd edn, London: Routledge.

Martin, J. R. (1992), *English Text: System and Structure*, Amsterdam: John Benjamins.

Martin, J. R. (ed.) (2018), 'Interpersonal Meaning: Systemic Functional Perspectives', Special issue of *Functions of Language* 25 (1): 2–19.

Martin, J. R., and Doran, Y. J. (eds) (2015), *Grammatical Descriptions*, London: Routledge, vol. 2.

Martin, J. R., Doran, Y. J. and Figueredo, G. (eds) (2020), *Systemic Functional Language Description: Making Meaning Matter*, London: Routledge.

Martin, J. R., Quiroz, B. and Figueredo, G. (eds) (2021), *Interpersonal Grammar: Systemic Functional Linguistic Theory and Description*, Cambridge: Cambridge University Press.

Martin, J. R., Quiroz, B., Wang, P. and Zhu, Y. (2021), *Systemic Functional Grammar: Another Step into the Theory – Grammatical Description*, Beijing: Higher Education Press.

Martin, J. R., and Rose, D. (2007), *Working with Discourse: Meaning beyond the Clause*, 2nd edn, London: Continuum.

Martin, J. R., and White, P. (2005), *The Language of Evaluation: Appraisal in English*, Houndmills: Palgrave Macmillan.

Matthiessen, C. M. I. M. (2018), 'The Notion of a Multilingual Meaning Potential: A Systemic Exploration', in A. S. Baklouti and L. Fontaine (eds), *Perspectives from Systemic Functional Linguistics*, 90–120, London: Routledge.

Mwinlaaru, I., and Xuan, W. W. (2016), 'A Survey of Studies in Systemic Functional Language Description and Typology', *Functional Linguistics* 3 (8): 1–41.

Simpson, P. (1993), *Language, Ideology and Point of View*, London: Routledge.

Toury, G. (2012), *Descriptive Translation Studies: And Beyond*, 2nd edn, Amsterdam: John Benjamins.

1

Functional language typology: Systemic Functional Linguistic perspectives

J. R. Martin
University of Sydney; Shanghai Jiao Tong University; Pontificia Universidad Católica de Chile
Beatriz Quiroz
Pontificia Universidad Católica de Chile

1 Language description

Although regularly cited in relation to its descriptions of English (e.g. Halliday 1985 and subsequent editions, Martin 1992), Systemic Functional Linguistics (hereafter SFL) has in fact inspired work on a wide range of languages throughout its history. Martin and Doran (2015) present a representative selection of foundational work; and the field as a whole is ably surveyed in Mwinlaaru and Xuan (2016). The current research takes Caffarel, Martin and Matthiessen (2004) as a key point of reference, especially its culminative survey of descriptive motifs and generalizations by Matthiessen (2004). Various publications (e.g. Martin 2018, Martin, Doran and Figueredo 2020, Martin, Quiroz and Figueredo 2021, Martin, Quiroz and Wang 2021) reflect this wide-ranging concern with the grammar of different languages. And Matthiessen (2014, 2018) relates this work to Translation Studies (hereafter TS) and the field of multilingual language studies in general.

In this chapter we draw particularly on an early draft of Matthiessen (2018) in which he outlines a model of multilingual similarity and difference across various dimensions of SFL theory and description. In order to focus the discussion we concentrate on the verbal group in two languages – English and Spanish[1] – zeroing in on their systems of TENSE in particular. Drawing on just a few texts for illustrative purposes, we will show how Matthiessen's model can be used to compare and contrast the English and Spanish TENSE systems and discuss some implications of this analysis for TS. For relevant work from an SFL perspective on TENSE in French, see Caffarel (1992); Wang (2018) develops an SFL description of TENSE in relation to other verbal group systems in Manchu.

2 The discourse function of TENSE systems

Over the decades since Catford's (1965) classic *A Linguistic Theory of Translation*, based on the birthing phase of SFL (essentially Halliday 1961), a number of major theoretical developments have taken place, which bear critically on research in the field of TS. A synoptic account of the contemporary model is presented in Matthiessen and Halliday (2009); and Martin (2016) reviews key aspects of its development. Here we assume the general model surveyed in Martin (2010), including the hierarchies of stratification, instantiation and individuation. More specifically we will assume a model founded on axial relations (system and structure), which bundles these relations in terms of rank, strata and metafunction. As far as metafunction is concerned, we will concentrate on ideational meaning – logical meaning in particular – which we circumscribe as involving all and only recursive systems realized by serial structures (Halliday 1979; Martin 1996). Of these we focus on TENSE in English and Spanish. This means that we are concerned with systems that position figures in relation to the moment of speaking (PRIMARY TENSE) and then potentially relocate those same figures relative to that positioning (SECONDARY TENSE).[2] With reference to Gleason's (1968) model of discourse, PRIMARY TENSE is involved in the realization of the discourse semantics of setting in time, and SECONDARY TENSE is involved in the realization of the discourse semantics of sequence in time.

By way of illustrating what we mean, consider the short phase of discourse in Example 1 (from Ridenhour 1994) taken from research reported in Martin (2012). The text's finite verbal groups are highlighted in bold:

> [1] When the choppers finally **scooped** us up on the fifth day, it **was** nearly dark again. We **did** not **make** it back to the coast that night, either. We**'d been** in the air only a few minutes when the pilot **changed** direction and **headed** for the nearest firebase, a primitive forward camp **had been gouged** into the mouth of the valley. A circle of bunkers and barbed wire less than a quarter mile across, it **was** the U.S. Army's point fort in the grand plan to staunch the flow of gooks through the valley. The battle on the south side of the valley **was** part of the plan. Now, our pilots **told** us, we **were going to be dumped** there for the night while they **headed** off as makeshift medevacs. There **were** some wounded who had to get out now, while there **was** some light left.

Their PRIMARY TENSE selection is exclusively past, since the war veteran turned journalist, Ron Ridenhour, is recounting some of his experiences in the Vietnam War, which took place many years before the essay was written. In addition, there are three SECONDARY TENSE selections, two for past and one for future. In Halliday's terms (e.g. Halliday and Matthiessen 2014), two verbal groups are 'past in past', and one is 'future in past'.

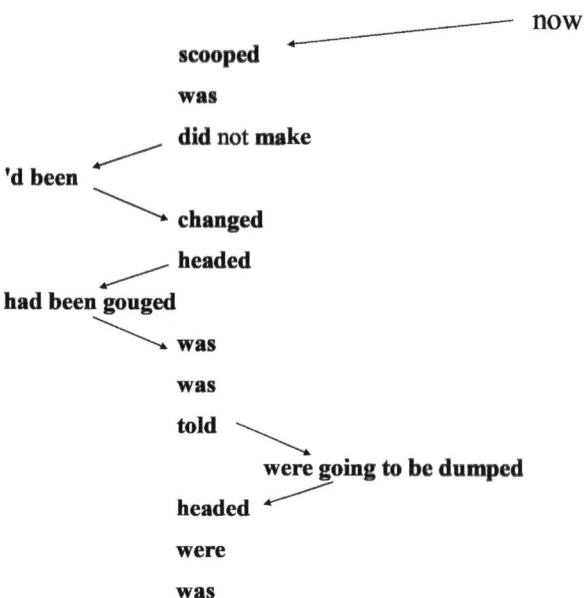

Figure 1.1 An outline of temporal relations (setting in time and sequence in time) construed by TENSE choices in Text [1].

[past]	*scooped, was, did ... make, changed, headed, was, was, told, headed, were, was*
[past in past]	*'d been, had been gouged*
[future in past]	*were going to be dumped*

As we can see, the PRIMARY TENSE selections locate what happened as taking place before the text was written (setting in time). The SECONDARY TENSE selections position occurrences in relation to that past time setting (sequence in time) as taking place earlier (*'d been* in relation to *changed*, and *had been gouged* in relation to *headed*), or later (*were going to be dumped* in relation to *told*). These relations are schematized in Figure 1.1 in relation to the 'here and now' of Ridenhour's composition of the essay (notated as 'now').

In this chapter we focus on the recursive TENSE systems of verbal groups in English and Spanish, exploring how these resources are taken up to position occurrences in time and position them in relation to one another; and we make suggestions about the implications of this perspective on tense for TS. We begin by briefly reviewing English TENSE systems (Section 3.1) and then turn to Spanish (Section 3.2), noting the most significant differences as we go.[3] We then consider some translation issues arising from a comparison of the instantiation of the two systems in short phases of discourse (Section 4). In conclusion we discuss the implications of this analysis for functional language typology (Section 5) and translation theory and practice informed by SFL (Section 6).

3 Two TENSE systems

3.1 English TENSE

As far as setting in time in relation to the 'here and now' of speaking or writing is concerned, English verbal groups distinguish [past], [present] and [future] as outlined in Figure 1.2 for PRIMARY TENSE. The [past] and [present] selections are realized morphologically at word rank through the choice of verb class – v-ed (simple past) or v-s (simple present); the [future] selection on the other hand is realized 'analytically' through two verbs: the auxiliary *will* followed by the v ('infinitive' dictionary entry) class.

English SECONDARY TENSE involves the same three options, but with distinctive realizations. Secondary [past] is realized by the auxiliary *have* followed by the v-en class of the following verb, secondary [present] by *be* followed by the v-ing class of the following verb and secondary [future] by *be going to* followed by the v class of the following verb. These axial relations are outlined in Figure 1.2.

The SECONDARY TENSE system is optional. So English indicative clauses accommodate the following verbal groups.

past: *showed*
present: *shows*
future: *will show*

past in past: *had shown*
past in present: *has shown*
past in future: *will have shown*

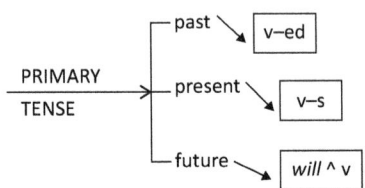

Figure 1.2 English PRIMARY TENSE.

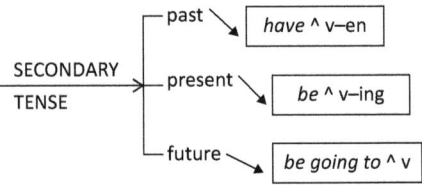

Figure 1.3 English SECONDARY TENSE.

present in past: *was showing*
present in present: *is showing*
present in future: *will be showing*

future in past: *was going to show*
future in present: *am going to show*
future in future: *will be going to show*

As outlined in Figure 1.4, choices from the SECONDARY TENSE system have to be understood in relation to choices from the PRIMARY TENSE system – as relative time. PRIMARY TENSE establishes the point in time with reference to which SECONDARY TENSE choices are interpreted. Its effect in discourse is to locate (PRIMARY TENSE) and sequence (SECONDARY TENSE) occurrences in time, as outlined in Figure 1.1 for Text [1] above (in Figure 1.4 '–' stands for past tense, '0' for present and '+' for future).

As introduced in Halliday (1976), SECONDARY TENSE is in fact a recursive system, which can be entered up to four times. Halliday (1991: 70) presumes a dialogic context for a verbal group with five tense selections along the following lines:

[2]
Can I use that machine?
–   Sorry, we use it ourselves in the mornings.
–   Are you using it now?
–   Yes we are.
–   Are you going to be using it this afternoon?
–   Well no, but it's going to be being tested.
–   What! It's been going to be being tested now for ages! It**'ll have been going to've been being tested** every day for about a fortnight soon!

An interpretation of this 'passive present in past in future in past in future' verbal group as a serial verb complex is presented below (using Greek letters alongside the following superscripts to represent elements of univariate structure: past, '–', present, '0', future, '+', passive, 'passive' and event, 'event').

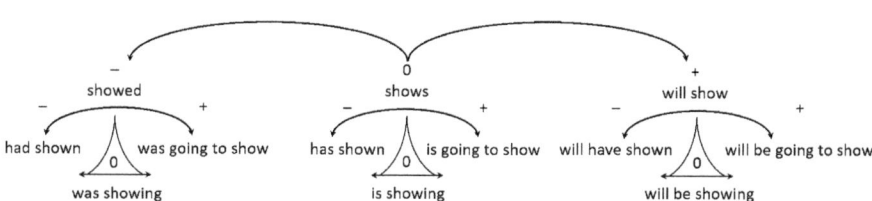

Figure 1.4 English SECONDARY TENSE in relation to PRIMARY TENSE options.

'll've been going to've been being tested

will	*have ^ v-en*	*be going to ^ v*	*have ^ v-en*	*be ^ v-ing*	*be ^ v-en*	*test*
future	past	future	past	present	passive	event
α^+	β^-	γ^+	δ^-	ε^0	$\zeta^{passive}$	η^{event}

passive 'present in past in future in past in future'

The build-up of tense selections in Text [2] (*use, are … using, are (using), are … going to be using, 's going to be being tested, 's been going to be being tested*) co-textualizing this maximally recursive example shows that English SECONDARY TENSE needs to be treated as a recursive system – as outlined in Figure 1.5. In this network, verb classes realizing tense choices are specified as follows (and illustrated for the verb *show*):

---

v-ed	*showed*
v-s	*show, shows*
will ^ v	*will show*
have ^ v-en	*have shown*
be ^ v-ing	*be showing*
be going to ^ v	*be going to show*

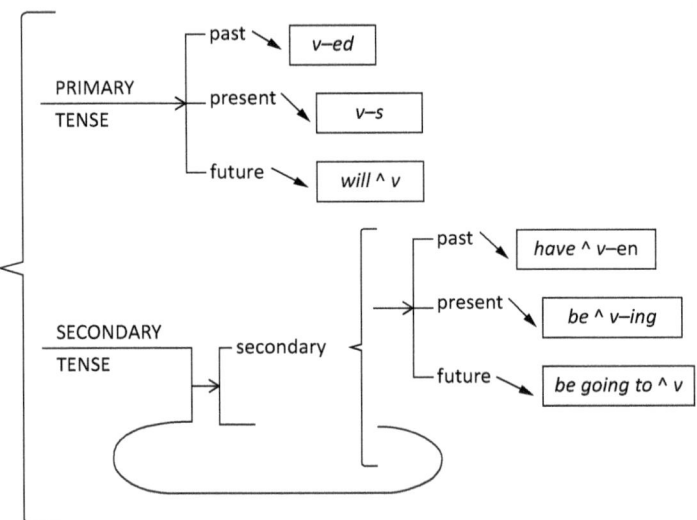

Figure 1.5 English SECONDARY TENSE as a recursive system.

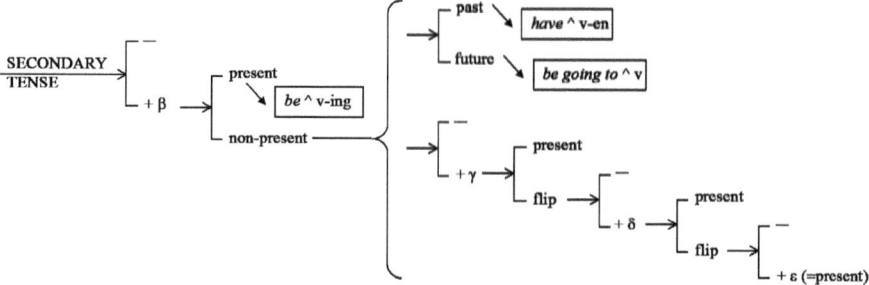

Figure 1.6 English SECONDARY TENSE system (incorporating stop rules).

As noted by Halliday (1976: 155), the SECONDARY TENSE system is not indefinitely recursive in that there are limits on possible combinations of tenses, which he presents as 'stop' rules. These stop rules are noted below.

1. secondary future can only be chosen once,
2. secondary present can only be chosen once, as the final choice and
3. the same secondary tense cannot be chosen twice in a row.

Halliday (1996: 11) formulates these restrictions as the network redrawn in Figure 1.6. In this network, the dash indicates an optional system, and the 'flip' option is used to stop the same tense being chosen twice consecutively. For complete paradigms of English TENSE choice see *Halliday's Introduction to Functional Grammar* (4th edn, 2014: 401–3).

3.2 Spanish TENSE

As far as setting in time in relation to the 'here and now' of speaking or writing is concerned, Spanish verbal groups distinguish [past], [imperfect], [present] and [future] as outlined in Figure 1.7 for PRIMARY TENSE. All tense selections are realized morphologically at word rank (Quiroz 2013).[4]

Spanish SECONDARY TENSE involves only three options, past, present and future, with different realizations.[5] Secondary [past] is realized by the auxiliary *haber* followed by the v-ado class of the following verb, secondary [present] by *estar* followed by the v-ando class of the following verb and secondary future by *ir a* followed by the v class of the following verb. These axial relations are outlined in Figure 1.8.

The verb classes that we are using in our description are outlined in Table 1.1, column 2. The names of classes are based (where relevant) on the third person affixation for *-ar* conjugation verbs; traditional terms for these classes have been included in column 1.

In common with English, the SECONDARY TENSE system is optional. But Spanish indicative clauses do not accommodate all possible co-selections of PRIMARY TENSE and SECONDARY TENSE (Quiroz 2017, 2018). As outlined for the verb *cantar* ('sing') below, neither the 'future in perfect'[6] nor 'future in future' combinations are possible.

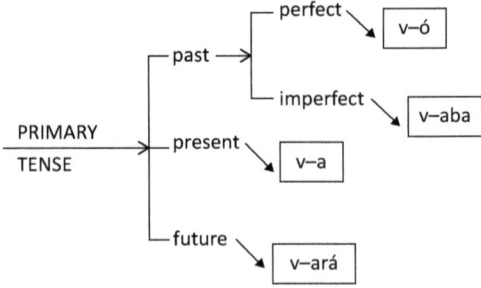

Figure 1.7 Spanish PRIMARY TENSE.

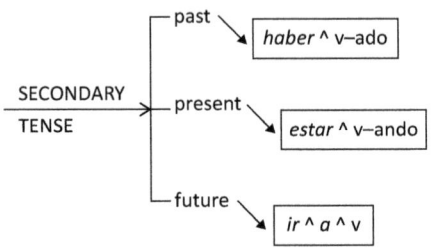

Figure 1.8 Spanish SECONDARY TENSE.

perfect	*cantó* 'sang'
imperfect	*cantaba* 'was singing'
present	*canta* 'sings'
future	*cantará* 'will sing'
past in perfect	*hubo cantado* 'had sung'
past in imperfect	*había cantado* 'had been singing'
past in present	*ha cantado* 'has sung'
past in future	*habrá cantado* 'will have sung'
present in perfect	*estuvo cantando* 'was singing'
present in imperfect	*estaba cantando* 'was singing'
present in present	*está cantando* 'is singing'
present in future	*estará cantando* 'will be winging'
future in perfect	–
future in imperfect	*iba a cantar* 'was going to sing'
future in present	*va a cantar* 'is going to sing'
future in future	–

Table 1.1 Terms used for Spanish verb classes, with examples

Traditional term	class	'be'	'have'	'go'	'be'	-ar verb	-er/-ir verb
'infinitive'	v	*estar*	*haber*	*ir*	*ser*	*cantar*	*recibir*
'imperative'	v-e	*esté*	*haya*	*vaya*	*sea*	*cante*	*reciba*
'present'	v-a	*está*	*ha*	*va*	*es*	*canta*	*recibe*
'perfect'	v-ó	*estuvo*	*hubo*	*fue*	*fue*	*cantó*	*recibió*
'imperfect'	v-aba	*estaba*	*había*	*iba*	*era*	*cantaba*	*recibía*
'future'	v-ará	*estará*	*habrá*	*irá*	*será*	*cantará*	*recibirá*
'participle'	v-ado	*estado*	*habido*	*ido*	*sido*	*cantado*	*recibido*
'gerund'	v-ando	*estando*	*habiendo*	*yendo*	*siendo*	*cantando*	*recibiendo*

Except for this, the relation between PRIMARY TENSE and SECONDARY TENSE is the same as that outlined in Figure 1.4 for English. So, choices from the SECONDARY TENSE system have to be understood in relation to choices from the PRIMARY TENSE system as relative time (i.e. the Spanish PRIMARY TENSE system establishes the point in time with reference to which SECONDARY TENSE choices are interpreted). The role of the secondary choices in discourse is to sequence occurrences in time. In Text [3], for example, which recounts a phase of an earthquake and tidal wave disaster in Chile, five primary tense selections position what happened before the moment it was written (three perfect and two imperfect selections):

perfect	*llegó* 'arrived'
imperfect	*estaban* 'were'
imperfect	*venía* 'came'
perfect	*transmitió* 'passed on'
imperfect	*perdía* 'lost'

In addition, Text [3] uses two 'past in imperfect' selections to sequence both what Jonathan told his mother Nora and what happened to his friend Gabriel as taking place before their arrival in Constitución.

past in imperfect	*había dicho* 'had told'
past in imperfect	*había llevado* 'had taken'

[3] Nora llegó a Constitución a las diez de la mañana, cuando los saqueos estaban en su apogeo. Venía acompañada de la madre de Gabriel. Durante la noche Jonathan, llorando, le **había dicho** que a Gabriel se lo **había llevado** la ola y Nora se lo transmitió a la madre. Pero ella no perdía la esperanza.

[3'] 'Nora arrived in Constitución at ten in the morning, when the looting was at its peak. She came accompanied by Gabriel's mother. During the night Jonathan,

Table 1.2a *había dicho*

había dicho		
v-a	*hacer* ∧ v-ado	*decir*
present	past	event
α^{--}	β^-	γ^{event}
'past in present'		
'has said'		

Table 1.2b *había llevado*

había llevado		
v-aba	*haber* ∧ v-ado	*llevar*
imperfect	past	event
α^{--}	β^-	γ^{event}
'past in imperfect'		
'had taken'		

crying, **had told** her that the wave **had taken** Gabriel and Nora passed this on to his mother. But she did not lose[7] hope.'

The secondary past tenses, *había dicho* 'had told' and *había llevado* 'had taken', are analysed as univariate structures in Tables 1.2a and 1.2b. For Spanish, we adopt the following superscripts for verbal group features: '0' for present, '-' for perfect and for secondary past, '--' for imperfect, '+' for future and 'event' for event.

Beyond the limitations on secondary future note above, the Spanish verbal group tense system is less delicate[8] than the English one. Future tense in fact can be selected only once; 'present in past in perfect' (*hubo estado cantando* 'had been singing') appears mainly in teaching materials for Spanish as a second or foreign language; and like English, secondary present can be chosen only once, as the final selection. This explains the gaps in the paradigm presented as Table 1.2, which offers Spanish speakers up to three secondary tense selections. Taking teaching materials into account this means that Chilean Spanish allows for twenty-four different tense combinations (compared to thirty-six in English). Since third and fourth rounds of tense selection are extremely rare and far more likely to occur in informal conversation, these limits on recursion would very rarely pose a challenge for translators and interpreters. More significant is the differences in the PRIMARY TENSE system, where Spanish has two 'past' time options instead of one, and the [imperfect] accommodates several more secondary tense selections than perfect does. We return to these challenges in Section 4.

4 Interlingual instantiation

In this section we will focus on four short texts, that is, two recounts and two phases of classroom interaction. The English texts were translated by Quiroz (a linguist and professional translator) in consultation with Martin (a linguist, with no training in translation); the Spanish texts were translated by Martin, in consultation with Quiroz. We begin with the English recount, Text [1], repeated below,[10] and its translation as [1TT]. Source texts are presented in italics and target texts in roman font for each pair of examples; finite verbal groups are in bold.

[1] *When the choppers finally **scooped** us up on the fifth day, it **was** nearly dark again. We **did not make** it back to the coast that night, either. We**'d been** in the air*

Table 1.3 Primary tense and secondary tense in Spanish

primary α	secondary β	secondary γ	secondary δ
perfect: v-ó *cantó* 'sang'	past: haber ∧ v-ado *hubo cantado* 'had sung'	present: estar ∧ v-ando *hubo estado cantando*[9] 'had been singing'	
	present: estar ∧ v-ando *estuvo cantando* 'was singing'		
imperfect: v-aba *cantaba* 'was singing'	past: haber ∧ v-ado *había cantado* 'had sung'	present: estar ∧ v-ando *había estado cantando* 'had been singing'	
	present: estar ∧ v-ando *estaba cantando* 'was singing'		
	future: ir *a* ∧ v *iba a cantar* 'was going to sing'	past: haber ∧ v-ado *iba a haber cantado* 'was going to have sung'	present: estar ∧ v-ando *iba a haber estado cantando* 'was going to have been singing'
		present: estar ∧ v-ando *iba a estar cantando* 'was going to be singing'	
present: v-a *canta* 'sings'	past: haber ∧ v-ado *ha cantado* 'has sung'	present: estar ∧ v-ando *ha estado cantando* 'has been singing'	
	present: estar ∧ v-ando *está cantando* 'is singing'		
	future: ir *a* ∧ v *va a cantar* 'is going to sing'	past: haber ∧ v-ado *va a haber cantado* 'is going to have sung'	present: estar ∧ v-ando *va a haber estado cantando* 'is going to have been singing'
		present: estar ∧-ando *va a estar cantando* 'is going to be singing'	
future: v-ará *cantará* 'will sing'	past: haber ∧ v-ado *habrá cantado* 'will have sung' present: estar ∧ v-ando	present: estar ∧ v-ando *habrá estado cantando* 'will have been singing'	
	estará cantando 'will be singing'		

only a few minutes when the pilot **changed** direction and **headed** for the nearest firebase, a primitive forward camp that grunts **had gouged** into the mouth of the valley. A circle of bunkers and barbed wire less than a quarter mile across, it **was** the U.S. Army's point fort in the grand plan to staunch the flow of gooks through the valley. The battle on the south side of the valley **was** part of the plan. Now, our pilots **told** us, they **were going to dump** us there for the night while they **headed** off as *makeshift medevacs. There **were** some wounded who **had to get** out now, while there **was** some light left.*

[1TT] Cuando los helicópteros finalmente **llegaron** a recogernos al quinto día, ya casi **estaba** oscuro. Tampoco **pudimos regresar** a la costa esa noche. **Llevábamos** en el aire apenas unos minutos cuando el piloto **cambió** de rumbo y **se dirigió** a la base más cercana, un rudimentario campamento de avanzada que los soldados **habían enclavado** en la entrada del valle. Formando un círculo de arcones y alambradas de menos de una milla de diámetro, **era** el puesto clave dentro del gran plan del ejército estadounidense para contener el flujo de vietnamitas por el valle. La batalla en el lado meridional del valle **era** parte del plan. Ahora, **nos dijeron** los pilotos, **nos iban a dejar** allí para pasar la noche mientras ellos **se retiraban** para prestar apoyo en operaciones de evacuación médica. **Había** algunos heridos que **tenían que sacar** ahora, mientras todavía **quedaba** algo de luz.

The most striking difference between the two texts is the PRIMARY TENSE contrast between English [past] and Spanish [imperfect] – itemized below.

past	*it **was** nearly dark again*
imperfect	ya casi **estaba** oscuro
past	*it **was** the U.S. Army's point fort*
imperfect	**era** el puesto clave del ejército estadounidense
past	*The battle on the south side of the valley **was** part of the plan*
imperfect	La batalla en el lado meridional **era** parte del plan.
past	*while they **headed** off as makeshift medevacs*
imperfect	mientras ellos **se retiraban** para prestar apoyo en operaciones de evacuación médica
past	*There **were** some wounded*
imperfect	**Había** algunos heridos
past	*who had to get out now,*
imperfect	que **tenían** que sacar ahora
past	*while there **was** some light left.*
imperfect	mientras todavía **quedaba** algo de luz.

This preference for the Spanish imperfect also holds where secondary tenses are involved, with 'past in imperfect' preferred over 'past in past' and 'future in imperfect' preferred over 'future in past'.

past in past	*a primitive forward camp that grunts **had gouged** into the mouth of the valley*
past in imperfect	que **habían enclavado** en la entrada del valle.
future in past	*they **were going to dump** us there*
future in imperfect	nos **iban a dejar** allí.

This shows the danger of equating English 'present in past' (e.g. *was being, were heading*) with Spanish [imperfect] (e.g. *estaba, era, retiraban*).

In one case imperfect is preferred to English 'past in past'.[11]

past in past	*We'd **been** in the air only a few minutes*
past	*when the pilot **changed** direction*
imperfect	**Llevábamos** en el aire apenas unos minutos
past	cuando el piloto **cambió** de rumbo.

The same pattern of difference is found for the translation of the phase of English classroom discourse presented as Text [4]. The teacher here is working on the structure of exposition with her Year 6 primary school students – focusing in particular at this point on the need to make sure that any arguments predicted by an exposition's introduction need to be developed in the text as it unfolds.

[4] *What some people **did** the other day **was** they all **had** these wonderful ideas in their introduction or thesis and I **was** all ready to read about them and I **got** to the end and they **hadn't talked** about all these things that they **had told** me they **were going to tell** me.*

[4TT] 'Lo que algunos **hicieron** el otro día **fue** que **tenían** todos ideas maravillosas en su introducción o tesis y yo **estaba** lista para leer de qué trataban y **llegué** al final y nadie **había mencionado** nada de todas esas cosas que me **habían dicho** que me **iban a decir**.'

past	*they all **had** these wonderful ideas*
imperfect	que **tenían** todos ideas maravillosas
past	*I **was** all ready*
imperfect	yo **estaba** lista

The English translation of the Spanish recount confirms the same pattern of difference, with [imperfect] the favoured host for secondary tense selections – the use of English 'past in past' (e.g. *had walked*) to translate Spanish 'past in imperfect' (e.g. *había caminado*) and English 'future in past' (*was going to get*) for Spanish 'future in imperfect' (*iba a llegar*). In this anecdote a scout leader talks about a frightening false alarm he experienced at a summer camp.

> [5] *Eeh el susto más grande **fue** ahora en campamento de verano. Lo que pasa es que **soy** dirigente de scout y de repente una niña **tuvo** un ataque respiratorio y claro **me tocó correr** cuatro cinco kilómetros buscando una ambulancia y en el momento **estaba** súper agotado, **había caminado** todo el día, pero por el puro golpe de adrenalina al final **corrí** los cinco kilómetros y cuando ya **iba a llegar** al teléfono como que **me avisaron** ya se **había mejorado**, que **había sido** algo momentáneo, que en el momento **no vimos** bien la situación y **llegamos** y **actuamos** no más* (PRESEEA, 2014–).

> [5TT] 'Ehm, the worse fright **was** now in summer camp. The thing is I **am** a scout leader and suddenly a girl **had** a breathing attack and of course I **had** to run four five kilometres looking for an ambulance and at that moment I **was** super exhausted, I **had walked** the whole day, but just because of the adrenaline rush in the end I **ran** the five kilometres and when I **was going to get** to a phone someone like **told** me she **had got** better already, it **had been** a momentary thing, that in that moment we **didn't check** the situation properly and we just **went** and **reacted**.'

imperfect	en el momento **estaba** súper agotado
past	at that moment I **was** super exhausted,
past in imperfect	**había caminado** todo el día
past in past	I **had walked** the whole day
past in imperfect	ya se **había mejorado**
past in past	she **had got** better already
past in imperfect	que **había sido** algo momentáneo
past in past	it **had been** a momentary thing
future in imperfect	cuando ya **iba a llegar** al teléfono
future in past	when I **was going to get** to a phone

The English translation of the Spanish classroom interaction below introduces another point of interest in relation to future action. Each of the Spanish 'future in present' tenses (e.g. *va a tomar*) was translated as English 'future in present' (e.g. *is going to take*) below. The teacher here is doing some work on Spanish grammar with a group of primary school students.

[6] Teacher: *Todas estas palabras que **tengo** aquí ¿**corresponden** a qué tipo de palabras? Hija, usted, ¿qué **hemos estado hablando** toda la clase? ¿**Corresponden** a qué tipo de palabras? ¿Qué **fue** lo que **recordamos** al principio de la clase?*

Student: *Verbos.*

Teacher: *Bien. Todas estas acciones que **escribimos** en la pizarra y con la que **trabajamos** en la línea de tiempo **corresponden** a acciones que están expresadas en los verbos. Para que nuestro aprendizaje quede aún más fijo en nuestra cabecita cada uno **va a tomar** el texto que **escribió** con lo que **hizo** hoy en la mañana y lo **va a transformar** a presente y luego lo **va a transformar** a futuro. O sea que las acciones que **hicieron** hoy día en la mañana las **van a hacer** ahora y luego las **van a hacer** después o en el futuro. Muy bien comencemos a trabajar. Léame su párrafo, el primero y luego el segundo.*

[6TT] Teacher: All of these words that I **have** here **correspond** to what kind of words? Child, you, what **have we been talking** about the whole lesson? What kind of words do they **correspond** to? What **was** it that we **reviewed** at the beginning of the lesson?

Student: Verbs.

Teacher: Good. All these actions we **wrote** on the board and which we **worked** with on the timeline **correspond** to actions that are expressed in the verbs. In order to consolidate our learning in our lovely heads each one of you **is going to take** the text you **wrote** with what you **did** today in the morning and **is going to change** it into present and then into future. That is, the actions that you **did** today in the morning you **are going to do** them now and then you **are going to do** them later or in the future. Very well, let's start working. Read me your paragraph, the first one and then the second one.

future in present	*cada uno **va a tomar** el texto*
future	each one of you **is going to take** the text
future in present	*lo **va a transformar** a presente*
future	**is going to change** it into present
future in present	*las **van a hacer** ahora*
future	you **are going to do** them now
future in present	*luego las **van a hacer** después o en el futuro*
future	then you **are going to do** them later or in the future

But the English could just as well have deployed primary future, as in [6TT], for example, *'ll take*. This removes any implication of immediacy inherent in the English 'future in present' selection, and either translation seems appropriate for this context.

[6TT] Teacher: Good. All these actions we **wrote** on the board and which we **worked** with on the timeline **correspond** to actions that are expressed in the verbs. In order to consolidate our learning in our lovely heads each one of you'**ll take** the text you **wrote** with what you **did** today in the morning and **will change** it into present and then into future. That is, the actions that you **did** today in the morning you'**ll do** now and then you'**ll do** them later or in the future. Very well, let's start working. Read me your paragraph, the first one and then the second one.

future in present	*cada uno **va a tomar** el texto*
future	each one of you'**ll take** the text
future in present	*lo **va a transformar** a presente*
future	**will change** it into present
future in present	*las **van a hacer** ahora*
future	you'**ll do** them now
future in present	*luego las **van a hacer** después o en el futuro*
future	then you'**ll do** them later or in the future

In spoken Chilean Spanish the 'future in present' selection is far more common than simple future, and it does not mean that an occurrence so positioned will imminently unfold. Chilean Spanish in other words neutralizes the distinction between following and following imminently – a distinction which obtains in English (and some other varieties of Spanish).

5 Defeasible language typology

Matthiessen (in a draft of Matthiessen, 2018) makes the critical point that diversification across languages can be usefully explored by asking how far it extends 'upwards' – along various dimensions of SFL theory. And he proposes a general fractal principle to guide this exploration – a cline from more similar to more different:

> In the comparison and representation of two or more languages, we can postulate a general fractal principle in the form of a cline from 'most similar' to 'most different'. The principle is fractal in the sense that it is manifested along a range of semiotic dimensions in the overall 'architecture' of language … The dimensions … are the hierarchy of stratification, the hierarchy of rank, the hierarchy of axis and the cline of delicacy. Matthiessen (2014: 43)

This principle is outlined in Figure 1.9, taken from Matthiessen's draft paper (but unfortunately omitted from its final publication).

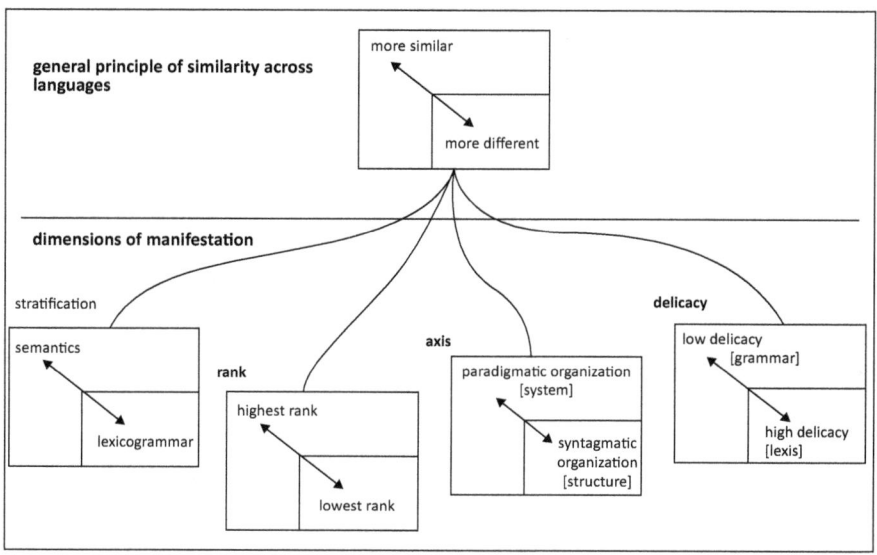

Figure 1.9 Fractal principle of similarity across languages (Matthiessen 2014: 43).

Taking this principle of 'ascent' as a guide, we can review differences between English and Spanish TENSE systems, drawing on and extending the discussion in Sections 2 to 4.

First axis. This fundamental dimension of SFL focuses on systems of choice in relation to their structural manifestations (the connection between paradigmatic relations and syntagmatic structures). Figures 1.2, 1.3, 1.5, 1.6, 1.7 and 1.8 formalized this axial perspective on TENSE as system networks with accompanying realization statements. Axis is relevant to ascent because languages tend to be more different in the way they realize systems in structures than with respect to the systems themselves.

A comparison of English and Spanish PRIMARY TENSE systems is illustrative here. English PRIMARY TENSE [future] is realized by the word syntagm *will* ^ v, whereas Spanish PRIMARY TENSE [future] is realized by the morpheme syntagm v-*ará*.[12] From the perspective of system the valeur is the same, but from the perspective of structure the future choice is realized at different ranks (involving verbal group structure versus verb morphology). So syntagmatic difference can be generalized as paradigmatic similarity. The axial (i.e. system/structure) relations in focus here are re-presented in Figure 1.10.

Next delicacy. Delicacy has to do with the dependence of finer grained distinctions on more general ones – for example the distinction between perfect and imperfect in relation to past in the PRIMARY TENSE system for Spanish (Figure 1.10). Delicacy is relevant to ascent because languages tend to be more different with respect to more delicate systems than more general ones.

A comparison of English and Spanish SECONDARY TENSE systems is illustrative here. As noted above, Spanish verbal groups involve just one future tense (see Table 1.2); for

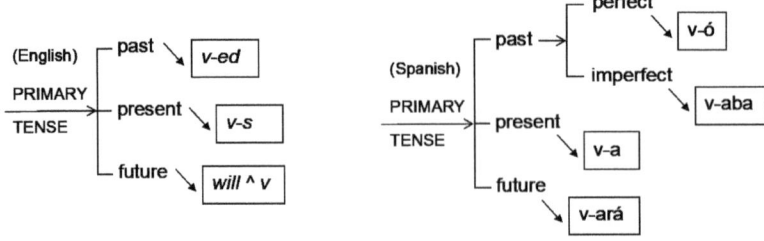

Figure 1.10 Comparison of PRIMARY TENSE system and structure in English and Spanish.

Table 1.4 SECONDARY TENSE delicacy for PRIMARY TENSE [future] in Spanish and English

primary α	secondary β	secondary γ	secondary δ
future: v-ará *cantará* 'will sing'	past: haber ^ v-ado *habrá cantado* 'will have sung'	present: estar ^ v-ando *habrá estado cantando* 'will have been singing'	
	present: estar ^ v-ando *estará cantando* 'will be singing'		
	future: be going to ^ v **will be going to sing**	**past: have ^ v-em** **will be going to have sung** **present: be ^ v-ing** **will be going to be singing**	**present: be ^ v-ing** **will be going to have been singing**

In English on the other hand the restriction on future is that it is chosen just once after PRIMARY TENSE. This means that English allows for 'future in future' (*will be going to sing*), 'past in future in future' (*will be going to have sung*), 'present in future in future' (*will be going to be singing*) and 'present in past in future in future' (*will be going to have been singing*) options that Spanish does not. From the perspective of PRIMARY TENSE these can all be considered future options; in this respect English and Spanish are comparable. But English verbal groups make finer grained distinctions that Spanish verbal groups do not. So, in this case, delicate differentiation can be generalized as less delicate superordination. The systemic delicacy relations in focus here are re-presented in Table 1.4 – taking primary future as the point of departure and treating English as if it were an elaboration of Spanish; the extra delicacy English affords is in bold.

Next rank. Rank organizes system networks and realization statements according to the size of the unit being described, for example, clause systems realized by group and phrase systems, realized in turn by word systems, realized in turn by morpheme system. Rank is relevant to ascent because systems and structures at lower ranks tend to be more different than systems and structures at higher ones.

As we saw above in relation to Text [1] and its translation into Spanish [1TT], English past tense verbal groups were regularly translated as Spanish imperfect rather than Spanish perfect tense. This is the favoured pattern for relational clauses (and this is true for Texts [2TT] and [3TT] as well) – a clause type construing relationships which typically endure for a longer period of time than do the occurrences realized through other more 'dynamic' types of clause for which perfect tense is often more appropriate (e.g. *tuvo un ataque* 'had an attack', *me tocó correr* 'had to run', *corrí* 'ran', *me avisaron* 'advised me', *no vimos* 'didn't check', *llegamos* 'went', *actuamos* 'reacted' in Text [3]). The relevant examples from Text [1] are repeated below.

past	*it **was** nearly dark again*
imperfect	ya casi **estaba** oscuro
past	*it **was** the U.S. Army's point fort*
imperfect	**era** el puesto clave del ejército estadounidense
past	*The battle on the south side of the valley **was** part of the plan*
imperfect	La batalla en el lado meridional del valle **era** parte del plan.
past	*There **were** some wounded*
imperfect	**Había** algunos heridos
past	*while there **was** some light left.*
imperfect	mientras todavía **quedaba** algo de luz.

As we can see, for English, positioning a relational clause in the past is sufficient to encode the meaning of a relatively unbounded state of affairs – and the choice of 'present in past' would be very strange (e.g.?*it **was being** nearly dark*). For Spanish, on the other hand, imperfect is a more suitable choice than perfect, for positioning relationships before the moment of speaking. In this case the same choice at clause rank has divergent implications for tense choice at the rank next below.

Finally, stratification. Stratification, as modelled in Figure 1.10, organizes system networks and realization statements according to levels of abstraction from phonic or visual substance, for example, genre realized through register, realized in turn through discourse semantics, realized in turn through lexicogrammar, realized in turn through phonology, graphology or sign. Stratification is relevant to ascent because languages tend to be more different at less abstract strata than at more abstract ones.

For the last of the examples listed above (repeated below) imperfect tense is just one of three resources construing the temporality of the clause. The Spanish translation includes the assessment adverb *todavía* 'still', indicating that pilots can continue to see even though night is approaching. So TENSE (*quedaba*) and ASSESSMENT (*todavía*) are co-construing temporality in a hypotactic 'while' (*mientras*) clause which also 'stretches' time.

past	*while there **was** some light left.*
imperfect	mientras todavía **quedaba** algo de luz.

The same type of dependent clause is perhaps in part responsible for the choice of imperfect tense (*retiraban*) for the material action clause below:

past	*while they **headed** off as makeshift medevacs*
imperfect	mientras ellos se **retiraban** para prestar apoyo en operaciones de evacuación médica

What these examples reveal is that choosing between [perfect] and [imperfect] as translations of English past, or choosing between [past] and [present in past] as translations of Spanish [imperfect] is not a matter of verbal group TENSE alone. Various clause rank systems come into play – including the kind of activity or relationship being construed, the choice of temporal assessment (e.g. *still, yet, already, finally, just* in English) and any temporal conjunctions relating the clause to connected relationships or goings on.

In order to coordinate and move towards generalizing across these 'temporal' systems we need to move upwards in our model and consider co-textual relations. The model of discourse semantic we are assuming here is presented in Figure 1.9 (based on Martin 1992; Martin and Rose 2003). Their CONJUNCTION system is renamed CONNEXION here, following Hao (2018, 2020), in order to more clearly distinguish discourse semantic and lexicogrammatical resources. CONNEXION is concerned with sequencing figures in discourse, and thus with coordinating conjunctive relations and tense selections as texts unfold. Variation in realization across languages with respect to this system are introduced in Gleason (1968).

Bringing assessment options into the picture (e.g. the *todavía* 'still' assessment flagged above) means casting our net wider still – in order to bring in temporal counter-expectation resources deriving from the ENGAGEMENT system in Martin and White's

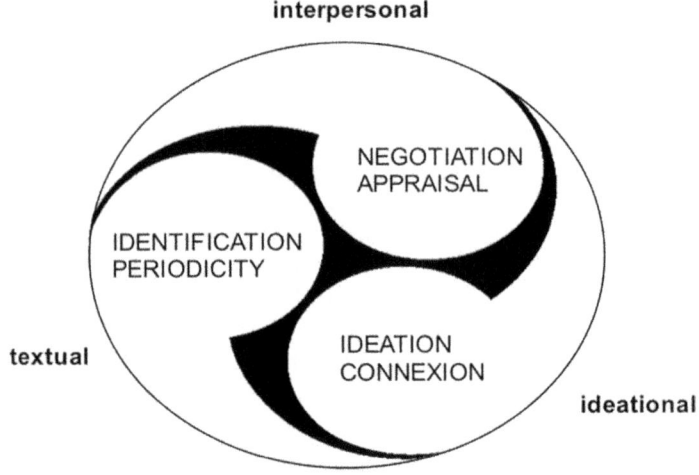

Figure 1.11 Discourse semantic systems.

(2005) appraisal framework, and also the extent and location in time resources associated with figures in Hao's IDEATION system (Hao 2020) and realized through circumstances in clause grammar. The temporal circumstantial resources we are drawing attention to here are highlighted in for Text [1], represented as Text [1TT] below.

[1TT] When the choppers finally scooped us up **on the fifth day**, it was nearly dark again. We did not make it back to the coast **that night**, either. We'd been in the air **only a few minutes** when the pilot changed direction and headed for the nearest firebase, a primitive forward camp had been gouged into the mouth of the valley. A circle of bunkers and barbed wire less than a quarter mile across, it was the U.S. Army's point fort in the grand plan to staunch the flow of gooks through the valley. The battle on the south side of the valley was part of the plan. **Now,** our pilots told us, we were going to be dumped us there **for the night** while they headed off as makeshift medevacs. There were some wounded who had to get out **now**, while there was some light left.

In order to coordinate IDEATION, CONNEXION and ENGAGEMENT we would have to move up another level still – at least to register (field and tenor in particular) and ultimately genre. The levels of stratification assumed here are outlined in Figure 1.12 (based on Martin 1992; Martin and Rose 2008). Detailed discussion of this step is beyond the scope of this chapter.

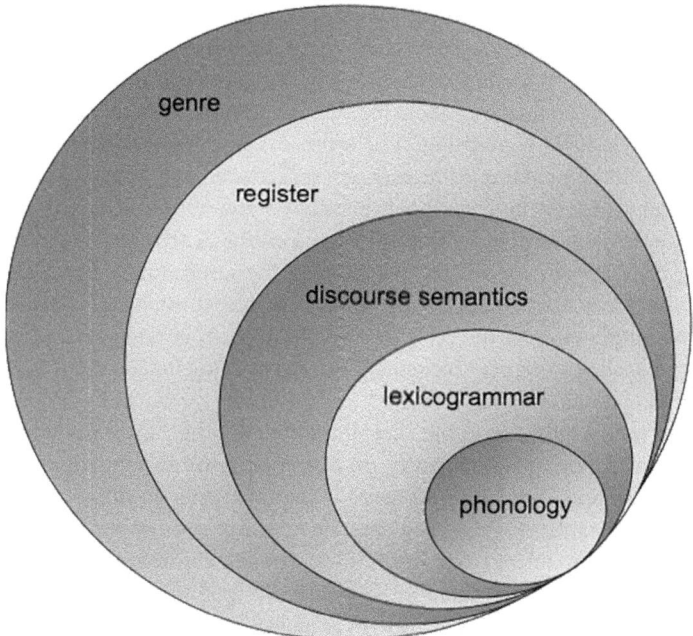

Figure 1.12 Stratification: phonology, lexicogrammar, discourse semantics, register and genre.

6 Realization, instantiation, individuation and translation

Summing up his discussion of choice in translation, Matthiessen (2014) poses a number of research questions which need addressing in future research informed by SFL:

- **what degree of systemic separation do choices produce in translation – minimal 'equivalence' or maximal 'shift'; and what are common shifts in terms of delicacy – more or less constant delicacy, increase in delicacy, decrease in delicacy?**
- to what extent are choices made within the same metafunction and to what extent do they entail a shift from one metafunction to another; and what are common shifts in metafunctional modes of meaning – are there favoured directions of shift such as the experientialization of meaning (as in grammatical metaphor)?
- **how far up do we have to ascend in terms of rank and in terms of stratification to locate the systems where meanings are located through choices in the target language?** (Matthiessen, 'Choice in Translation' 2014: 322)

In this chapter we have been particularly concerned with the first and third of these, exploring 'ascent' in terms of Matthiessen's 'fractal principle' of similarity and difference across languages elaborated in Figure 1.8. The relevance of this principle for TS lies in the abiding concern in this field with relative 'equivalence' as translators and interpreters move from source to target text. This of course brings SFL's cline of instantiation into the picture, as researchers and practitioners ask questions about how source language systems are instantiated in a particular text, and how these instances are related to target language systems for the purpose of re-instantiation. De Souza (2010) explicitly addresses translation as a process of re-instantiation, and outlines possible re-instantiation paths in the diagram reproduced as Figure 1.13.

Of particular interest in a model of this kind is the notion of ascent, in order to access source language systems of meaning that converge with target language systems. Discussing relations among different versions of the same story, Martin (2008a: 50) proposes the term 'distantiation' for a comparable intralingual re-instantiation process: 'We might suggest the term distantiation, for this metaphorical process of reaching up the cline to recover meaning potential (leaving instantiation in its normal sense of moving down).'

De Souza adopts this term for her interlingual re-instantiation context, with Figure 1.9 presenting possible paths of distantiation/re-instantiation during the process of translation. The basic idea here is that of letting go of instances, and the specific choices instantiated there, and opening up the meaning potential of the source language – moving in effect from structure to system, and then from more delicate options to less delicate ones and from lower ranks and strata to higher ones until appropriately comparable source and target language systems are found. Once located, the appropriate target language systems can be instantiated as the target text. This gives the paradigmatic orientation to the translation process we would expect from a model

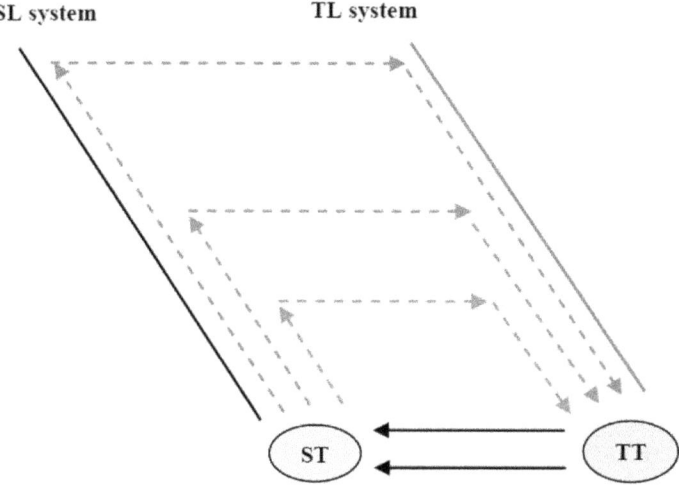

SL system   TL system

ST   TT

Figure 1.13 De Souza's model of interlingual re-instantiation.

of language such as SFL, and the systemic account it provides of the meaning making resources in the source and target languages in play.

As de Souza notes, there is inevitably some degree of shift involved; equivalence is always a matter of degree. This inevitably brings SFL's perspective on individuation into the picture (Martin 2010), with its focus on the allocation of resources to members of a culture (a translator's source and target language repertoire, for example), and the affiliation of those members into communities of various kinds (a translator's targeted readership, for example). Space precludes discussion of this 'ideological' dimension of the translation process. (For further reading on the interplay of instantiation and individuation in SFL see Martin 2008b, 2012.)

Clearly a distantiation/re-instantiation model of this kind draws attention to the need for ever more SFL descriptions of the source and target languages in focus in TS. The gap between what we have to hand and what we need is of course huge. But models of the kind of descriptions we need, taking axial relations as their foundation and bundling systems by rank, metafunction and strata are continuing to emerge. TS is one application of this work, and a field we hope can foster SFL descriptions – for the many languages SFL has yet to describe.

Notes

1. In order to focus the discussion we will restrict ourselves to a consideration of Chilean Spanish in this chapter, ignoring other varieties.
2. SFL's perspective on tense contrasts with tense and aspect models (e.g. the tense [past/present] ^ perfective ^ progressive analysis of English verbal groups popularized by Chomsky 1957). These models generally reject the idea that English grammar has a

future tense (either primary or secondary) and so verbal groups like *will dump* and *were going to dump* are not part of the picture.

3. The descriptive work on Spanish TENSE presented in this chapter has been partially funded by the Pontificia Universidad Católica de Chile (grant FRCAI1720) and by CONICYT-FONDECYT (grant 11170674).

4. There has of course been extensive discussion of perfect/imperfect opposition in Spanish (e.g. Bosque 1990; Bull 1960; García Fernández and Camus Bergareche 2004; Veiga 2004), and the precise difference in meaning and usage between imperfect (*acampaban*) and 'present in past' (*estaban acampando*) remains an outstanding issue.

5. We are developing here a particular model of Spanish verbal groups, which treats secondary present and secondary future as grammaticalized resources comparable to secondary past and passive. An alternative treatment of tense is possible, reinterpreting our analysis in relation to verbal group complexing (i.e. acknowledging the status of *estar* ˆ v-ando and *ir* ˆ *a* ˆ -ar as 'periphrastic' structures; cf. Olbertz 2011).

6. For example, *fuimos a ayudar* 'we went to help' would mean that we did go to help (with *fuimos* 'we went' realizing an Event, not a secondary future tense) – not that we simply intended to help; *fuimos a ayudar* is a verbal group complex, not a 'future in perfect' complex tense.

7. Note, in relation to the discussion of the Spanish imperfect tense above, our preference for the English past tense in the translation of the Spanish imperfect *perdía*.

8. As we will show in Sections 4 and 5, this does not mean that Spanish has a more limited meaning potential than English as far as positioning and repositioning of figures in relation to the moment of speaking. A range of resources are available in any language to this purpose, including those realizing IDEATION, CONNEXION and ENGAGEMENT alongside TENSE in Spanish. And our analysis of the meaning potential available is of course an 'artifact' of the particular model of secondary tense we are developing. This is comparable to our account of English and how Spanish treats secondary present (*estar* ∧ v-ando) and secondary future (*ir* ∧ *a* ∧ v-ar) as fully grammaticalized elements of verbal group structure.

9. The 'present in past in perfect' choice seems to appear almost exclusively in teaching materials for non-native speakers.

10. Two passive verbal groups have been changed to active voice for this exercise; translation of English passive verbal groups into Spanish warrants discussion beyond the scope of this chapter.

11. There is one further difference between the source text and its translation, involving a shift from English past tense (*did … make*) to Spanish past tense modality (*pudimos regresar* 'could return'); this shift takes us beyond our focus on tense in this chapter:

past	We **did not make** it back to the coast that night, either.
past modalized	Tampoco **pudimos regresar** a la costa esa noche

12. As noted in passing above, for Chilean Spanish this comparison is complicated by the fact that in most registers 'future in present' is used rather than simple [future] (e.g. *va a cantar* 'is going to sing' rather than *cantará* 'will sing').

References

Bosque, I. (ed.) (1990), *Tiempo y aspecto en español*, Madrid: Cátedra.

Bull, W. E. (1960), *Time, Tense and the Verb: A Study in Theoretical and Applied Linguistics, with Particular Attention to Spanish*, Berkeley: University of California Press.

Caffarel, A. (1992), 'Interacting between a Generalized Tense Semantics and Register-Specific Semantic Tense Systems: A Bi-stratal Exploration of the Semantics of French Tense', *Language Sciences* 14 (4): 385–418.

Caffarel, A., Martin, J. R. and Matthiessen, C. M. I. M. (eds) (2004), *Language Typology: A Functional Perspective*, Amsterdam: Benjamins.

Catford, J. C. (1965), *A Linguistic Theory of Translation*, Oxford: Oxford University Press.

Chomsky, N. (1957), *Syntactic Structures*, The Hague: Mouton.

de Souza, L. M. F. (2010), *Interlingual Re-instantiation: A Model for a New and More Comprehensive Systemic Functional Perspective on Translation*, PhD Thesis, Florianopolis: Federal University of Santa Catarina.

García Fernández, L., and Camus Bergareche, B. (eds) (2004), *El pretérito imperfecto*, Madrid: Gredos.

Gleason, H. A. (1968), 'Contrastive Analysis in Discourse Structure', *Monograph Series on Languages and Linguistics* 21 (Georgetown University Institute of Languages and Linguistics), 39–64.

Halliday, M. A. K. (1961), 'Categories of the Theory of Grammar', *Word* 17 (3): 241–92.

Halliday, M. A. K. (1976), 'The English Verbal Group', in G. Kress (ed.), *Halliday: System and Function in Language*, 136–58, Oxford: Oxford University Press.

Halliday, M. A. K. (1979), 'Modes of Meaning and Modes of Expression: Types of Grammatical Structure, and Their Determination by Different Semantic Functions', in D. J. Allerton, E. Carney and D. Holcroft (eds), *Function and Context in Linguistics Analysis: Essays Offered to William Haas*, 57–79, Cambridge: Cambridge University Press.

Halliday, M. A. K. (1985), *An Introduction to Functional Grammar*, London: Arnold (2nd edn, 1994; 3rd edn revised by C. M. I. M. Matthiessen, 2004; 4th edn revised by C. M. I. M. Matthiessen, 2014).

Halliday, M. A. K. (1991), 'Language System and Language Instance; The Corpus as a Theoretical Concept', in J. Svartvik (ed.), *Directions in Corpus Linguistics: Proceedings of the Nobel Symposium 82*, 61–78, Berlin: Mouton de Gruyter.

Halliday, M. A. K. (1996), 'On Grammar and Grammatics', in R. Hasan, C. Cloran and D. G. Butt (eds), *Functional Descriptions: Theory in Practice*, 1–38, Amsterdam: Benjamins.

Hao, J. (2018), 'Reconsidering "Cause Inside the Clause" in Scientific Discourse – from a Discourse Semantic Perspective in Systemic Functional Linguistics', *Text & Talk* 38 (5): 525–50.

Hao, J. (2020), *Analysing Scientific Discourse from a Systemic Functional Linguistic Perspective: A Framework for Exploring Knowledge Building in Biology*, London: Routledge.

Martin, J. R. (1992), *English Text: System and structure*, Amsterdam: Benjamins.

Martin, J. R. (1996), 'Types of Structure: Deconstructing Notions of Constituency in Clause and Text', in E. H. Hovy and D. R. Scott (ed.), *Computational and Conversational Discourse: Burning Issues – an Interdisciplinary Account*, 39–66, Heidelberg: Springer.

Martin, J. R. (2008a), 'Tenderness: Realisation and Instantiation in a Botswanan Town', *Odense Working Papers in Language and Communication*, 30–62 (Special Issue of Papers from 34th International Systemic Functional Congress edited by Nina Nørgaard).

Martin, J. R. (2008b), 'Innocence: Realisation, Instantiation and Individuation in a Botswanan Town', in N. Knight and A. Mahboob (ed.), *Questioning Linguistics*, 32–76, Cambridge: Cambridge Scholars.

Martin, J. R. (2010), 'Semantic Variation: Modelling System, Text and Affiliation in Social Semiosis', in M. Bednarek and J. R. Martin (eds), *New Discourse on Language: Functional Perspectives on Multimodality, Identity and Affiliation*, 1–34, London: Continuum.

Martin, J. R. (2012), 'Heart from Darkness: Apocalypse Ron', *Revista Canaria de Estudios Ingleses* 65, November 2012, 67–99 (Special issue on The Evaluative Uses of Language: The Appraisal Framework).

Martin, J. R. (2016), 'Meaning Matters: A Short History of Systemic Functional Linguistics', *Word* 61 (2): 35–58.

Martin, J. R. (ed.) (2018), 'Interpersonal Meaning: Systemic Functional Perspectives', Special issue of *Functions of Language* 25 (1).

Martin, J. R., and Doran, Y. J. (eds) (2015), *Grammatical Descriptions*, edited by J. R. Martin and Y. J. Doran, London: Routledge (Critical Concepts in Linguistics: Systemic Functional Linguistics, vol. 2).

Martin, J. R., Doran, Y. J. and Figueredo, G. (eds) (2020), *Systemic Functional Language Description: Making Meaning Matter*, London: Routledge.

Martin, J. R., Quiroz, B., and Figueredo, G. (eds) (2021), *Interpersonal Grammar: Systemic Functional Linguistic Theory and Description*, Cambridge: Cambridge University Press.

Martin, J. R., Quiroz, B., and Wang, P. (eds) (2021), *Systemic Functional Grammar: Another Step into the Theory – Grammatical Description*, Beijing: Higher Education Press.

Martin, J. R., and Rose, D. (2003), *Working with Discourse: Meaning beyond the Clause*, 2nd revised edn 2007, London: Continuum.

Martin, J. R., and Rose, D. (2008), *Genre Relations: Mapping Culture*, London: Equinox.

Martin, J. R., and White, P. R. R. (2005), *The Language of Evaluation: Appraisal in English*, London: Palgrave.

Matthiessen, C. M. I. M. (2004), 'Descriptive Motifs and Generalisations', in A. Caffarel, J. R. Martin and C. M. I. M. Matthiessen (eds), *Language Typology: A Functional Perspective*, 537–673, Amsterdam: Benjamins.

Matthiessen, C. M. I. M. (2014), 'Choice in Translation: Metafunctional Considerations', in K. Kunz, E. Teich, S. Hansen-Schirra, S. Neumann and P. Daut (eds), *Caught in the Middle – Language Use and Translation* (A Festschrift for Erich Steiner on the Occasion of his 60th Birthday), 271–334. Saarbrücken: Saarland University Press.

Matthiessen, C. M. I. M. (2018), 'The Notion of a Multilingual Meaning Potential: A Systemic Exploration', in Akila S. Baklouti and Lise Fontaine (eds), *Perspectives from Systemic Functional Linguistics*, 90–120, London: Routledge.

Matthiessen, C. M. I. M., and Halliday, M. A. K. (2009), *Systemic Functional Grammar: A First Step into the Theory*, Beijing: Higher Education Press.

Mwinlaaru, I. N., Matthiessen, C. M. I. M. and Akerejola, E. (2018), 'A System-Based Typology of MOOD in Niger-Congo Languages', in A. Agwuele and A. Bodomo (eds), *The Handbook of African Linguistics*, London: Routledge.

Mwinlaaru, I. N., and Xuan, W. W. (2016), 'A Survey of Studies in Systemic Functional Language Description and Typology', *Functional Linguistics* 3 (8).

Olbertz, H. (2011), *Verbal Periphrases in a Functional Grammar of Spanish*, Berlin: Gruyter.

PRESEEA (2014–), *Corpus del Proyecto para el estudio sociolingüístico del español de España y de América*. Alcalá de Henares: Universidad de Alcalá. Recovered on 21 August 2017 from http://preseea.linguas.net.

Quiroz, B. (2013), *The Interpersonal and Experiential Grammar of Chilean Spanish: Towards a Principled Systemic-Functional Description based on Axial Argumentation*. Unpublished PhD Dissertation. University of Sydney, Sydney. https://repositorio.uc.cl/handle/11534/22682.

Quiroz, B. (2017), 'Gramática interpersonal básica del español: una caracterización sistémico-funcional del sistema de MODO', *Lenguas Modernas* 49: 157–82. https://revistas.uchile.cl/index.php/LM/article/view/49231.

Quiroz, B. (2018), 'Negotiating Interpersonal Meanings: Reasoning about MOOD', *Functions of Language* 25 (1): 135–63. doi:10.1075/fol.17013.qui.

Ridenhour, R. (1994), 'Jesus Was Gook', in Dan Duffy and Kalí Tal (eds), *Nobody Gets Off the Bus: The Viet Nam Generation Big Book* 5. 1–4, 138–42, Woodbridge, CT: Viet Nam Generation, http://www.ridenhour.org/about_ron.html & http://www2.iath.virginia.edu/sixties/HTML_docs/Texts/Narrative/Ridenhour_Jesus_01.html.

Teruya, K., Akerejola, E., Anderson, T. H., Caffarel, A., Lavid, J., Matthiessen, C. M. I. M., Petersen, U. H., Patpong, P. and Smedegaard, F. (2007), 'Typology of Mood: A Text-Based and System-Based Functional View', in R. Hasan, C. M. I. M. Matthiessen and J. J. Webster (eds), *Continuing Discourse on Language: A Functional Perspective*, vol. 2, 859–920, London: Equinox.

Veiga, A. (2004), 'Cantaba y canté. Sobre una hipótesis temporal y alguna de sus repercusiones', *ELUA, Anexo 2 (El verbo)*, 599–614.

Wang, P. (2018), 'Verbal Groups in Manchu: A Systemic Functional Account', *Word* 64 (3): 157–76.

2

Textual instantiation, the notion of 'readings of texts', and translational agency

Erich Steiner

Universität des Saarlandes, Saarbrücken

The chapter begins by illustrating the central place of 'reading' in text analysis and translation. Assume that we have a text such as Example (1) with its original German translation (1b) and that our task is an analysis of lexical cohesion,[1] either in corpus-based work or within a pre-translational text analysis:

Example (1), Reading 1, lexical cohesion:

(1) THE HIDDEN GENETIC PROGRAM of COMPLEX ORGANISMS

Assumptions can be dangerous, especially in science. They usually start as the most plausible or comfortable interpretation of the available facts. But when their truth cannot be immediately tested and their flaws are not obvious, assumptions often graduate to articles of faith, and new observations are forced to fit them. Eventually, if the volume of troublesome information becomes unsustainable, the orthodoxy must collapse.

Published German translation:

(1b) Das verkannte Genom-Programm

Unbewiesene Annahmen entwickeln manchmal ein Eigenleben, was besonders in der Naturwissenschaft unangenehme Folgen haben kann. Am Anfang geht es gewöhnlich nur um eine plausible oder einfache Erklärung der Befunde. Wenn sie keine offensichtlichen Mängel aufweist und ihr Wahrheitsgehalt nicht unmittelbar überprüfbar ist, mutiert sie aber oft zum Glaubenssatz. Neue Beobachtungen werden dann passend interpretiert. Irgendwann jedoch muß das Dogma unter der Last eklatanter Widersprüche zusammenbrechen.

English gloss of (1b) word by word

The unrecognized Genome Programme
Unproven assumptions develop sometimes a life-of-their-own, which especially in the natural science uncomfortable consequences have can. At the beginning goes it usually only about a plausible or simple explanation of the findings. If it no obvious shortcomings displays and its truth-content not immediately testable is, mutates it however often to a dogma. New observations are then fittingly interpreted. At some time, however, must the dogma under the burden of blatant contradictions collapse.

In our Reading 1, we identify a lexical chain, indicated here through boldface, with an inferred superordinate concept such as **stages of science as a process and their properties**. The semantic relations (types of lexical cohesion in the sense of Halliday and Hasan 1976: 288) are *repetition, synonymy, part-of, have-a*. Reading 1, as any reading, crucially relies on interpretation and disambiguation by the reader/annotator. Simply assigning the lexical (potential) meanings based on some lexicon or dictionary look up will not suffice: LDOCE, for example (1995 edition), has two different readings for *assumption*, of which Reading 1 is the more plausible. WORDNET (searched 19 January 2018) gives seven senses, only three or four of which would fall into the lexical chain annotated in (1). Even if disambiguation by a reader is sufficient for deciding on the lexical chaining that occurs monolingually in English, in translation we need to decide on additional and/or different alignments between lexical items: there are at the time of look up (January 2018) fourteen different German lexical equivalents in *LEO* and seven different variants in the translation corpus *Linguee*.

For *interpretation*, LDOCE has two meanings, WORDNET has four readings, Linguee has eleven translations into German and LEO has seventy-two different translations. Once again, links between items will be different as will be the semantic relations on them depending on our readings. For example, are *assumptions, interpretations of the available facts, articles of faith, orthodoxy* lexically all hyponyms of *belief systems*, with, instantially, their phrases co-referring (cf. Section 4.3)? Furthermore, is *assumption* here part of a structured scientific process (*hypothesis, prediction*), or is it used more in its non-specialized meaning *belief, understanding, idea* …? These different readings exist for the English text independently of whether we are in a translation context or in a context of monolingual analysis of lexical cohesion. The translator, additionally, not only needs to decide whether the given lexical items belong in a chain in the source text, but also, and in interaction with this decision, on the translation into differently structured lexical fields of the target language. The resulting translations will be very different, depending on the outcome of these decisions about 'readings', and we shall see in Section 4.3 that more dimensions of meaning are involved than lexical experiential meaning only. The notion of 'reading', together with 'textual instantiation' and 'translational agency' will occupy a central place in this chapter.

1 The specificity of translation (studies)

What is distinctive about translation compared to other forms of text production? What does this distinctiveness have to do with 'equivalence'? Do we postulate equivalence between systems or instances, and where in all these relationships does the active role of the translator come into play? The assumption of distinctive properties of translation as product and as process has been one of the justifications of a discipline of Translation Studies (TS). Assume that by 'equivalence' we mean a relationship between source texts (STs) and target texts (TTs), or between smaller translation units as instances – an approximation along several dimensions of meaning. These dimensions will be ranked depending on the context of the translation brief, technically an aspect of the field of discourse of the translation under review. The approximation thus becomes a multidimensional optimization task, rather than one single right or wrong decision. What a notion of this kind requires, though, is a clear understanding of what the textual instance is to start with. It will be argued that some key properties of translation are largely due to the translator's search for equivalence. Moreover, the ST- and TT-instances, between which equivalence is sought, are 'readings' characterized by the specific double bind between ST and TT, so uniquely typical for translation.

Different notions of 'equivalence', or even the complete rejection of it, will lead to different notions of translation. The notion in its more precise variants allows us to make some important distinctions between translation and other forms of multilingual text production. The concept of equivalence has a long and important, yet controversial, history in TS (Koller 1995; Halverson 1997; Munday 2001: chapter 3; Steiner 2001b, 202; House 2015: 5–7). The requirement of equivalence has sometimes been shifted away from structural encoding towards processing and/or context. However, without explicit models of these, the burden of definition is simply shifted to other disciplines, or to common sense – not a promising strategy for TS. If the domain of equivalence is shifted to 'equivalent effect' in receptors of STs and TTs in some given context (Nida 1964: 159), the question arises of what contexts and effects are and in which way they can be equivalent. How do we assure comparability between source and target contexts and between receptors' patterns of behaviour in respect to which 'equivalent effect' is going to be measured? Likewise, if with relevance theory translation is considered as 'interlingual interpretive use' (Gutt 1991: 100), we again must assume some sort of equivalence between patterns of use in contexts and between assumptions, implicatures or propositions in which these can be expressed.

In view of such debates, the notion of equivalence has continuously been relativized and refined (Halverson 1997). Catford (1965), in his classic account building on Halliday et al. (1964), already diversified the notion across an entire range of linguistic ranks and levels. Matthiessen (2001, 2014) took that approach substantially further within a highly developed model of Systemic Functional Linguistics (SFL) (for applications to textual analyses cf. Halliday 2009, 2012). Transfer-based models of (machine-) translation (MT) relied on notions of equivalence-based transfer on a hierarchy of levels (EUROTRA as in Durand et al. 1991; Carl and Schaeffer 2017: 51–3), or in the extreme case on an interlingua which would neutralize language-dependent differences. More recent statistics-based MT models incorporate it under 'adequacy' (vs fluency) for MT evaluation (Banchs, D'Haro and Li 2015; Chungyu and Tak-Ming 2015), as do models of neural-networks-based MT with some modifications (cf. Gupta, Constantin and van Genabith 2015). For models of cognition in translation, removing equivalence altogether simply leaves us with notions of text production, text comprehension, bilingual processing – or a combination of these at best (Schwieter and Ferreira 2017a: 144–147; Shreve and LaCruz 2017: 129, 134–5 on the notion of 'transfer'). This also applies if we extend the notion of translation across different modes of meaning (Matthiessen 2001:50–60; Kress 2010, illustrating the notion of 'transduction' across modes). Multimodal semiotic objects increasingly are objects of translation posing a creative challenge to any form of text production (Hiippala 2012), but the very different codes employed in the different modalities require a motivated notion of 'equivalence across modes' which cannot simply be the unrefined everyday meaning of the term.

'Translation' is not a relationship between language systems, which is the object of contrastive linguistics. It is necessarily a relationship between instantiations of texts, more specifically a relationship between STs and TTs (or smaller translation units), which approximates equivalence in a combination of the dimensions of field, tenor and mode contextually and their realization as registers on the one hand, and ideational, interpersonal and textual meaning in terms of semantics and grammar on the other (Steiner 2001b, 2004, 2015). These dimensions will usually be ranked in importance depending on the context of the translation brief similar to the model of Koller (1997). Equivalence then is an approximation, a multidimensional optimization task. In addition, TTs may show traces of the process of understanding (e.g. explicitation) and other aspects of the translation process, in particular traces of contrasts between the language systems involved (interference, shining-through as in Teich 2003). Translation is different from paraphrase in respecting interpersonal and textual meanings in addition to experiential (propositional) and logical meaning. And translation is different from variation by keeping stable as many as possible of the parameters of variation. It is thus an approximation to a multifunctional paraphrase of the ST by some TT (rather than the mono-functional paraphrases of logic-oriented semantics) under the constraints of the process of understanding and of the typology of the language systems involved. Each individual translation as situated and instantiated language use is text production under the constraints of a source (con-)text.

In a slightly metaphoric way, we can think of the grammatical notion of 'quoting vs. reporting' (Halliday and Matthiessen 2014: 304) as an analogue to translation, exemplified in sentences (2) and (3), grammatical annotations in brackets:

(2) John said 'I'm hungry' (verbal: quote).
(3) John said that he was hungry (verbal: report).

In the sense of 'translation' advocated here, (4) is asking for a translation, whereas (5) is asking for some other form of multilingual text production:

(4) Tell them (in a different language) 'I'm hungry'.
(5) Tell them (in a different language) that I am hungry.

Partly as a consequence of the specifics of translation, translated texts exhibit properties such as simplification, normalization, levelling-out, explicitation and a few others. Explicitation in translated texts, both relative to their STs and relative to registerially comparable texts in their target culture, has received particular attention

(Hansen-Schirra, Neumann and Steiner 2012). One of the reasons for explicitation along ideational, interpersonal and textual dimensions may be the attempts by translators to maximally understand their ST in its context. This involves the unpacking of grammatical metaphors, which then is not completely reversed in TT production. This 'maximal understanding' is a deep, intense and attentive 'reading' of the ST.

And this is a crucial point at which the translator as an agent comes in: the ST-instance to be translated as '(translator's) reading of ST' is an idea we shall return to below, particularly in a review of the notion of 're-instantiation' as currently used in some SFL models. The activity of the translator has often been addressed in TS, and rightly so. However, the notion itself is not a powerful theoretical concept as long as it is taken in its unreconstructed everyday meaning ('What the translator does'). Nor does a superficial borrowing of the original sociological concept of 'role' bring much enlightenment, unless it is borrowed with its conceptual and methodological background from its empirical parent disciplines. Another source of concepts for modelling translators' activities is the notion of the 'implied reader/author' as in literary theory (Eagleton 1996: 64–6 on 'reception theory'), and it is here that semiotically based notions of 'reading' in SFL (e.g. Martin and Rose 2003; Martin and White 2005) can act as an interface to TS, as exemplified by Munday (2012). In different 'compliant, resistant, tactical' readings of texts translators unfold their (not necessarily conscious) activity and they are making choices, but choices which are contextualized and moulded (positively and negatively) by the double bind between ST and TT, so uniquely typical of translation.

As we have seen, an SFL perspective can be relevant for several key questions of translation (studies), such as 'equivalence' between texts, and such as 'reading' and translational agency. It will be seen, though, that such questions have to be situated within a maximally transparent modelling to unfold their potential, and this is what we shall turn to in the following sections.

2 SFL architectures for modelling translation: Abstraction and strata

This section briefly discusses SFL architectures for modelling translation, making a distinction between non-stratified models and stratified models of context. The distinction seems important for a model of translation in general, even if a comprehensive model of translation is not at issue here. However, the relationships between the linguistic strata involved and the precise characterization of 'instantiation' need further clarification because of our focus on the notion of 'reading' as the ultimate instance of a text. Thus we hope to lay the groundwork for our more detailed argumentation and exemplification in Sections 3 and 4.

Early scale-and-category-based models (cf. Halliday et al. 1964: 111–134; Catford 1965) usually focused on a rank-based translation model with the units *morpheme, word, group, clause, sentence*. In terms of stratification these models were grammatical, and in terms of instantiation discussions included the system and the instance. However, even these early models were in principle embedded within analyses of phonology/phonetics on one side and of context on the other, even if discussions often were programmatic and example-based rather than specific and empirical in a stricter sense. 'Meaning' was 'function in context' on all strata, and units were related to each other and to the instance through the scales of rank, delicacy and exponence, the latter closest to 'instantiation', as we shall discuss it later. Context was not stratified, and there was as yet no explicit mention of a 'reading' in relationship to 'exponence'.

2.1 Non-stratified context

Early SFL based modelling of translation was followed in the 1980-1990s by work with a more 'multifunctional' theoretical base (House 2015 with a first version 1977, several contributions in Steiner, Schmidt and Zelinsky-Wibbelt 1988; Bell 1991; Hatim and Mason 1990; Steiner 1996; Steiner and Yallop (eds) 2001), later leading on to empirical work on contrastive linguistics and translation (Steiner 2001a, b, 2004, 2019). This strand of work was related to a comprehensive and theoretical underpinning in Matthiessen (2001: 77), who presented an overall model for translation in terms of stratification, that is, abstraction into linguistic levels (context, semantics, lexicogrammar, phonology), instantiation (system versus sub-system versus textual instance), rank (clause, group/phrase, word, morpheme), delicacy (low versus high) and axis (system versus structure), all of these metafunctionally diversified (cf. also Matthiessen 2014) and embedded in a wider environment of translation. 'Context' in this strand of work was not further stratified, yet differentiated into 'contextual configuration in terms of field, tenor and mode' and 'register' as its semantic realization.[2] What elsewhere was treated as a separate and superordinate stratum of 'genre' (Martin 1992) was integrated here as 'goal orientation', or 'activity', under 'field of discourse'.

Within this line of work, translation was differentiated from other forms of text production as follows (Steiner 2001b: 179–185):

In this model, choosing the type of text production is up to the translator after due consideration of the contextual configuration of the text production task at hand, in particular through negotiation with the client. In semantic or grammatical translation,

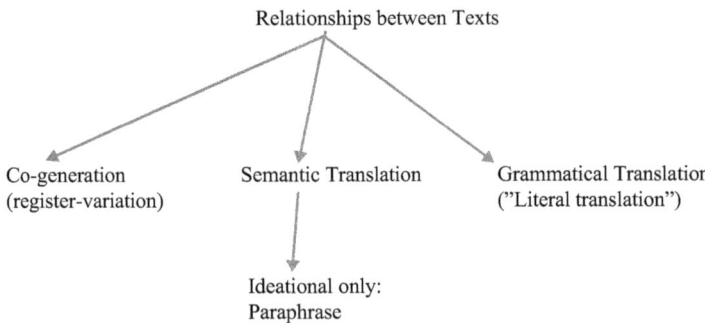

Figure 2.1 Translation and other relationships between texts.

rather than in co-generation, there is a strong commitment by the translator to the source text (ST) meaning, so translation is assumed to be, grammatically speaking, more like 'quoting' than 'reporting' (cf. Section 1).

In pre-translational ST-analysis, or 'reading' of the ST, the translator attempts to arrive at the (source-)contextually most plausible interpretation. Modelled on the level of lexicogrammar, this interpretation is conceptualized as involving 'de-metaphorization' in the SFL sense of 'grammatical metaphor'. In producing the target text (TT), the translator may not go back up all the TT-compatible way towards 're-metaphorization', for various reasons to do with the target language system, TT-registerial norms, pressures of time and so on, Figure 2.2 symbolizes this assumption:

The strand of work briefly characterized here explored strata and metafunctions to a considerable extent, leading in due course to extensive empirical testing on corpora (Steiner 2001a; Teich 2003; Hansen-Schirra, Neumann and Steiner 2012; Neumann 2014; Steiner 2015) and on the process of translation (cf. Alves et al. 2010; Serbina et al. 2017), and thus to motivated links between modelling, predictions and data – the instance. The perspective on registers and individual texts against the background of the language systems involved can be seen as a move along a cline of instantiation (to be explained in the following section), even if a distinction between (i) a textual instance and (ii) possible readings of it by the translator was not explicitly made.

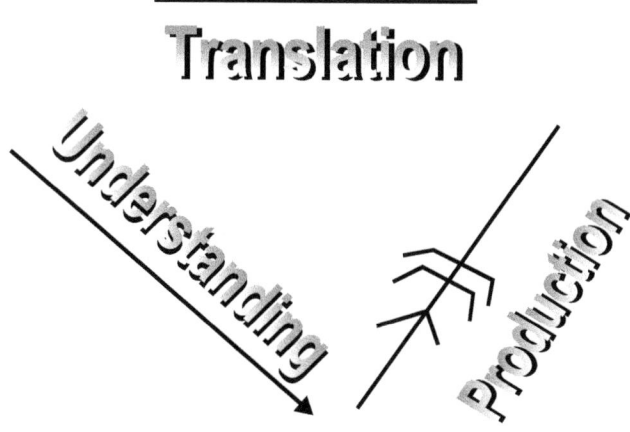

Figure 2.2 Incomplete re-metaphorization in the target language (from Steiner 2001a: 15).

2.2 Stratified context

Martin, since 1992 and earlier, has been pursuing an architecture with a notion of context stratified into *genre* and *register*, and in earlier versions also *ideology*,[3] to be realized in *discourse semantics* and then *lexicogrammar* and *phonology* as further, less abstract strata. Importantly, and as in the work referred to in Section 2.1, all of these strata instantiate (e.g. Martin 2006: 285; Tann 2017). Added to the notion of 'abstraction' applied to the realization hierarchy, there are the scales of *instantiation* and *individuation*, the latter one being unique to this version of the theory as a scale, although it is founded on the related notion of *code* in Basil Bernstein's sense.

Of particular importance for a modelling of translation within Martin's approach is the importance of 'instantiation', including 'reading', and of the active role of the translator which thus comes more clearly into view (de Souza 2010, 2013).[4] This approach uses a notion of *re-instantiation*, subclassified into *intermodal (transduction)*, *intralingual (elaboration)* and *interlingual (translation)* types. Elsewhere (Martin 2006), *intralingual* is in turn sub-classified into *quotation, paraphrasing and retelling*, and de Souza extends this sub-classification to *interlingual translation* (2013) This interlingual re-instantiation involves a process of distantiation from the end of the instance cline (the 'reading'). In looking for translational equivalents, a translator may 'ascend' from the reading-instance and apply *quotation, paraphrasing and retelling*, depending on the constraints of the translation situation. Distantiation leads to more generalized meanings, while instantiation yields more specific meanings, for example, readings of a textual instance (cf. Section 3.2 below).

In principle, translation can be modelled in terms of realization (systems), users (individuations, codes) and uses (instances) (de Souza 2013: 575); the latter two perspectives are foregrounded in the Martin and de Souza approaches. It is possible to hold a stratum constant (e.g. appraisal/ discourse semantics) and then explore effects when moving along the individuation and instantiation hierarchies. 'In intra- as in interlingual re-instantiation, a TT reconstructs the meaning potential of a given ST. In the latter, this reconstruction is enabled by the translator's reading of the ST, which in turn is informed by his/her repertoires in the two languages/cultures' (de Souza 2013: 580–1). We shall argue in Section 4 that, indeed, all texts still represent meaning *potentials*, whereas readings, contextually instantiated and thus annotated, are not potentials – they are fully disambiguated, at least in theory.

Martin et al. have introduced the notion of '(compliant, tactical, resistant) subjectified readings' of texts (Martin and Rose 2003: 269–70; Martin and White 2005: 206–7; Martin 2010; for translation Munday 2012: 37–40) as a further (and ultimate?) layer along the instantiation cline,[5] thus giving greater emphasis to the role of the reader than was usual before in SFL based models:

> Compliant readings accommodate the reading position naturalised by a text ... Resistant readings on the other hand work against the grain of this naturalisation process ... Tactical readings are readings which take some aspect of the evaluation a text affords, and respond to it in an interested way that neither accepts nor rejects communion with the text as a whole. (Martin and White 2005: 206)

It is this notion which de Souza exploits as the ultimate instance for a model of translation. As she says:

STs can thus be said to participate in both systems – in the SL system as an instance and in the TL system as one of its afforded readings. Likewise, TTs also participate in both language systems – in the SL system, as one of the readings afforded by the ST, and in the TL system, as an instance plus the new readings afforded by it ... This evidences the Janus-faced status of the translator's reading – it looks backwards to the ST and forward to the TT to be produced. (de Souza 2010: 150)

We shall suggest below that the translator's reading is tactical in the sense that his/her activity and goals are different from those of the primary audience. However, in producing the TT, the translator will choose between compliant, tactical or resistant readings to encode.

In the two sections to come, we shall attempt a critical review of the precise relationships between the linguistic strata involved, but above all a further clarification of the notions of 'instantiation' in both of the approaches in Sections 2.1 and 2.2. The notion of 'reading' as the ultimate instance of a text to be translated will receive our particular attention.[6]

3 Generalization and the scale of instantiation

We shall begin here with a few examples illustrating the importance of notions such as 'reading' and 'implicitness of meaning'. After a brief discussion of some general linguistic accounts of implicit meaning, of the notion of 'explicitation' in translation, and of the notion of 'reading' in literary studies, we shall discuss the SFL notion of 'instantiation', which is shared by the models in Sections 2.1 and 2.2. The notion of 'reading', embodied in Section 2.2, will be highlighted as the end point of the scale of instantiation. It is attractive in its potential for modelling phenomena such as ambiguity, vagueness and interpretation in studies of textuality generally, but also of ideology and evaluation in critical discourse analysis or translation. In particular, it allows us to focus on the active role of the translator as an intrinsic part of a model of translation. It also represents one possible way of re-conceptualizing the key notion of 'equivalence' (cf. Section 1), if it can be made sufficiently transparent and explicit. At the same time, it brings with it a number of open questions of conceptualization and operationalization which will be addressed in later sections.

Establishing the meaning(s) of a text requires the recognition that the mappings between different strata of textual encoding are not one to one. There are indeed different 'readings' of texts, as illustrated by Examples (6) to (7) and (8) in Section 4.3 in contexts of translation.[7]

(6) *Inmates will not be allowed to **leave** the grounds **unattended**.* (COCA)

German translations:

(6a) *Insassen dürfen das Gelände nicht **unbeaufsichtigt lassen**.*
(6b) *Insassen dürfen das Gelände nicht **unbeaufsichtigt verlassen**.*

The experiential ambiguity in (6) is due to a well-known ambiguity of attachment and scoping of the modifier *unattended*, which leads to two different readings. In reading (6a), it is the grounds which are left unattended; in (6b) it is the inmates. The translator into German has to decide between these two readings because the German verbal system (*lassen/verlassen*) forces the choice so that a (translationally ideal) ambiguity-preserving translation is not possible. There is no verbal superordinate in German for *lassen vs verlassen* which would allow the neutralization.

Example (7) has to do with scoping ambiguities in a case of cohesive reference:

(7) *And he answered them courteously that they should speak on, for he had not come so far and so wearily simply in order to turn back. Moreover he was charged by his father with a mission, which he might not reveal in that place. 'It is known to us already,' said the three damsels. [EO_FICTION_002]*

(7a) *Und er erwiderte ihnen artig, dass sie weitersprechen sollten, denn er habe die Mühsal und Beschwerden des weiten Weges nicht auf sich genommen, um nun kehrtzumachen. Und zudem habe sein Vater ihn mit einer Aufgabe betraut, die er an diesem Ort zu enthüllen nicht gesonnen sei. '**Dies** ist uns bekannt', sagten die drei Jungfrauen. [GTrans_FICTION_002].* (from Byatt, A. S. 1991, 152 *Possession*; translation by Melanie Walz 1994); detailed discussion in Steiner 2015: 360)

In Example (7), there is substantial ambiguity as to the antecedent of *It*, as well as to the scoping of the indirect speech and as to information distribution, especially in the relative clause. The constraints of German grammar and cohesion force the translator to choose between some of the possible readings compatible with the English ST in (7): the choice between coreferential pronouns *es* versus *dies* ('it' versus 'this') encoding personal or extended reference, respectively; the choice between indicative and conjunctive/subjunctive mood in the preceding main clauses as potential antecedents; and the choice of word order in the preceding relative clause, encoding informational markedness and thus status as an antecedent of the referential pronouns. Both (7) and (7a) are lexicogrammatical instances, that is, not yet fully instantiated textual readings, but the German translation (7a) resolves the ambiguities mentioned above by steering the readings in a certain direction.

Examples (1) and (8) and their different readings in terms of lexical cohesion, participant tracking, information structure and in appraisal provide detailed illustration of translators' choices when reading (see Section 4.3). Some of the ambiguities in (6)–(8), especially those to do with experiential meaning, will be reduced or even resolved given sufficient co- and context. Yet even some of these, and more so ambiguities related to information structure and interpersonal meaning, leave more space for choice by the reader, and by the translator in particular. The fact that textual encoding provides only constraints on readings (rather than full specifications) has been acknowledged and modelled across approaches to textuality, some of which we point to in the following section.

3.1 'Explicitation' and 'reading'

According to a widely accessible handbook article (Linke and Nussbaumer 2000: 4357), there are the following layers of implicit meaning of utterances:

1 Implicit meaning I (linguistic semantics)
    1.1 Semantic presuppositions
    1.2 Implications/ entailments
2 Implicit meaning II (dependent on usage/ context)
    2.1 Pragmatic presuppositions (world knowledge, procedural knowledge)
    2.2 Conversational Implicatures
    2.3 Illocution, perlocution etc.

In terms of the widespread 'Iceberg Metaphor' of meaning, a 'reading' of a piece of discourse is an enrichment of the linguistically encoded message with implicit meaning of type I, and then also with implicit meaning of type II. The former is part of linguistic semantics, the latter of pragmatics. Further layers of meaning are not excluded.[8]

Another well-known framework for modelling explicitated meanings of linguistic encoding is Relevance Theory (RT). In Carston's version of RT (Carston 2002: 15, 94), there is a basic distinction between linguistic structure (encoding, saying) and utterance meaning (relevance- and context-based inferencing on the basis of structure). Several mappings between levels of representation are posited such that

> **Linguistic meaning** *underdetermines what is meant.*
> **What is said** *underdetermines what is meant.*
> **Linguistic meaning** *underdetermines what is said.*

Linguistic meaning is the linguistic encoding itself. *What is said* is a propositional semantic representation, including referential instantiation and disambiguation, as well as some forms of 'pragmatic enrichment' (Carston 2002: 223), essentially implicit meaning of type 1 in Linke and Nussbaumer. *What is meant* is the full utterance meaning including all sorts of pragmatic implicature. There is then a much wider gap even between linguistic meaning and *what is said* than is commonly assumed, particularly in pragmatics. In terms of Carston's version of RT, a reading of an utterance is the linguistic encoding instantiated into 'what is said' and, on the basis of this, the inferred 'utterance meaning/ what is meant'.

Yet another context in which explicitation of meaning was modelled is Steiner (2001a: 15) and Hansen-Schirra, Neumann and Steiner (2012: 59) (cf. Figure 2.2). Here we define a notion of explicitation:

> We assume explicitation if a translation (or language-internally one text in a pair of register-related texts) realizes meanings (not only ideational, but including interpersonal and textual) more explicitly than its source text – more precisely, meanings not realized in the less explicit source variant but implicitly present

in a theoretically-motivated sense. The resulting text is more explicit than its counterpart. (Hansen-Schirra, Neumann and Steiner 2012: 59)

In terms of this definition, which can be applied intra- or interlingually, a reading (including referential instantiation and disambiguation) is based on relatively explicitated/congruent lexicogrammatical encodings of a ST segment/ translation unit.

Finally, the notion of 'reading' in the context of 'reception (theory) of texts' is a central focus of literary studies (cf. among many others Eagleton):

> To read at all, we need to be familiar with the literary techniques and conventions which a particular work deploys; we must have some grasp of its 'codes', by which is meant the rules which systematically govern the ways it produces its meanings. Recall once more the London Underground sign I discussed in the Introduction: 'Dogs must be carried on the escalator.' To understand this notice I need to do a great deal more than simply read its words one after the other. I need to know, for example, that these words belong to what might be called a 'code of reference' – that the sign is not just a decorative piece of language there to entertain travelers, but is to be taken as referring to the behavior of actual dogs and passengers on actual escalators. I must mobilize my general social knowledge to recognize that the sign has been placed there by the authorities, that these authorities have the power to penalize offenders, that I as a member of the public am being implicitly addressed, none of which is evident in the words themselves. I have to rely, in other words, upon certain social codes and contexts to understand the notice properly. But I also need to bring these into interaction with certain codes or conventions of reading – conventions which tell me that by 'the escalator' is meant *this* escalator and not one in Paraguay, that 'must be carried' means 'must be carried *now*' and so on. I must recognize that the 'genre' of the sign is such as to make it highly improbable that the ambiguity I mentioned in the Introduction is actually 'intended'. It is not easy to distinguish between 'social' and 'literary' codes here: concretizing 'the escalator' as 'this escalator', adopting a reading convention which eradicates ambiguity, itself depends upon a whole network of social knowledge. (Eagleton 1996: 67–8)

So, written and even spoken texts are not the ultimate 'instance', instead textual encodings become disambiguated and explicitated in their cultural and situative contexts along several dimensions of meaning by a reader (including the translating reader). This is not an isolated or, indeed, new insight, so what is the enrichment offered by an SFL perspective?

3.2 Development of 'instantiation' and 'reading' in SFL

As we saw in Section 2.2, de Souza (2013) extends Martin's notions of 'quotation, paraphrasing, retelling' from *intra*lingual re-instantiation to *inter*lingual re-instantiation. Elsewhere, she models the process of translation as follows:

For interlingual re-instantiation this could be rephrased as

1. start at the instance pole of the source language (SL) system, that is, an instance already produced (the ST),
2. distantiate
   a. move up the SL's cline so as to access meanings at a less committed level,
   b. move up the TL's cline so as to access meanings at a less committed level,
   c. find/forging points of convergence between the clines of the two systems, and then
3. re-instantiate the ST by managing semantic relations like those proposed in Martin (2008) and Hood (2008).

Of course, in practice, the three steps of distantiation, finding/forging points of convergence and re-instantiation happen simultaneously, but we have to artificially separate them in order to understand which elements are contributed by each to the final product, i.e., the TT. (de Souza 2010: 165–6)

This is shown in Figure 2.3 (Figure 3.12 in de Souza 2010: 169).

My understanding of moving along the scale of instantiation, always keeping stratum (here: semantics), axis, metafunctions and delicacy constant, is the following: the ultimate instance is a 'reading'. Moving upwards from a reading, we have a group/set of readings, that is, all and only those compatible with the lexicogrammatical text itself. This would presumably be like the readings of our text Examples (8) in Section 4.3. Thus when moving upwards from one reading to the set of readings compatible with ('afforded by' in Martin and White's 2005: chapter 4.1 terminology) one written/spoken text, we would not necessarily move upwards in delicacy. Moving upwards from there, we have a larger set of readings from a set of texts (text-type, cf. Section

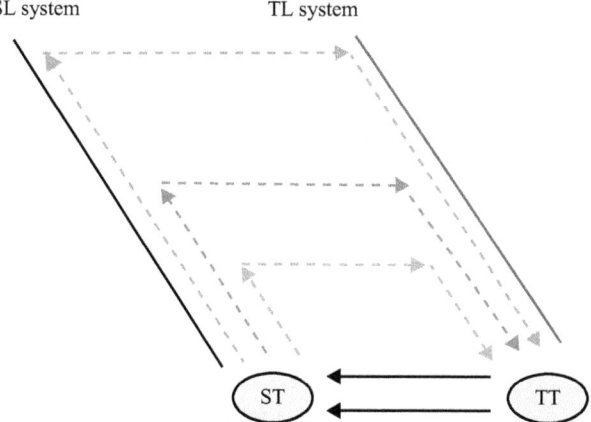

Figure 2.3 Possible distantiation/re-instantiation paths in interlingual re-instantiation (de Souza 2010: 169).

4.2). Some, but not all, of these types will also be sets of texts belonging to a register. All the registers and text types together constitute the possible set of texts of a language.

Now, is instantiation/distantiation in that sense clearly different from and in principle independent of 'delicacy'? Moves in delicacy lead to *under-/over-translation*, something which clearly happens in translation, but does not constitute a new approach to equivalence. An SFL based answer so far has involved 'shifts' (Matthiessen 2001: 78–9, 96–7; 2014) and 'compensation', that is, the selection of meanings elsewhere in the text for the loss of specificity through less delicate 'under-translation' in the particular translation unit (Steiner 1996: 621–2; Teich 2003: 219–20). De Souza's model, however, privileges distantiation along the scale/cline of generalization/instantiation rather than delicacy. This is precisely the sense in which our English Examples (1) and (8) would be different instances of a text, yet not differently delicate in most cases.

In my initial understanding of SFL, an instance is a (complete) path through linguistic system(s) plus realization statements, leading from less delicate to more delicate features. Text-type-specific or register-specific sub-systems are not *defined* by delicacy, but *imply* restricted and/or fewer paths in a systemic or delicacy perspective. The second understanding is 'exponence', that is, a lexicogrammatical wording compatible with such paths. Both notions have their own validities (Halliday and Matthiessen 1999: 382). Registers or text-types are defined as intermediate on a scale of instantiation (sub-languages) relatively independently of delicacy, an understanding compatible with both variants of SFL in the sense of Section 2. How, in a more precise sense, do we generalize from instances *other than through either exponence or through delicacy*? Sections 4.2 and 4.3 suggest some tentative answers.

The related notion of re-instantiation needs to engage with the traditional notion of equivalence in TS. If we conceive of translation as re-instantiation, what precisely is the 're-' here other than (a possibly better theorized) notion of 'equivalence'? Even metafunctionally diversifying 're-instantiate' into 're-construe, re-enact and re-present' (Matthiessen 2014: 277), a necessary and insightful SFL contribution to any model of translation, does not finally answer the question of 'equivalence' and 'cross-linguistic meaning'.

In summary, the notion of 'reading as (ultimate) instance' appears to be a plausible and possibly necessary part of a model of translation. And further discussion of 'individuation and subjectivization' (Martin, 2006; de Souza 2010, 2013), which we have not engaged with here, looks like another promising area to explore especially for a modelling of translational agency. But explicitly modelling a scale of instantiation, independently of delicacy and exponence, needs further clarification in both variants of SFL architecture. Section 4.2 attempts a tentative answer to the question of instantiation versus delicacy, whereas Section 4.3 explores exponence, the decisive step in going from the most specific 'type' (a worded text) to its 'token' (the fully contextualized instantiation in a given reading).

4 Translational agency: Levels of meaning, registers, text types and readings of texts

The clarifications suggested below will involve the notions of abstraction (strata of language) versus generalization (instantiation). Some empirical bottom-up analyses and classifications of texts will explore how 'text type' is different from 'register' on the scale of instantiation. It will then be argued with the help of some detailed examples that a 'reading' of a text can be modelled as its 'annotation', and that some types of reading/annotation are ultimate instances whereas others are more like yet another text, and thus possibly circular as far as the cline of instantiation is concerned. Phenomena covered will include lexical cohesion, participant tracking, information structure and appraisal. It will be seen that readings are instantiations of texts, forming a set of meanings on the semantic stratum, which together are compatible with ('afforded by') the written/spoken text. However, where we employ natural language for annotations, these are themselves parts of more delicate texts and thus not an ultimate instance. Where we use other representations of reading (chains, indices), these are not ambiguous. Translational agency is involved in choosing between priorities given to levels of textual encoding, registers and readings of texts, yet it has a particular commitment to the author's voice in the ST.

4.1 Clarification of the notions of 'abstraction' and 'generalization'

From the perspective of methodology, a proliferation of assumed levels and clines in a theory without clear operationalizations makes that theory non-transparent and prevents testable empirical predictions (cf. also Steiner 1991: 84–5; Hao 2015: 2–5; Williams, Russel and Irwin 2017).

Starting with 'strata' and 'abstraction', in what precise senses are

Subject – Finite – Predicator – Complement (Interpersonal Grammar)
Agent – Process – Goal (Semantics)
Activity – Sequence (Field in Contextual Configuration)

representations at the levels of grammar, semantics and contextual configuration, respectively, and in what sense are these levels 'abstractions' from each other within a roughly sketched non-stratified context architecture of SFL? The same would apply to analyses within a stratified context architecture:

Participant – Process – Circumstance
Occurrences – Entities – Qualities (Discourse Semantics)
Activities – Items – Properties (Field/ Register)

The strata here would be grammar, discourse semantics and register.

In the examples above, 'abstraction' cannot mean 'abstraction of common features from a set of classes to form a super-class' in the hyponymy sense, because this is covered in SFL by intra-stratum 'delicacy'. Assuming instead that the inter-stratal relationships are in terms of 'realization' and 'meta-redundancy' (Halliday and Matthiessen 1999: 25), how is that different from saying that they 'encode' each other? If with Halliday and Matthiessen (1999: 327) we maintain that *realization, instantiation* and *delicacy* are distinct scales of abstraction – then 'abstraction' seems to be used as a superordinate concept. The three scales, though, are inter-stratal, type-token and intra-stratal, respectively; hence subsuming them under a general concept of 'abstraction' may be intuitively useful, but not very precise. In addition, between the two variants of SFL it is not clear whether 'semantics' is a projection from lexicogrammar (in the sense of Halliday and Matthiessen 1999), involving grammatical cryptotypes as a motivating mechanism (Halliday and Matthiessen 1999: 27), or whether semantics is rather a 'discourse semantics' (Martin 1992), a semantic interpretation of patterns of cohesion, information structure and interpersonal meanings (on which cf. Hao 2015). In Halliday, Hasan and Matthiessen's writings, and in my own work to date, 'cohesion' is non-structural realization complementing the textual component of lexicogrammar within one stratum, whereas in Martin's account it is the backbone of 'discourse semantics'. On the other hand, this discourse semantics seems to include the 'ideation-base' semantics of Halliday and Matthiessen (1999) under ideation/experiential, alongside lexical cohesion. For a methodologically desirable unified model, which level is 'abstracted' from which and according to which principles?

Moving further upwards from 'semantics', can features of 'context' be derived from inside language, or from outside? If the latter, in what sense is linguistics capable of achieving it (see the discussion in Lukin et al. 2008; Bowcher 2017) rather than, say, anthropology or sociology? And how generalizable are networks of context across domains and sequences of activity (cf. also Wegener 2011: 118–19; Hao 2015)? Abstraction, then, is only vaguely defined, related to 'encoding', and the strata related through abstraction seem to be less clear as we move outwards from lexicogrammar through semantics to context.

The 'inside-out' approach to stratification attempts to work from units of structure at a given level towards features within one stratum (axis), and then through realization towards features at adjacent levels. To achieve this, a level-specific unit of structure, of realization, is needed, and what these units are beyond the grammar-to-semantics interface is unclear in both versions of the theory. Candidate units have been suggested as *clause, turn, interaction*, sometimes *message* (Butt in Lukin et al. 2008: 202), and *phase of episode*. Lukin et al. (2008: 192) quote Halliday as suggesting

> A 'rank scale' of structural units such as, possibly, text, subtext, semantic paragraph, sequence, figure, element; and metafunctional regions defined in topological fashion, construing the activity patterns and ideological motifs of the culture (clusters relating to technology, to social hierarchy, to the sphere of activities of daily life, and so on).

The discourse semantic unit of meaning for context in Martin (1992: 293) and in Hao (2015: 45–6) is *message-part*, yet its realizational relationship outwards to field of discourse is not clear. Martin and Matruglio (2013) and Hao (2015: 319) address these problems, especially in connection with working on stratal tension, indirectness of mapping and grammatical metaphor, but the status, operationalization and interaction of units of realization are currently still underspecified in the theory. As long as this is the case, the important notions of 'realization' and of 'abstraction' as superordinate concepts remain vague.

When it comes to 'generalization', both versions of SFL claim it to be the relationship of instantiation 'upwards' (*intra-stratal*), similar to 'delicacy' and different from 'realization' (*inter-stratal*). In a system network as an intra-stratal feature hierarchy, the move from more delicate to less delicate is one clear sense of (intra-stratal) 'generalization', where the daughter classes conjointly denote the same classes and elements as their less delicate parent class. However, what SFL seems to mean by 'instantiation/generalization' is the intra-stratal 'type-token' relationship: in a perspective taking the system and its instantiations together, a token/instantiation (one worded text/reading) is a (maximally delicate) feature selection/path-plus-realizational statements which jointly designate a set of readings, one reading only in the limiting case.

In set theory generally, instantiations of a class are (subsets of) members (elements). The class 'contains' its members (systemic instantiation) yet 'includes' its subclasses (systemic delicacy) – however all of the latter are classes/types, not instances. A move towards increased instantiation yields a set which has fewer members than the more general set: for example, a register or a text-type contains (is instantiated by) a subset of the possible texts of the language, a position which I believe to be compatible with Halliday and Matthiessen (1999: 382–3). *Instantiation* within a stratum (i.e. moving from the overall linguistic system through registers and text-types to texts and readings) successively narrows the sets of texts contained. Importantly for our discussion in Section 4.3, instances/readings should ideally not be ambiguous, because they are fully situated language.

By contrast, a move in *realization* across strata upwards or downwards designates identical sets of sentences. Within a stratum, *delicacy* sub-specifies a given class into its more specific (included) classes. Now, these sub-classes, in my view, are each also instantiated by smaller sets of sentences than the super-class – so do we have two separate notions of 'intra-stratal generalization'? An answer suggested in Halliday and Matthiessen is that more and less *delicate* classes are related *typologically*, whereas more or less *instantial* text types are related *topologically*, which I understand would be compatible with Martin's position on the issue. As a more formal version of this view, I would suggest that our text types hierarchically clustered in Figure 2.4 and any cluster derived from Figure 2.6 are examples of bottom-up classified text-types ('distantiations' in Martin's sense). They are clustered in terms of shallow lexical features and quantitative chain properties, and these features are not (necessarily) part of a system network or a realizational rule. The clustering also concerns frequencies, proportionalities and distinctiveness of features, whereas classification according to delicacy is usually in terms of presence/absence of features. In that sense, they may be different from features in systemic networks, and they are 'topological' rather than typological because the features used in our clustering are not (necessarily) features which are typologically related.

In summary, I suggest that *realization, delicacy* and *instantiation* are technical concepts of the theory. They may be referred to as subtypes of abstraction, but that latter term is much less strictly defined than the former three (cf. also Steiner 1996; Williams, Russel and Irwin 2017). *Instantiation*, either as any set of paths through systems or as their lexicogrammatical output through realization rules, is also clear enough. We have argued for one sense in which *instantiation/generalization* can be seen as independent of *delicacy* above, that is, topological rather than typological.

4.2 How is 'text type' different from 'register' on the scale of instantiation?

'Text type' and 'genre/register' meet up along the same cline of instantiation (Matthiessen 2001: 91–6; Martin and White 2005: 163) as bottom-up versus top-down perspectives. A text type is a class of texts to which the individual textual instance with its readings belongs. In my view, those text types which are contextually and culturally meaningful, are 'registers'. However, not all text-types are registers, as illustrated by Figure 2.4, and to some extent also Figures 2.5 and 2.6:

The HCA in Figure 2.4 shows a bottom-up classification of texts(-types) by properties of their lexical composition as indicators of lexical cohesion (for a fuller account, see Kunz et al. 2017b). The properties or 'shallow features' are lexical density, standardized type-token ratio, the role of most-frequent words, the role of top-content words relative to the next more general text-type, and the role of certain romance words. Texts belong to clusters according to (topological?) relationships in terms of these features. Figure 2.4 clearly shows that classifying bottom-up with shallow lexical features does not yield a classification by language, mode and register, and this is confirmed by the same type of analysis one level down in the corpus for texts within registers.

A second type of bottom-up analysis, this time by semantic relations (Figure 2.5) and properties of lexical chains (Figure 2.6), both from Kunz et al. (2016), further confirms this impression:

Cluster Dendrogram

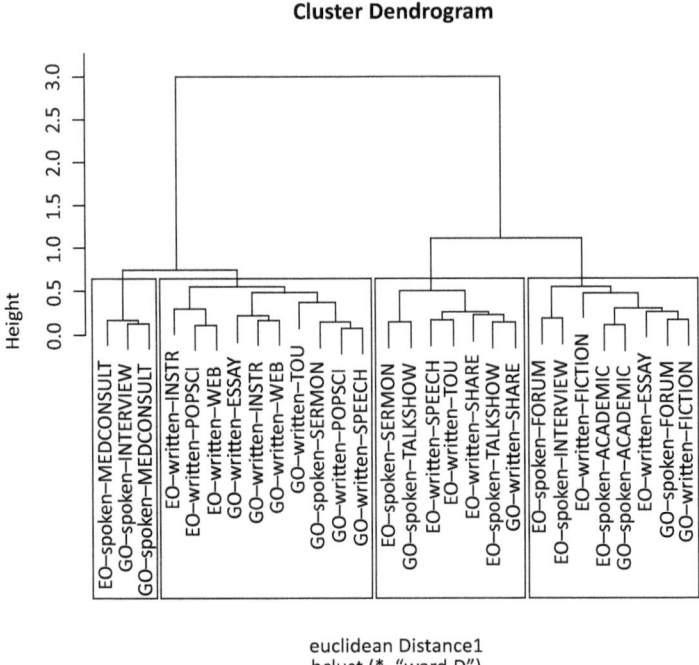

euclidean Distance1
hclust (*, "ward.D")

Figure 2.4 Hierarchical Cluster Analysis (HCA), based on 'shallow features' (Kunz et al. 2017b).

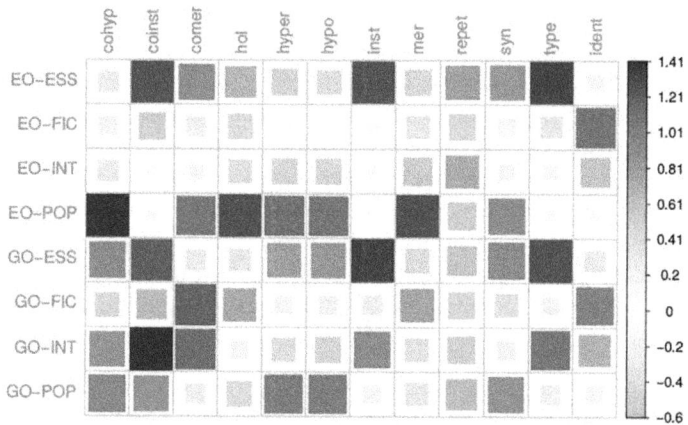

Figure 2.5 Associations between registers and semantic relations (Kunz et al. 2016).

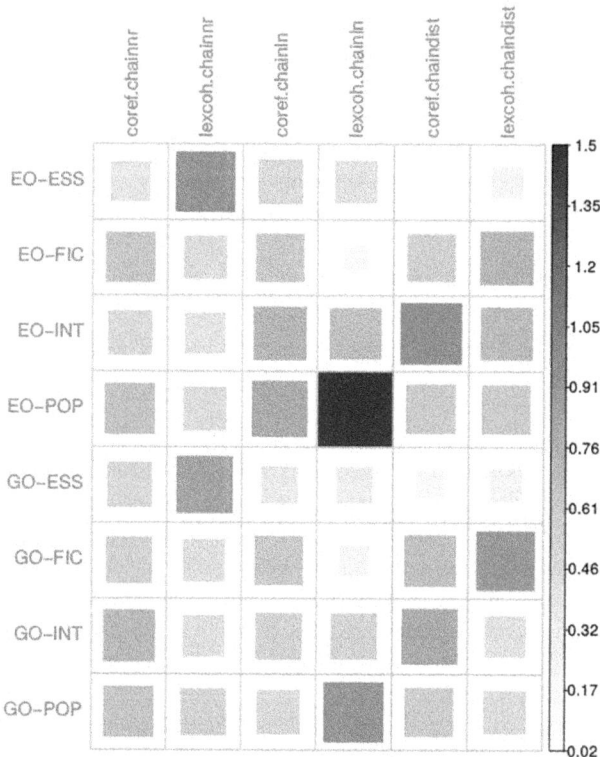

Figure 2.6 Associations between registers and chain properties (Kunz et al. 2016).

The analyses in Figures 2.4–2.6 show text-types bottom-up on the instantiation cline, and in terms of lexicogrammatical (4) versus semantic/cohesive (5, 6) features. Most importantly, we cannot assume a priori that text-types map one to one onto registers – which may be an empirical question for cultures and languages concerned. If we had not taken registers as an input to the classifications in Figures 2.5 and 2.6, we would get clusters more like in Figure 2.4. And if we look at how individual texts fall into types, as we often do in our empirical work, we see that not all of the bottom-up types correspond to registers. Both concepts of register and text-type can be operationalized for empirical research, but if and how they map onto each other, and on which stratum, is an empirical question. Generalization in this sense clearly depends on the features chosen.

4.3 Is 'reading' different from 'just another instantiated text'?

It will be argued here that 'readings' of a text can be modelled as its 'annotation', and that some types of reading/annotation are 'ultimate instances' whereas others are more like yet another text. The phenomena discussed will include lexical cohesion, participant tracking, information structure and appraisal in terms of Martin's discourse semantics. Readings are, indeed, instantiations of texts, forming a set of meanings which together are compatible with, or 'afforded by', the written/spoken text. However, where our annotations of a reading are in terms of natural language, these are themselves more delicate texts and thus potentially open to different readings. Where we use other representations (chains, indices), these are not ambiguous.

Let us assume that a reading of a text is a representation which has gone through

- grammatical and lexical disambiguation (leading to lexical chains, one aspect of *ideation*),
- referential indexing (leading to participant-tracking through *identification*),
- FOCUS/ NEW assignment (one aspect of *periodicity*) and
- annotations for *appraisal*

in the sense of Martin's discourse semantic systems (Martin 1992, updated summary in Hao 2015: 44–5), or leading to grammatical and cohesive instantiated representations in the sense of Halliday and Matthiessen (1999). Our guiding questions then are: In what sense are the readings of our examples below more instantiated than the (written or spoken) texts would be? In what sense are the latter generalizations of our readings? Are there remaining ambiguities in readings, or are they the 'ultimate instance', that is, the realization of fully instantiated paths through all the relevant system networks plus full contextual instantiation?

The processes of grammatical and lexical disambiguation, referential indexing and analyses of information structure have to some extent been modelled explicitly by schools of linguistics, such as those referred to in Section 4.1, work of the Prague School and others. Where, then, is the added value of an SFL perspective? The answer may largely lie in SFL's wider metafunctional spread, particularly in interpersonal meaning (appraisal), and in its domain of modelling, that is, comprehensive 'texts' rather than the typical sentence-pair examples often used in other approaches. The full potential of SFL approaches, though, can only be realized if at least some of the open questions raised in its architecture (cf. above) can be answered.[9] As an example of a first functional dimension along which meaning is stratified in SFL, we have already discussed Example (1) at the very beginning of this chapter, dealing with the phenomenon of lexical cohesion as an important aspect of ideational meaning. It was pointed out there that the questions of which lexical elements belong to which chains, and what that implies for translation, very much depend on the reading by the text analyst or translator.

Let us now move on to the second dimension of meaning selected here for the sake of illustration, that of participant tracking, co-reference resolution and identification. Example (1) will here be repeated as Example (8):

Example 8 (Reading 2, cohesive reference):

THE HIDDEN GENETIC PROGRAM of COMPLEX ORGANISMS

Assumptions *can be dangerous, especially in science.* **They** *usually start as* **the most plausible or comfortable interpretation of the available facts.** *But when* **their truth** *cannot be immediately tested and* **their flaws** *are not obvious,* **assumptions** *often graduate to* **articles of faith,** *and new observations are forced to fit* **them.** *Eventually, if the volume of troublesome information becomes unsustainable,* **the orthodoxy (?)** *must collapse.*

Reading 2 of our sample text shows an annotation for co-reference in boldface, realized in our GECCo-corpora with the help of co-indexation. Interestingly, the German translation (Example 1b above) has some changes in the co-reference chains relative to its English ST, both the English ST and its German translation encoding eight phrases as 'recoverable' (excluding the headline), though not entirely the same ones, and not with exactly the same antecedents. Note that most German translations would have somewhat fewer referential ambiguities than the English wording due to gender agreement in pronouns, yet the basic fact remains of readings as more instantiated than written/spoken texts.

Example 8 information distribution:

FOCUS/ NEW: Reading 3

THE HIDDEN GENETIC PROGRAM of COMPLEX ORGANISMS

Assumptions can be **dangerous**,// especially **in science**.// They usually **start** // as the most plausible or comfortable interpretation of the available **facts**.// But when their truth cannot be immediately **tested**// and their flaws are not **obvious**//, assumptions often graduate to **articles of faith**//, and new observations are forced to fit them//. **Eventually,**// if the volume of troublesome information becomes **unsustainable,**// the orthodoxy must **collapse.**//

FOCUS/ NEW: Reading 4

THE HIDDEN GENETIC PROGRAM of COMPLEX ORGANISMS
    Assumptions can be **dangerous,**// **especially** in science.// They **usually** start // as the most **plausible**// or **comfortable** interpretation of the available facts.// But when **their truth** cannot be immediately tested// and **their flaws** are not obvious//, assumptions often graduate to **articles of faith**//, and **new observations** are forced to fit them//. **Eventually,**// if the volume of **troublesome information** becomes unsustainable,// the **orthodoxy** must **collapse.**//

At this point, we are offering two readings for *Information*, not because this would be unique to information structure, but rather because many different readings corresponding to primary focus are compatible with a given written encoding, depending on context. Even when taking lexicogrammatical indicators for information structure into account, as we have done here, phonological indicators (stress) can still fall on a range of items and project differently onto phrases and phrasal extensions. Readings 3 and 4 are more instantiated than the written texts would be – they are closer to spoken mode through the annotation of information units and stress. There are remaining ambiguities only as to the extent of focus projection onto phrases, especially in unmarked cases. Otherwise, we would again have an ultimate instance. In the case of information structure, the translation seems to stay close to the original, although thematic progression does not.

Below we include Readings 5 and 6 as two possible appraisal analyses, yet at this point in terms of ATTITUDE (AFFECT, JUDGEMENT, APPRECIATION) and GRADUATION (cf. Martin and White 2005: 34–5) only.

Example 8 Appraisal

Appraisal/ attitude and graduation: Reading 5

THE **HIDDEN** *[judgement+graduation-neutral]* GENETIC PROGRAM of **COMPLEX** ORGANISMS *[appreciation+neutral]*
    Assumptions can be **dangerous** *[judgement, graduation-neutral]*, especially in science. They usually start as **the most plausible or comfortable** *[affect+graduation-raise]* interpretation of the available facts. But when their truth cannot be immediately tested and their **flaws** *[judgement+graduation-neutral]* are not obvious, assumptions often graduate to **articles of faith** *[judgement+graduation-neutral]*, and new observations are forced to fit them. Eventually, if the volume of **troublesome information** *[affect+graduation-neutral]* becomes **unsustainable** *[judgement+graduation-neutral]*, the **orthodoxy** *[involvement]* must collapse.

Appraisal/ attitude and graduation: Reading 6

THE **HIDDEN** *[judgement+graduation-raise]* GENETIC PROGRAM of **COMPLEX** ORGANISMS *[appreciation+raise]*

Assumptions can be **dangerous** *[judgement, graduation-raise]*, especially in science. They usually start as the most **plausible or comfortable** *[affect+graduation-raise]* interpretation of the available facts. But when their truth cannot be immediately tested and their **flaws** *[judgement+graduation-raise]* are not obvious, assumptions often graduate to **articles of faith** *[judgement+graduation-raise]*, and new observations are forced to fit them. Eventually, if the volume of **troublesome information** *[appreciation+graduation-raise]* becomes **unsustainable** *[judgement+graduation-raise]*, the **orthodoxy** *[involvement]* must collapse.

Our annotation reflects questions of deciding between Readings 5and 6 such as: Is *hidden* to be read as '(intentionally, dangerously, unjustifiably) hidden' *hidden*? The German translation *verkannte* represents a dubious reading there. Is *complex* neutral, or more like *complicated, highly-developed, ...*? Is *dangerous* literally *dangerous*, or else *uncomfortable* (as in the German translation), or stronger like *disastrous*? Note that these differences in meaning become nowhere more apparent than in translation, where translational choices have to be made, as in the case of lexical cohesion.[10] Similar questions apply to the other phrases marked in Readings 5 and 6. Overall, the two readings are different in that Reading 5 is neutral as a prosody dispersed throughout the text, whereas Reading 6 is stronger in terms of appraisal, both positive and negative. The German translation (1b) is an instance of Reading 5.

Readings 5 and 6 are thus two of several possible readings of Example 1, the source text. There are no remaining ambiguities as to appraisal, assuming that the terms used as appraisal categories are not themselves ambiguous – which is, indeed, a major question.

The conclusion from our example analyses is that instantiations of texts are, indeed, readings. They form a set, all of whose elements are compatible with the written/ spoken text. Readings/annotations for co-reference and for information structure are more instantiated than the written text, yet not more delicate along the scale of delicacy: English (and largely German) does not offer more delicate mechanisms of encoding co-reference, hence the reading has to fall back on meanings additional to purely systemic ones (on which see *accessibility theory* as in Ariel 2001). The readings are part of *what is said* and *linguistic meaning type I* in terms of Section 3.1. And so are readings/annotations for lexical cohesion and for appraisal, yet these may also involve changes in delicacy if the language system offers means of encoding this, for example, in lexical taxonomies. Where we need natural-language categories for annotation, these are themselves more delicate texts. Where we use other representations of reading (chains, indexes), these are ultimate instantiations.

Finally, readings across multifunctional dimensions may seem to be independent of each other. However, in terms of plausible textuality they are not: meanings across the metafunctional dimensions strongly co-select each other, as in our case *ideation/ identification, periodicity, appraisal*, so that we have coupled syndromes of meanings.[11]

4.4 Translational agency

A defining feature of translation is the translator's attempt at rendering the reading of the (implied) author in his/her target text production. This is a compliant reading, or 'quotation', in the sense of Martin (2006: 286) in a new target context. In the usual case of translation, the translator's main goal is that of re-instantiating a compliant reading, not that of trying to align the TT-audience with his/her own set of goals. Other forms of multilingual text production are of course frequent and may be pragmatically valid, but calling them 'translation' would be unethical in my view. The translator's own reading in pre-translational text analysis basically is a tactical one (for discussion cf. de Souza 2010; Munday 2012: 37–8). As a translational agent and in choosing translation strategies (procedures, methods), the translator must choose which level and metafunction of meaning to prioritize in his/her translation, how to negotiate register differences between situations and cultures and which readings to prioritize in his/her text. A translator is thus like Hasan's and Bourdieu's 'impartial spectator', who 'seeks to understand for the sake of understanding' (Hasan 1999: 240 quoting Bourdieu 1990: 31). In my view, this impartiality is an important prerequisite for understanding, although it is not yet in itself social agency. Social agency ideally presupposes understanding but itself arises from being partial to some cause and thus goes beyond translating.

5 Conclusions

1. **A reading can be represented** as a text plus annotations (indices, co-reference chains, lexical chains, focus-bolding). These annotated texts are 'more instantiated' than 'worded texts' (e.g. on paper, on the screen, etc). Each individual reading is no longer ambiguous in terms of identification, co-reference and lexical cohesion. Where our annotations themselves use natural language (*appraisal, decisions on readings of lexical items*), they reduce ambiguity if well operationalized but do not fully abolish it.

2. **An annotated text ('reading') is lower in 'generality' than the worded text** because it denotes a one-member set, whereas the non-annotated worded text still is compatible with a possibly open set (type, class) of readings of the worded instance.

3. **Text-types clustered ('generalized') bottom-up are examples of distantiations** in Martin's sense. The features on which the clustering is based are not (necessarily) part of a system network or a realizational rule (e.g. length or density of chains). The clustering is also in terms of frequencies, proportionalities and distinctiveness of features, whereas classification in terms of delicacy is usually in terms of presence/absence of features. In that sense, they may be different from features in systemic networks, and they are topological because they are not (necessarily) typologically related.

4. *Realization, delicacy* and *instantiation* **are technical concepts of the theory.** They may be referred to as subtypes of *abstraction*, but that latter term is much less strictly defined than the former three.

Notes

1. Text from CroCo-Gecco-Corpus, cf. Hansen-Schirra, Neumann and Steiner (2012); Kunz et al. (2017a, b); Information about the corpora: http://www.gecco.uni-saarland. de/GECCo/index.html.
2. A distinction which I sometimes blurred in my own work, although I distinguished 'situation' and 'register' in my own work fairly early on (Steiner 1991).
3. For the later treatment of 'ideology' within a scale of 'individuation' cf. Martin (2010).
4. Martin presented this view in a talk at UNSW Round Table on Translation, November 2016, where he also addressed notions of 'ascent' by stratum, rank, delicacy, axis, and 'traversal' across languages, metafunctions and modalities.
5. The recognition of 'reading', in a somewhat different formulation, may already be implied in Hasan (1999: 230–231) as a contextually disambiguated instantiation of a lexicogrammatical 'text'.
6. Other SFL inspired approaches to translation that encompass the notions of genre and register include Bell (1991); House (2015); Hatim and Mason (1991, 1997). Whereas these would belong with the 'stratified-context' variant of SFL broadly speaking, none of them has used contextual stratification in the theoretically motivated sense of this section.
7. Examples from our Croco/Gecco corpora (cf. http://www.gecco.uni-saarland. de/ GECCo/index.html), except Example 5 from COCA.
8. For a related discussion under the topic of text representation and understanding, cf. Smith (2003: 49–51).
9. For our example analyses below, the annotations for lexical cohesion and for co-reference are technically realized in our GECCo-corpora (footnote 7), interactions with information structure and the Prague Discourse Tree Bank are explored in Menzel, Lapshinova-Koltunski and Kunz (eds) (2017). Appraisal analyses have so far not been undertaken in our own work and will only be sketched here.
10. *Graduation-neutral* is not an option in Martin and White (2005). It has to be *raise, lower*. I have also not marked whether the attitude is direct or indirect (*invoked, evoked*). *Involvement* is another discourse semantic system, alongside negotiation and appraisal, within the interpersonal semantics. Some of our analysis is based on indirect rather than direct encoding of appraisal (Martin and White 2005: 61ff).
11. Martin suggests (personal communication 2018) that moving upwards on the scale of instantiation may undo precisely such couplings.

References

Alves, F., Pagano, A., Neumann, S., Steiner, E. and Hansen-Schirra, S. (2010), 'Translation Units and Grammatical Shifts: Towards an Integration of Product- and Process-Based Translation Research', in G. Shreve and E. Angelone (eds), *Translation and Cognition*, 109–42, Amsterdam: John Benjamins.

Ariel, M. (2001), 'Accessibility Theory. An Overview', in T. J. M. Sanders, J. Schilperoord and W. Spooren (eds), *Text Representation: Linguistic and Psycholinguistic Aspects*, 29–87, Amsterdam: John Benjamins.

Banchs, R. E., D'Haro, L. F. and Li, H. (2015), 'Adequacy – Fluency Metrics: Evaluating MT in the Continuous Space Model Framework', *IEEE/ACM Transactions on Audio, Speech and Language Processing* 23 (3): 472–82.

Bell, R. T. (1991), *Translation and Translating*, London: Longman.

Bourdieu, P. (1990), *The Logic of Practice*, trans. Richard Nice, London: Polity Press.

Bowcher, W. L. (2017), 'Field, Tenor and Mode', in T. Bartlett and G. O'Grady (eds), *The Routledge Handbook of Systemic Functional Linguistics*, 391–403, London: Routledge.

Carl, M., and Schaeffer, M. J. (2017), 'Models of the Translation Process', in J. W. Schwieter and A. Ferreira (eds), *The Handbook of Translation and Cognition*, 50–70, Hoboken, NJ: Wiley Blackwell.

Carston, R. (2002), *Thoughts and Utterances: The Pragmatics of Explicit Communication*, Oxford: Blackwell.

Catford, J. C. (1965), *A Linguistic Theory of Translation*, Oxford: Oxford University Press.

Chungyu, K., and Tak-Ming, B. W. (2015), 'Evaluation in Machine Translation and Computer-Aided Translation', in Ch. Sin-Wai (ed.), *The Routledge Encyclopedia of Translation Technology*, 213–36, London: Routledge.

de Souza, L. M. F. (2010), *Interlingual Re-instantiation: A Model for a New and More Comprehensive Systemic Functional Perspective on Translation*, Tese submetida ao Programa de Pós-graduação em Língua Inglesa da Universidade Federal deSanta Catarina paraa obtenção doGraudeDoutor em Língua Inglesa, https://www.sapili.org/livros/en/cp151824.pdf.

de Souza, L. M. F. (2013), 'Interlingual Re-instantiation – a New Systemic Functional Perspective on Translation', *Text &Talk* 33 (4–5): 575–94.

Durand, J., Bennett, P., Allegranza, V., van Eynde, F., Humphreys, L., Schmidt, P. and Steiner, E. (1991), 'The Eurotra Linguistic Specifications: An Overview', in V. Allegranza, S. Krauwer and E. Steiner (eds), *Special Issue of Machine Translation on Eurotra*, 6 (2): 103–47.

Eagleton, T. (1996), *Literary Theory – An Introduction*, 2nd edn, London: Blackwell.

Gupta, R., Constantin, O. and van Genabith, J. (2015), 'ReVal: A Simple and Effective Machine Translation Evaluation Metric Based on Recurrent Neural Networks', in *Proceedings of the 2015 Conference on Empirical Methods in Natural Language Processing*, Lisbon, Portugal, 17–21 September 2015. Association for Computational Linguistics, 1066–72.

Gutt, E. A. (1991), *Translation and Relevance*, Oxford: Basil Blackwell.

Halliday, M. A. K. (2009), 'The Gloosy Ganoderm: Systemic Functional Linguistics and Translation', republished in J. Webster (ed.) (2017), *Halliday in the 21st Century. Vol.11 in the Collected Works of M. A. K. Halliday*, 105–26, London: Bloomsbury.

Halliday, M. A. K. (2012), 'Pinpointing the Choice: Meaning and the Search for Equivalents in a Translated Text', re-published in J. Webster (ed.) (2017), *Halliday in the 21st Century. Vol.11 in the Collected Works of M.A.K. Halliday*, 143–54, London: Bloomsbury.

Halliday, M. A. K., McIntosh, A., and Strevens, P. (1964), *The Linguistic Sciences and Language Teaching*, London: Longman

Halliday, M. A. K., and Hasan, R. (1976), *Cohesion in English*, London: Longman.

Halliday, M. A. K., and Hasan, R. (1989), *Language, Context and Text: Aspects of Language in a Social-Semiotic Perspective*, Oxford: Oxford University Press.

Halliday, M. A. K., and Matthiessen, C. M. I. M. (1999), *Construing Experience through Meaning: A Language-Based Approach to Cognition*, London: Cassell.

Halverson, S. (1997), 'The Concept of Equivalence in Translation Studies: Much Ado about Something', *Target* 9 (2): 207–33.

Hansen-Schirra, S., Czulo, O., and Hofmann, S. (eds) (2017), *Empirical Modelling of Translation and Interpreting*, Berlin: Language Science Press.

Hansen-Schirra, S., Neumann, S., and Steiner, E. (2012), *Cross-Linguistic Corpora for the Study of Translations. Insights from the Language Pair English–German*, Berlin: Mouton de Gruyter.

Hao, J. (2015), *Construing Biology: An Ideational Perspective*, PhD Thesis, University of Sydney.

Hasan, R. (1999), 'Speaking with Reference to Context', in M. Ghadessy (ed.), *Text and Context in Functional Linguistics: Systemic Perspectives*, 219–328, Amsterdam: John Benjamins.

Hatim, B., and Mason, I. (1990), *Discourse and the Translator*, Language in Social Life Series, London: Longman.

Hatim, B., and Mason, I. (1997), *The Translator as Communicator*, London: Routledge.

Hiippala, T. (2012), 'The Localisation of Advertising Print Media as a Multimodal Process', in W. Bowcher (ed.), *Multimodal Texts from around the World: Cultural and Linguistic Insights*, 97–122, Basingstoke: Palgrave Macmillan.

Hood, S. (2008), 'Summary Writing in Academic Contexts: Implicating Meaning in Processes of Change', *Linguistics and Education* 19: 351–65.

House, J. (2015), *Translation Quality Assessment*, London: Routledge.

Koller, W. (1995), 'The Concept of Equivalence and the Object of Translation Studies', *Target* 7 (2): 191–222.

Koller, W. (1997), *Einführung in die Übersetzungswissenschaft*, 5, Aktualisierte Auflage, Wiesbaden: Quelle und Meyer.

Kress, G. (2010), *Multimodality: A Social Semiotic Approach to Contemporary Communication*, London: Taylor and Francis.

Kunz, K., Degaetano-Ortlieb, S., Lapshinova-Koltunski, E., Menzel, K. and Steiner, E. (2017a), 'GECCo – an Empirically-Based Comparison of English-German Cohesion', in G. De Sutter, I. Delaere and M. Lefer (eds), *New Ways of Analysing Translational Behaviour in Corpus-Based Translation Studies*, 265–312, Berlin: Mouton De Gruyter.

Kunz, K., Lapshinova-Koltunski, E. and Martinez-Martinez, J. M. (2016), 'Beyond Identity Coreference: Contrasting Indicators of Textual Coherence in English and German', *Proceedings of Corbon at NAACL-HLT2016*, 23–31, San Diego.

Kunz, K., Lapshinova-Koltunski, E., Manuel Martínez-Martínez, J. M., Menzel, K. and Steiner, E. (2017b), 'Shallow Features as Indicators of English-German Contrasts in Lexical Cohesion', *Languages in Contrast* 18 (2): 175–206. (Electronic publication: http://doi.org/10.1075/lic.16005.kun).

Linke, A., and Nussbaumer, M. (2000), 'Konzepte des Impliziten: Präsuppositionen und Implikaturen', in K. Brinker, G. Antos, W. Heinemann and S. F. Sager (eds), *Linguistics of Text and Conversation: An International Handbook of Contemporary Research*, 435–48, Berlin: Walter De Gruyter.

Lukin, A., Moore, A., Herke, M., Wegener, R. and Wu, C. (2008), 'Halliday's Model of Register Revisited and Explored', *Linguistics and the Human Sciences* 4 (2): 187–243.

Martin, J. R. (1992), *English Text: System and Structure*, Amsterdam: John Benjamins.

Martin, J. R. (2006), 'Genre, Ideology and Intertextuality: A Systemic Functional Perspective', *Linguistics and the Human Sciences* 2 (2) special issue: 275–98.

Martin, J. R. (2008), 'Tenderness: Realisation and Instantiation in a Botswanan Town', in N. Norgaard (ed.), *Systemic Functional Linguistics in Use*, 30–62, Odense: Odense Working Papers in Language and Communication, vol. 29.

Martin, J. R. (2010), 'Semantic Variation – Modelling Realisation, Instantiation and Individuation in Social Semiosis', in M. Bednarek and J. R. Martin (eds), *New Discourse on Language: Functional Perspectives on Multimodality, Identity, and Affiliation*, 1–34, London: Continuum.

Martin, J. R., and Matruglio, E. (2013), 'Revisiting Mode: Context In/dependency in Ancient History Classroom Discourse', in G. Huang, D. Zhang and X. Yang (eds), *Studies in Functional Linguistics and Discourse Analysis V*, 72–95, Beijing: Higher Education Press.

Martin, J. R., and Rose, D. (2003), *Working with Discourse: Meaning beyond the Clause*, London: Continuum.

Martin. J. R., and White, P. (2005), *The Language of Evaluation: Appraisal in English*, London: Palgrave Macmillan.

Matthiessen, C. M. I. M. (2001), 'The Environments of Translation', in E. Steiner and C. Yallop (eds), *Exploring Translation and Multilingual Text Production: Beyond Content*, 41–126, Berlin: Mouton de Gruyter.

Matthiessen, C. M. I. M. (2014), 'Choice in Translation: Metafunctional Considerations', in K. Kunz, E. Teich, S. Hansen-Schirra, S. Neumann and P. Daut (eds), *Caught in the Middle – Language Use and Translation: A Festschrift for Erich Steiner on the Occasion of his 60th Birthday*, 271–334, Saarbrücken: Saarland University Press.

Menzel, K., Lapshinova-Koltunski, E. and Kunz, K. (eds) (2017), *New Perspectives on Cohesion and Coherence: Implications for Translation*, Berlin: Language Science Press.

Munday, J. (2001), *Introducing Translation Studies: Theories and Applications*, 4th edn, London: Routledge.

Munday, J. (2012), *Evaluation in Translation: Critical Points of Translator Decision Making*, London: Routledge.

Neumann, S. (2014), *Contrastive Register Variation: A Quantitative Approach to the Comparison of English and German*, Berlin: de Gruyter Mouton.

Nida, E. A. (1964), *Toward a Science of Translating: With Special Reference to Principles and Procedures Involved in Bible Translation*, Leiden: Brill.

Schwieter, J. W., and Ferreira, A. (2017a), 'Bilingualism in Cognitive Translation and Interpreting Studies', in J. W. Schwieter and A. Ferreira (eds), *The Handbook of Translation and Cognition*, 144–64, Hoboken, NJ: Wiley Blackwell.

Schwieter, J. W., and Ferreira, A. (eds) (2017b), *The Handbook of Translation and Cognition*, Hoboken, NJ: Wiley Blackwell.

Serbina, T., Hintzen, S., Niemietz, P. and Neumann, S. (2017), 'Changes of Word Class During Translation – Insights from a Combined Analysis of Corpus, Keystroke Logging and Eye-tracking Data', in S. Hansen-Schirra, O. Czulo and S. Hofmann (eds), *Empirical Modelling of Translation and Interpreting*, 177–208, Berlin: Language Science Press.

Shreve, G., and Lacruz, I. (2017), 'Aspects of a Cognitive Model of translation', in J. W. Schwieter and A. Ferreira (eds), *The Handbook of Translation and Cognition*, 127–43, Hoboken, NJ: Wiley Blackwell.

Smith, C. S. (2003), *Modes of Discourse. The Local Structure of Texts*, Cambridge: Cambridge University Press.

Steiner, E. (1991), *A Functional Perspective on Language, Action, and Interpretation*, Berlin: Mouton De Gruyter.

Steiner. E. (1996), 'A Fragment of a Multilingual Transfer Component and Its Relation to Discourse Knowledge', in M. Berry, C. Butler, R. Fawcet and G. Huang (eds), *Meaning and Form: Systemic Functional Interpretations*, 601–36, Norwood, NJ: Ablex.

Steiner, E. (2001a), 'Translations English – German: Investigating the Relative Importance of Systemic Contrasts and of the Text-type "Translation"', in *Papers from the 2000*

Symposium on Information Structures across languages, in *SPRIK-Reports* No. 7, 1–49, *Reports from the Project 'Languages in Contrast' University of Oslo*. http://www.hf.uio. no/ilos/forskning/prosjekter/sprik/sprikreports.html updated version in Steiner 2004.

Steiner E. (2001b), 'Intralingual and Interlingual Versions of a Text – How Specific Is the Notion of Translation', in E. Steiner and C. Yallop (eds), *Exploring Translation and Multilingual Textproduction: Beyond Content*, Series Text, Translation, Computational Processing, 161–90, Berlin: Mouton de Gruyter.

Steiner, E. (2004), *Translated Texts: Properties, Variants, Evaluations*, Frankfurt/M: Peter Lang Verlag.

Steiner, E. (2015), 'Contrastive Studies of Cohesion and Their Impact on Our Knowledge of Translation (English-German)', in J. Munday and M. Zhang (eds), *Special Issue Discourse Analysis in Translation Studies. Target* 27 (3): 351–69.

Steiner, E. (2019), 'Theorizing and Modelling Translation', in W. Bowcher, L. Fontaine, J. Y. Laing and G. Thompson (eds), *The Cambridge Handbook of Systemic Functional Linguistics*, 739–66, Cambridge: Cambridge University Press.

Steiner, E. (2020), 'Translation, Equivalence and Cognition', in F. Alves and A. L. Jakobsen (eds), *The Routledge Handbook of Translation and Cognition*, London: Routledge. 344–59.

Steiner, E., Schmidt, P., and Zelinsky-Wibbelt, C. (eds) (1988), *From Syntax to Semantics – Insights from Machine Translation*, London: Frances Pinter.

Steiner, E., and Yallop, C. (eds) (2001), *Exploring Translation and Multilingual Textproduction: Beyond Content*, Berlin: Mouton de Gruyter.

Tann, K. (2017), 'Context and Meaning in the Sydney Architecture of Systemic Functional Linguistics', in T. Bartlett and G. O'Grady (eds), *The Routledge Handbook of Systemic Functional Linguistics*, 438–56, London: Routledge.

Teich, E. (2003), *Cross-linguistic Variation in System and Text – A Methodology for the Investigation of Translations and Comparable Texts*, Berlin: Mouton de Gruyter.

Wegener, R. (2011), *Parameters of Context: From Theory to Model and Application*, PhD Thesis, Macquarie University Sydney.

Williams, J., Russel, N. and Irwin, D. (2017), 'On the Notion of Abstraction in Systemic Functional Linguistics', *Functional Linguistics* 4 (13): 1–22, doi:10.1186/ s40554-017-0047-3.

3

Register and translation

Stella Neumann

RWTH Aachen University

1 Introduction

One of the key insights of Systemic Functional Linguistics (SFL) is that language use cannot be divorced from the cultural, social and situational context in which it occurs (e.g. Halliday 1978, 1999; Hasan 1973, 2009; Martin 1992, 1999; Bartlett 2017; Bowcher 2019). Register is the theoretical construct that specifies the role of situational context in the systemic functional conceptualization of language (e.g. Halliday and Hasan 1989; Matthiessen 1993; Halliday 1999). It captures a 'configuration of meanings' (Halliday and Hasan 1989: 39) which co-varies with the context of use (Matthiessen 2019: 14). This co-variation has been shown to be a major factor affecting the choice, and consequently the patterning, of linguistic features also at the other strata as these realize meaning (Halliday and Hasan 1989: 39). Assuming that contexts of situation represent a selection from or instantiate particular cultures (Bowcher 2019: 151) and that cultures are realized in and construed by languages (Halliday 1999: 8), there is potential for differences between registers across lingua-cultures if the respective contexts of situation (partially) differ.

If such differences apply between the source and target language registers involved in translation, the translator will have to respond to these in his or her linguistic choices when producing the target text. The outcome of the translator's response to similarities or differences between the source and target language registers can be related to variation in translation, that is, in relation to given source texts/languages, but also in comparison to non-translated texts in the target language.

Can we expect translators to know or be aware of these differences a priori? Does the awareness come into existence by translator training/practice and consequently as part of the professional expertise, or is it something that every human develops (Ferguson 1982: 58) in the course of their language development? Do register-related patterns simply reflect specific linguistic choices, that is, probabilities, of different registers as subsystems of the (respective) language system? Or, can we identify further-reaching patterns in the linguistic behaviour of translators which can still be linked to the influence of register? If this were the case, we should, for instance, observe differences in how typical properties of translations such as normalization, interference/shining through, explicitation and so on, play out across registers (Neumann 2012; Kruger and Van Rooy 2012). To what extent do translators deviate from the target register? If they are not aware of register conventions or deem it fit to depart from them, we might be able to observe dilution of register features in translated texts. And finally, can the investigation of the language of translation provide us with insights that we can use to refine our theory (initially register theory, but beyond this also language theory)?

In this chapter I will examine some of these questions with the goal of exploring the extent to which (systemic functional) register theory can inform translation (theory). To this end, I will briefly review the role of register in Translation Studies (TS). Note that research into the language of translation is often agnostic towards language theory and therefore tends to use linguistic terms in a pre-theoretical way. Outside of SFL the notion of register is often used interchangeably with the notion of genre, referring to groups of texts that share some similarities and ignoring the theoretical implications of both notions. Approaches that do not specify what the place of register (or genre) in language is might suggest that groups of texts are something that may or may not occur, in the sense that speakers may or may not conform to the features typical for a register. In order to delineate these commonsense uses from the theoretical notion of register in SFL, I will use small caps to indicate the technical terms whereas commonsense uses will not be indicated by formatting.

I will then introduce SFL-based REGISTER theory with a focus on explicating my specific perspective, as there is a considerable range of variation between views (Section 3). It is beyond the scope of this chapter to review all the different positions, but I hope that explicating my view may at least be seen as a contribution to an ongoing debate about the interaction between (situational) context and (functional) language variation. Section 4 will briefly review some methodological considerations relevant to translation-related REGISTER analysis. In Section 5, I will then discuss how some of the questions raised above have been investigated empirically, and how such investigations contribute to our understanding of translation. Finally, the chapter closes with some concluding remarks in Section 6.

2 From text types to register in TS

In an early and influential publication, Reiß (1976) derives text types from Bühler's functions of language (Bühler 1934). Bühler's organon model of language identifies three functions of language, namely the representational ('Darstellung'), expressive ('Ausdruck') and conative ('Appell') functions, claiming that all three operate simultaneously. Reiß (1976) maps these directly onto functions of texts yielding three types: the informative text type foregrounds the representational function, the expressive type foregrounds the language function of the same name and the operative text type foregrounds the conative function, that is, language use oriented towards the addressee. In recognition of the specific characteristics of texts combining different modalities (note that this is the year 1976!) she suggests a fourth, mixed text type which she calls 'audio-medial'. She then proposes differential translation strategies for each of these text types, according to which the functional type is kept invariant (potentially at the expense of other features of the text).

In their discussion of proposals for functions of language, Halliday and Hasan (1989: 15–16) also address Bühler's functions of language. However, they emphasize that function is not simply use but a fundamental property of language (Halliday and Hasan 1989: 17). Since functions are 'interwoven in the fabric of the discourse' (Halliday and Hasan 1989: 23), individual linguistic features in a text such as the presence of imperatives are not treated as direct indicators of a single function of a text.[1] This is a crucial move as it underlines the complexity and multifunctionality of language use. Each linguistic unit is examined simultaneously in three metafunctional perspectives to understand how it functions with respect to the ideational, interpersonal and textual metafunctions proposed. Consequently, a text can be characterized in these functional perspectives simultaneously, summarizing the ideational, interpersonal and textual resources it draws on primarily. Against this background, we might argue that Reiß's approach oversimplifies matters by narrowing down the function of a text and the corresponding translation strategy to just one functional aspect, as interesting as the suggested link to translation strategy might be. Prioritizing one functional dimension over the others can lead to exaggerating the emphasis of some aspects of the meaning of a text while neglecting the contribution of other functional dimensions. Nevertheless, Reiß's achievement is drawing attention to this important aspect of translating. Nord (2005) further contributes to spreading awareness of the requirements of genres by including the identification of a text's genre in her pre-translational text analysis.

Such suggestions have been highly influential in (German) translation departments where translator trainers to the best of my knowledge routinely teach students to analyse source texts (STs) not only for linguistic features but crucially also for characteristic features of groups of texts. Practitioners specialize in the translation of certain types of texts and, if asked to translate a text from a type they are not experienced in – as we did in translation experiments, for example, in Heilmann et al. (2020) – they will first want to inspect a number of comparable texts in order to get an (informal) idea of the make-up of this type of text.

In studies of the role of register in translation, scholars often draw on the SFL notions of REGISTER, but do not necessarily commit to any further-reaching assumptions and conclusions in the light of language theory (e.g. Hatim and Mason 1990; Baker 1992; House 1997; Trosborg 1997). That a deeper link is possible becomes evident, among others, in Steiner's work on translation-related REGISTER analysis (Steiner 2001; and papers collected in 2004; see also Hansen-Schirra and Steiner 2012 for a more detailed discussion of the place of translation in SFL). Corpus-based research further highlights the importance of REGISTER on translation (based on SFL, see Teich 2003; Neumann 2003, 2012, 2013, 2014). Even if scholars do not commit to a theoretical stance, their empirical studies still demonstrate the influence of register[2] on translation (Kruger and Van Rooy 2012, 2018; Delaere 2015; Redelinghuys and Kruger 2015; Redelinghuys 2016). Their findings will be discussed in more detail in Section 5.

Unlike other approaches, the systemic functional notion of REGISTER, that is, the configuration of meanings typically associated with a particular situational configuration (Halliday and Hasan 1989: 39), is theoretically motivated in terms of the language system (Bowcher 2018: 3). Context, according to this approach, is in a realization relationship with language (Halliday 1999; Hasan 2009) and in this way makes REGISTER a richer concept than a notion of text type or a pre-theoretical notion of genre (*Textsorte* in German) as it is often used in TS.

Translation scholars tend to be wary of linking claims about translation more generally to language (theory). Nevertheless, I would claim that it is specifically through a link to theorizing language in all its (social) complexity that we can start to understand translation. This point was aptly made by Hasan (1992). Although she discussed limitations of Bakhtin's approach to speech genres, I believe that it can also be read in the light of theorizing translation:

> It seems to me that some consistent means of linking the social situation and the language of the utterance (i.e., what the utterance manifests, and what manifests the utterance) is a necessity in the theory of genre. Assertions about the nature and attributes of utterance/text will tend to create a 'mystification', unless they are grounded in the social and verbal systems. If 'stylistic effect', almost as a rule, is not produced by the functioning of the categories of the system of language in context, then by implication its source is mysterious, and in explaining its appearance, we may need to appeal to something akin to the individualistic subjectivism, which Bakhtin so categorically rejected as having no basis in reality. (Hasan 1992: 510–11)

The effect REGISTER has on translation can be understood most clearly if its central role in the architecture of language as a subsystem of the language system (Matthiessen 1993) is taken into consideration. In this architecture, REGISTER can be viewed as a gatekeeper preselecting lexico-grammatical resources 'at risk' in a given context (Taverniers 2019: 84). This gatekeeping may yield different preselections across cultures to which the translator responds.

3 Theory-driven REGISTER analysis

A first step towards understanding the role of REGISTER is to acknowledge that variation is a central motif of language and that this variation falls into types (Halliday 1978). Dialectal variation refers to geographic or social patterns across speech communities. It is linked to the speakers' provenance and, as Halliday (1978: 185) suggests, represents different (linguistic) ways of saying the same thing. The type of variation most relevant in the context of this chapter is not linked to the speakers' background but to situations: based on the (diverging) features of different situations, we use language differently. Rather than representing differences in the use of language between entire groups of speakers, we are now concerned with functional variation where one and the same speaker adapts their language use depending on the specifics of the context of situation. Halliday (1978: 185) relates this functional language variation to social order, or, more specifically, to the diversity of social processes. Matthiessen (2019: 16–17) adds to this codal variation, that is, semantic variation within a culture by class or other socio-economic variables (see Hasan 1973, 1989). For the sake of completeness, we might add a last type of variation, namely diachronic or phylogenetic variation. This, however, is a different order of variation, as it is normally not at the individual speaker's disposal but rather something we can only observe over longer stretches of time.

My focus in this chapter is on the role of functional language variation for translators and, more specifically, how systemic functionally informed REGISTER analysis can help us understand the way translators respond to STs produced in various situational contexts. The SFL perspective is of particular interest here because, as Bowcher (2018: 2) points out, context is a construct used for understanding the nature of the language system and more specifically the role of language as a social activity. Although functional variation has been investigated extensively over the past decades, systemic functional approaches diverge substantially, especially with respect to the conceptualization of context. An important alternative approach to the one adopted here is Martin's genre-based approach (e.g. 1992, 1999, 2014), according to which context is stratified with GENRE (now as a theoretical concept) as supervenient to REGISTER as an 'emergently complex pattern of field, tenor and mode configurations' (Martin 2014: 17).

As Moore (2017: 418) writes, the interest 'masks a persistent conflation of disparate views' including its location and centrality in a functional theory of language. It will therefore be necessary to first summarize my specific approach before studying translation-related questions in more detail.

It has become customary to use the term REGISTER when referring to functional language variation. Steiner (2001: 163) characterizes REGISTER as 'a theoretically motivated view of contexts of situation'. In the words of Ure and Ellis (1977: 197), 'Register is a certain kind of language patterning regularly used in a certain kind of situation.' They stress the fact that speakers show their awareness of social situations by making use of register patterns and define REGISTER as:

> A subdivision of a given language, a 'situational variety' constituted by a selection of choices from among the total linguistic options offered by that specific language. (Ure and Ellis 1977: 198)

This definition alludes to the central theoretical status of REGISTER as a subsystem of the language system by constraining choices from the language system (Matthiessen 1993). Nesbitt and Plum (1988) elaborate that the language system represents the possible choices in a given language, whereas the REGISTER specifies the probabilities of certain choices to be made (see also Halliday 2013: 21–4). Halliday and Hasan (1989: 39) describe REGISTER as a semantic concept, a configuration of meanings. Semantics is conceptualized in SFL as one of several strata, which are in a realization relationship with each other. It is realized by the stratum of lexico-grammar and this in turn by phonology/graphology, which means that, ultimately, the configurations of meanings of a given register correspond to, or rather are realized by, lexico-grammatical and phonological/graphological configurations (for a discussion of complementary approaches to semantics in SFL, see Taverniers 2019). In contrast to approaches not grounded in any theoretical framework that identify typical features of genres (drawing on a pre-theoretical notion, see above) based on their perceived importance in an ad hoc manner, the SFL-based approach locates relevant features in their place in the language system and hence facilitates a principled methodological approach and theoretical generalizations.

There are two important features in the definition of REGISTER which have to be examined in more detail: reference to situations and reference to 'patterning', that is, the recurring character of linguistic features.

Reference to situations means that I follow Halliday and Hasan (1989: 8) in linking REGISTER to context of *situation* rather than social context. According to Firth (1957: 182), situations involve the following aspects:

A. The relevant features of participants: persons, personalities.
  (i) The verbal action of the participants.
  (ii) The non-verbal action of the participants.
B. The relevant objects.
C. The effect of the verbal action.

Halliday and Hasan (1989: 8) elaborate on this by characterizing the personalities as 'what sociologists would regard as statuses and roles of the participants'. By including the relevant features of situations and not just of the participants, this notion of context is at the same time more comprehensive and more constrained, as only those features of the participants are relevant which have a bearing on their behaviour in situations.

Reference to patterning means that we are looking at an essentially quantitative phenomenon. Given that any kind of human behaviour *inevitably* takes place in some concrete situation, at the most concrete possible level, there cannot be any language use outside of situations. Moreover, situations will have a strong tendency to recur – not in identical ways, but displaying such clear similarities that participants will recognize them as *another* occurrence of something they experienced before – meaning that it will be hard to find unique situations which involve working out ad hoc appropriate linguistic behaviour. Rather, the likelihood of similar situations to recur will result in a tendency of language users to develop a conventionalized set of behaviours appropriate to what we can then call a type of situation. We will expect a certain spectrum in which the specific values for features vary due to individual traits and the particular combination of participants and setting, but, when describing instances of similar situations, values for specific features can be described in terms of density with a large number of occurrences concentrating around one particular value. As a consequence, initiated speakers will recognize a particular situation as an instance of a type. We are looking at something which is best characterized in terms of types: types of situations, types of participants in situations and typical linguistic features captured as frequencies of occurrence beyond the individual instance. It is crucial for the translator to respond to the distribution of linguistic features in the subsystem of the source and target languages that is a realization of a particular type of situation.

This has implications for the most suitable methods for analysing REGISTER, namely quantitative methods, as well as for its theoretical conceptualization. Particular situations are rarely novel: communities develop novel types of situations only under specific circumstances such as the advent of virtual assistants.³ A speaker's individual interaction with her virtual assistant will then count as an instance of this new type of situation, which can be characterized by a specific linguistic configuration of patterns (cf. the discussion of metastability as the interplay of stability across strata with gaps and contradictions which provide room for innovation in Taverniers 2019: 67). This means that situation-specific language use results in distributional patterns of the options of the language system, which can be described in *probabilistic* terms (Halliday 2013). Consequently, REGISTERS have to be conceptualized as configurations of (conditional) probabilities of features. This implies that some features may be altogether blocked in a given situational context, whereas others are very likely to be chosen (Matthiessen 1993).

Referring to Malinowski's observations based on his anthropological fieldwork, Halliday and Hasan (1989: 5–8) argue that situations do not occur in isolation, but are embedded in the context of a particular culture (see also the conceptualization of text in context as a manifestation of culture in Martin 1992: 493). Halliday (1999: 5) elaborates on the interplay between language and culture: 'Since language evolved as part ... of every human culture, it functioned as the primary means whereby the deepest perception of the members, their joint construction of shared experience into social reality, were constantly reaffirmed and transmitted.' It appears obvious to assume that types of situations will unfold differently across cultures. For example, in some cultures the social relationship between those acquiring or accumulating knowledge (e.g. students) and those dispensing knowledge or facilitating its acquisition (e.g. university lecturers) will be highly hierarchical. In other cultures the relationship will be fairly casual, meaning that students and lecturers will meet outside of the university context and hence also develop more contact, that is, reduced social distance. As a result, consultations between students and lecturers will unfold differently. If this is true, the expertise to recognize differences between similar contexts of situation across cultures will be crucial for translation.

The notion of REGISTER has been criticized as too general and vague to serve as a useful category for classifying groups of texts (in the context of translation e.g. Trosborg 1997: 7). I would argue that this ignores work on the multidimensional character of REGISTER (Halliday and Hasan 1989: chapter 4; more recently Hasan 2014; see also the discussion in Neumann 2014). Halliday and Hasan (1989) group Firth's features of situations into the contextual parameters of field, tenor and mode. These are assumed to capture the main situational dimensions that have a bearing on what is chosen linguistically by interactants.

Field is concerned with 'the nature of the social activity', that is, 'both the kind of acts being carried out and their goals' (Halliday and Hasan 1989: 56). According to Gregory and Carroll (1978: 78), field is determined by 'the ways in which a society organises, analyses and names its experience and orders it in systems of knowledge'. Field cannot simply be equated with topic or subject matter, as one and the same topic, say, explaining a particular biological phenomenon, will be negotiated in quite different ways in a university lecture, at a scientific conference or in parent–child interaction.

Tenor is primarily interested in capturing how the characterization of interactants as members of a social group or community shapes situation-specific language use.

Our concern is to capture who the typical participants in a particular situation type are, to what extent there is inequality in some participants' control over others and whether participants typically have a shared communicative history.

Finally, mode refers to the way language is put to use in types of situation. This involves the role language typically plays in the type of situation (as compared with other ways of conveying meaning), the transmission channel, whether participants are speaking or writing and so on.

Referring to developments over time, Moore (2017: 420) points out that 'Halliday's view of register has consistently been that of ... a multifunctional, multidimensional construct that cannot be reduced to a single feature or cline such as "degree of formality" or "degree of spoken/writtenness" ...'. Halliday and Hasan (1989: chapter 4) address some more specific aspects such as agent role, channel and medium. In a later work on contextualization system networks, Hasan specifies these as semiotic domains which narrow down choices in situations (e.g. Hasan 2014; see also Bowcher 2017). Such specifications also have methodological advantages: for systematic analysis, the linguist will want to link linguistic indicators as unequivocally as possible to the REGISTER parameters. This is best done by specifying field, tenor and mode into subdimensions which are explicit enough to establish plausible and robust relations between linguistic operationalizations and the abstract concepts (see, e.g. Steiner 2001: 163).

Analysis based on this systematic approach yields a detailed characterization of situation-specific language use in the form of REGISTER profiles with specific values for each of the dimensions (see Neumann 2013: chapter 10). In addition to the methodological advantages of specifying subdimensions, their use also allows the analyst to identify similarities and differences between types of situations in more delicate ways. Two REGISTER profiles can then be said to be similar along *n* dimensions and to be different along *m* dimensions. Space limitations do not permit a more detailed discussion whether the six subdimensions Neumann (2013) uses in her analysis (i.e. experiential domain, goal orientation, social role relationship, social distance, language role and medium) are the most important ones. What appears important in this context is the basic idea of capturing the multidimensional character of REGISTER in all its complexity. This implies that empirical studies potentially require application of multivariate statistical techniques. REGISTER analysis based on such a principled, multidimensional organization is far from vague and instead highly informative for translation.

Given the quantitative character of REGISTER, we might simply adopt Biber's multidimensional analysis (Biber 1995; Biber and Conrad 2009), which is highly influential in corpus linguistics. While there is substantial overlap between his approach and the one advocated here, Biber's approach concentrates on descriptive facts resulting from the multivariate statistical analysis of corpora. Using a heavily inductive method, Biber's multidimensional analysis is at the mercy of the respective corpus and the features selected for analysis. This can be exemplified by the fact that Biber's (1995) study of register variation in English is simply a more generalized interpretation of his study of variation in speaking and writing (Biber 1988). While the features he analyses cover a wide range of register-related features, they were originally selected for the analysis of medium rather than the more general analysis of register variation. It is therefore at least possible that the dimensions he arrives at on the basis of the statistical technique of factor analysis are biased towards the spoken–written continuum because of this bias in features. In more recent work (Biber and Conrad 2009), a more comprehensive feature catalogue is proposed to capture features of situations. The inclusion of corpus-based findings on variation between registers in the *Longman Grammar of Spoken and Written English* (Biber et al. 1999) is a major breakthrough in our understanding of language. However, there is no theoretical commitment to the position that the language system is organized into subsystems with their specific rearrangements of lexico-grammatical features of the language, even though the grammar provides very clear evidence for this.

O'Donnell (1999) points out that a dynamic model is required to analyse the dynamic character of unfolding interactions. This raises the question whether this dynamism, or, rather, a change in the speakers' behaviour in the course of an interaction, leads to a change in REGISTER. This appears to be a question of granularity of the analysis and granularity of the scope of terms. We might claim that a type of situation can also be characterized in terms of its typical degree of dynamism. For instance, when considering a meeting between friends in a cafe, aspects such as interaction between the friends *as well as* interactions with a waiter/waitress will be expected; they should be analysed as a typical characteristic of this type of REGISTER rather than a change in REGISTER (cf. Hasan 1999 on complex texts). The number of turns, the topic of the interaction and so on, are all constrained by the overall situation, which includes all interactions in the cafe. Rather than assuming a change in REGISTER, it appears plausible to analyse texts not as synoptic entities but as wholes consisting of parts with specific dynamics unfolding over the course of instantiated situations (Dourish 2004: 22). With the support of enhanced computational techniques, such analyses are indeed possible (see, e.g. Ströbel et al. 2016) and, when applied to REGISTER analysis, could give us a more detailed handle on the dynamic unfolding of situations.

4 Methodological considerations

There are two main strands of research that involve register. The first is when register is used as an analytical tool to investigate other research questions (e.g. House 1997 on translation quality; Evert and Neumann 2017 on properties of translations): here, register is used as a predictor variable to explain something else (e.g. Redelinghuys 2016). The second is when register (variation) is the object of research. Strictly speaking, only this second type is concerned with REGISTER proper. The first one presupposes that register is a factor that influences some other linguistic phenomenon. For the purposes of this chapter, both types are of interest, but they should still be kept apart. Focussing on the latter type of research (register variation as the object of research) we will have to specify how we can determine registers. As pointed out by Moore (2017: 420), this cannot be achieved by analysing individual features even if they are highly salient, as REGISTER is a complex multidimensional construct capturing the various strands of meaning which realize the contextual parameters. Analysing a single group of texts assumed to represent a REGISTER also won't do, because REGISTER-specific features only emerge by comparison with other REGISTERS (see Neumann 2014).

Crucially, eyeballing text based on the analyst's assessment may not yield reliable results, even if the analyst works with an elaborate catalogue of subdimensions. Such an approach exploits the analyst's initiated, naïve speaker intuition rather than actual language use by different speakers. One of the main achievements of SFL is its clarity in linguistic analysis, in showing that what speakers mean can be analysed based on their paradigmatic choices of the features of a language (note, however, that this may not hold for unexpressed implicit meanings or particular readings by addressees, see Steiner this volume). The architecture of SFL provides the analytical tools for specific, explicit analyses that are replicable by other scholars (even if they might diverge on the exact classification of certain features, but these are coding practices, cf. O'Donnell, Zappavigna and Whitelaw 2008). There may be alternative ways of going about the specific, replicable analysis based on different assumptions about the exact conceptualization of the relationship between situational context and semantics and lexico-grammar leading to differences in the exact features that will be taken into consideration in the analysis.

In general, the multidimensionality of functional language variation can be seen by linguists as too complex for a comprehensive research approach and might therefore lead to a fragmented research agenda with a host of individual studies on specific aspects. However, concentrating on specific aspects might yield findings that understate the role of factors controlled for (or even overlooked) that might altogether change the results. This has happened in corpus-based TS: studies often focus on individual linguistic features in specific language pairs and keep the variable register constant. This has resulted in seemingly contradictory findings, not least because the impact of REGISTER variation was not assessed. Translations are affected by a range of factors: therefore, their empirical analysis requires a methodology that accounts for this multifactorial character (cf. De Sutter and Lefer 2020), especially with respect to the differential influence of REGISTER (see Section 5).

The focus in such a multifactorial analysis is on bringing out typical characteristics. With respect to understanding how REGISTERS can be seen as subsystems on the cline of instantiation filtering the options of the language system as the meaning potential in light of the specific sub-potential of the context of situation, such generalizations are essential. At the same time, corpus-based analysis may exaggerate the focus on general trends in terms of typical features including typical absences of features. I would claim that this disadvantage can be alleviated by reporting as much information as possible alongside the analysis, for instance, detailed statistical information including indications of the variability of the data set. Comparing mean values for groups of texts may give an idea of differences between registers, but it leaves implicit the potentially differential range of variation within a REGISTER. Evert and Neumann (2017) use a multivariate quantitative procedure which involves inspection of visualizations. In these visualizations each corpus text is represented individually as a vector of its comprehensive linguistic characterization in multidimensional space and can be examined for its individual contribution to the emerging picture of a group of texts.

This sheds light on continuities between clusters of texts (see also Neumann 2020) and makes sense as REGISTERS can be seen as 'areas of density' of similar texts and overlaps with similar REGISTERS, rather than shoebox categories with clear dividing boundaries with other REGISTERS. Interpretation of these clusters and their overlaps can be further facilitated by comparing them to a reference corpus (Neumann 2013) or an overview of the register variation in a given language (e.g. Biber 1995).

5 Empirical investigations of the interaction between translation and register

Having clarified the concepts, I will now discuss empirical research that might give an answer to some of the questions raised in Section 1. Evert and Neumann (2017) use REGISTER analysis as the framework for text analysis. Their exploratory statistical analysis is concerned with examining how translations on the whole (i.e. when characterized by a comprehensive set of linguistic features derived as operationalizations from the type of REGISTER dimensions sketched out in this chapter) display specific properties. They find a difference in translation direction: whereas translations from German into English across a range of five (fairly similar) registers from the CroCo Corpus (Hansen-Schirra, Neumann, and Steiner 2012) are overwhelmingly similar to non-translated texts in the same language, translations into German are clearly different from German non-translated texts and thus display shining-through of English features (Teich 2003). Drawing on Toury's (2012) law of interference, they interpret this in terms of unequal status of the two languages involved in the respective target lingua-cultures.

Let us come back to one of the questions raised in Section 1, namely whether awareness for REGISTER-specific language use is developed in the process of becoming a professional, experienced translator or whether translators simply draw on knowledge they have in the target language anyway. The latter is not implausible because language users who are not language professionals also adapt their linguistic behaviour to the requirements of the situation. However, Redelinghuys's (2016) study of the interaction between expertise and register suggests that there is indeed a development in the way translators adapt to register requirements. Her corpus-based study shows that experienced translators still do not entirely adapt to the respective register in all respects, but inexperienced translators deviate even more. Part of translation expertise then is an active effort to make the translated text similar to comparable texts in the target language.

Kruger and Van Rooy (2012) test generally for typical properties of translations and, more particularly, whether register specificity is levelled out in translation. Focussing on specific properties such as explicitation, normalization and simplification, the authors find evidence for explicitation of the complementizer *that* and simplification in the form of a lower standardized type-token ratio in translations. Moreover, they find that translators tend to adapt to the register at hand and interpret this as an indication of exaggerating target language norms. This is investigated in more detail by Delaere (2015) and will be discussed below.

In my own prior work (Neumann 2013), a pattern of linguistic features conforming to target REGISTER conventions was found. On the basis of a comprehensive analysis of linguistic indicators of six subdimensions of field, tenor and mode in the two registers Fiction and Letters to Shareholders, I conclude that there are only local deviations of translations from the REGISTER features of the target language. This means that statistically significant differences in the relative frequency of individual features were found, but did not alter the interpretation for the given subdimension because other features supported the comparable interpretation. It should be noted, however, that the REGISTERS captured by the CroCo Corpus (Hansen-Schirra, Neumann and Steiner 2012) do not reflect any obvious cultural differences and thus permit translation without forcing adjustments. REGISTERS such as court decisions, which are incomparable due to more serious cultural differences in the respective legal systems, are not included (in the case of court decisions because this type of text is only translated in one of the two translation directions). Presumably, such incomparable REGISTERS are generally infrequent in this language pair.

The findings reported so far all simply show that translators conform to the exigencies of the relevant contexts of situation in the target language except for those cases where the translation serves a purely informative, documentary purpose, that is, where the translation is 'overtly' recognizable as such (House 1997). This is, for instance, the case when German court decisions are translated into English because they touch upon internationally relevant questions such as the role of the NATO, international terrorism and so on. While the original has a legal status in Germany, the translation only serves to inform international stakeholders – who might still have a very vital interest in the proceedings – about the decision.

This is not the only way in which REGISTER is of relevance to understand translation. Automatic machine learning techniques reach high levels of accuracy in classifying translated and non-translated texts (Volansky, Ordan and Wintner 2015). This high accuracy corroborates assumptions about typical properties of translations that make them distinct from non-translated texts (Baker 1995; Toury 2012), and suggest that translations systematically deviate from non-translated texts to the extent that they might be identified as a separate variety in the target language (Kruger 2018). But the overall relevance of REGISTER in the language system and translators' proven awareness thereof could lead to the assumption that there are more specific ways in which translators respond to the exigencies of the context.

Arguably, some contexts allow for more variability than others – not just for original speakers/writers but also for translators. Although the main aim of Xiao and Dai's (2014) investigation of original and translated Chinese is not to ascertain the role of register in translation, they still show that some specific properties of the translations in their corpus vary across registers. Delaere (2015) makes register[4] together with the assessment of source language influence the main aims of her study of conformity to descriptive and prescriptive norms in Dutch translated language. Her study of selected lexico-grammatical features in a corpus of Dutch originals and translations using the Dutch Parallel Corpus (Macken, De Clercq and Paulussen 2011) shows that register explains variation between translations in the extent to which they conform to target language descriptive/prescriptive norms. For instance, register is shown to affect the choice of formal versus neutral lexemes, and of loan words in translation. Registers also differ as to whether they show a tendency to use standard rather than non-standard items: in effect this means that Delaere did not find there was a general trend to conform to target language norms. Even if Delaere's approach is not grounded in SFL, her findings can still be interpreted in light of SFL assumptions about language. Translators (as language users) draw on detailed experience with situation-dependent language use. The accumulated knowledge even extends to the amount of liberty that they may take in a given context.

At the same time, comparison across REGISTERS also reveals evidence of insensitivity towards REGISTER characteristics (Neumann 2014). It seems that in some REGISTERS features of original texts are diluted so that the translated REGISTER loses its distinctive character in comparison to the comparable register in the source language. More work is required to compare this loss of register distinctiveness with Baker's 'levelling out' (Redelinghuys 2016).

All these findings on deviating patterns in certain registers or language pairs are important for corpus-based TS because they show that properties of translations seem to be largely determined by a range of factors including more general social factors, that is, the prestige of the languages involved and the specific social and situational context. Any idea of these properties operating uniformly, that is, 'universally' (Baker 1995), clearly has to be rejected. Toury (2004) draws on Halliday's claims about the probabilistic character of language (Halliday 1991; see also Taverniers 2019: 70–1) to assert that translation properties as the result of the translators' linguistic choices and conditioned by various factors must be probabilistic, too. Based on this summary of empirical findings, we can conclude that REGISTER has been proven to be an important factor.

How can practitioners use information on register for translating? Optimally, they could use a resource that contains profiles of the REGISTERS they typically translate. This could replace the current practice of translators who collect comparable target language texts in order to get an indication of typical language use in this particular type of texts. REGISTER profiles can summarize the information in a systematic way. This does not mean, however, that translators can use such profiles in a very direct way to adapt the exact number of times a particular REGISTER feature is used in a translation. If the resource comprises comparable descriptions of REGISTERS across languages, translators can assess to what extent the ST they are about to translate represents a typical exemplar of the given REGISTER. If it does not, the translator may decide to adapt their translation strategy to this deviation of the ST. REGISTER profiles which break down the characterization of a REGISTER into the individual subdimensions will allow the translator to locate the more specific point where REGISTERS in a given language pair display differences. For instance, social dynamics are likely to play out differently across cultures, and detailed REGISTER profiles can inform the translator that, say, expressions of reduced social distance do not necessarily correlate to expressions of non-hierarchical social roles. This suggests that the collection of comparative REGISTER profiles may be meaningful for future work.

Remaining open questions in a systemic functional perspective include the following: do translations into the L1 and the L2 show the same extent of REGISTER sensitivity (for experienced translators)? What role is played by more general social phenomena such as the (translators') attitude towards the two languages they work with and how does this affect their response to REGISTER conventions (cf. Evert and Neumann 2017)? To what extent will our understanding of REGISTERS already empirically investigated change if we add a dynamic component and analyse how textual parts contribute to their overall description?

6 Conclusions and outlook

In this chapter, I hope to have shown that an SFL take on REGISTER is indeed relevant for TS. Generally speaking, an approach to theorizing translation informed by (functional) language theory is crucial in order to make sense of observations (and to make assumptions explicit). We now have clear empirical evidence that translators do not just conform to the specificities of REGISTER, but that they actually respond to it in different ways, that is, taking more liberty to diverge from conventions in some registers compared to others. This cannot be reduced to a general lack of awareness of the requirements of REGISTER given the overall trend to conform to REGISTER conventions. While no particular theoretical alignment is required for these findings (as long as register is recognized as a factor) an SFL-based approach will allow the translation scholar to embed insights on translation-related aspects of REGISTER in a wider theoretical context and ultimately to achieve deeper explanations for their observations.

SFL can learn from translation-related findings on REGISTER that REGISTERS across languages may display different linguistic patterns even in cases where the general semantic characterization of field, tenor and mode might still yield fairly similar descriptions. Taking translations into consideration forces the REGISTER theorist to clarify the place of culture in relation to instantiation. While the role of REGISTERS as subsystems of the respective language system seems obvious when investigating translations, the interaction with culture still needs to be worked out in more detail. That it is relevant is shown by the empirical studies that report a differential effect of individual languages and REGISTERS.

Acknowledgements

The author gratefully acknowledges support of the German Research Foundation (DFG) project TRICKLET (Translation Research in Corpora, Keystroke Logging and Eye Tracking), research grant no. NE1822/2-2.

Notes

1. Bühler (1934), too, suggests that all three language functions are present in an act of linguistic communication. This important aspect is, however, often backgrounded by scholars who draw on his ideas.

2. Drawing on Biber's (1995) use of the term in the sociolinguistic tradition (Matthiessen 2019: 26).
3. The Covid-19 pandemic unfolding during production of this book represents a very salient example of such specific circumstances: It forced entire societies to develop new ways of negotiating social processes.
4. In fact, Delaere uses the notion of genre, but in a way that is most similar to usage in the sociolinguistic tradition of register analysis.

References

Baker, Mona (1992), *In Other Words: A Coursebook on Translation*, London: Routledge.
Baker, Mona (1995), 'Corpora in Translation Studies: An Overview and Some Suggestions for Future Research', *Target* 7 (2): 223–43.
Bartlett, Tom (2017), 'Context in Systemic Functional Linguistics: Towards Scalar Supervenience?' in Tom Bartlett and Gerard O'Grady (eds), *The Routledge Handbook of Systemic Functional Linguistics*, 375–90, London: Routledge.
Biber, Douglas (1988), *Variation across Speech and Writing*, Cambridge: Cambridge University Press.
Biber, Douglas (1995), *Dimensions of Register Variation*, Cambridge: Cambridge University Press.
Biber, Douglas, and Conrad, Susan (2009), *Register, Genre, and Style*, Cambridge: Cambridge University Press.
Biber, Douglas, Johansson, Stig, Leech, Geoffrey, Conrad, Susan and Finegan, Ed (1999), *The Longman Grammar of Spoken and Written English*, London: Longman.
Bowcher, Wendy L. (2017), 'Field, Tenor and Mode', in Tom Bartlett and Gerard O'Grady (eds), *The Routledge Handbook of Systemic Functional Linguistics*, 391–403, London: Routledge.
Bowcher, Wendy L. (2018), 'The Semiotic Sense of Context vs the Material Sense of Context', *Functional Linguistics* 5 (1): 5. https://doi.org/10.1186/s40554-018-0055-y.
Bowcher, Wendy L. (2019), 'Context and Register', in David Schönthal, Geoff Thompson, Lise Fontaine and Wendy L. Bowcher (eds), *The Cambridge Handbook of Systemic Functional Linguistics*, 142–70, Cambridge: Cambridge University Press. https://doi.org/10.1017/9781316337936.008.
Bühler, Karl (1934), *Sprachtheorie. Die Darstellungsfunktion der Sprache*, Jena: Fischer.
De Sutter, Gert, and Lefer, Marie-Aude (2020). 'On the Need for a New Research Agenda for Corpus-Based Translation Studies: A Multi-Methodological, Multifactorial and Interdisciplinary Approach', *Perspectives* 28 (1): 1–23. https://doi.org/10.1080/09076 76X.2019.1611891.
Delaere, Isabelle (2015), 'Do Translators Walk the Line? Visually Exploring Translated and Non-Translated Texts in Search of Norm Conformity', PhD diss., University of Ghent.
Dourish, Paul (2004), 'What We Talk about When We Talk about Context', *Personal and Ubiquitous Computing* 8 (1): 19–30. https://doi.org/10.1007/s00779-003-0253-8.
Evert, Stefan, and Neumann, Stella (2017), 'The Impact of Translation Direction on Characteristics of Translated Texts: A Multivariate Analysis for English and German', in Gert De Sutter, Marie-Aude Lefer and Isabelle Delaere (eds), *Empirical Translation Studies: New Theoretical and Methodological Traditions*, 47–80, Berlin: de Gruyter.

Ferguson, Charles A. (1982), 'Simplified Registers and Linguistic Theory', in Loraine K. Obler and Lise Menn (eds), *Exceptional Language and Linguistics*, 49–66, New York: Academic Press.

Firth, J. R. (1957), *Papers in Linguistics 1934–1951*, London: Oxford University Press.

Gregory, Michael, and Carroll, Susanne (1978), *Language and Situation: Language Varieties and Their Social Contexts*, London: Routledge & Kegan Paul.

Halliday, M. A. K. (1978), *Language as Social Semiotic: The Social Interpretation of Language and Meaning*, London: Arnold.

Halliday, M. A. K. (1991), 'Towards Probabilistic Interpretations', in Eija Ventola (ed.), *Functional and Systemic Linguistics: Approaches and Uses*, 39–61. Berlin: de Gruyter.

Halliday, M. A. K. (1999), 'The Notion of "Context" in Language Education', in Mohsen Ghadessy (ed.), *Text and Context in Functional Linguistics*, 1–24, Amsterdam: John Benjamins.

Halliday, M. A. K. (2013), 'Meaning as Choice', in Lise Fontaine, Tom Bartlett and Gerard O'Grady (eds), *Systemic Functional Linguistics: Exploring Choice*, 15–36, Cambridge: Cambridge University Press.

Halliday, M. A. K., and Hasan, Ruqaiya (1989), *Language, Context, and Text: Aspects of Language in a Social-Semiotic Perspective*, Oxford: Oxford University Press.

Hansen-Schirra, Silvia, Neumann, Stella and Steiner, Erich (2012), *Cross-Linguistic Corpora for the Study of Translations – Insights from the Language Pair English-German*, Berlin: de Gruyter Mouton.

Hansen-Schirra, Silvia, and Steiner, Erich (2012), 'Towards a Typology of Translation Properties', in Silvia Hansen-Schirra, Stella Neumann and Erich Steiner, *Cross-Linguistic Corpora for the Study of Translations*, 255–79, Berlin: de Gruyter Mouton.

Hasan, Ruqaiya (1973), 'Code, Register and Social Dialect', in Basil Bernstein (ed.), *Class, Codes and Control*, 253–92, London: Routledge & Kegan Paul.

Hasan, Ruqaiya (1989), 'Semantic Variation and Sociolinguistics', *Australian Journal of Linguistics* 9 (2): 221–75. https://doi.org/10.1080/07268608908599422.

Hasan, Ruqaiya (1992), 'Speech Genre, Semiotic Mediation and the Development of Higher Mental Functions', *Language Sciences* 14 (4): 489–528.

Hasan, Ruqaiya (1999), 'Speaking with Reference to Context', in Mohsen Ghadessy (ed.), *Text and Context in Functional Linguistics*, 219–328, Amsterdam: John Benjamins.

Hasan, Ruqaiya (2009), 'The Place of Context in a Systemic Functional Model', in M. A. K. Halliday and Jonathan Webster (eds), *Continuum Companion to Systemic Functional Linguistics*, 166–89, London: Continuum.

Hasan, Ruqaiya (2014), 'Towards a Paradigmatic Description of Context: Systems, Metafunctions, and Semantics', *Functional Linguistics* 1 (1): 9. https://doi.org/10.1186/s40554-014-0009-y.

Hatim, Basil, and Mason, Ian (1990), *Discourse and the Translator*, London: Longman.

Heilmann, Arndt, Serbina, Tatiana, Freiwald, Jonas and Neumann, Stella (2020), 'Animacy and Agentivity of Subject Themes in English-German Translation', *Lingua*, March, 102813. https://doi.org/10.1016/j.lingua.2020.102813.

House, Juliane (1997), *Translation Quality Assessment. A Model Revisited*, Tübingen: Gunter Narr Verlag.

Kruger, Haidee (2018), 'Expanding the Third Code: Corpus-Based Studies of Constrained Communication and Language Mediation. Keynote Lecture', in *5th Using Corpora in Contrastive and Translation Studies Conference*, Louvain-la-Neuve, Belgium.

Kruger, Haidee, and Van Rooy, Bertus (2012), 'Register and the Features of Translated Language', *Across Languages and Cultures* 13 (1): 33–65. https://doi.org/10.1556/Acr.13.2012.1.3.

Kruger, Haidee, and Van Rooy, Bertus (2018), 'Register Variation in Written Contact Varieties of English', *English World-Wide* 39 (2): 214–42. https://doi.org/info:doi/10.1075/eww.00011.kru.

Macken, Lieve, De Clercq, Orphée and Paulussen, Hans (2011), 'Dutch Parallel Corpus: A Balanced Copyright-Cleared Parallel Corpus', *Meta: Journal des traducteurs* 56 (2): 374–90. https://doi.org/10.7202/1006182ar.

Martin, J. R. (1992), *English Text*, Amsterdam: John Benjamins.

Martin, J. R. (1999), 'Modelling Context: The Crooked Path of Progress in Contextual Linguistics', in Mohsen Ghadessy (ed.), *Text and Context in Functional Linguistics*, 25–61, Amsterdam: John Benjamins.

Martin, J. R. (2014), 'Evolving Systemic Functional Linguistics: Beyond the Clause', *Functional Linguistics* 1 (1): 3. https://doi.org/10.1186/2196-419X-1-3.

Matthiessen, C. M. I. M. (1993), 'Register in the Round: Diversity in a Unified Theory of Register Analysis', in Mohsen Ghadessy (ed.), *Register Analysis. Theory and Practice*, 221–92, London: Pinter.

Matthiessen, C. M. I. M. (2019), 'Register in Systemic Functional Linguistics', *Register Studies* 1 (1): 10–41. https://doi.org/10.1075/rs.18010.mat.

Moore, Alison Rotha (2017), 'Register Analysis in Systemic Functional Linguistics', in Tom Bartlett and Gerard O'Grady (eds), *The Routledge Handbook of Systemic Functional Linguistics*, 418–37, London: Routledge.

Nesbitt, Christopher, and Plum, Guenter (1988), 'Probabilities in a Systemic-Functional Grammar: The Clause Complex in English', in Robin P. Fawcett and David Young (eds), *New Developments in Systemic Linguistics: Theory and Application*, 2:6–38, London: Pinter.

Neumann, Stella (2003), *Textsorten und Übersetzen: Eine Korpusanalyse englischer und deutscher Reiseführer*, Frankfurt: Peter Lang Verlag.

Neumann, Stella (2012), 'Register-Induced Properties of Translations', in Silvia Hansen-Schirra, Stella Neumann and Erich Steiner, *Cross-Linguistic Corpora for the Study of Translations: Insights from the Language Pair English-German*, 191–209. Berlin: de Gruyter Mouton.

Neumann, Stella (2013), *Contrastive Register Variation: A Quantitative Approach to the Comparison of English and German*, Berlin: de Gruyter Mouton.

Neumann, Stella (2014), 'Cross-Linguistic Register Studies: Theoretical and Methodological Considerations', *Languages in Contrast* 14 (1): 35–57. https://doi.org/10.1075/lic.14.1.03neu.

Neumann, Stella (2020), 'On the Interaction between Register Variation and Regional Varieties in English', *Language, Context and Text* 2 (1): 121–44. https://doi.org/10.1075/langct.00023.neu.

Nord, Christiane (2005), *Text Analysis in Translation: Theory Methodology, and Didactic Application of a Model for Translation-Oriented Text Analysis*, 2nd edn, Amsterdam: Rodopi.

O'Donnell, Michael (1999), 'Context in Dynamic Modelling', in Mohsen Ghadessy (ed.), *Text and Context in Functional Linguistics*, 63–99, Amsterdam: John Benjamins.

O'Donnell, Mick, Zappavigna, Michele and Whitelaw, Casey (2008), 'A Survey of Process Type Classification over Difficult Cases', in Carys Jones and Eija Ventola (eds), *From*

Language to Multimodality: New Developments in the Study of Ideational Meaning, 47–64, London: Equinox.

Redelinghuys, Karien (2016), 'Levelling-Out and Register Variation in the Translations of Experienced and Inexperienced Translators: A Corpus-Based Study', *Stellenbosch Papers in Linguistics* 45 (July): 189–220. https://doi.org/10.5774/45-0-198.

Redelinghuys, Karien, and Kruger, Haidee (2015), 'Using the Features of Translated Language to Investigate Translation Expertise: A Corpus-Based Study', *International Journal of Corpus Linguistics* 20 (3): 293–325. https://doi.org/10.1075/ijcl.20.3.02red.

Reiß, Katharina (1976), *Texttyp und Übersetzungsmethode. Der operative Text*, Kronberg/ Ts.: Scriptor-Verlag.

Steiner, Erich (2001), 'Intralingual and Interlingual Versions of a Text – How Specific Is the Notion of "Translation"?' in Erich Steiner and Colin Yallop (eds), *Exploring Translation and Multilingual Text Production. Beyond Content*, 161–90, Berlin: de Gruyter Mouton.

Steiner, Erich (2004), *Translated Texts: Properties, Variants, Evaluations*, Frankfurt: Peter Lang Verlag.

Ströbel, Marcus, Kerz, Elma, Wiechmann, Daniel and Neumann, Stella (2016), 'CoCoGen – Complexity Contour Generator: Automatic Assessment of Linguistic Complexity Using a Sliding-Window Technique', in *Coling 2016 Workshop on Computational Linguistics for Linguistic Complexity*, 23–31. Osaka. http://aclanthology. info/papers/cocogen-complexity-contour-generator-automatic-assessment-of-linguistic-complexity-using-a-sliding-window-technique.

Taverniers, Miriam (2019), 'Semantics', in David Schönthal, Geoff Thompson, Lise Fontaine and Wendy L. Bowcher (eds), *The Cambridge Handbook of Systemic Functional Linguistics*, 55–91, Cambridge: Cambridge University Press. https://doi. org/10.1017/9781316337936.005.

Teich, Elke (2003), *Cross-Linguistic Variation in System and Text: A Methodology for the Investigation of Translations and Comparable Texts*, Berlin: de Gruyter Mouton.

Toury, Gideon (2004), 'Probabilistic Explanations in Translation Studies: Welcome as They Are, Would They Qualify as Universals?' in Anna Mauranen and Pekka Kujamäki (eds), *Translation Universals: Do They Exist?*, 15–32. Amsterdam: John Benjamins.

Toury, Gideon (2012), *Descriptive Translation Studies – and beyond: Revised Edition*, 2nd edn, Amsterdam: John Benjamins.

Trosborg, Anna (1997), 'Text Typology: Register, Genre and Text Type', in Anna Trosborg (ed.), *Text Typology and Translation*, 3–23, Amsterdam: John Benjamins.

Ure, Jean, and Ellis, Jeffrey (1977), 'Register in Descriptive Linguistics and Linguistic Sociology', in Oscar Uribe-Villegas (ed.), *Issues in Sociolinguistics*, 197–243, The Hague: Mouton.

Volansky, Vered, Ordan, Noam and Wintner, Shuly (2015), 'On the Features of Translationese', *Digital Scholarship in the Humanities* 30 (1): 98–118. https://doi. org/10.1093/llc/fqt031.

Xiao, Richard, and Dai, Guangrong (2014), 'Lexical and Grammatical Properties of Translational Chinese: Translation Universal Hypotheses Reevaluated from the Chinese Perspective', *Corpus Linguistics and Linguistic Theory* 10 (1): 11–55.

4

Systemic Functional Linguistics as a framework for the analysis of translator/interpreter intervention

Jeremy Munday
University of Leeds

1 Introduction

This chapter focuses on Systemic Functional Linguistics (SFL)-based models used in Translation Studies (TS) for the analysis of source text–target text pairs. Its main aim is to critically assess current applications of SFL by TS and to discuss in detail the potential of the increasingly popular system of Appraisal for the investigation of translator 'intervention' (Munday 2007). Appraisal is all about identifying linguistic expressions of value and positioning, while intervention relates to the active involvement of the translator(s) and other actors in shaping the target text; in both cases, there is a negotiation of values, individual and societal, with the possibility of a shift in value in the target text. The essence of the chapter can be captured by three direct questions: What are the reasons for using an SFL-based model to analyse the translator's choices? How successful is it? and How might the model be best applied?[1] The discussion will mark an advance in the understanding of linguistic models of translation and provide an enhanced conceptual framework for future TS-SFL research.

The chapter is organized as follows: Section 2 will discuss the shared values underpinning SFL and TS; Section 3 will evaluate the importance of Appraisal as a means of identifying critical points of translation; Section 4 will examine the link to the TS procedure of explicitation before Section 5 concludes by considering the future of a refined and blended model of analysis specifically geared to the characteristics of translated texts.

2 Values underpinning SFL and TS

Even before the heralded 'cultural turn' of the 1980s and 1990s, scholars were challenging the structuralist models that had held sway in previous decades. Thus, the early taxonomies of translation shifts – notably Vinay and Darbelnet (1958) and the Firth-inspired Catford (1965) – along with the Chomskyan calculation of different forms of equivalence (Nida 1964), were attacked by those intent on moving TS towards Gender Studies, Postcolonial Studies and so on (Gentzler 1993). At the same time, the deconstructionists questioned the very feasibility of achieving equivalence of meaning and challenged its stability in philosophical terms (Graham 1985).

The collaboration between linguistics-oriented TS and the discipline of Linguistics has itself often been unequal. While quantitative calculations are central to statistical machine translation programmes, to experiments in cognitive TS and to some corpus-based TS, the linguistic theories adopted by TS often derive their multifaceted approach from various trends of discourse analysis and pragmatics. Here it is important to note that SFL and TS both place a premium on language as functional communication, although this is tackled somewhat differently in the two fields.

2.1 SFL

The SFL perspective is that language is a system of choices at each level, related to communicative function (Bartlett and O'Grady 2017). The identification of typical language patterns means the system has the power to predict what will occur in specific contexts and genres. This is manifested in a number of ways: so, the predictive power of the theory enables description of typical genre configurations and, using that knowledge, to reliably determine the components of similar communicative situations such as the famous service encounters analysed in Halliday and Hasan (1989). On the other hand, it is possible to describe the language system as a whole using SFL's grammatical categories and functions. Over the years, SFL grammars or studies have been produced for a range of languages including Chinese, Japanese, Korean, French and Spanish (see Martin and Quiroz, this volume). This is vital because the range of semiotic resources available to each language (its 'meaning potential' in Halliday's terms) needs to be understood before a solid comparison can be made between a source text and its target text. For instance, how can we evaluate whether there has been an obligatory or optional translation shift if we do not fully understand the resources available to each language system for adding emphasis through word order?

SFL has been a useful model of **discourse analysis** for TS partly because of its emphasis on language as communication but also because it provides a thorough, context-linked model that can be applied comparatively to source and target text. Halliday himself (1994: xv) saw two possible levels where discourse analysis may successfully operate: the first is in the **understanding** of the text, by showing how it means what it does; and the second is in the **evaluation** of the text, whether it is an effective text for its own purposes. Evaluation is much more difficult to ascertain than is understanding, stresses Halliday (1994: xv), because it requires the establishment of the relationship between context and text. For example, the selection of formal or informal, inclusive or exclusive, pronouns in a political speech will depend on the hierarchical relationship between the speaker and the audience and the speaker's purpose.

2.2 TS

SFL models, including critical discourse analysis (Fairclough 1989, 2003), have been used in TS for more than three decades. This has encompassed the work of House (1977, 1997, 2015), Hatim ([1997] 2020), Hatim and Mason (1990, 1997), Baker ([1992] 2018) and Bell ([1991] 2016), all active at the end of the 1980s, followed since then by some of the contributors to the present volume. To date, some of the most prominent work in TS written from an SFL standpoint has employed Register analysis. This is achieved by drawing up ST profiles of the three parameters of Register (field, tenor, mode) and, on the discourse semantic level, the three related metafunctions of language (ideational, interpersonal and textual) in order to see how these vary in the target text. In her work, House has used these 'mismatches' to make a statement about the quality of the translation (see also Halliday 2001).

For quality statements in TS as well as in professional translation, two texts (existing source and new, finished target) are always in play. Sometimes the number of texts is higher, as in the case of a re-translated text (existing source and target texts plus new target) or a source text which includes 'synonymy points' where there are potentially two or more translation equivalents (the existing source plus two or more different target options). The latter is almost a default in the process a translation. For written translation, texts are analysed typically:

1. **Pre-translation**. This covers an analysis of the source text and the mental construction of a strategy for producing the future target text. It should be noted that, despite what is generally taught in the translation classroom (i.e. that a full analysis be made of the source text prior to commencing translation), the translator often reads the text for the first time in detail while translating it.
2. **Intra-translation**. Here, as the target text emerges through the various drafts and revisions of the translation process, the translator is constantly readjusting his/her position and using bilingual competence to ascertain those 'critical points' in the text that may need further revision or research.
3. **Post-translation**. In this stage, the finished target text product is compared to the source text in order to evaluate it and/or ensure translation quality. If it is a descriptive research study (Toury [1995] 2012), the aim is to identify non-judgmentally the patterns of shifts and the translation strategy that has been adopted.

What contribution can SFL make in these situations? Based on his plenary speech in 1998 at the 'Twenty-Fifth International Systemic Functional Congress' in Cardiff, where 'modelling language in use' was the major theme, Halliday's 'Towards a Theory of Good Translation' (2001) is an attempt to bring together SFL and translation theory in the analysis of translation. He concludes the paper arguing that 'a good translation is a text which is a translation (i.e. is equivalent) in respect of those linguistic features which are most valued in the given translation context' (Halliday 2001: 17). As Halliday points out, this raises the question of what is valued and why, as well as how and why it varies according to situation. Translation theory has long responded to these questions by highlighting key parameters that are linked to what in SFL terms is the 'context of situation': thus, 'equivalence in meaning' is considered to be a key objective using Nida's 'dynamic equivalence' (1964), which seeks the closest natural equivalent in the target language, but the form of equivalence would vary depending on the context of situation, which normally includes the target text function (Nord [1991] 2005) and the text type and purpose for which it will be used (its *Skopos*, to use Vermeer's terminology).

Halliday notes that the default is for the translation of ideational equivalents to take prominence, and he importantly questions why the interpersonal and textual realms have been afforded less importance. Clearly, the ideational metafunction, divided into experiential and logical, deals with the main subject matter of the text; this aligns itself with what TS calls the 'content' and includes technical terminology. Interestingly though, much research work in TS incorporating an SFL perspective has been conducted on Register configurations as a whole (Neumann, this volume) and on the textual function, notably cohesion (see Steiner, this volume, and Baker [1992] 2018). The study of cohesion has benefited from the growth of Corpus Linguistics, which is well suited to frequency and collocation analysis of large data sets. What has been somewhat overlooked, until quite recently in TS, has been the interpersonal metafunction, specifically the development of the system of Appraisal. Yet, as we shall see in the next section, it has much potential for illuminating writer and reader or speaker and listener intervention and intention.

3 The system of Appraisal

Appraisal has been developed in numerous publications, one of the earliest being 'Beyond Exchange: Appraisal Systems in English' (Martin 2000). This later led to the seminal publication of the co-authored monograph *The Language of Evaluation: Appraisal in English* (Martin and White 2005), where we see the following description of what the authors understand by Appraisal and the interpersonal function in general:

> This book is concerned with the interpersonal in language, with the subjective presence of writers/speakers in texts as they adopt stances towards both the material they present and those with whom they communicate. It is concerned with how writers/speakers approve and disapprove, enthuse and abhor, applaud and criticise, with how they position their readers/listeners to do likewise. It is concerned with the construction by texts of communities of shared feelings and values, and with the linguistic mechanisms for the sharing of emotions, tastes and normative assessments. (Martin and White 2005: 1)

The focus on subjectivity and stance has also become of great interest in TS, with a shift in recent years towards the role of the translator as interested participant in the communicative event rather than as a transparent conduit and impartial mediator. The positioning of the translator may well be different to that of the original author, even more so in the case of the interpreter who may be physically present in the room with the speakers and employed by one side in the meeting. In addition, as can be seen in the above quote, there is a whole gamut of emotions and reactions that fall under this umbrella[2]; and the text may perform many functions including the transmission of values which are again open to modification and alteration in translation. The advantage of using a model drawn from SFL is that there is a clearly defined link between lexico-grammatical realizations and communicative effect; in the case of attitude, there are very specific linguistic triggers that enter into play when a value judgement is made. And, of course, that judgement reflects the position of the speaker/writer and his/her relationship to others. In translation contexts it allows the investigation of translator stance and positioning.

Appraisal expanded on the Register dimension of tenor and, in discourse semantic terms, the interpersonal function of language. This function does not have the crucial, field-filling, terminology-coining role of the ideational function. It is conveyed through mood and modality, the choice of subject pronouns and forms of address, and most obviously through what Halliday calls 'evaluative epithets' (*good, bad, beautiful* ...).

There are three dimensions of Appraisal resources: **attitude, graduation** and **engagement**. **Attitude** is at the core and by far the most overt. It covers evident points of evaluation, divided by Martin and White into three categories: **Affect** (*happy*), **Judgement** (*wrong*) and **Appreciation** (*beautiful*), which themselves are further subdivided. Thus, Judgement has two subcategories ('social esteem' and 'social sanction') and five sub-subcategories ('normality', 'capacity', 'tenacity', 'veracity' and 'propriety'). The profile of an individual text involves classification of Appraisal terms according to these categories in order to identify the main tendencies, whether these are predominantly an emotional response (Affect), an ethical evaluation (Judgement) or an aesthetic comment (Appreciation) (see Martin 2017).

In my experience, it is decidedly more straightforward to work with Affect and Appreciation. Judgement is problematic from the point of view of classification, simply because the concepts are more subtle or abstract. For example, is it really possible to reliably distinguish between Affect and Judgement with a word such as *humbled*? On the one hand it conveys a clear sense of Judgement, deriving from the dictionary description of the adjective *humble* as 'not proud or haughty: not assertive or aggressive'.[3] This could be categorized as subtype social sanction, +propriety (ethics) of Judgement (see Martin and White 2005: 53). However, it might also be considered to be part of social esteem, negative capacity; in that case it would be classed as negative capacity (the president is faced with an enormous task) even though the overall message from the text is that his humble demeanour is admirable. That is, he is *humbled* because he is aware of the enormity of the responsibility and the challenge this represents to his own capacity. Furthermore, the epithet *humbled* may also belong to the category of Affect, insecurity, since there is an underlying lack of confidence which is classified as a kind of unhappiness. In short, a complication of the model is that the same epithet may be classified into multiple categories (e.g. propriety/capacity) and the positive/negative distinction does not always correspond to a good/bad classification (cf. Martin 2020. To counteract this, the context and clustering of Appraisal must be taken into account as an important contributor to the reading of attitude and the reader response. As we shall see below, individual examples must not be treated in isolation.

The second dimension of Appraisal are the resources of **graduation**, which may either intensify or downplay the degree of attitude. If we pursue the case of *humble/ humbled*, the *Oxford Dictionary* gives the example 'I felt very humble when meeting her', where the intensification achieved by the adverb *very* is clear. Similarly, in the online resource *Oxford Lexico*, synonyms or 'similar' verbs for *humble* are almost all intensifiers (*humiliate, abase, demean, belittle, lower, degrade*).[4]

The third dimension of Appraisal is **engagement**, which in essence deals with the commitment of the writer/speaker (A) to the truth of what he/she says, along with the construction by (A) of more or less space for the reader/listener (B) to challenge (A)'s ideas. In other words, does the writer of an article or a politician in an interview present material as fact when it is only opinion? Or, how much freedom does (B) really have to challenge (A)'s statement? This is signalled by a variety of means, including the expression of modality but also reporting verbs and the labelling of institutions and individuals. At the moment, engagement is relatively under-referenced in TS.

The use of a methodology centred around Appraisal has raised many questions in TS analysis. For a start, there is the difficulty of terminology and the abundance of categories. We mentioned the case of *humbled* above, but in reality the tricky methodological problem of classification occurs with any data analysis. Martin and White (2005) discuss comprehensively subcategories such as 'unhappiness', 'insecurity' and 'dissatisfaction'. Each of these has a positive and negative pole: *the captain felt sad* is –happiness (negative happiness); *happy* is +happiness, and so on. An example is given of the range of intensity between a lower and higher value of emotion: thus, the 'dislike' scale goes from low value *disliked* to median *hated* to high *detested*, a classification which mimics the cline of modality in SFL. Feelings are also described in a way that is linked to the categories of process used by SFL in its analysis of action and the ideational function of language. Thus, the expressions of emotion may be behavioural (*cries*), mental (*upset*), a surge of behaviour (*wept, tremble*) or a state/ disposition (*wary, fearful*). This approach may be useful in drawing up a profile of the text or of a character in the narrative, who may be more or less active or cerebral. This is what may be referred to as the specific 'mind style' (Leech and Short 2007). The categorization of emotive response that is found in the system of Appraisal can help understand the stylistic choices and the way the narrative perspective is constructed. However, there are a number of questions that mitigate against the straightforward application of this methodology. One, which we have alluded to above, relates to the difficulty of categorizing consistently and in analysing objectively. For example, attitude depends very much on the context and co-text in which it is used. A word such as *humbled* acquires a positive or negative attitude that is linked to its semantic prosody (Partington 2004) or to the cultural value associated with it.

Take an epithet such as *brash*, which many dictionary definitions classify as 'impertinent' or 'impudent' (or some close variant of this), both of which would be categorized as negative judgement (specifically the sub-category of propriety). Yet this is an example of a word that is contextually and culturally dependent, since it clearly has the capacity to convey a more positive attitude: witness the couplet *brash and exciting*,[5] which was used to describe Sydney in an online review. This corresponds to one of three senses, found in the online dictionary.com, which is 'energetic and high-spirited, especially in an irreverent way'.[6] On other occasions, *brash* may be paired in other couplets that are more negative:

> Brash and brassy it may be, as any Melburnian will cheerfully remind you, but Sydney has got a lot to crow about. Golden beaches, weather of the gods and a twinkling harbor that's the envy of the world.[7]

This appears in an online travel article that praises Sydney's virtues, as can be seen in the intense appreciation in the second sentence above (*golden beaches*). In this instance, *brash and brassy* must be seen as the negative contrast to Sydney which *has got a lot to crow about*: this is signalled by the adversities of the conjunction *but* and the modal *it may be* which has a similar function. However, the negativity is not intense: the couplet has an amusing literary alliteration and a playful jibe from the rival city of Melbourne. This all seems light-hearted and does not detract from the spectacular appreciation of the second sentence and, indeed, the rest of the article.

The potential for the shift in attitude (a negative epithet changing to playfully positive, signalled by the grammatical structure and contextual situation) is more problematic for translation, and subjective for any analysis, although the automatic computer-assisted analysis of semantic prosodies using tools such as Sketch Engine[8] helps achieve a more objective perspective. The problem, in fact, encompasses tricky questions of the relationship between explicit and implicit attitude. Terminology is overtly complex on this point: Martin and White (2005) use the term 'inscribed' to refer to explicit attitude and 'invoked' or 'evoked' to speak about implicit attitude. But there are further sub-terms, including 'provoked', which concern the use of devices such as metaphor that encourage a certain response from the audience. However, the difference between the various terms ('invoked', 'evoked', 'provoked', not to mention 'invite', 'flag', 'afford' 'associated') is sometimes not clearly delineated and is hard to justify rigorously.

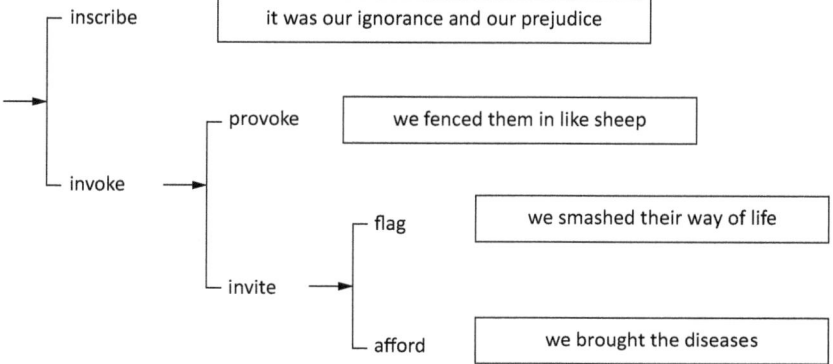

Figure 4.1 *Strategies for inscribing and invoking attitude,* adapted with examples from Martin and White (2005: 67).

The various strategies for inscribing or invoking attitude are outlined in Figure 4.1, based on an example text from Martin and White about the treatment of Aboriginals in Australia. Options can be usefully read top-down from 'inscribed' to 'afford' according to the degree of freedom allowed to the readers/audience in aligning with the values that underlie the text. Thus, 'inscribe' categorically exposes the attitude with its direct reference to *our ignorance and prejudice*, making it difficult for the reader to challenge this opinion. At another point on the scale, the more sophisticated lexical metaphor and non-core vocabulary have the effect of intensifying feeling, as can be seen in the examples of 'provoke' (*we **fenced** them in like sheep*) and 'flag' (*we **smashed** their way of life*).

Other questions that arise with this type of analysis are how far is a particular phenomenon genre-specific, language-specific or idiosyncratic to the individual speaker/writer. It is difficult to tackle such questions without a good corpus of textual evidence; that is, instances of attitude measured against a reference corpus of the language in which it is possible to better gauge the markedness of the individual text choices.

The use of Appraisal has been focused on a number of genres and fields, notably academic texts, the political interview, the history textbook, tourist material and other advertising and writing with similar functions. There is certainly a language or culture element involved too. This manifests itself either through interference from the source language configurations or through cultural difference, in which there is variation in the conventional use of Appraisal; for example, an email from a prospective student to a potential supervisor which is overly flattering, rendering it unsuitable for a UK academic setting, where the relationship between teacher and student is generally less hierarchical. Then there is the idiosyncratic use of Appraisal resources, either 'upscaling' or 'downscaling'. Downscaling would be the stereotypical hard-to-please teacher for whom an epithet such as *not bad* represents a high degree of approval (Appreciation in attitudinal terms). Upscaling's proponents will include the overexcited football commentator screaming *Goal! Goal! Goal!* at the top of their voice and with an exaggerated lengthening of the syllable, which goes to show that attitude and graduation need to incorporate multimodal functions of visual and spoken communication (cf. Hao and Hood 2019; Martin et al., 2021). Meanwhile, a figure such as President Trump has an idiosyncratic way of presenting himself that almost descends into parody with his exaggerated selection of upscaled and highly graduated evaluation markers. Take the following example, where President Trump is attacking the spread of on-land wind turbines, which he, quixotically, refers to as *windmills* and *monsters*:

ST1

We'll have an economy based on wind. I never understood wind. You know, I know windmills very much. I've studied it better than anybody I know. It's very **expensive**. They're made in China and Germany mostly – very few made here, almost none. But they're manufactured tremendous – if you're into this – tremendous fumes. Gases are spewing into the atmosphere. You know we have a world, right? So the world is **tiny** compared to the universe. So tremendous, tremendous amount of fumes and everything. You talk about the carbon footprint – fumes are spewing into the air. Right? Spewing. Whether it's in China, Germany, it's going into the air. It's our air, their air, <u>everything</u> – right?[9]

This is an extract from the President's remarks at the Turning Point USA Student Action Summit, West Palm Beach, 22 December 2019. The words and expressions underlined correspond to graduation, all increased (*very much, better, mostly*) since even those which show a reduction in attitude still present this with intensification (*never, very few*). Increased intensification may of course be a bad thing: so, *tremendous* is repeated four times and is collocated with *fumes*, therefore something very undesirable. *Spewing*, used three times, is a non-core word that energizes its negative attitude by appearing with common collocates in a combined grammatical pattern that may be expressed as:

Tremendous amount of fumes/gases are spewing into the atmosphere/air.

As well as the intensity of the graduation, there is also invoked attitude (negative appreciation) inherent in the image of environmental contamination. It should be noted that everything Trump says constitutes indirect evaluation, since at no point in the example does he state explicitly that the production of wind turbines is polluting. This indirectness is compounded by the transitivity structures, part of the Register variable field and the ideational metafunction of discourse semantics: thus, the fumes/gases appear to act without human intervention (*fumes/gases are spewing …*) and the listener or reader needs to work to make the link to producers in China and Germany.

This propensity to intensification is clearly not specific to the genre or language, since the intensity of graduation can be compared to similar speeches by other previous US presidents. It is particular to President Trump, his idiosyncratic 'Appraisal signature' (cf. Martin and White 2005: 203) if you like, the equivalent of the written stylistic fingerprint analysed by researchers working on style in fiction (Leech and Short 2007). The question becomes, 'How does or should translation deal with such a phenomenon?' Should the translator and interpreter reproduce this in-your-face, and mainly off-the-cuff, bravado, or should they opt for downscaling and moulding the speech in an effort to produce something that conforms to the expected conventions of the genre? The real crux of the matter centres on this intensity of attitude. It is expressed through the number of attitudinal markers, through graduation of various types (including non-core vocabulary, voice volume and pitch) and through the use of stand-out attitudinal terms, unexpected evaluation or else indirect/implicit/negotiable Appraisal resources. In all cases the values at stake need to be carefully controlled by the translator or interpreter. Target texts 1.1 and 1.2 illustrate this in Table 4.1.

The sources for these target texts are the Spanish version of *RT* news (formerly *Russia Today*) and the Spanish conservative daily *ABC*. What is visible above all is the fact that in this type of hard news journalism the words of the president are often paraphrased and reframed rather than reproduced in a more conventional translation format. Both extracts demonstrate this with a paraphrase, summary and interpretation of his words: TT1.1 (*RT*) issues a direct statement of the contamination produced by the turbines, while TT1.2 (*ABC*) introduces the quote with a clear negative evaluation

Table 4.1 Target Texts 1.1 and 1.2

TT 1.1 (Bold highlight in the original)	*[Back translation of target text 1.1]*
Mientras se burlaba del llamado Green New Deal (un conjunto de medidas propuestas para combatir el calentamiento global), el mandatario aseveró que 'nunca entendió' el atractivo de las plantas de energía eólica, alegando que la producción de sus turbinas causa grandes emisiones de carbono.	*While he was mocking the so-called Green New Deal (a group of measures proposed to combat global warming), the president affirmed that 'he never understood' the attraction of wind energy plants, claiming that the production of its turbines causes high carbon emissions.*
'Nunca entendí el viento', señaló. 'Sé mucho sobre los molinos de viento, los he estudiado mejor que nadie. Sé que son muy caros. En su mayoría se fabrican en China y Alemania, muy pocos se fabrican aquí, casi ninguno, pero [...] **producen enormes vapores y gases, que están siendo arrojados a la atmósfera'.**[a]	*'I never understood wind', he indicated. 'I know a lot about windmills, I have studied them better than anyone. I know that they are very expensive. The majority are manufactured in China and Germany, very few are manufactured here, but [...]* ***they produce enormous fumes and gases, which are being hurled into the atmosphere'.***

TT 1.2 (Bold highlight in the original)	*[Back translation of target text 1.2]*
Pero fueron sus comentarios laberínticos y a menudo absurdos sobre las turbinas eólicas lo que causó mayor sorpresa. «Se fabrican en China y Alemania principalmente», de los cuales hay más de 57.000 en todo EE.UU., según la Asociación Americana de Energía Eólica. «**Pero se fabrican generando tremendos humos que están lanzando a la atmósfera.** Sabes que tenemos un mundo, ¿verdad? Así que el mundo es diminuto comparado con el universo. Así que una tremenda, tremenda cantidad de gases y todo».[b]	But it was his labyrinthine and often absurd comments about wind turbines which caused most surprise. 'They are manufactured in China and Germany mainly', of which there are more than 57,000 in the whole of the United States, according to the American Association of Wind Energy. '**But they are manufactured generating tremendous fumes that they are throwing into the atmosphere.** You know that we have a world, right? So the world is tiny compared with the universe. So tremendous, tremendous amount of gases and everything'.

Note: [a]https://actualidad.rt.com/actualidad/337784-viento-trump-arremeter-molinos.

[b]https://www.abc.es/economia/abci-trump-carga-contra-molinos-viento-porque-ruidosos-y-matan-miles-aves-201912251803_noticia.html.

of Trump's comments (*labyrinthine and often absurd*). When it comes to the actual translation of the quotations, the trend is that a more or less literal translation is provided, the difference being that TT1.1 offers syntax that is more in line with conventional structures and stricter cohesion; TT1.2 follows somewhat more closely the structure and repetition of the original spoken language (*so ... So ... Tremendous, tremendous*). What these examples show is that the application of the system of Appraisal to translated texts is far from straightforward. Indeed, the more conventional forms of Appraisal (*labyrinthine ...*) form only part of an interlocked system. Thus, the translator needs to negotiate meaning from features, such as reporting verbs, and decide whether or not to adhere to the structure of the spoken language.

4 Implicitation and explicitation

From the comparison of Appraisal resources and translation theory concepts, it seems clear that there are opportunities for collaboration in the general area of translating intervention. Appraisal is precisely concentrated on those features which reveal the stance or attitude of the writer or speaker which, in the target text, is represented by the linguistic choices of the translator. At a more precise level, there is a strong link between indirect/direct attitude and the translation theoretical concept of explicitation (Pym 2005).

Explicitation has its logical counterpart in implicitation or implication. Yet the latter is rarely mentioned in translation theory. Implicitation runs counter-intuitive to long-held tenets of theory which state that in most instances the translator will explain ('explicate') an idea that is implicit in the source text. It is a given that the target text audience will lack some background information or specialist knowledge that is bound to the culture or field of the source text.

But not all theorists agree. For those who locate translation within relevance theory (Gutt 2000; Smith 2000), communication in such a scenario may be achieved satisfactorily without full explicitation; instead, the translator would assess what information is required for the target audience to understand the meaning of the source text. However, there are multiple questions surrounding how meaning is transmitted and how the audience is assessed. Audience design is critical to TS (Mason 2000) and in most cases a translator will have in mind the core audience to which he or she directs the translation. This audience also provides a benchmark against which to grade or determine the amount of explicitation that is appropriate at a given point in the text. This will alter according to various factors, including whether we are dealing with translation, interpreting or with audiovisual translation. Each has specific constraints which limit the possible responses; for example, a written translation facing a delayed date of publication or interpreting that is delivered simultaneously with the source speech. To give an idea of how this works out in practice, think of the first inaugural speech of President Obama (analysed in Munday, 2012), when he refers to critical battles of American history. These names should have triggered in the audience references to the wars in which these battles took place and, as a further step, the values which the United States was projecting in those wars. Thus,

- **Concord (1775)** – marked the start of the American Revolutionary War against the British colonists. The unexpected victory paved the way for the founding of the United States of America.
- **Gettysburg (1863)** – the key battle in the American Civil War, in which the Union prevailed over the Confederates. The defeat signalled the end for slavery, on which the South depended.
- **Normandy (1944)** – the seaborne landings by the Allied forces led by the United States, which took place in the north of France and opened a second front for the defeat of Nazi Germany.
- **Khe Sanh (1968)** – a defensive battle against the North Vietnamese Army in which the United States defended the siege of its base for over three months before reinforcements arrived.

The values projected are those of solidarity and standing up for the rights of the people against the colonialist British, the slave-owning South, the Nazi dictatorship and Communism (the North Vietnamese army and proxy opponents, the USSR).

However, the values represented by the battles can only be meaningfully understood if the audience is able to recognize the triggers of the evoked attitude. It would be interesting to study how many Americans would actually know or recognize all four of those battle names mentioned in the speech. Two questions arise: (i) Do they need to recognize all the battles in order to receive the core of the message, which is that the United States has always been a defender of human rights and freedoms across the world? (ii) What is the extent to which the expressive function of language in these passages might serve to compensate for any lack of historical knowledge from the audience?

Example 2 is full of reference and allusion to the waves of migrants who separately and together formed the wealth and success of the United States in the nineteenth and twentieth centuries.

ST2

For us, they packed up their few worldly possessions and travelled across oceans in search of a new life. For us, they toiled in sweatshops, and settled the West, endured the lash of the whip, and plowed the hard earth. For us, they fought and died in places like Concord and Gettysburg, Normandy and Khe Sanh.[10]

When we come to examine the various translations and interpreted versions and how these might affect explicitation in the target texts, we note a difference of realization. For the three simultaneous, Spanish language interpreters (from CNN, Telemundo and the Peruvian Canal N) who were studied for Barack Obama's speech, it was the lack of time, and perhaps the failure to recognize these unexpected problems, which led to the omission of one or more battle names with no obvious attempt to mitigate this by compensation. Amongst translations, however, with the translators working from a written version of the speech and knowing that the audience will be able to study the translation for longer than a piece of interpreting, the preference was to retain all the names. These were sometimes supported by a mention between parenthesis of the battles and wars to which each name refers. The difference in the amount of explicitation in the various target texts shows that there is no seamless deterministic link between any problem of knowledge and the translation solution. Explicitation remains a general tendency in translation (one of Toury's 'translation universals' or 'laws') because of the hierarchy in the communicative situation; the translator, however good he or she may be, is working normally on a secondary text, on a derivative of the source text. There are obvious exceptions to this hierarchy, especially when the translator is a well-known writer in their own right in the target culture or when they are adapting a literary text that is long dead, but in most non-literary translation, and certainly as an interpreter or translator of the words of a leading contemporary statesman/woman, the translator/interpreter will minimize risk by opting for a safe translation at crucial points in the text. A bad translation error can give rise to a diplomatic incident, famously when in December 1977 President Carter's interpreter told a Polish audience that the president lusted after them[11] or where a translator averts a clash by downscaling, in Appraisal terms, a potential insult or what might be interpreted as a derogatory remark.

Political discourse is full of such instances. Spanish-language reporting on the debate in Westminster about Brexit, the United Kingdom's departure from the European Union, included ad hoc translations for the following controversial remarks: Prime Minister Johnson calling the leader of the opposition 'you great big girl's blouse'[12] and his chief aide, Dominic Cummings, appealing for a new breed of civil servant, one category of which he named 'weirdos and misfits with odd skills'.[13] The first of these examples is an old English idiom meaning 'a weak and cowardly (= not brave) man'.[14] Here it is used as a comment on the opposition leader's fear of an election; it would be appraised as judgement, negative tenacity and is an example of invoked or provoked attitude, a metaphor that is now an idiom in certain circles.

It does not seem that the type of attitude at this juncture really affects the translation. Rather, it is the overall profile of attitudinal resources in the text which positions it emotionally, ethically and aesthetically. The translation problems begin when a particularly important attitudinal marker does not have a ready-made, contextually appropriate equivalent in the target language. In the case of 'you great big girl's blouse', one Spanish news outlet found the clever solution of *nenaza*, combining an informal word for a child, *nene*, and the rather humorous suffix *-aza*;[15] it is as sexist and idiomatic as the source text, and also with the same degree of invokedness. It is worth noting the equivalent proposed by one of the main translation resources websites: *inútil*[16] (useless), which lacks the image but also shifts the attitude from negative tenacity to negative capacity.

The other example introduced above (*weirdos and misfits ...*) is an intertextual reference to the 1960s American comedy, *The Munsters*.[17] It is unusual in that the evaluation is enacted through the two non-core nouns rather than epithets. They fit into the ideational metafunction (part of field), but also into the interpersonal, because of their evaluation expressed through what Fairclough (2003) and Baker (2006) termed 'labelling'. The label, or evaluative name, endeavours to cast the subject with (on this particular occasion) a negative connotation (judgement, negative normality, in Appraisal terms). But the negativity is to be seen from the comfortable, conventional reader's standpoint; for Cummings, the author, such a reaction would be anticipated and welcomed because he wants to shake up what he considers to be a complacent civil service by recruiting unconventional young people who are often dismissed with such labels by institutions. Spanish-language news outlets and corpora tended to standardize *weirdos and misfits* to *gente rara* (strange people), *gente loca* (crazy people), *bicho raro* (strange creature) or *inadaptados* (unadapted).[18] These variations in interpretation, triggered in both source and target texts, show how much the Appraisal analysis depends on the individual reader's response. This includes the translator's reading, which appears as intervention in the target text through the selection of specific interpretations at key moments in the text.

5 Conclusion

This chapter raises important issues about the relationship between SFL and TS. While SFL is being used effectively in TS for the analysis of power differentials along the lines of CDA, there are still significant differences of opinion over the usefulness of SFL to account for translation phenomena. One problem is the preponderance of labels that for some make SFL a daunting model of analysis. The problem is not that SFL is too detailed but that many of the categories pose little problem for the translator, meaning that a large part of the analysis of a text pair is irrelevant if there are no shifts in the translation process. For example, while there is a point in differentiating subcategories of attitude for the understanding of the source text in English, in practice very few of these categories change in translation. The model would be better if refined, simplified and repeated, incorporating and evaluating factors that are more likely to occur in translation than in source language writing. In Appraisal, often the most interesting and fluid feature is graduation and forms of intensification rather than the attitudinal categories themselves.

There are various areas of research which will profit from the pursuit of this line of thought: one, which we have proposed and foregrounded in this chapter, is the continued development and application of a blended model of analysis that brings together the most relevant characteristics of SFL and TS. In the current study, that model is emphatically the system of Appraisal and the TS concept of explicitation based on the perceived needs of the reader and the individual interpretations of the translator. The interesting point for further investigation is how far explicitation as a translation tendency is matched to specific types of Appraisal resources. So, for example, we look for those indicators of attitude that are susceptible to change in transfer to the target culture. In day-to-day translation, it is unusual for the type of attitude to alter except in those situations where the attitudinal expression conveys a different value in the two linguacultures. One example would be culturally sensitive lexicalized concepts such as *humble/humility, silence/silent, modest/modesty, assertive/ assertiveness, respect for the elderly, frugality*, and so on. Here we are entering the realm of cross-cultural communication; translation is intimately related to such cultural concepts and TS, working with SFL, should find rich fields to study how texts of all sorts – visual and verbal – mould themselves to the circumstances of context.

Notes

1. For ease of reference, I use the superordinate *translator, translation* and so on, to cover written translation, spoken interpreting and audiovisual subtitling/dubbing and so on.
2. There is a strong link between Appraisal and sentiment analysis, but space constraints prevent an exploration of the link in this chapter.
3. https://www.merriam-webster.com/dictionary/humble.
4. https://www.lexico.com/en/definition/humble.
5. https://www.tripadvisor.co.uk/ShowUserReviews-g255060-d5452878-r385985972-Ester_Restaurant-Sydney_New_South_Wales.html.

6. https://www.dictionary.com/browse/brash.
7. https://edition.cnn.com/travel/article/sydney-worlds-greatest-city-reasons/index.html.
8. https://www.sketchengine.eu/.
9. https://www.whitehouse.gov/briefings-statements/remarks-president-trump-turning-point-usa-student-action-summit-west-palm-beach-fl/.
10. https://obamawhitehouse.archives.gov/blog/2009/01/21/president-barack-obamas-inaugural-address.
11. https://www.newsweek.com/3-minor-interpreting-mistakes-world-leaders-had-big-implications-i-desire-1026312.
12. https://www.theguardian.com/politics/2019/sep/04/you-great-big-girls-blouse-boris-johnson-appears-to-insult-corbyn-during-pmqs.
13. https://dominiccummings.com/.
14. https://dictionary.cambridge.org/dictionary/english/a-big-great-girl-s-blouse.
15. https://www.elespanol.com/mundo/20190904/matonismo-boris-johnson-jeremy-corbyn-nenaza-colorada/426708562_0.html.
16. https://context.reverso.net/traduccion/ingles-espanol/you+big+girl%27s+blouse.
17. Series 1, Episode 22, *Dance With Me, Herman.*
18. https://context.reverso.net/traduccion/ingles-espanol/a+lot+of+weirdos; https://www.elmundo.es/internacional/2020/01/07/5e14ea8221efa00a458b45c9.html.

References

Baker, M. ([1992] 2018), *In Other Words: A Coursebook on Translation*, 3rd edn, Abingdon: Routledge.

Baker, M. (2006), *Translation and Conflict*, London: Routledge.

Bartlett, T., and O'Grady, G. (eds) (2017), *The Routledge Handbook of Systemic Functional Linguistics*, Abingdon: Routledge.

Bell, R. ([1991] 2016), *Translation and Translating: Theory and Practice*, London: Routledge.

Catford, J. C. (1965), *A Linguistic Theory of Translation*, Oxford: Oxford University Press.

Fairclough, N. (1989), *Language and Power*, London: Pearson.

Fairclough, N. (2003), *Analysing Discourse: Textual Analysis for Social Research*, London: Routledge.

Gentzler, E. (1993), *Contemporary Translation Theories*, London: Routledge.

Graham, J. (ed.) (1985), *Difference in Translation*, Ithaca, NY: Cornell University Press.

Gutt, E.-A. (2000), *Translation and Relevance*, 2nd edn, Manchester: St Jerome.

Halliday, M. A. K. (1994), *Introduction to Functional Grammar*, 2nd edn, London: Arnold.

Halliday, M. A. K. (2001), 'Towards a Theory of Good Translation', in E. Steiner and C. Yallop (eds), *Exploring Translation and Multilingual Text Production: Beyond Content*, 13–18, Berlin: Mouton de Gruyter.

Halliday M. A. K., and Hasan, R. (1989), *Language, Context and Text*, Oxford: Oxford University Press.

Hao, J., and Hood, S. (2019), 'Valuing Science: The Role of Language and Body Language in a Health Science Lecture', *Journal of Pragmatics* 139: 200–15.

Hatim, B. ([1997] 2020), *Communication across Cultures: Translation, Theory and Contrastive Text Linguistics*, Exeter: University of Exeter Press.

Hatim, B., and Mason, I. (1990), *Discourse and the Translator*, Harlow: Longman.

Hatim, B., and Mason, I. (1997), *The Translator as Communicator*, London: Routledge.

House, J. (1977), *A Model for Translation Quality Assessment*, Tübingen: G. Narr.

House, J. (1997), *Translation Quality Assessment: A Model Revisited*, Tübingen: G. Narr.

House, J. (2015), *Translation Quality Assessment: Past and Present*, Abingdon: Routledge.

Leech, G., and Short, M. (2007), *Style in Fiction: A Linguistic Introduction to English Fictional Prose*, 2nd edn, London: Routledge.

Martin, J. R. (2000), 'Beyond Exchange: Appraisal Systems in English', in S. Hunston and G. Thompson (eds), *Evaluation in Text*, 142–75, Oxford: Oxford University Press.

Martin, J. R. (2017), 'The Discourse Semantics of Attitudinal Relations: Continuing the Study of Lexis', *Russian Journal of Linguistics* 21 (1): 22–47.

Martin, J. R. (2020), 'The Effability of Semantic Relations: Describing Attitude', *Journal of Foreign Languages (China), Special Issue on Appraisal* 43 (6): 2–20.

Martin, J. R., Painter, C., Smith, B., Zappavigna, M., Ngo, T., and Hood, S. (in press for 2021), *Modelling Paralanguage Using Systemic Functional Semiotics: Theory and Application*, London: Bloomsbury Academic.

Martin, J. R., and White, P. (2005), *The Language of Evaluation: Appraisal in English*, Houndsmills: Palgrave Macmillan.

Mason, I. (2000), 'Audience Design in Translation', *The Translator* 6 (1): 1–22.

Munday, J. (ed.) (2007), *Translation as Intervention*, London: Continuum.

Munday, J. (2012), *Evaluation in Translation: Critical Points of Translator Decision-Making*, Abingdon: Routledge.

Nida, E. (1964), *Toward a Science of Translation*, Leiden: Brill.

Nord, C. ([1991] 2005), *Text Analysis in Translation*, trans. C. Nord and P. Sparrow, Amsterdam: Rodopi.

Partington, A. (2004), '"Utterly Content in Each Other's Company": Semantic Prosody and Semantic Preference', *International Journal of Corpus Linguistics* 9.1: 131–56.

Pym, A. (2005), 'Explaining Explicitation', in K. Károly and A. Fóris (eds), *New Trends in Translation Studies*, 29–34, Bern: Peter Lang.

Smith, K. G. (2000), *Bible Translation and Relevance Theory: The Translation of Titus*, unpublished PhD Thesis, Stellenbosch University.

Toury, G. ([1995] 2012), *Descriptive Translation Studies – and Beyond*, Amsterdam: John Benjamins.

Vinay, J.-P., and Darbelnet, J. (1958), *Stylistique comparée du français et de l'anglais: Méthode de traduction*, Paris: Didier.

5

Corpus-Based Translation Studies and Systemic Functional Linguistics

Ekaterina Lapshinova-Koltunski

Universität des Saarlandes, Saarbrücken

1 Introduction

The main goal of the present chapter is to explore collaboration between Corpus-Based Translation Studies (CBTS) (De Sutter, Lefer and Delaere 2017) and Systemic Functional Linguistics (SFL) (Halliday 2004; Halliday and Matthiessen 2014). The main concepts that are relevant for this collaboration will be presented here. We explore current and potential directions in CBTS and show an interaction between the latter and not only SFL but also Genre/Register theories and studies on translationese.

We specify two interaction directions: top-down and bottom-up. In the first case, existing theories are used as a background for translation-relevant corpus-based analysis. So, we show how SFL can be used as a theoretical background for formulations of research questions and hypotheses for translation phenomena. Research questions and hypotheses can then be operationalized in terms of linguistic features, for example lexicogrammatical or cohesive patterns. These patterns, or the frequencies of their distributions, are then extracted from corpora, and are analysed from the point of view of language and Register properties, specificities and distinctiveness in translated and non-translated texts. In this way, a number of research questions in the area of translation may be investigated from a contextual perspective. In this case, we can speak about theory-driven CBTS.

We also show the other interaction direction, where SFL is used for the interpretation of corpus-based findings. In some cases, corpus-based studies proceed bottom-up starting with the data rather than theories and use a number of shallow (or 'easy-to-get') features, for example, n-grams of words or parts of speech, in their analysis. However, the interpretation of the findings often requires a solid framework. And in this case, SFL will facilitate interpreting quantitative and qualitative results. We call this type of study data-driven CBTS. Overall, the chapter aims to extensively describe the existing collaboration between CBTS and SFL. Beyond that, it will hopefully serve as an inspiration for further collaboration between SFL and TS, illustrating possible research questions, linguistic phenomena, as well as existing available resources at hand.

The chapter is organized as follows: In Section 2, we introduce the main concepts related to the goals of the chapter. In Section 3, we describe the resources needed and address the two methodological directions of the interaction between SFL and CBTS. In Section 4, we show two studies representing examples of the two interaction directions. In Section 5, we conclude.

2 Main concepts

2.1 Corpus-based studies

According to Biber, Conrad and Reppen (1998), the corpus-based approach has a number of specific characteristics. For instance, corpus-based studies are empirical and they analyse the actual patterns of use in natural texts. The basis for this kind of analysis is a collection of natural texts (a corpus), which are intended to be an adequate representation of naturally occurring discourse, including multiple texts from any given variety. They make extensive use of computers for analysis, using both automatic and interactive techniques. Corpus-based analyses depend on both quantitative and qualitative (interpretive) analytical techniques.

2.2 Corpus-Based Translation Studies (CBTS)

The area of CBTS is mostly related to the hypothesis that translated texts have certain linguistic characteristics in common which do not occur to the same extent in non-translated texts.

This kind of study was inspired by Mona Baker who claimed that there exist 'features which typically occur in translated text rather than original utterances and which are not the result of interference from specific linguistic systems' (Baker 1993: 243). Baker emphasized on the general effects of the process of translation, the so-called **translation universals**, which are independent of the influence of the specific language pairs involved in the process of translation. Toury ([1995] 2012) and Chesterman (2004) uses other terms – **laws** or **regularities**. Another frequent designation is **translationese** and **translationese features**, coined by Gellerstam (1986). These features can be classified according to different parameters:

1. **normalization** – how translations conform to the characteristics of the target language and target textual varieties (Bernardini and Ferraresi 2011);
2. **shining through** – how translations reflect characteristics of the source language (Teich 2003);
3. **explicitation** – how translations are more explicit than register-comparable original texts or their STs (Olohan and Baker 2000);
4. the opposite process of **implicitation** (Becher 2011);

5. **under-representation** – how translations exhibit fewer unique items (Tirkkonen-Condit 2004);
6. **simplification** – how translators simplify the language used in translated texts and
7. **levelling out** – how translations are linguistically more homogeneous than originals (Olohan 2004).

For the latter, **convergence**, another term proposed by Laviosa (2002), is also used. It implies a relatively higher level of homogeneity of translated texts with regard to their own universal features, for example, lexical density, sentence length and so on. These characteristics of translations, although not being completely universal and being dependent on different factors, have been studied for a long time and for many different language pairs, for example, by Laviosa (1996) for English translations from a variety of source languages, by Mauranen (2000) for English-Finnish, by Teich (2003), Steiner (2004), Hansen-Schirra, Neumann and Steiner (2012) and House (2014) for English and German.

Baroni and Bernardini (2006), Ilisei et al. (2010) and Koppel and Ordan (2011) have all shown that it is possible to automatically predict whether a text is an original or a translation. Furthermore, automatic classification of original versus translated texts found application in machine translation, especially in studies showing the impact of the nature (original versus translation) of the text in translation and language models (used in statistical or neural machine translations). Kurokawa, Goutte and Isabelle (2009) show that a machine translation (MT) system trained on English-to-French data performs better than a system trained on French-to-English translations. However, the 'better performance' of an MT system is mostly automatically measured with the help of 'compliance' scores that, in fact, indicate to which extent an MT output complies with a reference translation produced by humans. Two translations (one produced by a machine and the other by a human) seem to comply better than a translated and non-translated text. The impact of the source language on French-English phrase-based statistical MT was also shown by Ozdowska and Way (2009). Inspired by Kurokawa, Goutte and Isabelle (2009)'s work, Lembersky, Ordan and Wintner (2012) show that language models trained on translated texts fit better to human translations in terms of perplexity. In fact, this only indicates that machine translations comply more with translated rather than non-translated texts produced by humans.

2.3 Recent trends in CBTS

Recent developments in Translation Studies show that these specific features can be attributable to different, sometimes language-external, factors (De Sutter, Lefer and Delaere 2017). These factors include register or text type, source language and translator's educational background (see e.g. Kruger and van Rooy 2012; Lapshinova-Koltunski 2013; Neumann 2013). For instance, Mauranen (2000) states that translated academic texts tend to adopt the norms of the target language more strongly than do translated popular non-fiction texts. The author also claims that similar registers in different languages tend to have similar communicative needs, meaning that they would also have similar contexts of use resulting in similar register variation. In the case of such cross-linguistic similarities, translations should also be similar to both their STs and the comparable originals in the target language. Neumann (2013: 104) claims that where there are interlingual registerial differences, the results for the translations by default should lie somewhere between the STs and the comparable originals in the target language. In the present study, eight registers were analysed in English and German focussing on how translations were adapted to the requirements of these different registers. The default situation also includes more pronounced tendencies towards either the source or the originals in the target language. In cases of cross-lingual differences, varying degrees of both shining through and normalization in the translations were stated by Teich (2003). However, translations may also vary from non-translated texts independently of the influence of language contrasts and register differences (see Neumann 2013: 105). Kruger and van Rooy (2012) suggest that translated texts reveal less register variation or sensitivity to register as a consequence of translation-specific effects. However, their findings provide limited support for this hypothesis. In the context of automatic identification of translated texts, Rabinovich and Wintner (2015) also report the influence of registers – the accuracy of translation detection deteriorates when the classifier is trained on texts from one register but is tested on a text from another register.

The difference between translated and non-translated texts may also co-vary with further parameters influencing translation process and, as a result, translation product: for example, the use of computer-aided or machine translation, time pressure, editorial control and others. For this reason, when we compare translations and non-translations, we should keep in mind that we are dealing with multifactorial phenomena. There is a need in such investigations to find out which factors affect linguistic behaviour in both categories of text. However, as De Sutter, Lefer and Delaere (2017: 1) point out, multifactorial investigations into the linguistic behaviour of translators remain rather scarce. To our knowledge, the following are the factors that have been taken into consideration so far: experience and proficiency of translators, where non-translated texts are compared to translations by professionals and novice translators (see e.g. Rubino, Lapshinova-Koltunski and van Genabith 2016; Kunilovskaya and Kutuzov 2018); translation mode, which may involve a comparison of translated and interpreted texts (Ferraresi and Miličević 2017); and editorial intervention, where originals are compared with translated and edited versions of the texts (Bisiada 2016; Kruger 2017).

Furthermore, there exist studies that observe interactions of more than one factor at the same time. For instance, Jenset and McGillivray (2012) pay attention to the interaction between register, translator and source language in translated English. They analyse affix use and state that the correlation between affix and register seems to be a much better explanatory structure than affix and translator or affix and source language. Similarly, Jenset and Hareide (2013) analysed interaction between register, author and translator with the help of sentence alignment patterns. Delaere and De Sutter (2017) include the influence of the source language and register onto translated Dutch, comparing translations from English or French. Lapshinova-Koltunski and Vela (2015) pay attention to the differences between human and machine translations from English into German analysing how they comply with non-translated texts in terms of registers. Lapshinova-Koltunski (2017) combines language, register, translation method and translator experience to analyse English–German translations. The types of translations distinguished by these factors, or dimensions, are here called **translation varieties**.

3 Methodological directions

3.1 Corpus-based and corpora

Corpus-based studies include empirical analyses of actual patterns of use in natural texts (see Biber, Conrad and Reppen 1998: 4). They make extensive use of automatic and interactive techniques assisted by computers. At the same time, corpus-based studies go beyond simple counts of linguistic features and include qualitative interpretations of the quantitative pattern, depending in this way on both quantitative and qualitative (interpretive) analytical techniques. They explore the importance of the quantitative findings for learning about the patterns of language use. These kind of studies can be based on an adequate representation of naturally occurring discourse, including analysis of complete texts, multiple texts from any given variety, and inclusion of multiple spoken and written varieties for comparative purposes.

One of the important aspects of corpus-based studies is the utilization of a large and principled collection of natural texts (the corpus). Sinclair (1991: 171) defines corpus as a collection of naturally occurring language texts chosen to characterize a state or variety of a language. In the past thirty-five years, this term has been increasingly applied to a body of language material which exists in electronic form and which may be computationally processed for various purposes.

Corpora may be thus monolingual bilingual or multilingual. For the analysis of translations or translation-related phenomena, we need either parallel or comparable corpora. The former contains STs in at least one language and their translations into another language, for example, English sources and their translations into German are required for our analysis of German–English translations. In parallel corpora, STs are aligned (connected) to their translations on various levels, for example, on the level of the sentence, in this way building parallel ST-TT blocks. A corpus containing translations in one direction only (like our example of English–German translations) is called unidirectional. If we add German sources and their translations into English, then we deal with a bidirectional parallel corpus. Comparable corpora may also consist of original texts or translations. Their main feature is the comparability of their texts. For instance, if our English–German corpus contains English and German STs that belong to the same register or genre, and that describe the same topics and originate from the same time spans, then it can also be called comparable (see Figure 5.1).

For the English–German language pair, there exist a number of corpora available for academic purposes, for instance, those available within the OPUS project (Tiedemann 2012),[1] a growing collection of translated texts from the web. This project is an attempt to constantly collect free online data, to convert and align sources and translations,

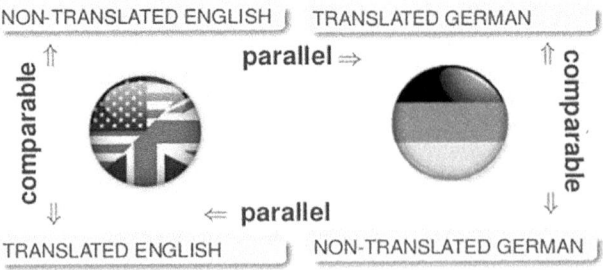

Figure 5.1 Corpus structure.

to add linguistic annotation and to provide the linguistic community with a publicly available parallel corpus. All text annotations are done automatically and do not contain manual corrections. The tools used are open-source products, and the corpora are also delivered as an open-content package. OPUS contains several corpora for the English–German pair that can be selected with the help of the search mask available. Some of them are extensively used for both linguistic and computational studies, for example, EUROPARL and TED talks.

However, not all these corpus resources contain information about translation direction. In case of a unidirectional corpus, a corresponding comparable part should be found, which is sometimes not an easy task. Further information, commonly stored in metadata, is also often missing (information on translator background, translation settings, such as tools used and time pressure, editorial interventions, etc.). These problems have led to the creation of translation corpora aimed at a specific research task.

These resources, however, remain scarce for the translations from or into German – language pairs we are specifically interested in. Some examples known to us include the corpora listed in Table 5.1.

As mentioned above, corpus-based analyses are empirical and thus require observations of actual patterns of use in a certain language. To automatize a process of analysis/to make it interactive, we need to apply a number of appropriate corpus processing tools. Having linguistic information in the form of annotation, we can then extract frequencies and distributions of these actual patterns and perform quantitative and qualitative analysis of our data. These patterns mostly represent linguistic features, which may be of different types – both shallow, such as type-token–ratio (TTR) or lexical density, and complex structures, for example, passive constructions of verbs.

3.2 Top-down or theory-driven

As already mentioned in Section 1, interaction between CBTS and SFL or other existing theories and frameworks may proceed either top-down or bottom up. In the case of a top-down interaction, SFL is used as a background for translation-relevant corpus-based analyses.

Table 5.1 Translation corpora for German

Resource	Languages	References
MeLLANGE LTC	A number of different languages including German	http://corpus.leeds.ac.uk/mellange/ltc.html
PACTE	Catalan and Spanish translated into/from English, German and French	Hurtado Albir (2017)
KOPTE	French-German	Wurm (2016)
translated and edited versions of Harvard Business Review	English-German	Bisiada (2018)
CroCo	English-German	Hansen-Schirra, Neumann and Steiner (2012)
VARTRA	English-German	Lapshinova-Koltunski (2013)
ParCorFull	English-German	Lapshinova-Koltunski, Hardmeier and Krielke (2018)

We know that contextual factors systematically influence linguistic variation and in this way registers arise. So, the theoretical background from SFL in combination with the knowledge provided by some registers studies (e.g. Biber 1995) offer an appropriate framework for register analysis. In terms of SFL, registers are referred to as linguistic variation according to use in context. These contexts influence the distribution of particular lexicogrammatical patterns which manifest language registers. SFL provides three variables characterizing the level of context: *field, tenor* and *mode* of discourse. These variables are associated with particular lexicogrammatical features. Field of discourse relates to processes and participants (e.g. Actor, Goal, Medium), as well as circumstantials (Time, Manner, Place, etc.). Linguistically it is realized in terms of patterns, functional verb classes, such as activity (*approach, supply*, etc.) and communication (*answer, inform, suggest*, etc.), argument structure and adverbial types. Tenor of discourse relates to roles and attitudes of participants, and is realized linguistically in stance expressions used by speakers to convey personal attitude to the given information: adverbs such as *actually, certainly* and *importantly*; adjectives (*amazing*) or modality expressed by modal verbs such as *can, may* and *must*. Mode relates to the role of the language in the interaction and is realized at the grammatical level in Theme-Rheme and Given-New constellations as well as cohesive relations at the textual level. Generally speaking, in lexicogrammar, the contextual variables correspond to sets of specific lexicogrammatical features: different registers vary in the distribution of these features.

To explore these features that are formulated as abstract concepts (e.g. processes and participants, textual cohesion) we define a number of operationalizations, which represent lexicogrammatical patterns. What is being extracted from corpora are text instances of these patterns, particular tokens, sequences of tokens or part-of-speech tags. Particular analysis tasks impose restrictions on the definition of specific features. Thus, in a register-independent study, features should be content-independent, that

Table 5.2 Features and patterns from SFL and Register Theory

Contextual parameter	Feature	Language pattern
FIELD	participants and processes	nominal and verbal chunks nominal and verbal parts of speech
	vocabulary and style	*ung*-nominalizations in German and general nouns (*fact, plan*)
	Voice	verbs in passive/active
TENOR	Modality	obligation/necessity (*must, ought to, should*) permission/possibility/ability (*can, may*) volition/prediction (*will, would, shall*)
	Evaluation	evaluative patterns (*it is interesting to know*)
MODE	textual cohesion	coreference (including distribution of pronominal/nominal reference, personal/demonstrative pronouns) conjunctive relations (additive, causal, etc.), substitution (*one, those, ein/e/r*) ellipsis (*We have the Dee river on one side of the peninsula and the Mersey on the other*) lexical cohesion (synonyms, hyponyms, etc.)

is, they should not contain terminology or keywords. Table 5.2 illustrates examples of the patterns for register-sensitive analysis of translations. The first column contains the corresponding contextual parameter of variation, the second column shows examples of features formulated in abstract categories and the third column provides examples of language patterns serving as operationalizations for the features. Nearly the whole set of these registerial features was used in the analysis of variation in both human and machine translation by Lapshinova-Koltunski (2017) and Lapshinova-Koltunski and Vela (2015).

The contextual parameter of mode expressed in textual cohesion delivers good indicators of variation along the dimension of 'language'. Lapshinova-Koltunski (2015) and Lapshinova-Koltunski et al. (2016), for instance, used them to analyse contrasts between languages. The main categories of textual cohesion include cohesive reference, conjunction, substitution, ellipsis and conjunction. A number of distinguished subtypes (type or functional columns in Table 5.3) reflect general structural groupings of cohesive devices that exist in English and German. These features can also be used for a cross-lingual register analysis of English and German (Kunz and Lapshinova-Koltunski 2015). Besides that, variation in translation can also be analysed if distributions of cohesive features across translated and non-translated texts are compared (Lapshinova-Koltunski 2015).

Differences between translated and non-translated texts are commonly analysed with the help of translation features (see Section 2.2 on the clarification of translationese or translation universals). Some of the language patterns used to operationalize these features coincide with those inspired by SFL that we presented in Table 5.2. We discussed this overlap in (Lapshinova-Koltunski 2017). Table 5.4 illustrates examples of such features indicating this overlap.

Table 5.3 Cohesive devices and their subtypes

Device	Type	Func
Reference	Personal	head, modifier, *it*-endophoric
	Demonstrative	head, modifier, local, temporal, pronadv
	Comparative	particular, general
Conjunction	connects, subjuncts, adverbials	additive, adversative, causal, temporal, modal
Substitution	nominal, verbal, clausal	
Ellipsis	nominal, verbal, clausal	
Lexical cohesion	general nouns, semantic relations	

Table 5.4 Overlap between SFL and translation features

	Lexicogrammatical patterns	SFL	Corpus-based Translation Studies
1	content versus total words	mode	Simplification
2	nominal versus verbal parts of speech and phrases (np.chunk, vp.chunk)	field	shining through/normalization
3	ung-nominalization (ungnom)	field	shining through/normalization
4	nominal (all.np) versus pronominal (pronnp) and demonstrative versus personal reference (perspron, dempron)	mode	explicitation, shining through/normalization
5	abstract general nouns (gen.nouns) versus all other nouns	field	Explicitation
6	logico-semantic relations: additive, adversative, causal, temporal, modal	mode	Explicitation
7	modality: obligation, permission, volition	tenor	shining through/normalization
8	evaluation patterns	tenor	shining through/normalization

The first column shows the lexicogrammatical patterns, the second column presents the correspondence of these patterns to the context parameters (field, tenor and mode of discourse) and the third column links the lexicogrammatical patterns with the translation features discussed in Section 2.2. Content words and their proportion to the total number of words in a text (Table 5.4, row 1) represent lexical density, which is related to information density in a text. This corresponds to the mode parameter in register theory and simplification in translationese studies (lexical richness of translations). The number of nominal and verbal parts of speech as well as their groupings into nominal and verbal phrases or chunks (row 2) reflect the parameters of participants in the field, shining through and normalization: languages use different grammatical structures and these differences are reflected in translations. For instance, English tends to use more verbal structures than German (Steiner 2012), and if a translation from English into German contains more verbal structures than a comparable German non-translated text would do, we observe shining through. For the same reasons, field and shining through and normalization can also be analysed via the distribution of nominalizations (*ung*-nominalizations[2] in row 3). Reference expressed either in nominal phrases or in pronouns (row 4) reflects textual cohesion in the parameter of mode. From the point of view of Translation Studies, this feature can point to explicitation, as pronouns are less explicit than nouns or nominal phrases. Moreover, preferences for personal or demonstrative pronouns in different languages (in our case English and German) can be reflected in shining through and normalization. The distribution of abstract or general nouns and their comparison to other nouns (row 5) give information about lexical choices (parameter of field) and preferences for more concrete or abstract words in translations (explicitation). Conjunctions (including both grammatical conjuncts such as *und* [and], *aber* [but] and multiword expressions like *aus diesem Grund* [that is why], for which we analyse distributions of logico-semantic relations (row 6), belong to the parameter of Mode as they express cohesion, and at the same time to the explicitation feature, as they explicitly mark relations in discourse. Modal verbs, such as *können* [can], *müssen* [must] (row 7), express modality, that is, the parameter of tenor. They are grouped according to different meanings, and also reveal cross-linguistic contrasts, as described by Teich (2003) and König and Gast (2012) for differences between English and German. That is why their distribution in translation also reflects normalization and shining through. Similarly, these phenomena (tenor and shining through/ normalization) are reflected in evaluation patterns (e.g. *es ist interessant/wichtig zu wissen* ... [it is interesting/important to know], row 8).

Operationalizations of abstract linguistic categories include particular lexicogrammatical patterns, that is, sequences of tokens or part-of-speech tags, often enhanced with contextual restrictions, for example, sentence or phrase position. For the empirical analysis of translations, text instances of these patterns are extracted from appropriate corpora along with their distributional information. One of the existing tools allowing for this kind of extraction is Corpus Query Processor (CQP, Evert and the CWB Development Team 2016), which is a part of Corpus Workbench (CWB), an open source resource.[3] This query tool allows definition of language patterns in the form of complex regular expressions based on string, part of speech and chunk and further available tags, which are beneficial for the extraction of linguistically motivated features. Such regular expressions can match on various annotation strings, test for membership in user-specific word lists, include special operations on feature sets and have constraints to specify dependencies. So, it is possible to define a set of candidate lexicogrammatical patterns derived from SFL and TS, as described above, and formulate them as CQP queries.

Table 5.5 provides examples for two queries to extract SFL-inspired features. Query (1) is a simple lexical search with a positional constraint – here, we find all instances of 'additive' conjunctions when acting cohesively (in principle a closed class the members of which we know). Query (2) is a syntactic pattern search – here we find all instances of the pattern with an evaluative adjective (in principle, an open class of which we know some members). Queries deliver concordances, that is, text instances which can be sorted according to the texts, registers and subcorpora they occur in. The information on distributions can, on the one hand, be extracted for particular patterns.

Table 5.5 CQP query for conjunctive relations and evaluative patterns

	Query building blocks	Description	Extracted text instances
(1)	<s> []{0,2} [lemma=RE($additive)]	sentence start fol- lowed by two optional words conjunctions from the 'additive' list	*and, moreover, in addition,* etc.
(2)	[word="[I|i]t"] [lemma="be"] [pos="JJ.*"] [word="that|to"]	*it* verb *be* adjective subjunct *that*/ particle *to*	*It* *is* *important* *that*

For instance, the frequencies of the connectives *and* or *in addition* are sorted according to their occurrences in different registers of the English subcorpus. On the other hand, the frequencies of more abstract features can be generalized with the help of the formulated queries, since frequencies are extracted not only of *and* or *in addition* but also all other additive conjunctions in the predefined list. In this way, information on the distributions of all additive conjunctions in English texts may be obtained. These distributions can be compared to the distributions of all additive conjunctions in German and the extracted distributional information can then be saved in tables and used for statistical analyses.

Since CWB also provides tools for annotation, we propose a method of adding a more abstract annotation level to a corpus using pattern-based extraction. In the CWB formalism, there is no conceptual difference between extraction queries and annotation rules other than their function. Query results deliver not only concordances of the searched structures but also information on their corpus positions. So, a set of semi-automatic procedures can be elaborated that contains an iterative extraction–annotation process based on the YAC framework[4] described by Kermes and Evert (2002). This allows the re-importation of the information on queried data back into the corpus. Lapshinova-Koltunski and Kunz (2014) employ such procedures to semi-automatically annotate cohesive devices in English and German. The annotation of such linguistic categories as cohesion, voice, modality and others provides a different level of abstraction to a corpus and facilitates the access to abstract linguistic information for less experienced users. Moreover, it makes the extraction of more complex linguistic phenomena easier and more efficient. While for some phenomena simple queries on lemma and part-of-speech information are sufficient, other cases require more complex queries including lexical or contextual restrictions or the combination of several simple queries. In this case, annotation can help to simplify the queries and to make the extraction process more efficient, which is especially valuable in a multilingual corpus study.

It follows that theoretical frameworks serve as a starting point for corpus-based translation analyses as they provide a background for designing linguistic features and thus language patterns for such analyses.

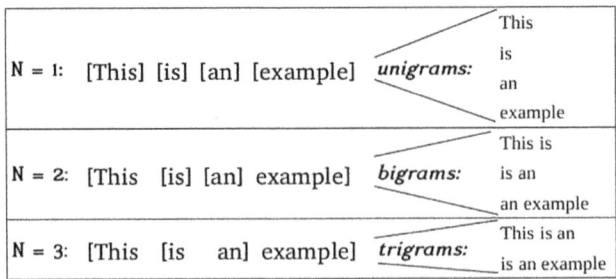

Figure 5.2 Token n-gram representation.

3.3 Bottom-up or data-driven

In linguistic bottom-up, or 'data-driven', approaches, existing theories commonly facilitate interpretation of the findings. In this kind of interaction, SFL is used to facilitate interpretation of quantitative and qualitative results in the corpus-based analyses. These analyses do not operate with frequencies and distributions of complex linguistic structures, but utilize more shallow features, such as bag-of-words, that is, n-grams or some automatically retrieved 'easy-to-get' features used mostly without any theoretical justification.

N-grams can be calculated on the basis of different structures, that is, token/word, lemma, part of speech or syntactic tree. Basic linguistic annotations, therefore, are still required to pre-process the corpora under analysis. An example of n-grams calculated on the level of tokens is given in Figure 5.2.

However, this type of feature is not content-dependent, which means that they are not suitable for multilingual or translation-relevant register or genre analysis. It is possible to utilize (semi-)delexicalized features, as Zampieri and Lapshinova-Koltunski (2015) do in their analysis of variation in translation. The authors substitute all nouns in the texts under analysis with place-holders. This results in a semi-delexicalized text representation, which is supposed to minimize topic variation, and thus, content-dependence of the features. This type of representation lies between fully delexicalized representations, such as the one proposed by Diwersy, Evert and Neumann (2014) for the study of variation in translation and diatopic variation of French texts, and the fully lexicalized representation, common in most approaches to automatic text classification, which uses all words in text without any substitution. Semi-delexicalized representation minimizes topic variation. Previous studies have shown that certain nouns, especially proper nouns, significantly influence the performance of text classification systems (Zampieri, Gebre and Diwersy 2013).

Part-of-speech n-grams reduce content-dependency of features even more, and may also consist of bigrams, trigrams, 4-grams and so on. In Example (1), we illustrate the representation of the sentences in parts of speech. Example (1a) represents a sentence from a corpus, which can underlie a token-based representation of, for example, trigrams *Die weltweiten Herausforderungen, weltweiten Herausforderungen im, Herausforderungen im Bereich* and so on. Example (1b) shows the representation, where all nouns are substituted with the placeholder *PLH* resulting in what we call a semi-delexicalized text representation. Trigrams in this case would be *Die weltweiten PLH, weltweiten PLH im, PLH im PLH* and so on. In (1c), a fully delexicalized representation of the sentence is shown, for which automatic part-of-speech annotation is used. The corresponding trigrams would be *ART ADJA NN, ADJA NN APPRART, NN APPRART NN* and so on. Zampieri, Gebre and Diwersy (2013) show that classification experiments using POS and morphological information as features can not only be linguistically informative but may also achieve good performance in discriminating between texts written in different Spanish varieties. Therefore, this representation can be also used to analyse variation within translated texts, as shown by Lapshinova and Zampieri (2018). The authors decided to use these features for investigating translation variation influenced by both register/genre and translation method. Example (1d) illustrates a syntactic tree representation, which can be obtained with the help of an automatic parser. The corresponding trigrams would contain the information on the tree brackets (e.g. *TOP (S (ART*, which indicates an article at a sentence start, or *(S (ART (ADJA* corresponding to an article at sentence start followed by an adjective, or *(ART (ADJA (NN* indicating a nominal phrase that contains a determiner and an adjectival modifier.

(1a) *Die weltweiten Herausforderungen im Bereich der Energiesicherheit erfordern über einen Zeitraum von vielen Jahrzehnten nachhaltige Anstrengungen auf der ganzen Welt.*

(1b) *Die weltweiten PLH im PLH der PLH erfordern über einen PLH von vielen PLH nachhaltige PLH auf der ganzen PLH.*

(1c) *ART ADJA NN APPRART NN ART NN VVFIN APPR ART NN APPR PIAT ADJA ADJA NN APPR ART ADJA NN.*

(1d) *(TOP (S (ART (ADJA (NN (APPRART (NN (ART (NN))))))) (VVFIN) (APPR (ART (NN (APPR PIAT ADJA)))) (ADJA (NN (APPR (ART (ADJA (NN))))))))).*

Semi- and fully delexicalized patterns can then be interpreted in terms of more abstract linguistic categories, for example, ART ADJA NN in (1c) represents a definite nominal phrase with an adjectival modifier and so on. Their frequent usage in specific contexts, for example, in a specific register, provides us with some information about this register, and theoretical frameworks, in our case SFL, help us to understand and interpret this information.

In this way, we have shown that theoretical frameworks facilitate interpretation of the findings from bottom-up and data-driven approaches that operate with frequencies and distributions of shallow features such as bag of words or n-grams.

4 Examples of studies

In the present section, we will show two examples of studies in which SFL interacts with CBTS using the two directions described above: theory-driven and data-driven.

4.1 Theory-driven

Lapshinova-Koltunski (2017) investigates the interplay between two dimensions influencing translation variation – text register and translation method. This is achieved by a corpus-based analysis which involves the extraction of a set of SFL-inspired linguistic features occurring in multiple translations of the same texts. These translations differ, on the one hand, in the registers to which the texts belong, and on the other, in the translation method applied (human versus machine translation). The author also relates the SFL-inspired features with those derived from CBTS. The quantitative analysis is supported with unsupervised statistical techniques that help to trace the degree of variation caused by the two variation dimensions. Moreover, they help to identify the dimension having a greater impact on the translations. The results of this analysis shed light on the main factors influencing translation and also deliver explanations for translation errors. In addition, further factors affecting linguistic features of translations (the experience involved) are also traced in this analysis. In this way, the study contributes to a better understanding of both translation product and translation process, and provides information which is useful for both evaluation of translation and improvement.

As already mentioned, Lapshinova-Koltunski (2017) selected a set of features derived from SFL/register theory and corpus-based studies on translationese. These features represent lexicogrammatical patterns of more abstract concepts, for example, textual cohesion expressed via pronominal or nominal reference or evaluative patterns expressed via certain syntactic constructions. The selected features were chosen because they reflect linguistic characteristics of all texts under analysis, are content-independent (they do not contain terminology or keywords) and are easy to interpret, thereby yielding insights into the differences between the two dimensions under analysis. The author excluded certain feature types, for example, token n-grams, as they are rather content-dependent, and reflect domains (register). As the dataset under analysis contains multiple translations of the same texts, this kind of feature is not suitable for the analysis. The set of the selected features used by Lapshinova-Koltunski (2017) is outlined and described in Table 5.4.

The corpus used for this analysis (VARTRA, Lapshinova-Koltunski 2013) contains different English-German translation variants (called varieties) produced by

1. professional humans (PHT, Professional Human Translation);
2. student translators (SHT, Student Human Translation);
3. a rule-based MT system (RBMT, Rule-Based Machine Translation) and two statistical MT systems;
4. Google Statistical Machine Translation (GSMT) and
5. Moses Statistical Machine Translation (MSMT).

The dataset contains multiple translations of the same texts, which cover seven registers of written language: political essays (ESSAY), fictional texts (FICTION), manuals (INSTR), popular-scientific articles (POPSCI), letters to shareholders (SHARE), prepared political speeches (SPEECH) and tourism leaflets (TOU).[5] The total number

Table 5.6 Queries for feature extraction

	Feature category	CQP query
1	personal	[pos="PP.*"]
	demonstrative	[pos="PD.*"]
2	*ung*-nominalization	[pos="NN.*"&lemma=".*ung.*"]
3	obligation	[pos="VM.*"&lemma="müssen|sollen"]
	permission	[pos="VM.*"&lemma="können|dürfen"]
	volition	[pos="VM.*"&lemma="wollen|mögen"]
4	additive	$additive-conjunction
	adversative	$adversative-conjunction
	causal	$causal-conjunction
	temporal	$temporal-conjunction
	modal	$modal-conjunction
5	abstract nouns	[pos="NN.*"&lemma=$abstract_nouns"]
6	evaluation patterns	"es|Es"[pos="VAFIN"][pos!="$.\|$,"]{0,3}[pos="AD.*"][]?"da(ss|ß|\"s)"
		"es|Es"[pos="VAFIN"][pos!="$.\|$,"]{0,3}[pos="ADJ.*"] []?"zu|wenn|f(ü|\"u)r"
		"(A|a)m" [pos="AD.*"&word=".*ste.*"]

of tokens is around 600,000. All subcorpora are tokenized, lemmatized and tagged with part-of-speech information, segmented into syntactic chunks and sentences (annotations obtained with Tree Tagger, Schmid 1994). The corpus can be queried with the help of CQP (see Section 3.2), which allows the definition of language patterns in the form of regular expressions based on string, part of speech and chunk tags among others. Table 5.6 outlines a number of query examples used in this study. For instance, query 1 is used to differentiate between personal and demonstrative reference. In the second and the third query, lexical information is added.

For evaluation patterns more morpho-syntactic restrictions in the form of parts-of-speech sequences and lexical elements are added. Extracted distributions were then sorted according to the texts, registers and translation methods.

Lapshinova-Koltunski (2017) applied an unsupervised technique – hierarchical cluster analysis (HCA, Baayen 2008) for her analysis. This kind of data analysis allows discovering 'interesting structures' in the data. In this study, these structures are represented by translation clusters which are formed according to different dimensions, that is, translation method and register. In this way, the interplay of variation dimensions and the predominance of one of the dimensions (whichever has a greater impact on the clustering of translations) was traced in this study. In hierarchical cluster analysis, a set of dissimilarities for the translated texts are calculated. In this study, Euclidean distance is used, which is one of the most straightforward and generally accepted ways of computing distances between objects in a multidimensional space. This calculated distance indicates the distance between the subcorpora under analysis. The results are represented graphically in a branching diagram that represents the relationships of similarity among a group of entities. Its leaves present the variables (subcorpora), and the branches represent the clusters. The arrangement of the branches indicates which leaves are most similar to each other. The height of the branches indicates how similar or different they are from each other: the greater the height, the greater the difference. Highly correlated clusters are near the bottom of a dendrogram.

To analyse the interplay between translation methods and registers, and to find out which of these two dimensions causes greater variation in VARTRA, Lapshinova-Koltunski (2017) calculated the distances between registers of all translations (thirty-five dependent variables) that underlie the hierarchical clustering. The clustering results are represented in Figure 5.3 (Lapshinova-Koltunski 2017: 223).

The dendrogram clearly reveals two very distinct groups: the bottom group seems to consist of two more distinct clusters, while the clustering of most classes in the upper group is more levelled out. Looking at the tree from the outermost nodes, a clear

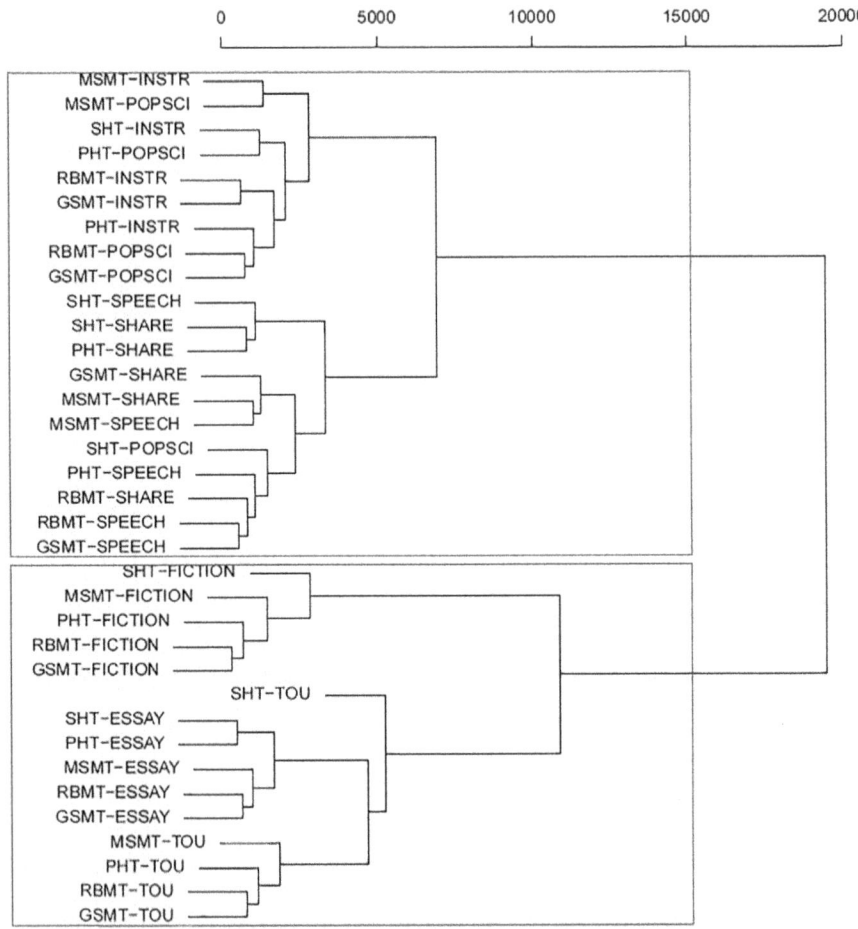

Figure 5.3 Clusters representing translation methods and registers.

predominance of register features for the clustering of fictional texts, tourism leaflets and political essays can be observed.

Besides the groupings indicating the prominence of register variation in translation data, Lapshinova-Koltunski (2017) analyses the features contributing to the register classification (clustering). Table 5.7 presents the original feature set for each of the seven clusters represented with median values for the variables used in the cluster analysis which are broken up by the cluster groups. These values change if a different number of clusters is selected. Comparing the figures across clusters helps to characterize each cluster according to the set of features specific to it. For instance, cluster 1 (political essays) is characterized by an average distribution of nominal and verbal parts of speech and phrases and a relatively low number of conjunctive relations. The amount of pronominal reference here is also lower than average. General nouns, *ung*-nominalizations, as well as modal verbs expressing obligation are more frequent here than on average. Modality, especially with the meaning of obligation, is one of the indicators of argumentative goal orientation. Argumentative texts contain significantly more modality than texts pursuing other goals. Qualitative analysis by Lapshinova-Koltunski (2017) shows that the verbs are used more in their meaning of personal obligation than of logical necessity. The main distinctive features of cluster 2 include first a prevalence of pronominal reference, which is expressed

Table 5.7 Features contributing to cluster definition

Cluster	1	2	3	4	5	6	7
content.words	7037	4407	9469	10351.5	11098	6633	8568.5
np.chunk	4651	3384	6274	7039	7332	4115	5506
vp.chunk	1712	1570	2344	2593.5	2908	1381	1495
Nominal	8885	5679	11483	13239	13772	7993	10535.5
Verbal	4197	3485	5857	6396.5	7124	3361	4177
Additive	726	622	717	1041.5	1169	752	880
Adversative	313	250	502	413.5	453	232	274
Causal	115	169	271	133	179	65	79
Temporal	384	332	614	565.5	628	213	307.5
Modal	96	146	248	130.5	159	57	89
Pronnp	39	154	82	66.5	62	35	21
all.np	3399	2717	4602	5121	5140	2799	3969
gen.nouns	121	52	107	138.5	138	37	48.5
all nouns	3464	1852	4816	5291.5	5701	3394	4417
Obligation	72	32	46	71.5	76	8	13
Permission	76	38	174	96	162	81	64.5
Volition	18	35	32	21.5	30	5	6
Evaluation	11	4	8	12	12	5	7
Ungnom	685	94	422	786	756	134	210.5
Perspron	521	1127	781	1140.5	1084	288	407.5
Dempron	122	102	175	262.5	252	43	68

with personal pronouns in most cases. This usually characterizes spoken language (FICTION contains conversations). Moreover, pronouns also correspond to one of the characteristics of narrative texts. Further characteristics include description of events in clausal structures rather than in nominal structures, which leads to a lower proportion of nominalizations in this cluster. Again, the features characterizing cluster 2 correspond to those of fictional texts as stated, for example, by Steiner (2012) or Neumann (2013). The heterogeneous cluster 3 (containing instruction manuals and popular-scientific texts) is characterized by conjunctive relations and modal verbs indicating the argumentative goal. SHARE and SPEECH, which compose cluster 4, have a number of commonalities. According to Neumann (2013), these two registers seem to be closer in English than in German, which might indicate the influence of the STs on the translations in the corpus. Cluster 5 is characterized by a large number of both nominal and verbal classes, general nouns and nominalizations, as well as additive and temporal conjunctive relations. These are the same features which also characterize cluster 4, and thus the other translations of the register SHARE. However, translations in cluster 5 reveal a greater amount of conjunctive relations and modality meanings than those in 4.

Overall, it can be said that the features contributing to the cluster formation correspond (with some exceptions) to the features specific to the registers involved. Yet, the dimension of register seems to have more influence on variation in the TTs than that of translation method. However, influence of both dimensions is present in the corpus; a clear prevalence of the register dimension is observed for certain translations only (fiction, tourism texts and political essays) and variation in translation method can be detected within register-specific clusters. This deepens the knowledge of the linguistic properties of translated texts, which, in turn, furthers the understanding of variation processes in translation. The example study illustrates a top-down interaction between SFL and CBTS: enhanced by the knowledge from register studies, SFL is used to operationalize variation that has been analysed in translation corpora.

4.2 Data-driven

Lapshinova-Koltunski and Zampieri (2018) also analyse dimensions influencing translation. The underlying idea is that if these dimensions are 'recognizable' via feature profiles, analysis with 'known' (theory-driven) features delivers the anticipated results – the corpus-based analysis confirms what is described in theories. For instance, in the study by Lapshinova-Koltunski (2017) described in Section 4.1, the dimension of register variation seems to prevail over the dimension of translation method. This outcome may be influenced by the fact that the underlying features are supposed to reflect registers as they are derived from a framework describing contextual variation. Therefore, the study adopts 'unknown' (data-driven) features in the form of delexicalized n-grams represented by part-of-speech tags, at all the time believing that a data-driven approach will help to discover new language structures reflecting variation in translation. They use supervised techniques derived from text classification. For this, they train human classifiers to distinguish translated texts according to either their register or method of translation, using the same corpus as in Lapshinova-Koltunski (2017). Applying text classification, researchers are mostly interested in the reliability of classification methods to attribute correct labels to a set of texts. Lapshinova-Koltunski and Zampieri (2018) are interested more in levelling out interesting linguistic features than the classification results per se.

Before classification was carried out, the corpus was split into sentences. This splitting generated enough data points for text classification and made the task more challenging. The length of each sentence varied between 12 and 24 tokens. This resulted in a dataset containing 6,200 instances. The features used in the experiments were based on the combinations of POS tags arranged in form of bigrams, trigrams and 4-grams. The evaluation of the classifiers is performed with standard metrics (e.g. accuracy) that indicate how well the corpus data support the predefined classes. Indeed, it is much harder to differentiate between translation methods than between different registers even if a data-driven approach (not theoretically motivated n-gram features) is used. This result goes in hand with the results obtained by Lapshinova-Koltunski (2017) with theory-driven features: register dimension is stronger than that of translation method in translation variation.

Text classification allows not only measuring how well certain texts are distinguished from each other but also which individual features contribute to this distinction. For instance, it is possible to find out which features are responsible for the distinction between human and machine translations and which are useful for distinguishing fiction from popular science or from touristic texts. Therefore, Lapshinova-Koltunski and Zampieri (2018) analyse the output features resulting from the classification in this section. This step is manual and carried out by looking through the most informative features that are thus discriminative for certain registers and translation methods in the translations under analysis. The authors concentrate on trigrams (trigram models achieved the best results in classification), for example, (1) *ART NN VMFIN* (2). *KON PPER* and so on. Intuitively, for the given trigrams we can recognize more categories on a more abstract level of linguistic description, for example, the category of modality expressed through modal verbs, discourse-building devices such as discourse markers and co-reference and so on. Thus, Example (1) represents a finite clause containing a full nominal phrase, and Example (2) represents a pattern related to the level of discourse: a connector in sentence-initial position followed by a personal pronoun that likely has an anaphoric function.

The features contributing to the distinction between registers differ from those contributing to the differentiation of translation methods. These part-of-speech sequences may be interpreted in terms of more abstract categories referring to register studies and SFL. Thus, the features specific for distinguishing translation method include discourse and modality features, and some of them concern the preferred typology of phrases which can be related to the style of writing: nominal versus verbal. The analysis of register-specific features is performed pairwise: it is necessary to analyse the results of several classification steps, for example, fiction versus popular science, fiction versus tourism, fiction versus political speeches and so on, to identify the features that are specific for fiction.

Fiction seems to be well 'recognizable' with the help of discourse-related devices occurring in translated texts under analysis, that is, discourse markers expressing conjunctive relations (*so dass* [*so that*], *auch wenn* [*even if*]) or pronouns triggering cohesive reference (*er, sie, es* [*he, she, it*]). Discourse-structuring devices normally indicate narrative texts, which the fictional texts belong to. Some specific features that are informative in classifying fiction against one certain register only include also adjective and adverb modification. We know from other studies on registers that predicative adjectives are also indicators of narration and of a casual style specific for fictional texts.

5 Conclusion and discussion

The goals of the present chapter were to explore the current and potential directions in the collaboration between CBTS and SFL. Two directions of collaboration were presented. We showed the features based on the language-contextual parameters of SFL (field, tenor and mode), as well as their correspondences with existing translation features (translationese). We also showed that the results of the corpus analyses operating with shallow features such as token or part-of-speech n-grams can also have an interaction with SFL which is used as a framework for the quantitative interpretation of the result. We illustrated these with two recent example studies and summarized the existing translation corpus resources that are currently used, specifically for the language pair English–German.

However, no matter the direction in which we proceed, we need to keep in mind that in both cases we might well be influenced by the procedures we opt for. For instance, using a set of features derived from a specific framework, we may get the results which are expected as the selection of features underlying our analysis is already influenced by the framework. For instance, if we use a set of features designed to describe contextual variation of language in terms of register, we will see the prominence of register variation in the analysed data. If we proceed bottom-up, and decide for a set of 'unknown' structures, as we did in the case of part-of-speech n-grams, we are still influenced by the knowledge of existing frameworks that we possess.

A combination of the two directions (top-down and data-driven) may bring us new insights into the phenomena, which we were not aware of at the beginning of the analysis. Indeed, we believe that this will find more applications in the future collaboration between SFL and CBTS and hope that this chapter may inspire new research questions and analyses.

Notes

1. http://opus.nlpl.eu/.
2. Nominalizations with the suffix -ung which form nouns from verbs describing either an event in which an action is carried out, or the result of that action.
3. http://cwb.sourceforge.net/.
4. YAC is a fully automatic recursive chunker based on a symbolic regular expression grammar written in the CQP query language.

5. The texts were imported from the CroCo corpus (Hansen-Schirra, Neumann and Steiner 2012), and all the details on register definition can be found in the description of the corpus.

References

Baayen, H. (2008), *Analyzing Linguistic Data: A Practical Introduction to Statistics Using R*, Cambridge: Cambridge University Press.

Baker, M. (1993), 'Corpus Linguistics and Translation Studies: Implications and Applications', in M. Baker, G. Francis and E. Tognini-Bonelli (eds), *Text and Technology: In Honour of John Sinclair*, 233–50, Amsterdam: John Benjamins.

Baroni, M., and Bernardini, S. (2006), 'A New Approach to the Study of Translationese: Machine-Learning the Difference between Original and Translated Text', *Literary and Linguistic Computing* 21 (3): 259–74.

Becher, V. (2011), *Explicitation and Implicitation in Translation: A Corpus-Based Study of English-German and German-English Translations of Business Texts*, PhD Thesis, Universität Hamburg.

Bernardini, S., and Ferraresi, A. (2011), 'Practice, Description and Theory Come Together: Normalization or Interference in Italian Technical Translation?' *META* 56: 226–46.

Biber, D. (1995), *Dimensions of Register Variation: A Cross Linguistic Comparison*, Cambridge: Cambridge University Press.

Biber, D., Conrad, S. and Reppen, R. (1998), *Corpus Linguistics: Investigating Language Structure and Use*, Cambridge: Cambridge University Press.

Bisiada, M. (2016). '"Lösen sie schachtelsätze möglichst auf": The Impact of Editorial Guidelines on Sentence Splitting in German Business Article Translations', *Applied Linguistics* 37 (3): 354–76.

Bisiada, M. (2018), 'The Editor's Invisibility: Analysing Editorial Intervention in Translation', *Target* 30 (2): 288–309. doi:10.1075/target.16116.bis.

Chesterman, A. (2004), 'Beyond the Particular', in A. Mauranen and P. Kujamäki (eds), *Translation Universals: Do they Exist?*, 33–49, Amsterdam: John Benjamins.

De Sutter, G., Lefer, M.-A. and Delaere, I. (2017), *Empirical Translation Studies: New Methodological and Theoretical Traditions*, Berlin: Mouton de Gruyter.

Delaere, I., and De Sutter, G. (2017), 'Variability of English Loanword Use in Belgian Dutch Translations: Measuring the Effect of Source Language and Register', in G. De Sutter, M.-A. Lefer and I. Delaere (eds), *Empirical Translation Studies: New Methodological and Theoretical Traditions*, 81–112, Berlin: Mouton de Gruyter.

Diwersy, S., Evert, S. and Neumann, S. (2014), 'A Semi-Supervised Multivariate Approach to the Study of Language Variation', in B. Szmrecsanyi and B. Wälchli (eds), *Linguistic Variation in Text and Speech, within and across Languages*, 174–204, Berlin: Mouton de Gruyter.

Evert, S., and the CWB Development Team (2016), The IMS Open Corpus Workbench (CWB). CQP Query Language Tutorial. CWB Version 3.4.

Ferraresi, A., and Miličević, M. (2017), 'Phraseological Patterns in Interpreting and Translation. Similar or Different?' in G. De Sutter, M.-A. Lefer and I. Delaere (eds), *Empirical Translation Studies: New Methodological and Theoretical Traditions*, 157–82, Berlin: Mouton de Gruyter.

Gellerstam, M. (1986), 'Translationese in Swedish Novels Translated from English', in L. Wollin and H. Lindquist (eds), *Translation Studies in Scandinavia*, 88–95, Lund: CWK Gleerup.

Halliday, M. A. K. (2004), *An Introduction to Functional Grammar*, 3rd edn, London: Arnold.

Halliday, M. A. K., and Matthiessen, C. M. I. M. (2014), *Halliday's Introduction to Functional Grammar*, 4th edn, London: Routledge.

Hansen-Schirra, S., Neumann, S. and Steiner, E. (2012), *Cross-Linguistic Corpora for the Study of Translations: Insights from the Language Pair English-German*, Berlin: Mouton de Gruyter.

House, J. (2014), *Translation Quality Assessment. Past and Present*, London: Routledge.

Hurtado Albir, A. (ed.) (2017), *Researching Translation Competence by PACTE Group*, Amsterdam: John Benjamins.

Ilisei, I., Inkpen, D., Corpas Pastor G. and Mitkov, R. (2010), 'Identification of Translationese: A Machine Learning Approach', in A. Gelbukh (ed.), *Computational Linguistics and Intelligent Text Processing, Proceedings of* CICLing 2010, LNCS 6008: 503–511, Berlin: Springer.

Jenset, G. B., and Hareide, L. (2013), 'A Multidimensional Approach to Aligned Sentences in Translated Text', *Bergen Language and Linguistic Studies* 3: 195–210.

Jenset, G. B., and McGillivray, B. (2012), 'Multivariate Analyses of Affix Productivity in Translated English', in M. P. Oakesand M. Ji (eds), *Quantitative Methods in Corpus-Based Translation Studies*, 301–24, London: John Benjamins.

Kermes, H., and Evert, S. (2002), 'YAC – A Recursive Chunker for Unrestricted German Text', in M. G. Rodriguez and C. P. Araujo (eds), *Proceedings of the Third International Conference on Language Resources and Evaluation*, 1805–12.

König, E., and Gast, V. (2012), *Understanding English-German Contrasts. Grundlagen der Anglistik und Amerikanistik*, 3rd, extended edn, Berlin: Erich Schmidt Verlag.

Koppel, M., and Ordan, N. (2011), *Translationese and Its Dialects: Proceedings of the 49th Annual Meeting of the Association for Computational Linguistics* (ACL-2011), June.

Kruger, H. (2017). 'The Effects of Editorial Intervention: Implications for Studies of the Features of Translated Language', in G. De Sutter, M.-A. Lefer and I. Delaere (eds), *Empirical Translation Studies: New Methodological and Theoretical Traditions*, 113–56, Berlin: Mouton de Gruyter.

Kruger, H., and van Rooy, B. (2012), 'Register and the Features of Translated Language', *Across Languages and Cultures* 13 (1): 33–65.

Kunilovskaya, M., and Kutuzov, A. (2018), 'Universal Dependencies-Based Syntactic Features in Detecting Human Translation Varieties', in *Proceedings of the 16th International Workshop on Treebanks and Linguistic Theories* (TLT16), 27–36, Charles University, Prague, Czech Republic.

Kunz, K., and Lapshinova-Koltunski E. (2015), 'Cross-Linguistic Analysis of Discourse Variation Across Registers', *Special Issue of Nordic Journal of English Studies* 14 (1): 258–88.

Kurokawa, D., Goutte, C. and Isabelle, P. (2009), 'Automatic Detection of Translated Text and its Impact on Machine Translation', in Proceedings of MT-Summit XII.

Lapshinova-Koltunski, E. (2013), 'VARTRA: A Comparable Corpus for Analysis of Translation Variation', in *Proceedings of the Sixth Workshop on Building and Using Comparable Corpora*, 77–86, Sofia, Bulgaria, Association for Computational Linguistics.

Lapshinova-Koltunski, E. (2015), Exploration of Inter- and Intralingual Variation of Discourse Phenomena', in *Proceedings of the Second Workshop on Discourse in Machine Translation*, 158–67, Lisbon, Portugal, Association for Computational Linguistics.

Lapshinova-Koltunski, E. (2017), 'Exploratory Analysis of Dimensions Influencing Variation in Translation: The Case of Text Register and Translation Method', in G. De Sutter, M.-A. Lefer and I. Delaere (eds), *Empirical Translation Studies: New Methodological and Theoretical Traditions*, 207–34, Berlin: Mouton de Gruyter.

Lapshinova-Koltunski, E., Hardmeier, C. and Krielke, P. (2018), 'ParCorFull: A Parallel Corpus Annotated with Full Coreference', in *Proceedings of the Eleventh International Conference on Language Resources and Evaluation* (LREC 2018), 7–12 May, 423–8, Miyazaki, Japan.

Lapshinova-Koltunski, E., and Kunz, K. (2014), 'Annotating Cohesion for Multilingual Analysis', in *Proceedings of the 10th Joint ACL - ISO Workshop on Interoperable Semantic Annotation, Reykjavik*, 57–64, 26 May 2014.

Lapshinova-Koltunski, E., Kunz, K. and Nedoluzhko, A. (2016), 'From Interoperable Annotations towards Interoperable Resources: A Multilingual Approach to the Analysis of Discourse', in *Proceedings of LREC-2016*, Portoroz, Slovenia: ELRA.

Lapshinova-Koltunski, E., and Vela, M. (2015), 'Measuring "Registerness" in Human and Machine Translation: A Text Classification Approach', in *Proceedings of the Second Workshop on Discourse in Machine Translation*, 122–31, Lisbon, Portugal: Association for Computational Linguistics.

Lapshinova-Koltunski, E., and Zampieri, M. (2018), *Linguistic Features of Genre and Method Variation in Translation: A Computational Perspective*, Berlin: Mouton de Gruyter.

Laviosa, S. (1996), *The English Comparable Corpus (ECC): A Resource and a Methodology for the Empirical Study of Translation*, Manchester: UMIST PhD thesis.

Laviosa, S. (2002), *Corpus-based Translation Studies: Theory, Findings, Applications*, Amsterdam: Rodopi.

Lembersky, G., Ordan, N. and Wintner, S. (2012), 'Language Models for Machine Translation: Original vs. Translated Texts', *Computational Linguistics* 38 (4): 799–825.

Mauranen, A. (2000), 'Strange Strings in Translated Language: A Study on Corpora', in M. Olohan (ed.), *Research Models in Translation Studies: Intercultural Faultlines: Textual and Cognitive Aspects*, 119–41, Manchester: St. Jerome.

Neumann, S. (2013), *Contrastive Register Variation: A Quantitative Approach to the Comparison of English and German*, Berlin: De Gruyter Mouton.

Olohan, M. (2004), *Introducing Corpora in Translation Studies*, London: Routledge.

Olohan, M., and Baker, M. (2000), 'Reporting That in Translated English: Evidence for Subconscious Processes of Explicitation?' *Across Languages and Cultures* 1: 141–58.

Ozdowska, S., and Way, A. (2009). 'Optimal bilingual data for French-English PB-SMT', in *Proceedings of the EAMT 2009 - 13th Annual Conference of the European Association for Machine Translation*, Barcelona, Spain, 96–103.

Rabinovich, E., and Wintner, S. (2015), 'Unsupervised Identification of Translationese', *Transactions of the Association for Computational Linguistics* 3: 419–32.

Rubino, R., Lapshinova-Koltunski, E. and van Genabith, J. (2016), 'Information Density and Quality Estimation Features as Translationese Indicators for Human Translation Classification', in *Proceedings of NAACL HT 2006*, San Diego, California, 960–970.

Schmid, H. (1994), 'Probabilistic Part-of-Speech Tagging Using Decision Trees', in *International Conference on New Methods in Language Processing*, 44–9, Manchester.

Sinclair, J. (1991), *Corpus, Concordance, Collocation*, Oxford: Oxford University Press.

Steiner, E. (2004), *Translated Texts: Properties, Variants, Evaluations*, Frankfurt/M: Peter Lang Verlag.

Steiner, E. (2012), 'A Characterization of the Resource Based on Shallow Statistics', in S. Hansen-Schirra, S. Neumann and E. Steiner (eds), *Cross-Linguistic Corpora for the Study of Translations: Insights from the Language Pair English-German*, 71–90, Berlin: Mouton de Gruyter.

Teich, E. (2003), *Cross-Linguistic Variation in System und Text. A Methodology for the Investigation of Translations and Comparable Texts*, Berlin: Mouton de Gruyter.

Tiedemann, J. (2012), 'Parallel Data, Tools and Interfaces in OPUS', in *Proceedings of the 8th International Conference on Language Resources and Evaluation* (LREC 2012).

Tirkkonen-Condit, S. (2004), 'Keywords and Ideology in Translated History Texts: A Corpus-Based Analysis', in A. K. Mauranen and P. Kujamäki (eds), *Translation Universals: Do They Exist?*, 177–84, Amsterdam: John Benjamins.

Toury, G. ([1995] 2012), *Descriptive Translation Studies and Beyond*, Amsterdam: John Benjamins.

Wurm, A. (2016), 'Presentation of the KOPTE Corpus', Technical report, Universität des Saarlandes. Version 2.

Zampieri, M., Gebre, B. G. and Diwersy, S. (2013), 'N-gram Language Models and POS Distribution for the Identification of Spanish Varieties', in *Proceedings of TALN2013*, 580–7, Sable d'Olonne, France.

Zampieri, M., and Lapshinova-Koltunski, E. (2015), 'Investigating Genre and Method Variation in Translation Using Text Classification', in *Proceedings of TSD2015*, Lecture Notes in Artificial Intelligence, Springer-Verlag.

6

A descriptive study on Chinese–English translation choices for logical meanings

Xueying Li
Hangzhou Dianzi University
and
Mira Kim
University of New South Wales

1 Introduction

Translation Studies (TS) still lacks agreement about fundamental questions such as what translation is and how to evaluate translations (cf. Koby et al. 2014). There is general consensus that any form of translation is a decision-making process (cf. Munday 2012). Following Levý ([1967] 2000), who pioneered the idea, Wilss (1996) argued that translation is a knowledge-based activity during which translators solve problems and make decisions. From an SFL perspective, Matthiessen (2014: 272) also characterizes translation as 'the recreation of meaning in context through choice – choice in the interpretation of the original text and choice in the creation of the translated text'. In the same vein, Kim (2009) and Kim, Heffernan and Jing (2016) view translation as the product of translators' decision-making processes in which translators take many variables into consideration when producing a TT and then make negotiated or trade-off choices to convey multidimensional meanings of the ST – prioritizing one domain of meaning over another within context when it is not possible to translate all the multidimensional meanings of the ST simultaneously. In terms of SFL's notions of instantiation and distantiation (Martin 2008a), De Souza (2010) explains translation as a process of re-instantiation, as detailed in Martin and Quiroz's chapter in this volume. These studies have provided theoretical underpinning for the concept of translation as a decision-making process, following an approach grounded in close analysis of the translation product. This contrasts with other translation process research over the past decade that has followed an experimental path (e.g. Li Defeng, Lai Cheng and He 2019).

In this chapter, we will investigate translation choices made in four different English translations of the Chinese novel *Hong Lou Meng* (henceforth *HLM*) – with a particular focus on logical meaning, which is created when one experience is linked to another.

SFL models discourse semantics in terms of three kinds of meaning: ideational, interpersonal and textual. Ideational meaning is composed of experiential and logical meaning. Experiential meaning construes human experience, while logical meaning builds relations between one human experience and another.

The selection of this particular domain of meaning is motivated by the translation challenges caused by typological differences between Chinese and English in the realization of logical meanings. The most prominent difference is that, more often than in English, clauses in Chinese are linked in an implicit way through juxtaposition without any conjunctions making explicit the relation between the two clauses (e.g. Kim, Heffernan and Jing 2016), such as in Example 1 below.

Example 1 (Kim, Heffernan and Jing: 24)

小王子 是 存在的，
xiao wangzi shi cunzai de
little prince be exist SUB
'The Little Prince exists,'

证据 就是 他 那么 可爱。
zhengju jiu shi ta name keai
evidence FOC be he so cute
'the evidence is he is so cute.'

This typological difference raises challenging questions for Chinese–English (C–E) translators – such as whether or not the implicitness of logical meaning in the Chinese ST should remain in the English TT when clauses are linked without a conjunction, and which of the potential interpretations should be chosen when the implicit logical meaning can be interpreted in different ways. Such challenges have been investigated in a number of studies (e.g. Liu 2006), but none has systematically examined the comprehensive range of translation choices available.

Against this background, this study will survey C–E translation choices for logical meanings that have been made in the four TTs of *HLM*, and present them as a system of choices to address some of the research questions that Matthiessen (2014) has proposed for future SFL-informed translation studies. We are particularly interested in the following: a) to what extent choices are made within the same metafunction; and b) to what extent they involve a shift in other metafunctions (i.e. experiential, interpersonal and textual). We will start with a brief account of the underlying theory and methodology, and then describe our findings in relation to our research questions.

2 Theoretical framework

Our study focuses on logical meaning, which has been accounted for at two different strata in SFL: 1) through the system of CLAUSE COMPLEXING in the lexicogrammar (Halliday and Matthiessen 2014: 438–51) and 2) through the system of CONNEXION[1] in discourse semantics (Martin 1992: 159–279; Hao 2015: 228–55). The present study focuses on discourse semantics because the system 1) allows for the analysis of logical meanings within or between clause complexes in lexicogrammar, avoiding the issue of ambiguous clause complex boundaries in Chinese; and 2) identifies the type of logical meaning based on how experiential meanings are logically related in the text, which makes the analysis of implicit logical relations more feasible – see details in (Li 2019: Chapter 3).

The system of CONNEXION outlines elements used by writers or speakers to link figures. A figure is a discourse semantic unit referring to a state of affairs or 'an going-on in discourse semantics' (Hao 2015: 193). Its grammatical equivalent in the unmarked case is a clause. But the figure is different from the clause in that it encompasses experiential meanings, which can be realized by nominal groups involving grammatical metaphor. There are mainly two types of figures – occurrence figures construing something going on and state figures construing static relationships. A connexion is 'a relationship between figures' (Hao 2015: 193, 228). As mentioned above, logical meaning as defined in the system of CONNEXION can be identified either within a clause complex or between clause complexes; both are treated as a means for developing the logic of discourse (Martin 1992: 163).

The system of CONNEXION involves three systems: TYPE, EXPLICITNESS and EXTERNALITY. However, only EXPLICITNESS and TYPE are analysed in this chapter. The reasons for the choice of these two are primarily because (1) the present study has the particular aim of exploring typological differences in the EXPLICITNESS of connexion between English and Chinese; (2) the TYPE of connexion tends to be the most discussed dimension in this system and (3) an exploration of all three dimensions (i.e. including EXTERNALITY) would exceed the limits of this single chapter.

The system of EXPLICITNESS in Figure 6.1 has two features: explicit and implicit. A connexion is explicit if it is overtly marked by a conjunctive element, and it is implicit if figures are logically connected without any conjunctive elements.[2] The system of TYPE presents four types of connexion: addition, comparison, time or consequence. Addition involves extending one figure with another, through additive and alternative relations; comparison is the type of connexion in which one figure is similar to or different from other figures; time refers to simultaneous or successive temporal connexions between figures and consequence deals with relations of means, consequence, condition, purpose and concession.

There are two different grammatical ways of realizing a figure and a connexion in the discourse semantic system of CONNEXION: congruent or metaphorical. A congruent realization refers to the type of realization that typically happens in most cases, while an incongruent or metaphorical realization achieves the 'same' semantic purpose through grammatical metaphor, creating stratal tension between lexicogrammar and discourse semantics (Martin 2008b). A figure can be congruently realized through a clause; it can also be metaphorically realized by an embedded clause or a group/phrase (e.g. *[[That chytrids were present within the sample]] may have been due to the prolonged storage.*), a nominalization (e.g. *The survival of small but not large spores supports the importance of size in fracture initiation dynamics.*) or a textual reference (e.g. ... *This allows materials to be more readily degraded by fungi and bacteria.*) (Hao 2015: 250).

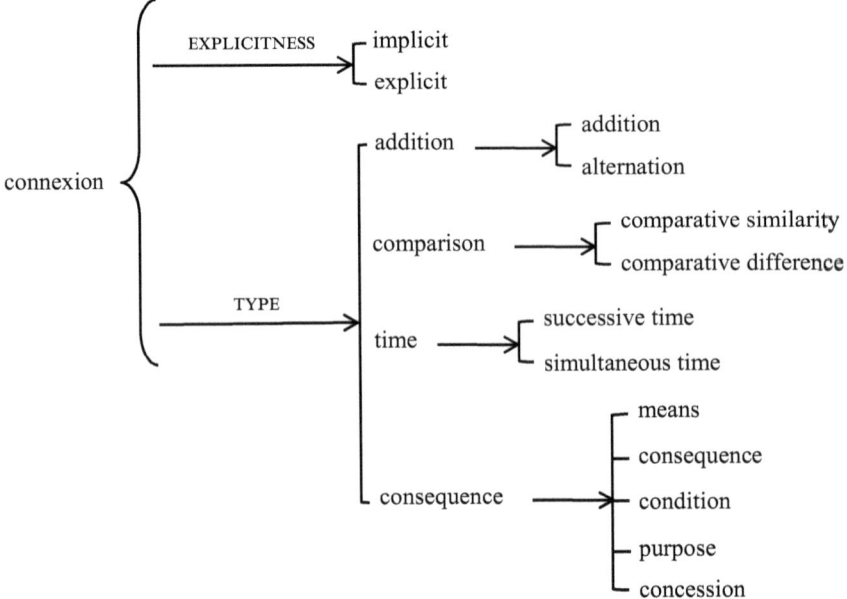

Figure 6.1 System of CONNEXION.

A connexion is congruently realized through a conjunction, but there are a number of ways to achieve realization when grammatical metaphor is present. For example, a connexion can be realized by a Circumstance if the Circumstance is realizing a figure (e.g. *Smaller fungal spores are more likely to retain integrity and viability, **due to** the ability to more easily avoid maceration.*). And a connexion can be realized as a Process if one or more of its Participants is realizing a figure (e.g. *Calibration of a pipette **allows** the relationship between theoretical volumes and those actually obtained to be determined.*). These two types of metaphorical realizations are frequently observed in our data; see Hao (2015: 251) for other metaphorical realizations of a connexion.

3 Methodology

The data analysis was conducted in three stages: (1) selecting texts; (2) analysing instances for translation choices and (3) examining the translation choices from two different angles in order to identify (a) common choices across the four translations and (b) differences between the TTs. Each stage will be explained in detail below.

3.1 Selecting texts

In the initial stage, Chapter One of *HLM* was selected as the Chinese ST and its four English translations as the TTs. *HLM*, which narrates a tragic love story, is one of the

Table 6.1 Four TTs of *HLM*

	Title	Translator	Translation time[a]
TT1	*A Dream of the Red Mansions*	Xianyi Yang Gladys Yang	In the 1960s and 1970s
TT2	*The Story of the Stone*	David Hawkes John Minford	In the 1970s and 1980s
TT3	*Red Chamber Dream*	B. S. Bonsall	In the 1950s
TT4	*The Dream of Red Chamber*	Henry B. Joly	In the 1890s

Note: [a]Translation time rather than dates of publication are provided in Table 6.1 because it took translators years to translate this long novel before turning it into a publication.

'Four Great Classical Novels' of China. The rationale for this choice of texts lies in its genre, the multitude of its available translations and the suitability of its language.

First of all, the novel *HLM* belongs to the story genre, which is more likely to be translated in a freer manner than other genres, and therefore may result in a variety of translation choices.

Second, the number of English translations of *HLM* makes it possible to compare translation choices between different TTs. Among the more than ten English translations of *HLM*, the four translations selected for this study are full translations of the novel rather than adaptations or translations of excerpts. Some basic information on these four TTs is presented in Table 6.1.

Finally, the language of *HLM* is suitable for the exploration of translation from Mandarin Chinese into English. Written in the mid-eighteenth century, *HLM* displays linguistic features in common with Chinese *baihuawen* (白话文); it is less classical than ancient Chinese but more classical than contemporary Mandarin. The selected text has features of contemporary Mandarin in terms of logical meaning, as commented by Ziqing Zhu in the preface to Wang (1943: 7): 'Even though over 200 years have passed since the appearance of *HLM*, the grammar is almost the same as modern Mandarin with only a few changes in vocabulary.'

3.2 Analysing instances for translation choices

The second stage of the investigation was the analysis of instances of translation choices:

i. First, the ST was divided into figures, and then connexions between contiguous figures were identified.
ii. Second, each connexion was analysed according to the dimensions of TYPE and EXPLICITNESS in the system of CONNEXION. Within the dimension of EXPLICITNESS, there are choices of implicit and explicit connexion; within TYPE, connexions are categorized into addition, alternation, comparative similarity, comparative difference, successive time, simultaneous time, means, consequence, condition, purpose or concession.

iii. Third, the translations corresponding to all the instances selected from the ST were identified in each of the four TTs, and these were then analysed and classified under the different categories of translation choices.

iv. Finally, the categories of translation choices were consolidated as a system network.

Note that only connexions involving two or three contiguous figures were included in order to investigate the phenomenon in question carefully and explain it in a systematic way before moving on to the more complex instances. In addition, indeterminate connexions, where the identification and/or type of connexion can be interpreted in different ways, were excluded, in order to observe the translation choices as objectively as possible. In total, 180 instances of connexions were identified in the ST. Since four TTs are included, this means that 720 translation instances were analysed for the Chinese logical meanings.

3.3 Investigating the translation choices from two angles

In the final stage, we examined the translation choices from two different angles: (a) common choices across the translations and (b) differences between the four translations.

4 Overview of translation choices

Based on the analysis of 180 connexions in the ST and their translations in the four TTs, a variety of English translation choices for Chinese logical meanings have been uncovered. We present them, beginning with less delicate options, and then consolidating the entire system towards the end of this section. To begin with, translation choices can be divided into 'no shift' and 'shift', as presented in Figure 6.2:

The concept of 'translation shift' derives from Catford (1965: 73), where it is defined as a 'departure[s] from formal correspondence in the process of going from SL [Source Language] to TL [Target Language]'. In our study, it specifically refers to discourse semantic changes in the domain of logical meaning between the ST and its TT.

'No shift' means a translation choice of maximal equivalence, as exemplified below in Example 2. Such a case was found when connexions are both explicit and implicit in the ST. In Example 2, the explicit additive connexion realized through the conjunction 且 *qie* 'and' was translated to an explicit connexion by addition, realized by the approximately equivalent conjunction *and* in English.

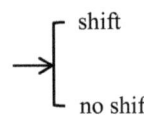

shift

no shift

Figure 6.2 Shift and no shift.

Example 2[3]

ST	Addition	a	千部 共 出 一套， qian bu gong chu yi tao thousand MEAS total come out one pattern 'A thousand (books) came out a single pattern,'
		b	**且** 其中 终 不能 不 涉于 淫滥 **qie** qizhong zhong bu neng bu she yu yinlan **and** therein finally NEG can NEG involve at indecency '**and** none of them can escape from indecency'
TT	Addition	a	a thousand are written to a single pattern
		b	**and** none escapes bordering on indecency.

Example 3 includes an implicit connexion between two Chinese figures. The connexion remains implicit in the TT, as one of the figures is realized through a non-finite clause *being next to the temple*.

Example 3

ST	Consequence	a	甄家 在 隔壁， zhen jia zai gebi Zhen home at next door 'The Zhens' house was next door,'
		b	(所以) 早已 烧成 一片 瓦砾场。 (suoyi) zao yi shao cheng yi pian wali chang (so) early already burn become one MEAS rubble square '(so) (it) was burnt to a heap of rubble a long time ago.'
TT	Consequence	a	The Zhens' home, being next to the temple,
		b	was reduced to a pile of rubble.

Connexions that were translated with a shift can be further divided into two categories, depending on whether the connexion has been removed or adjusted. When connexions were removed, we observed three distinct patterns: (1) certain elements of a figure, a whole figure or several figures in the ST are omitted from the TT, (2) the experiential meanings of figures in the ST are greatly shifted in the TT or (3) a figure in the ST was translated metaphorically, as shown in Figure 6.3.

In Example 4, the TT omits the first figure altogether and just translates the second figure, so that the connexion in the ST has been removed from the TT.

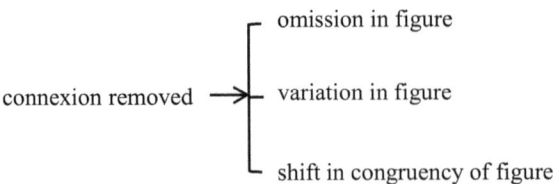

Figure 6.3 Connexion removed.

Example 4

ST	Successive time	a	石头 听了， shitou ting le stone listen/hear ASP 'The stone listened/heard,'
		b	(然后) 喜 不 能 禁 (ranhou) xi bu neng jin (then) happy NEG can help '(then) (it) couldn't help being happy'
TT		a	The stone was delighted.

In Example 5, there are variations in figures. The first figure of the ST is an occurrence figure, containing the occurrence 听 *ting* 'listen/hear'; the second figure is a positioned figure, in which the positioning part is 知 *zhi* 'know' and the positioned part is a state figure 是疯话 *shi fenghua* 'be mad words' (for the types of figure assumed here, see Hao 2015). The elements of the two figures in the ST are reorganized and integrated into a single positioned figure in the TT: the positioning part is *realize*, and the positioned part is an occurrence figure *he was listening to the words of a madman*. The variations have significantly changed the experiential meanings and accordingly removed the connexion between the figures.

Example 5

ST	Successive time	a	士隐 听了 (之后)， shiyin ting le (zhihou) Shiyin listen/hear ASP (after) '(After) Shiyin heard (some words),'
		b	知 是 疯话 zhi shi feng hua know be mad words '(he) knew (they) were mad words'
TT		a	Shi-yin realised that he was listening to the words of a madman

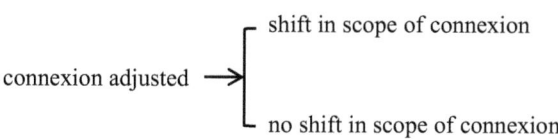

Figure 6.4 Connexion adjusted.

In Example 6, the ST connexion is absent in the TT due to a shift from a congruent to a metaphorical realization of figure. In the ST, the two figures in a consequential connexion are congruently realized through two clauses. In the TT, however, the realization of the second figure has been shifted to an embedded clause *recorded here* to modify *your tale*.

Example 6

ST	Consequence	a	你 这 一段 故事，有些 趣味， ni zhe yi duan gushi, you xie quwei you this one MEAS story, have some interest 'This story of yours, has some interest,'
		b	<u>故</u> 编写 在 此 **gu** bianxie zai ci **so** compile at here '**so** (it is) compiled here'
TT		a	Your tale [[recorded here]] is interesting enough.

We now discuss instances where connexions have not been removed but adjusted in various ways. They can first be categorized in regard to the scope of connexion as with or without a shift, as shown in Figure 6.4.

'Shift in scope of connexion' means the figures that are logically connected in the ST are connected with other figure(s) in the TT. For example, in Example 7, the first figure in the ST functions to provide the time when the second and third figures take place; and the second and the third figure are connected by condition, marked by the correlative conjunctions 只 … 便*zhi … bian* 'as long as … then'. In the TT, however, the connexion of simultaneous time exists only between the first figure and the second one (as suggested by the full stop after the second figure), while the conditional connexion is expanded to cover the relationship between all the other three figures.[4]

Example 7

ST	Simultaneous time	a	到 那 时 (之时)， dao na shi (zhishi) come that time (when) '(When) the time comes,'

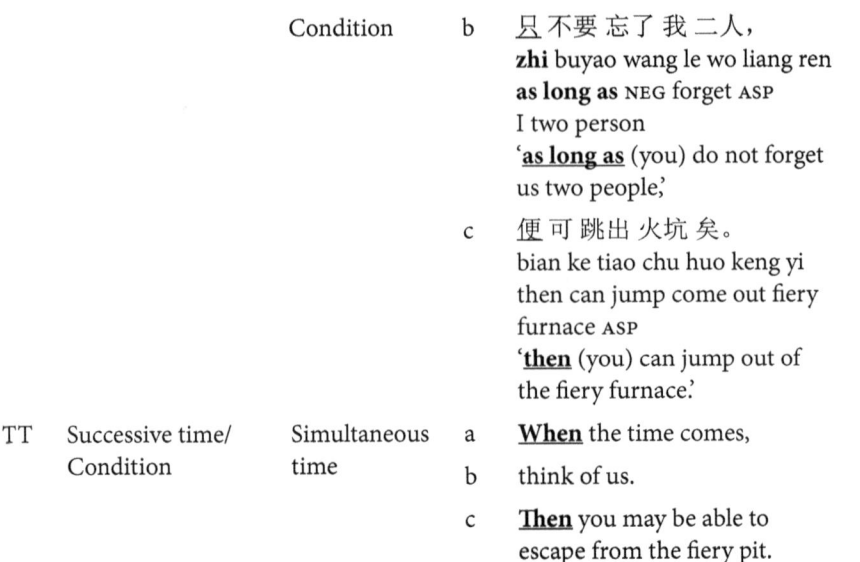

	Condition		b	且 不要 忘了 我 二人， **zhi** buyao wang le wo liang ren **as long as** NEG forget ASP I two person '**as long as** (you) do not forget us two people,'
			c	便 可 跳出 火坑 矣。 bian ke tiao chu huo keng yi then can jump come out fiery furnace ASP '**then** (you) can jump out of the fiery furnace.'
TT	Successive time/ Condition	Simultaneous time	a	**When** the time comes,
			b	think of us.
			c	**Then** you may be able to escape from the fiery pit.

When the scope of connexion is not shifted, there are three possible other shifts: 1) 'shift in congruency of connexion', 2) 'shift in explicitness of connexion' and 3) 'shift in type of connexion'; and they can occur singly or in a combination with another, as shown in Figure 6.5:

'Shift in congruency of connexion' has to do with whether or not a congruent realization of connexion in the ST has been translated in a metaphorical way in the TT or the other way around. In the ST of Example 8, the concessive connexion is congruently realized through the correlative conjunctions 虽 ... 然 *sui ... ran* 'although ... but'.[5] By contrast, in the TT the connexion is metaphorically realized by the conjunctive element *in spite of* within the Circumstance *in spite of his poverty*. As a result, Example 8 can be said to show a shift from a congruent realization to a metaphorical realization of connexion.

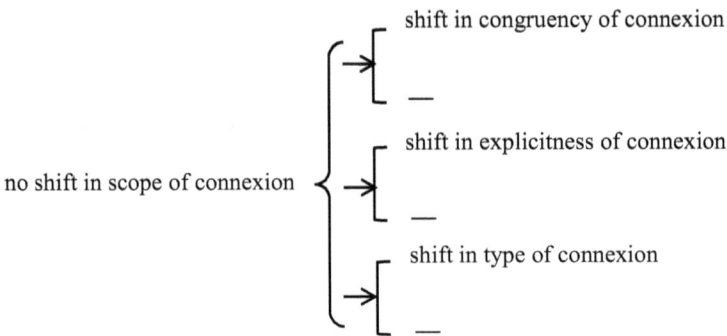

Figure 6.5 Shift in congruency, type and/or explicitness of connexion.

Example 8

ST	Concession	a	虽 是 贫窘，
			sui shi pinjiong
			although be poor
			'**Although** (he) was poor,'
		b	然 生 得 腰圆背厚⁶， 面阔口方
			ran sheng de yao yuan bei hou mian kuo kou fang
			but be born DEG waist-round-back-thick
			face-wide-mouth-square
			'**but** (he) had a manly physique'
TT	Concession	a	**In spite of** his poverty,
		b	he was naturally endowed with a round waist, a broad back, a fat face, and a square mouth.

'Shift in explicitness of connexion' includes two sub-categories: (i) a shift from an implicit connexion to an explicit connexion and (ii) a shift from an explicit connexion to an implicit connexion. In Example 9, the implicit connexion in the ST is shifted to an explicit one marked by *then*.

Example 9

ST	Successive time	a	思忖 半晌，
			sicun banshang
			think half day
			'(He) thought for a while,'
		b	(然后) 将 一 这 《石头记》 再 检阅 一遍。
			(ranhou) jiang yi zhe shitouji zai jianyue yibian
			(then) make one this stone tale again read one MEAS
			'(then) (he) read *Tale of the Stone* again.'
TT	Successive time	a	The Reverend Void thought it over,
		b	**then** carefully reread The Tale of the Stone.

For 'shift in type of connexion' three particular patterns have been observed as the most common: (i) a shift between successive time and simultaneous time; (ii) a shift between counter-expectant types (e.g. concession) and others and (iii) a shift between a sub-type of time (e.g. successive time) and a sub-type of consequence (e.g. condition). The first pattern is a shift between two types of temporal connexion. In the ST of Example 10, the occurrence 看见 *kanjian* 'see' in the first figure takes place before the occurrence 哭 *ku* 'cry' in the second figure. This connexion of successive time is marked by 便 *bian* 'then'. In the TT, the connexion has been shifted to overlapping time, marked by the conjunctive element *when*.

Example 10

ST	Successive time	a	看见 士隐 抱着 英莲, kanjian shiyin baozhe yinglian see Shiyin hold ASP Yinglian '(A monk and a Taoist) saw Shiyin holding Yinglian,'
		b	那僧 **便** 大哭 起来 naceng **bian** daku qilai that monk **then** big cry stand up '**then** the monk began to cry aloud'
TT	Simultaneous time	a	**When** they saw the child in his arms,
		b	the monk burst into lamentations.

The second pattern is between counter-expectant connexions and others. Readers tend to have certain expectations of logical development; when the development meets readers' expectations, the logic is expectant, and if it goes against normal expectations, it is counter-expectant (Martin and Rose 2007: 117–20). With regard to the type of connexion in the data, expectant connexions involve addition and successive time while counter-expectant ones involve comparative difference and concession. Example 11 illustrates a shift from counter-expectant comparative difference to expectant successive time. In the ST, it is expected that Shiyin will stay and accompany his guests after 另具一席 *ling ju yixi* 'prepar[ing] another table' in the first figure. Hence, 步月至庙中 *bu yue zhi miaozhong* 'walk under the moon to the temple' in the second figure counters readers' normal expectations. However, in the TT there is no counter-expectation marked (we simply have the additive connexion marker *and*).

Example 11

ST	Comparative difference	a	另 具 一席 于 书房, ling ju yi xi yu shufang another prepare a table at study room 'Shiyin prepared another table in the study room,'
		b	却 自己 步 月 至 庙 中 **que** ziji bu yue zhi miao zhong **but** self walk moon reach temple inside '**but** (he) himself walked under the moon to the temple'
TT	Successive time	a	Shiyin had another table laid in his study
		b	**and** strolled over in the moonlight to the temple

The third pattern deals with a shift between a sub-type of time and a sub-type of consequence. In Example 12, the first figure in the ST functions as the cause of the second figure, and this consequential connexion is marked by the correlative conjunctions 因 ... 便 *yin ... bian* 'because ... so'. In the TT, the type of connexion is shifted to simultaneous time as the figures linked by the conjunctive element *while* are realized as taking place at the same time. The type of connexion has been shifted from consequence to simultaneous time.

Example 12

ST	Consequence	a	半夜 中，霍启 因 要 小解，
			banye zhong, huoqi **yin** yao xiaojie
			midnight in, Huo Qi **because** want urinate
			'At midnight, <u>**because**</u> Huo Qi wanted to urinate,'
		b	便 将 英莲 放 在 一家 门槛 上。
			bian jiang yinglian fang zai yi jia menkan shang
			so make Yinglian put at one home doorstep on
			'<u>**so**</u> (he) put Yinglian on the doorstep of someone's house.'
TT	Simultaneous time	a	Towards midnight Huo Qi set the little girl down on a doorstep
		b & c	<u>**while**</u> he stepped round the corner to urinate.

The C–E translation choices for logical meanings are integrated in the system in Figure 6.6.

Starting from the left-hand side of the network, translation choices are categorized into 'no shift' and 'shift'. The choices of shift are further categorized depending on

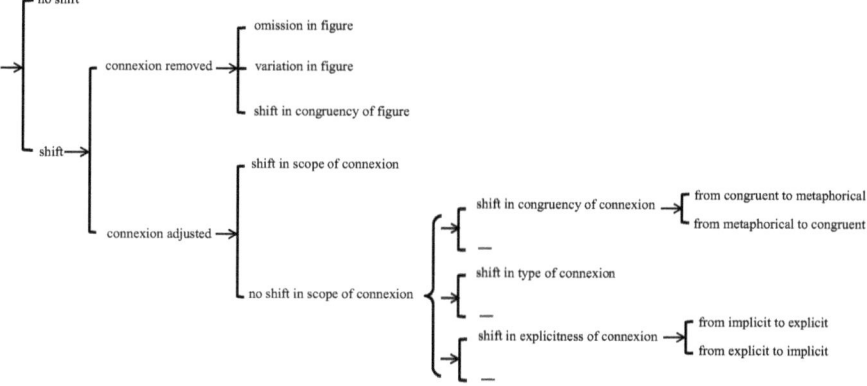

Figure 6.6 System of C–E translation choices for logical meanings.

whether the connexion has been removed or adjusted. The connexion can be removed by omitting a figure completely, varying some experiential elements of a figure or metaphorizing a figure. The connexion can be adjusted in terms of scope, congruency, type and/or explicitness of connexion. In the next section, we will explain the frequency of each choice in the TTs.

5 The frequency of translation choices

Out of 720 instances in the 4 TTs, 62 per cent of them were translated with a kind of shift, and only 38 per cent of them were translated without any shift. This means the translators chose to remove or adjust a connexion in 6 out of 10 instances on average. Adjusting a connexion (47%) is three times more frequent than removing a connexion (15%). When a connexion has been adjusted, the majority of the instances maintain the connexion between the figures that are logically connected in the ST except for the limited instances of translation shifts of scope (6%). Among such instances, the overriding translation shift has to do with the explicitness of the connexion. This choice occurs by itself in 159 instances (22%), or together with a shift in the type of connexion in 41 instances (6%), congruency in 8 instances (1%) and a combination of type and congruency in 12 instances (2%) – which account for 31 per cent of the total number of shifts. The detailed data are presented in Table 6.2.

Note: [a]'Congruency' is the abbreviation for 'shift in congruency of connexion', which is a sub-type of 'connexion adjusted'. This differs from 'shift in congruency of figure', which is a sub-type of 'connexion removed'.

It is interesting to note that instances of 'shift in explicitness of connexion' include fifty-two instances involving a shift from an explicit connexion to an implicit connexion. In other words, the translators chose to translate the explicit connexion

Table 6.2 Comparison of the translation choices in the overall data (four TTs)

			Number	Percentage
No shift (276, 38%)			276	38%
Shift (444, 62%)	Removed (108, 15%)	Omission	60	8
		Variation	22	3
		Congruency of figure	26	4
	Adjusted (336, 47%)	Scope	44	6
		No scope (292, 41%) Congruency[a] alone	20	3
		Type alone	52	7
		Explicitness alone	159	22
		Congruency & type	0	0
		Congruency & explicitness	8	1
		Type & explicitness	41	6
		Congruency & type & explicitness	12	2
Total			720	100

Table 6.3 Comparison of shifts in explicitness of connexion

	Number	Percentage
From implicit to explicit	168	76
From explicit to implicit	52	24
Total	220	100

implicitly even though they could have translated it explicitly. Such instances account for 24 per cent of the shifts in explicitness of connexion as shown in Table 6.3.

Although the percentage of 'shift from explicit to implicit' is relatively small, it is higher than originally expected – as English uses more explicit markers than Chinese in terms of logical meaning, and a higher degree of explicitness is commonly found to be characteristic of translated texts (Steiner 2004). The frequent pattern of this shift is because the removal of the explicit conjunction of the ST often occurs together with the replacement of a comma with a full stop. For example, in Example 13 the explicit connexion marked by the conjunction 遂 *sui* 'so' in the ST becomes an implicit one in the TT; at the same time, the comma is shifted to a full stop.

Example 13

ST	Consequence	a	忽 听得 窗外 有 女子 嗽声,
			hu ting de chuang wai you nüzi sou sheng
			sudden hear get window outside have female cough sound
			'Suddenly (he) heard there was a woman's cough out of the window,'
		b &	雨村 遂 起 身
		c	Yucun **sui** qi shen
			Yucun **so** rise body
			'**so** Yucun got up'
			往 窗外 一看
			wang chuang wai yi kan
			toward window outside one look
			'(he) looked out of the window'
TT	Consequence	a	Suddenly he heard a woman's cough outside the window.
		b &	Yu-ts'un got up
		c	and looked out.

When a connexion has been removed, there is a shift in experiential meaning, as discussed with Examples 5, 6 and 7 in Section 4. When a connexion has been adjusted, the shift is mostly made within the same logical metafunction, making changes in terms of the scope, explicitness, type and congruency of the connexion. Such shifts might also entail a slight shift of experiential meaning as well. The most common adjustment is found in explicitness (220 instances), of which 24 per cent (53 instances) involve a shift in type, which means two out of ten shifts in explicitness entail a shift in type. As discussed in Section 4 with Examples 10, 11 and 12, the most common shifts in type occur between successive time and simultaneous time; between expectant types (e.g. addition) and counterexpectant types (e.g. concession); and between a sub-type of time (e.g. successive time) and a sub-type of consequence (e.g. condition). A translation shift in congruency of connexion is found in 40 instances, of which 12 instances entail a shift in type.

6 Differences of translation choices between the four TTs

We now compare the frequency and types of translation shifts among the TTs. Numbers and percentages of translation choices in all 180 instances of each TT are shown in Table 6.4.

Overall, TT1 shows the highest percentage in the four types of shift including 'omission in figure', 'shift in congruency of figure', 'shift in scope of connexion', 'shift in congruency of connexion' and accordingly shows the lowest percentage for 'no shift' (17%). While TT2 and TT4 show average percentages of translation shifts in nearly all categories, TT1 and TT3 show noticeable contrasts. The striking difference is found in the category of 'omission in figure' (17% versus 1%), as exemplified in Example 14. TT1 has made the choice of 'omission in figure', omitting the entire first figure in the TT and so removing the connexion of successive time. For the same connexion in the ST, however, TT3 has only shifted the connexion from implicit to explicit.

Table 6.4 Comparison of translation choices across the four translations

	Average (%)	TT1 (%)		TT2 (%)		TT3 (%)		TT4 (%)	
No shift	38	53	29	60	33	97	54	66	37
Omission	8	30	17	20	11	2	1	9	5
Variation	3	9	5	8	4	3	2	1	1
Congruency of figure	4	9	5	8	4	2	1	7	4
Scope	6	14	8	9	5	9	5	10	6
Congruency	6	12	7	11	6	4	2	13	7
Type	15	18	10	25	14	29	16	33	18
Explicitness	31	52	29	54	30	52	29	62	34
Total	100	180	100	180	100	180	100	180	100

Note: The three kinds of shift – shifts in congruency, type and explicitness of connexion – may occur either alone or together. In Table 6.4, one kind of shift is discussed with all the occurrence options included. The purpose of this table is not to compare between different choices, but to compare the use of a particular choice across different translations.

Example 14

ST	Successive time	a	士隐 听 了,
			shiyin ting le,
			Shiyin listen/hear ASP,
			'Shiyin listened/heard,'
		b	(然后) 大 叫: "..."
			(ranhou) da jiao: ..."
			(then) big shout, "..."
			'(then) (he) shouted loudly, "..."'
TT1		a	"..." cried Shiyin.
TT3	Successive time	a	"..." cried Shiyin with a loud voice,
		b	**after** he had heard these lines.

As briefly mentioned earlier in Section 2, TT1 was translated by a source language (SL) native speaker together with a target language (TL) native speaker, and all the others by TL native speakers. This difference may explain why TT1 includes more shifts than the others as they might have negotiated logical meanings drawing on each translator's strength (i.e. the Chinese translator's interpretation of the ST, and the English translator's representation of that interpretation in the TT).

Other than the contrasts presented above, there is no large variation in the translation choices and the frequency of each choice in each TT. For example, in all four TTs 'shift in explicitness of connexion' accounts for a large number of the variations while 'variation in figure' accounts for the least.

7 Conclusion

This chapter has explored the concept of translation as a decision-making process in a descriptive study of translating logical meanings from Chinese into English. We used the system of CONNEXION in the SFL model as a framework and Chapter One of the Chinese novel *Hong Lou Meng* and its four English translations as data. We examined 180 instances of logical connexions of the ST and their translations in the four TTs and integrated all the choices observed in a system network. We described the choices one by one with instances and compared the numbers and percentages of the translation choices from two different angles, that is, common translation shifts across the translations and differences between the translations.

It is very clear that more than half of the logical connexions were translated with a kind of shift based on the average percentage of connexions translated with no shift (61%), and the results of the translation choices across the four translations presented in Table 6.4 indicate high percentages of shifts of various kinds (TT1 71%, TT2 67%, TT3 46% and TT4 63%). Out of 444 instances of shift, 76 per cent (336 instances) took place in the same metafunction and 25 per cent (108) involved a shift of experiential metafunction. These results show that the majority of shifts occurred in the same metafunction but the percentage of instances that involved a shift in experiential metafunction is not negligible at all. These results are concrete evidence to show that translating logical meanings from Chinese into English is not straightforward but does require careful consideration, which is why it has been known to be a great challenge among Chinese translators.

The most common shifts occurred in explicitness (31%, 220 instances) followed by type (15%, 105 instances) and congruency of connexion (6%, 40 instances). An interesting observation is that the translators not only make implicit connexions explicit but also explicit ones implicit, which clearly suggests that the translators did not determine their translation decisions based on visible linguistic resources exclusively. They even chose different types of connexions, the most common being: 1) a shift between successive time and simultaneous time; 2) a shift between counter-expectant types (e.g. concession) and others; and 3) a shift between a sub-type of time (e.g. successive time) and a sub-type of consequence (e.g. condition).

This study has shown that it is possible to categorize the various kinds of shift involved in the translation of logical meanings into a system network based on discourse semantics. At the initial stage of research when a lexicogrammatical approach was taken, the way forward seemed too daunting, as discussed in Li (2019; Chapter 3). However, when this phenomenon was approached from a discourse semantic perspective, it became feasible to classify seemingly unlimited translation shifts into three to five levels as shown in Figure 6.6. After the first level of shift versus no shift, the system network orders translation shifts from a general level of discourse semantics that has been impacted by shifts to a more specific level such as type and explicitness as it goes down the delicacy cline. The only grammatical aspect included in the network is grammatical metaphor.

Our descriptive study has reinforced the view that translation is a decision-making process during which various aspects of discourse semantics are negotiated, and the newly negotiated meanings are represented through translation shifts. A number of questions remain for future research, such as, a) To what extent are shifts obligatory purely due to the typological differences, and to what extent are they optional? b) What are the motivations for optional choices? and c) To what extent do they depend on factors such as translation brief and genre? These questions could be efficiently studied drawing on comparable descriptions of source and target languages in SFL. A series of such descriptive translation studies can be a solid basis on which general theories of translation can be built.

Notes

1. This system was initially proposed by Martin (e.g. 1992) under the name CONJUNCTION, and then renamed CONNEXION by Jing Hao in order to avoid the terminological confusion of using the same term for discourse semantic and lexicogrammatical systems.
2. In this study, conjunctive elements are defined as not only conjunctions (e.g. *because*) but also continuatives (e.g. *soon*), conjunctive settings (e.g. *from then on*) or

conjunctive occurrences (e.g. *enable*). Note that, although finiteness in English and aspect in Chinese can also indicate a connexion (e.g. Hao 2019), they are considered as covert markers in implicit connexions.

3. Tables are used to present examples of translation choices. In these tables, the first column shows whether the text is the ST or the TT; the second column shows the type of the connexion; the third column shows the order of figures in the text and the fourth column shows the text itself, aligned according to the placement of figures. In examples of explicit connexions, conjunctive elements are displayed in <u>underline</u> and **bold**. In instances of implicit connexions, conjunctive elements are added (in parentheses) based on the interpretation of the specific context. The purpose is to show how such implicit connexions have been interpreted in the TTs.

4. As noted in Section 2, logical meaning as defined in the system of CONNEXION can go beyond a clause complex in the lexicogrammar. Therefore, in the TT of Example 7, a connexion can be identified between the first two figures and the third figure, even though we can see a full stop after the second figure.

5. Unlike English, some certain conjunctions in Chinese are typically used together as correlative conjunctions, such as 虽 … 但 *sui … dan* 'although … but' and 因 … 便 *yin … bian* 'because … so'.

6. In the case of idioms in the Chinese ST, word-to-word translations are provided for each Chinese character, and they are linked by hyphens.

References

Catford, J. C. (1965), *A Linguistic Theory of Translation*, London: Oxford University Press.

De Souza, L. M. F. (2010), 'Interlingual Reinstantiation: A Model for a New and Comprehensive Systemic Functional Perspective on Translation', PhD diss., Universidade Federal de Santa Catarina, Florianopolis.

Halliday, M. A. K., and Matthiessen, C. M. I. M. (2014), *An Introduction to Functional Grammar*, 4th edn, London: Arnold.

Hao, J. (2015), 'Construing Biology: An Ideational Perspective', PhD diss., University of Sydney, Sydney.

Hao, J. (2019), 'Construing Relationship between Scientific Activities through Mandarin Chinese', in J. R. Martin, Y. J. Doran and G. Figueredo (eds), *Systemic Functional Language Description: Making Meaning Matter*, 238–72, London: Routledge.

Kim, M. (2009), 'Meaning-Oriented Assessment of Translations: SFL and Its Application to Formative Assessment', in C. V. Angelelli and H. E. Jacobson (eds), *Testing and Assessment in Translation and Interpreting Studies: A Call for Dialogue between Research and Practice*, 123–58, Amsterdam: John Benjamins.

Kim, M., Heffernan, J. and Jing, B. (2016), 'Translation Choices of Embedded Clauses: A Systemic Functional Linguistics Perspective', *Journal of Translation Studies* 17: 11–49.

Koby, G. S., Fields, P., Hague, D., Lommel, A. and Melby, A. (2014), 'Defining Translation Quality', *Tradumàtica* 12: 413–20.

Levý, L. ([1967] 2000), 'Translation as a Decision Process', in L. Venuti (ed.), *The Translation Studies Reader*, 148–59, London: Routledge.

Li, D., Lai Cheng, V. and He, Y. (eds) (2019), *Researching Cognitive Processes of Translation*, Frankfurt: Springer.

Li, X. (2019), 'A Study on Translation Choices for Logical Meanings from Chinese into English from a Systemic Functional Linguistic Perspective', PhD diss., University of New South Wales, Sydney.

Liu, B. (2006), *xin bian han ying duibi yu fanyi* [Chinese-English Contrastive Studies and Translation], revised edn, Beijing: China Translation and Publishing Corporation.

Martin, J. R. (1992), *English Text: System and Structure*, Amsterdam: John Benjamins.

Martin, J. R. (2008a), 'Tenderness: Realisation and Instantiation in a Botswanan Town', in N. Norgaard (ed.), *Systemic Functional Linguistics in Use (vol.29)*, 30–62, Odense: Odense Working Papers in Language and Communication.

Martin, J. R. (2008b), 'Incongruent and Proud: De-vilifying "Nominalization"', *Discourse and Society* 19 (6): 801–10.

Martin, J. R., and Rose, D. (2007), *Working with Discourse: Meaning beyond the Clause*, 2nd edn, London: Continuum.

Matthiessen, C. M. I. M. (2014), 'Choice in Translation: Metafunctional Considerations', in K. Kunz, E. Teich, S. Hansen-Schirra, S. Neumann and P. Daut (eds), *Caught in the Middle-Language Use and Translation: A Festschrift for Erich Steiner on the Occasion of His 60th Birthday*, 271–333, Saarland: Saarland University Press.

Munday, J. (2012), *Evaluation in Translation: Critical Points of Translator Decision-Making*, Abingdon: Routledge.

Steiner, E. (2004), *Translated Texts: Properties, Variants, Evaluations*, Frankfurt am Main: Peter Lang Verlag.

Wang, L. (1943), *zhongguo xiandai yufa* [Modern Chinese Grammar], Beijing: Commercial Press.

Wilss, W. (1996), *Knowledge and Skills in Translator Behaviour*, Amsterdam: John Benjamins.

7

Modality, point of view and translation: A systemic functional analysis of the Arabic translations of J. M. Coetzee's *Waiting for the Barbarians*

Komail Al Herz

King Faisal University

1 Introduction

This chapter explores the collaboration between Systemic Functional Linguistics (SFL), Translation Studies (TS) and Narratology in the investigation of narrative point of view in translation. The narrative 'voice', as the linguistic presence of the translator, is woven into the fabric of the translated text, yet it is often backgrounded in research (Hermans [1996] 2009) while the other narrative techniques, aspects, existents and order of events in the source text (ST) are transferred intact into the target text (TT). Nevertheless, over the years a number of studies within the realm of TS have questioned these assumptions and sought to highlight the shock to the original perspectivization brought about by translation (e.g. van Leuven-Zwart 1989, 1990; Bosseaux 2007; Munday 2008; Hewson 2011; Bernaerts, De Bleeker and De Wilde 2014). Many of these studies depend on the SFL model of research in Descriptive Translation Studies (DTS). It is concerned with re-mapping the lexicogrammatical and discourse semantic systems (e.g. TRANSITIVITY, MODALITY and THEME) of the ST onto those of the TT in order to locate micro-level shifts that may lead to the alteration of the narrative in translation at the macro-level point of view (Munday 2008: 31), the angle from which the story is relayed. Adopting the SFL framework is of paramount importance in avoiding the 'unprincipled impressionism' that is predominant in literary studies in designating narrative viewpoints (Simpson 2007: 118), and it is able to account for foregrounded, motivated choices made by the author. That is, the proliferation of metaphorical interpretation or impressionistic remarks by literary critics when determining points of view or a 'style' of a narrative text is rarely grounded in a transparent set of linguistic rules that can be systemically substantiated and replicated in the same or other texts (Simpson 2004: 4). The present model also helps to introduce more objectivity to the ST–TT comparison. One significant manifestation of this is the search for consistency through the systematic selection of linguistic features for a comparative analysis, premised on explicit terms and rigorous criteria.

For the English–Arabic pair, however, this line of research remains relatively under-researched. Thus, contributing to these studies, this chapter aims to explore the translation of modal patterns that realize point of view on the psychological plane. Particularly, it concentrates on comparing modal expressions from an SFL perspective in Chapters 3 and 4 of J. M. Coetzee's *Waiting for the Barbarians* ([1980] 2004) to those of its two Arabic translations by ʔibtisām ʕabdullāh (2004) and Ṣaḥr Al-Ḥājj Ḥusayn (2004), in an endeavour to identify, classify and explain the lexicogrammatical shifts. The selection of these two chapters was guided by varying degrees of involvement of the narrator-character, and they are characterized by different modal patterns, which then account for different types of viewpoints on the psychological plane. Hence, it would enable us to see how well the two translators retain such a variety of modal resources, or what types of modality systems are foregrounded in translation. For the grammaticization of the modal meanings in Modern Standard Arabic (MSA), the present study draws on Bardi's (2008) SFL typological description of MSA. This avoids the danger of forcing foreign terms/theory onto MSA by developing it based on natural discourse, a very important step in the SFL description of any language, as pointed out by Matthiessen (2009: 48). Finally, I will use Simpson's (1993) modal grammar of point of view to examine whether these translational alterations have potentially affected the original psychological perspective of the novel.

2 SFL categories of modality

The system of modality is a major exponent of the interpersonal metafunction of the language (the clause as exchange). Modality, in SFL, refers to the area of possibility or of uncertainty principally quantified in a scale between two opposing polarity extremes: *yes* (positive) and *no* (negative) (Halliday and Matthiessen 2014: 176). The system of modality is broken down into two main categories: modulation and modalization. Modulation is concerned with different grades of interpersonal meanings construing proposals (goods-and-services exchange: commands and offers) that are located on a continuum, the extremes of which are positive 'do it' and negative 'don't do it'. It includes the systems of **obligation** and **inclination** (including modal expressions of willingness and ability). Modulation can be congruently expressed through a Finite modal/quasi-modal operator (e.g. *may*), or the expansion of the Predicator (e.g. *are supposed to*).

The other type of modalization refers to the gradient of interpersonal meanings of propositions (information exchange: statements and questions) situated on a scale between the positive 'it is so' and negative 'it isn't so' poles. This type involves the system of **probability**. It also includes intermediate possibilities characterizing degrees of usuality: 'sometimes/usually/always'. In the present chapter, modal expressions triggering usuality meanings were not studied, chiefly because based on Simpson's model they are not considered linguistic signals of point of view on the psychological plane (see below). The system of probability is typically realized through a Finite modal/quasi-modal operator (e.g. *can*) and a modal Adjunct (e.g. *perhaps*). Modal meanings can also be expressed through interpersonal metaphor beyond the clause simplex, which is the incongruent realization of modality (e.g. 'But **I think** he is wrong').[1] The primary, mental process clause (*I think*) serves as a 'modal clause'. It functions as making explicit the personal source of modality, whereas the main proposition lies in the secondary projecting clause 'he is wrong' (Halliday and Matthiessen 2014: 184, 687). The incongruent form of realization (*I think*) corresponds to the congruent form of the modal Adjunct *probably* in a clause simplex. Hence, the underlying utterance can be paraphrased as 'Probably, he is wrong'. On the other hand, such an utterance as 'I do not even **know** whether to read from right to left or from left to right'[2] does not represent the qualification of the proposition, since it can be tagged as 'I do not even know whether to read from right to left or from left to right, do I?' (Halliday and Matthiessen 2014: 687). By contrast, the modal clause (*I think*) cannot be tagged, otherwise a marked clause will be generated (Thompson 2004: 70). This is also clearly shown in making the proposition negative 'I do not think he is wrong'. It is natural in English that the modal clause is negated while the main proposition remains unaffected. Again, this can be evidenced in tagging the sentence that generates an unnatural English construction: 'I do not think he is wrong, isn't he?'.

Furthermore, Halliday and Matthiessen (2014: 78) divide this area of uncertainty between the two poles into three basic regions: high, median and low, representing the values assigned to the modal judgement. Construing as one of the variables that control the production of modality, the intensity or forcefulness of modal expressions triggers to what extent the language user is committed to the state of affairs or to the truth-value of his/her proposition. Table 7.1 offers a brief overview of the SFL modality systems, their realization and three main degrees.

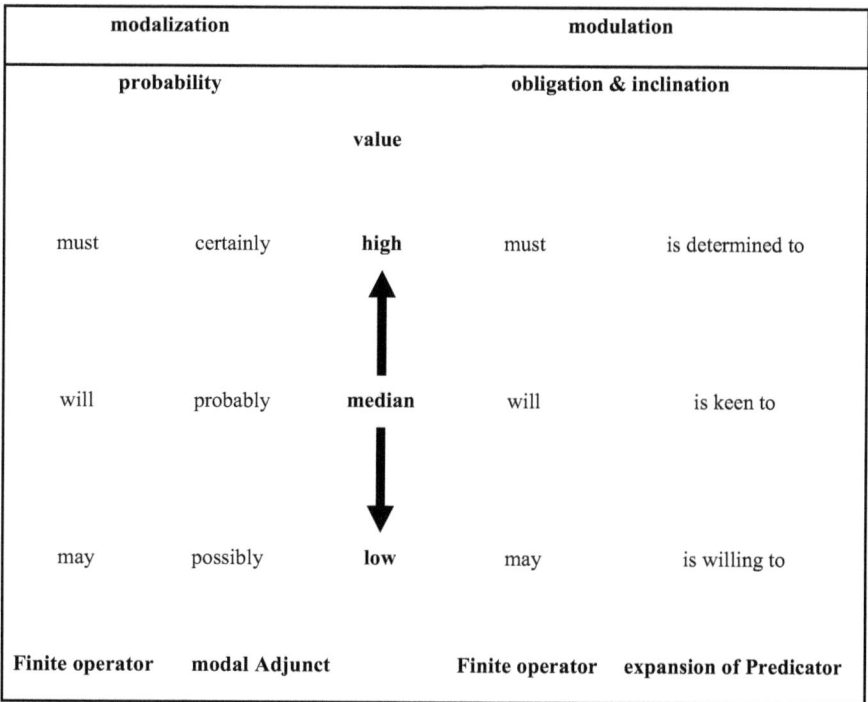

modalization			modulation	
probability			**obligation & inclination**	
		value		
must	certainly	**high**	must	is determined to
will	probably	**median**	will	is keen to
may	possibly	**low**	may	is willing to
Finite operator	**modal Adjunct**		**Finite operator**	**expansion of Predicator**

Table 7.1 SFL categories of modality adapted from Halliday and Matthiessen (2014: 691)

Thompson (2004: 69) points out that, although considered paramount in scrutinizing how far the language user is responsible for what she conveys, these scalar points should be viewed in terms of delicacy as intermediate points with a variation within the same region, rather than as absolute ones. For instance, in an **epistemic** sense, the Finite modal operator *will* can be considered extremely close to the scalar point occupied by *must*, as in '*John will have arrived by now*', compared to '*John must have arrived by now*'.

In comparison to English, in which modality is 'highly grammaticalized' as it develops into a small set of modal auxiliaries that share formal features and their 'periphrastic correspondents' (i.e. '*can – be able to*') (Halliday and Matthiessen 2014: 183–4), MSA does not have such a distinct grammatical category, but certainly employs different strategies to express interpersonal meanings of modality, among which are lexical verbs and prepositional phrases:

Example 7.1[3]

خطط [...]	عن	السياسات	صانعو	يكشف	أن	من المحتمل	إذ
ḥiṭṭin **plans**	ʕan about	al-siyāsāti the-policies	ṣāniʕū maker-(plural)	yakšifa discover	ʔan that	mim al-muḥtamal of-the-probable	ʔiḏ so
Adjunct		Subject		Predicator	–	modal Adjunct: probability	–
			Carrier			Attribute	–
			Rheme			topical/interpersonal Theme [marked]	textual

'So, it is probable that the policy makers reveal plans [...]'

Frequently employed to express modality in MSA, the modal Adjunct *min al-muḥtamal* (of-the-probable [probable/it is probable that]) realized by a prepositional phrase construes a probability meaning. This common strategy is considered congruent and non-metaphorical. In respect of orientation, this clause is represented as explicitly objective, since the source of conviction is explicitly stated by the language producer and does not include a subjective evaluation on his/her part encoded by the use of personal pronouns (Halliday and Matthiessen 2014: 181). Furthermore, the modal Adjunct *min al-muḥtamal* (of-the-probable [probable/it is probable that]) realizing the proposition here serves as marked Theme in MSA 'relational' clauses. It is assigned as an attributive to other elements in the clause functioning as Carrier. As an equivalent to the TL prepositional phrase *min al-muḥtamal* (of-the-probable [probable/ it is probable that]), the English clause *it is probable that* functioning as an expression of modality realizes explicitly objective propositions in clause nexus. It is deemed a metaphorical realization of *probably* in clause simplex. This English 'relational' clause *it is probable that* is construed/mapped into MSA 'at phrase level', rather than at clause rank, by a propositional phrase (i.e. *min al-muḥtamal*) in clause simplex (Bardi 2008: 505).

In English, the notion of indeterminacy is characteristic to the modal auxiliaries (Coates 1983: 9); that is, one particular form of the English modal auxiliary such as *will* can carry different shades of meaning (i.e. probability, obligation and inclination meanings). By contrast, this notion is less identified with the MSA modal expressions (Badran 2001: 48; Abdel-Fattah 2005: 44). This, Badran (2001) argues, springs from the fact that most MSA modal expressions that are considered equivalents to the English modal auxiliaries closely correspond to 'the clearer English paraphrase of these relatively' ambiguous Finite modal operators. For instance, the SL modal Adjunct *probably*, which is synonymous with the modal auxiliary *could* in its epistemic meaning, closely concurs to the TL modal Adjunct *min al-muḥtamal* (of-the-probable [probably/it is probable that]) or the Predicator *yuḥtamal* ((be)-probable-(it) [probably/it is probable that]). In this respect, Abdel-Fattah (2005: 44) argues that the paraphrase of the English modal auxiliaries can be one of the fruitful procedures that the translator should adopt to overcome the fussy nature of these finite closed sets of grammatical categories when translating into MSA.

Similarly to English, the determination of the value attached to some MSA modal expressions such as the Predicator *yajib* (must-(it) [must/should]) should not be interpreted as an absolute fixed point on the modality scale. They are highly influenced by the interpretation of the context in which they are employed. For instance, the value of the obligation modal expression *yajib* is unstable and hugely determined by the power relations between the addresser and addressee (Bardi 2008: 116–17). Hence, it is plausible that it is interpreted as expressing low necessity as is the case with an employee addressing a senior official, or a high necessity if the situation is the opposite.

3 Simpson's modal grammar of point of view

Lexicogrammatical realizations of modality form the basis of Simpson's influential narrative viewpoint framework. Modal expressions, Simpson (1993: 51) posits, are not equally dispersed throughout the viewpoint types in narrative texts. For instance, the modal expressions relating to knowledge and perception are prominent in the genre of horror fiction, while, scarce or absent in other types of narrative such as 'hard boiled' detective novels, in which subjective judgment is suppressed (Simpson 1993: 60–1). For instance, his stylistic framework centres around how different categories of point of view on the psychological plane are determined, premised on particular principled linguistic triggers, modality meanings prominent in narrative texts. Such modal characteristics can pertain to the narrating voice in fiction. To facilitate the identification of point of view, Simpson (1993) provides a four-part typology of modality in English, distinguishing two core categories of modality and their closely related peripheral categories: (1) deontic modality and its closely linked, (2) boulomaic modality, (3) epistemic modality and its subcategory and (4) perception modality (the typical linguistic patterns, according to which these types of modality are grammaticized, are shown in Table 7.2).

Table 7.2 Simpson's taxonomy of modality in English (adapted from Simpson 1993: 51)

Modality type	Linguistic manifestation
Deontic (obligation, duty and commitment)	– You **must** leave – It **is possible** for you to leave – you **are obliged** to leave
Boulomaic (desire)	– I hope that you **will** leave – It is hoped that you **will** leave – Hopefully, **you'll** leave
Epistemic (knowledge, belief and cognition)	– You **must** be alright – I **think** you are right – It **is certain** that you're right
Perception (perception)	– It's **clear** that you are right – **Apparently**, you are right – It **appears** you are right

Deontic modality refers to the grammaticization of the language user's varying levels of involvement in setting out degrees of obligation, while boulomaic modality concerns the expression of desire (Simpson 1993: 47). Boulomaic modality is very closely linked to the deontic type in terms of the performativity expressed in a speaker's utterance. That is, the two types of modality imply events performed by the act of speaking (Lyons 1977: 826). By contrast, epistemic modality preoccupies 'the speakers' assumptions or assessment of possibilities and ... indicates the speaker's confidence (or lack of confidence) in the truth of the proposition expressed' (Coates 1983: 18). As for perception modality, building on Perkins (1983: 81), Simpson (1993: 46) contends that the difference between the two lies in 'the fact that the degree of commitment to truth of a proposition is predicated on some reference to human perception, normally visual perception.' In other words, this type of modality designates that the language producer makes his/her judgement premised upon sensory evidence, upon what is being or 'has been observed' (Palmer 2001: 36). Although best considered a subsystem of epistemic modality, perception modality is distinguished in Simpson's account, since it is a fundamental linguistic resource for registering the external or internal narratorial point of view.

As can be seen, Simpson's categories of modality are broadly associated with those of SFL. The deontic and boulomaic categories are closely correspondent with modulation, while epistemic and perception modalities are linked to modalization. It is important to point out, however, that the analysis will be based on SFL modality types rather than embracing fully Simpson's taxonomy, which appears to be selective and of a condensed nature, simply because the study adopts the SFL framework for the examination of the ST–TT pair. Another reason is that the SFL account of modality can aid in the investigation of values attached to different modal expressions. This can be of significance in checking how degrees of commitments to the truth-value of propositions and states of affairs, on part of the I-narrator, are treated in translation. Finally, as mentioned above, leaning on the SFL framework adds a certain degree of objectivity, particularly to the process of selecting the lexicogrammatical elements for conducting a comparative analysis.

Now let us see how Simpson's four-part typology of modality can help designate the types of point of view on the psychological plane in a literary text. In his point of view framework, Simpson (1993: 50) divides the narrative mode into two main categories: Category A and Category B. Category A is a first-person-oriented mode in which the narrator is located within the story, while Category B is a third-person-oriented mode. Here, I will limit myself to the Category A narrative, since it is manifested in the ST. This category is further split into three basic subdivisions on the ground of the types of modal patterning distinguished: *positive shading, negative shading* and *neutral shading modalities* (Simpson 1993: 50–1). Fictional narratives with positive shading (A+ve) are dominated by deontic and boulomaic modal expressions, whereas epistemic and perception modalities are absent. In SFL terms, A+ve form is marked by the presence of obligation and inclination systems, while the probability system is not prominent. These narrative texts thus foreground the narrator's desires, duty and obligation, as regards the actions, events and other characters. They are also rich in generic sentences that hold 'universal or timeless references'; in *verba sentiendi* (verbs denoting thoughts, feelings and perceptions) such as *feel, suffer*, and so on; and in evaluative adjectives and adverbs (Simpson 1993: 36, 52). On the other hand, the epistemic and perception modal expressions, the probability system in SFL sense, are predominant in narrative texts with negative shading (A–ve) exhibiting estranging features and bewilderment. These narrative texts are additionally (Simpson 1993: 58) abundant in 'words of estrangement' (Uspensky 1973: 85) such as *seem, appear* and *as if*, which signal the narrator's limited knowledge. The final subcategory (Category A neutral) is concerned with neutrally shaded fictional narratives that are marked with a total absence of narratorial modality; unmodalized categorical assertions are dominant throughout these texts. Although scarce, such fictional narratives are characterized as objective forms of narration. Evincing no trace of subjective assessment on actions or other characters, the participant character aims to provide a physical description rather than the psychological one. It is worth mentioning that these subcategories are not mutually exclusive and may co-exist in narrative texts. In the remaining sections, the discussion will centre around the TT renderings of the ST modal patterns and their implications for shifting the ST psychological point of view.

4 Quantitative findings

The difference in the total number of modal expressions between the original and Al-Ḥājj Ḥusayn's translation (TT1) is slight; on the other hand, there is a notably higher number in ʕabdullāh's (TT2), with eighty-five TL modal expressions added as shown in Figure 7.1.

The ST expressions subsumed under the probability system are outnumbered by those of other modality systems. In large part, this may be attributed to the choice of simultaneous present as the narrative tense. The narrator-character has no privilege to 'survey the whole field of action in a synoptic manner in light of later developments

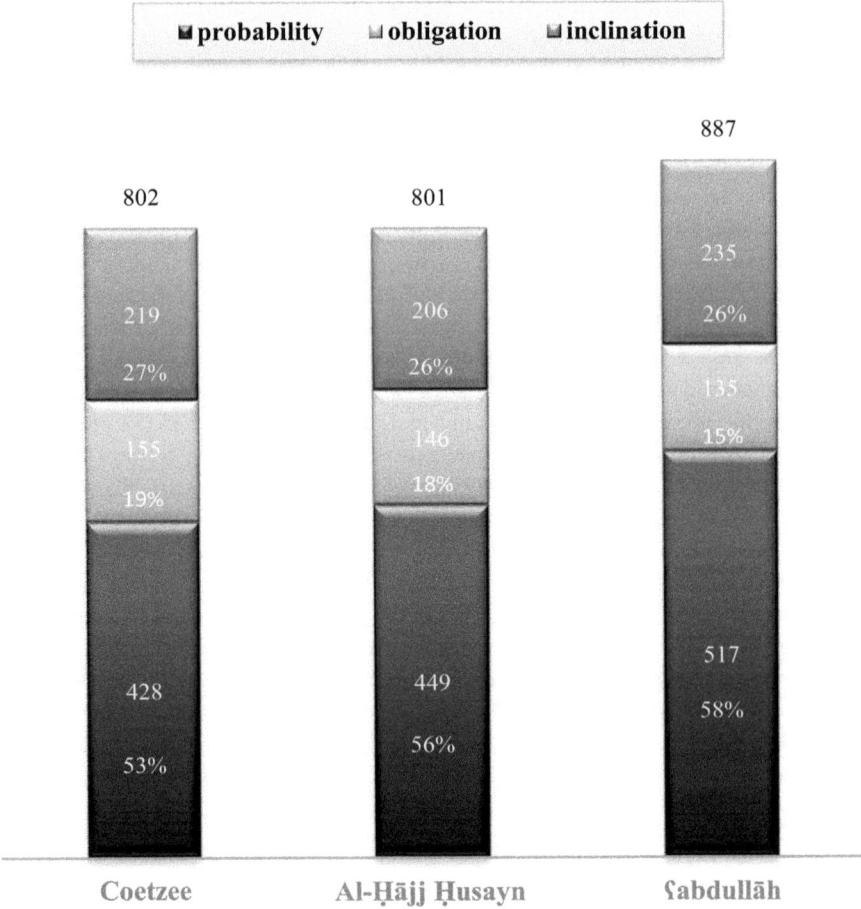

Figure 7.1 Distribution of modality systems in ST and TTs.

and final out-comes' (Margolin 1999: 51). Instead, his/her limited knowledge results in grounding the narrative propositions as they relate to the events and actions in the realm of uncertainty between positive and negative polarity. That is, at the moment of narration the events are not yet concluded because of the employment of on-the-scene reporting narrative technique. This explains why the narrator-character lacks a degree of confidence in the commitment to the truth-value of the propositions. TT1 and TT2 both feature more epistemically modalized utterances, amounting to fifteen and eighty-three occurrences, respectively. It thus appears that this aspect of uncertainty is over-determined in the two translated texts. On the other hand, the two TTs reveal reductionist propensities in the rendition of ST expressions of the obligation and inclination systems. By contrast, TT2 exhibits more reduction in modal obligation expressions, with 135 instances in comparison to 155 of the ST as well as to the 146 of the TT1. These numbers suggest that the narrator-character's capabilities and duties are less stressed in translation. The same observation is also reported by Bosseaux (2007: 187), who finds that Wajsbrot's French translation of Virginia Woolf's *The Waves* undermines the reflector's personal obligations, capacities and abilities, and therefore the shading of the original text is affected.

While it is true that the increase in the total number of the modal expressions in TT2 discernibly implicates the presence of shifts, this is unclear in TT1, which shows only one omission. However, it is this discrepancy in the frequency of the modality systems in the ST and TTs that undoubtedly signifies the existence of shifts that can be attributed to the translator's stylistic preferences and interpretation. Hence, it is very useful to examine the translation of each individual occurrence of the ST modal expressions in order to identify the recurrent patterns occurring in the two TTs. This will be the focus of the next section.

5 Types of modality shifts

On a closer inspection of the ST and TTs modal patterns, not all the translation shifts recorded may be interpreted as **optional shifts**, which are regarded as unnecessary deviations from the ST modal patterns, since they are attributed to the translators' propensities and stylistic preferences (Bakker, Koster and van Leuven-Zwart 2008: 271). There are also **obligatory shifts** registered, which are inevitable alterations to the ST modal patterns as a result of the systemic differences between the two languages; thus, they cannot be considered to be indicators of the two translators' stylistic inclination and linguistic repertoire. The analysis shows that a very small number of obligatory shifts is found in the two TTs, amounting to one percent in each, in contrast to those of the optional type. TT1 exhibits a higher number of optional shifts, amounting to almost thirty percent, as opposed to the slightly smaller number of optional shifts, namely 202 (22%) in TT2.

Examination of the obligatory shifts indicates that the two translators either render the ST categorical assertions as modalized utterances or leave out the ST modal expressions, as these additions and omissions are necessitated by the formal differences between the two languages. These motivated shifts can be classified into two categories:

1. Omission of the modal auxiliary *will*.
2. Lack of grammatical categories in the TL that correspond to those of the SL.

In each TT, there are only five obligatory shifts each that fall under the first category; whilst all the remaining shifts in each TT are subsumed under the second category. With regard to the omission of the modal auxiliary *will*, there is some flexibility in either preserving or omitting the SL future operator in MSA. It is very likely that in MSA making a prediction or assumption about future events may be (though not necessarily) expressed without recourse to the use of the operator *sawfa* or its abridged form *sa* (will/would). The interpretation of an MSA utterance as a future does not always require the presence of the particle, because the use of the imperfect form of the verb can be adequate for making such a modal judgement (Bahloul 2008: 113).

There is also a strong link between the omission of the MSA future operators and the existence of lexicalized futurity expressions such as the circumstantial Adjunct of time *ġadan* (tomorrow). The more these lexicalized expressions are attendant in the clauses, the more the MSA user leaves out the future operator (ibid.). However, it is also possible to use these operators regardless of whether the proposition contains lexicalized futurity references (Abu-Chacra 2007: 109). By contrast, the lack of TL correspondent grammatical categories leads to the rendering of the ST categorical assertions as qualified factual statements. It is noticeable that the two translators, for example, expand the ST lexical item *unimaginable* and *unidentifiable* that include the morphemes *able*, into modalized hypotactic clauses as *la yumkin taḥyyulahā* (not (be)-probable-(it) imagining-it [it cannot be imagined]) and *la yumkin al-taʕarruf ʕalyyhā* (not (be)-probable-(it) [it cannot be recognized]). It is quite possible that their choices stem from the fact that MSA lacks this grammatical category that corresponds to the ST. Thus, their options are regarded as obligatory shifts.

Nevertheless, it should be noted that not every omission of the modal auxiliary *will* in its probability sense can be accounted for as an inevitable change of the ST modal instance in this study. In fact, the omission of *will* might obscure the interpretation of the ST modal meaning.

Example 7.2 (ST Coetzee 2004: 97)
It **will** only bring disgrace on my warders.
Example 7.2a (Al-Ḥājj Ḥusayn 2004: 126)

حراسي.	بحق	عار	هذا
ḥurāsī	biḥqi	ʕārn	hāḏā
guards-my	with-right	disgrace	this
	Adjunct	Complement	Subject
		Residue	Mood
'This is a disgrace for my guards.'			

Here, as a translation of the English ST utterance, the translator opts for a nominal-initial segmentation that does not include a predicator/relational process. In doing so, he omits the ST Process *will bring*; its rendering may help the readers to interpret the truth-value of the ST proposition. So, the TT clause does not contain any imperfective form that might be crucial to express the prediction (Bahloul 2008: 113). What also contributes to the blurring of the interpretation of the ST clause is the absence of any lexicalized futurity expressions. Such a shift can be described as an optional rather than an obligatory one. Likewise, it is not always the case that wherever an English morpheme *-able* is suffixed to a lexical item it is turned into a modalized utterance in the TTs. In fact, the two translators adopt other strategies when dealing with such cases: by the omission of the ST lexical items or the use of the MSA expression *ġayr qabil* 'not susceptible/liable to' as a translation of the morpheme. This is the reason behind the fact that the total numbers of the obligatory shifts are very slightly different in the two translations.

5.1 Categories of optional modality shifts

The analysis of the translation of the ST modal expressions, as mentioned above, shows that more than twenty percent of the two TT modal expressions are shifted. It also represents recurrent patterns of shifts, which can be grouped under four different types: (1) demodalization; (2) inserted modal; (3) inter-modal and (4) and intra-modal shifts. The frequencies for the occurrences of each type of shift are shown in Figure 7.2. In the following subsections, the discussion will revolve around each type of shift, mainly to identify the modality systems that involve more shifts, uncover major trends in the translational changes and the nature of the modal expressions that are problematic in translation.

5.1.1 Demodalization shift

This type designates instances of shifts where the ST modalized utterances are rendered as purely categorical assertions. It also involves all instances where the ST-qualified utterances or modal expressions are left out in translation. Generally, the TT1 comprises a relatively higher number of demodalization shifts, amounting to 114 (50%) occurrences, in contrast to the TT2, which registers sixty-four (32%) instances, as shown in Figure 7.2. The analysis shows a clear disparity between the two translators in terms of the retention of the different ST modality systems. This type of shift is particularly manifested in the modal expressions that belong to the probability and the inclination systems, whilst there is a small number of occurrences in the obligation system. The TT1 comprises fifty-four shifts of demodalization that occur in the probability system and forty-one other occurrences in the inclination system, in contrast to the TT2 which has thirty-six and nineteen occurrences in the probability and inclination systems, respectively. In the two TTs, there is also a small number of occurrences (one in the TT1 and five in the TT2) where the whole qualified ST clauses, which include modal operators, are not rendered.

Through the examination of the demodalization shifts, it becomes apparent that most of these shifts are related to the positioning of the modal expressions within the ST clauses; that is, more than half the total number of demodalization shifts occur in the modal expressions located within the hypotactic-related clauses. This reveals a truncation trend since the two translators seemingly aim to reduce the ST clauses in translation by deleting modal expressions alongside other ST lexical items. The ST clauses appear to be less condensed in translation. Thus, it can be posited that in the present data, the more complex the ST structure, the more it is trimmed in the TTs, and the more modal expressions are omitted. The most deleted ST modal expressions are modal auxiliaries, totalling more than half of the demodalization shifts in the TTs, whereas this category of shift occurs less in the other modal expressions. The omission of the modal auxiliary *can* registers the highest occurrences among other modal auxiliaries. Overall, there are forty-one omissions of *can* in the TT1: thirty-five of *can* in its ability sense and six in its probability sense. By contrast, TT2 omits twenty-four occurrences of *can*, eighteen of which express ability meanings while the remainder carry probability meanings. TT1 shows an inclination to leaving out the

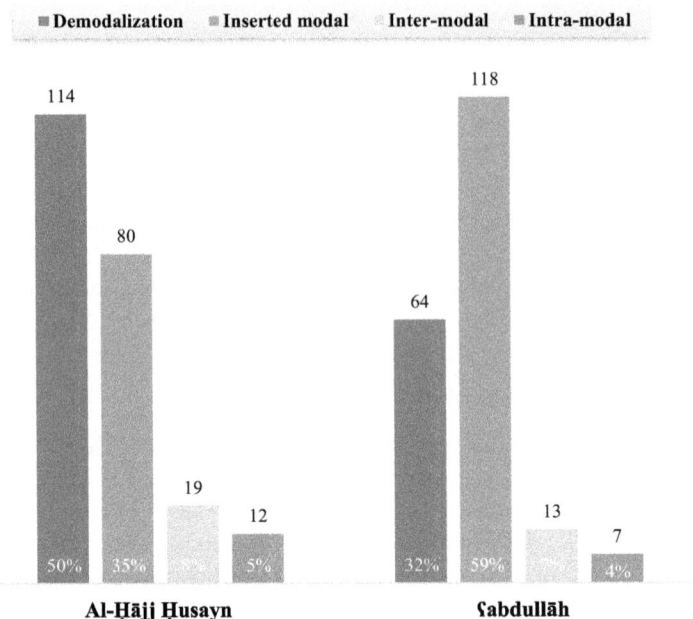

Figure 7.2 Frequency of types of modality optional shifts.

modal auxiliary *can* in the clauses that involve either mental processes of perception and recognition (e.g. *see* and *know*) or processes lying on its fringes (behavioural processes), as exemplified in Example 7.3.

Example 7.3 (ST Coetzee 2004: 107)
[…] I [Finite:] can [Process: mental:] see two boys quietly playing marbles under the mulberry trees.
Example 7.3a (Al-Ḥājj Ḥusayn 2004: 138)

التوت	شجر	تحت	الكلة	يلعبان	ولدين	أرى […]
al-tūti the-mulberry	šajri trees	taḥta under	al-kalata the-marbles	yalʕabān play-dual-(they)	waladyyn boy-dual	ʔara saw-(I)
	Adjunct		Complement	Predicator-Subject	Complement	Predicator-(Subject)
Location: spatial			Scope	material process	Actor	mental process-(Sensor)
'I saw two boys playing marbles under the mulberry trees.'						

Here the ST includes a mental process of perception (i.e. *see*) preceded by the modal auxiliary: the abilitive expression *can*, while in its TT counterpart, the ST modal expression is not rendered. In particular, out of the total number of demodalization occurrences in the ST modal auxiliary *can* (thirty-five), there are nineteen occurrences in which the ST clauses involve mental or behavioural processes. By contrast, the TT2 is more consistent in retaining this ST modal auxiliary with mental or behavioural process clauses, as only three instances of omission are found. It is also noted that this is the case with other ST modal auxiliaries (i.e. nine occurrences of omission in the TT1, while six occurrences are to be found in TT2). There are, however, other occasions where the two translators add ability modal expressions when rendering the unmodalized ST mental or behavioural clauses. Hence, it appears that these changes are unsystematic and likely affected by the translators' interpretation of the context and their attempts to create a stylistic effect, as will be discussed in subsection 7.5.1.2.

The MSA preferences for thematizing modal Adjuncts (Anghelescu 1999: 134; Bardi 2008: 191) may constitute a significant factor in the omissions of the ST modal Adjuncts, since they are located within the rhematic stretch of the clause. The data show that in TT1, there are just two out of thirteen omission occurrences in which the modal Adjuncts are not medially or finally positioned. Likewise, the TT2 shows a small number of omissions of the ST modal Adjuncts (four occurrences), all of which are located within the rhematic parts of the ST clauses, except for one occasion. It seems that the omissions of the ST modal Adjuncts/Themes in translation serve to enhance the readability of the TTs.

5.1.2 Inserted modal shift

This type refers to instances of shift, where the ST unmodalized clauses are rendered as modalized ones by the insertion of modal expressions that are non-existent in the ST. The analysis indicates that this kind of shift occurs more in ʕabdullāh's TT compared to Al-Ḥājj Ḥusayn's, accounting for 118 occurrences and eighty occurrences, respectively. More added modal expressions fall under the probability system in the TTs in contrast to other modality systems. The most frequently added modal expression is the emphatic *ʔinna* (indeed/verily), amounting to eighty-four occurrences in the TT2, in contrast to thirty occurrences in the TT1. These additions could be intended to intensify the truth-value of the ST utterances:

Example 7.4 (ST Coetzee 2004: 116)
'**You** are depraving these people!'
Example 7.4a (Al-Ḥājj Ḥusayn 2004: 151)

«الناس.»	هؤلاء	تفسد	إنك»
al-nnāsa	hāʔulaʔ	tūfsdu	ʔinnaka
the-people	these	spoil-(you)	indeed-you
	Complement	Predicator	particle-Subject
'Indeed, you are spoiling these people'.			

As it stands, the ST utterance is qualified in translation, since the translator seemingly attempts to amplify the meaning of the ST messages. In the ST example, the narrator-character stands up against Colonel Joll, who is about to lay down his hammer on the barbarian prisoners; he makes the colonel realize the immorality of his action; that is, he is corrupting the dwellers of the town. So in its TT counterpart, it would be possible to posit that by adding the MSA particle, the translator tries to intensify this ST proposition, emphasizing the villainous side of the colonel. A similar conclusion has been made from the study of German particles in literary translation (Winter 2013). In her parallel corpus that includes Fitzgerald's *The Beautiful and Damned* and its two German TTs, Winter (2013: 438) investigates eight German modal particles and points out that there is a difference in the frequency of modal particles in the two translations, which yields different impacts such as the change of the stress degree in the utterances. In addition, her study reveals that the use of the German modal particle *whol* substantially leads to modification of point of view and explicitly mark superiority in the relationship between the two characters Gloria and Bloeckman (ibid.: 440).

In addition, twenty occurrences of inserted modal shifts in the TT1 and fifteen occurrences in the TT2 are probably employed to enhance the interpretation of the ST clauses; they are added to sustain aspects of the narrator-character's narrative discourse, while highlighting more involvement on the part of the narrator-character. At the same time, they can provide the TL reader with what seems to be a better understanding of the ST narrative scene. The following examples can provide an opportunity to examine the enhancement of the ST interpretations:

Example 7.5 (ST Coetzee 2004: 95)
'Ssh,' I say, 'I will keep you warm.'
Example 7.5a (Al-Ḥājj Ḥusayn 2004: 165)

||| «سأدفئك» ||	سأدفئك،	هس « ||	همست |||
sa-ʔudafiʔuki	sa-ʔudafiʔuki	hus	hamastu
will-warm-you-(I)	will-warm-you-(I)	huss	whispered-(I)
Operator-Predicator-(Subject)	Operator-Predicator-(Subject)	-	Predicator-(Subject)

I whispered: 'Sssh, I will warm you, I will warm you.'

Example 7.6 (ST Coetzee 2004: 106)
I flatten myself [...]
Example 7.6a (ʕabdullāh 2004: 138)

نفسي [...]	أبسط	أن	علي
nafsī	ʔūbsiṭa	ʔan	ʕalayya
self-my	flatten-(I)	that	on-me
Complement	Predicator-(Subject)	-	modal Adjunct
'I must flatten myself [...].'			

The willingness of the narrator-character is reinforced in Example 7.5a, in which the TT modalized clause as a translation of that of the ST 'I will keep you warm' is repeated. It seems as if the translator attempts to add a dramatic sense to the scene by stressing the I-narrator's volitive act of continuing to keep the barbarian girl warmed. In the remaining TT Example (7.6a), the I-narrator straightens his body under the bed in order to remain hidden. Again, this situation is intensified in the translation by inserting a sense of obligation that emanates from within the I-narrator himself; he is obliged to flatten himself, otherwise he will be discovered.

There is a small number of other modal addition shifts in the TTs frequencies, such as the translator's choice of creating a stylistic effect by repeating the ST modal expression of ability:

Example 7.7 (ST Coetzee 2004: 96)
Some of what is said I can hear clearly.
Example 7.7a (ʕabdullāh 2004: 127)

بوضوح |||	سماعه	أستطيع |||	ما قيل،]]	[[بعض]]	سماع	أستطيع |||
bi-wūḍūḥn	samāʕahu	ʔastaṭīʕu	Qīla mā	baʕḍa	samāʕa	ʔastaṭīʕu
with-clarity	hearing-it	(be)-able-(I)	said-(it) that	some	hearing	(be)-able-(I)
Adjunct	Complement	Predicator-(Subject)	Complement			Predicator-(Subject)
Residue		Mood	Residue			Mood
Rheme		Theme	Rheme			Theme
'I can hear some of what is said; I can clearly hear it.'						

In translated Example 7.7a, the addition of the Predicator *ʔastaṭīʕu* (be-able-(I) [I can/I am able to]) is probably construed as an endeavour to create a stylistic effect of rhetorical parallelism (Hatim and Munday 2019: 51). The translator opts for the inclusion of the TT modal expression *ʔastaṭīʕu* at the beginning of the TT clause. This choice sacrifices the ST-marked thematic option in order to repeat the lexical item *ʔastaṭīʕu* (be-able-(I) [I can/I am able to]), a device that exerts a rhetorical impact by creating a parallel structure (Dickins, Hervey and Higgins 2002: 108–9). Other occurrences (four), can probably be attributed to mistranslation on the part of the translator. For instance, in his letter to the provincial governor, the narrator-character explains his purposes in undertaking a visit to the barbarians' territory. The ST purposive clause (*to repair some of the damage*)[4] included in the letter is mistranslated, since its TT equivalent utterance is made to express a medium obligation that the provincial governor is commended by the narrator-character to fix the crack in the relationship with the barbarians: *ʕalyyka ʔiṣlāḥ baʕḍa al-ʔaḍrār* (on-you repairing some the-damages [you should repair some of the damage]).

5.1.3 Inter-modal and Intra-modal Shifts

The inter-modal type of shift occurs when an ST modal expression is translated into another different modality system. The intra-modal type of shift, by contrast, occurs within the same modality system, either altering the intensity of the ST modal expressions or alternating between potentiality/ability and volition in translation. In the two TTs in Figure 7.2, these two categories of shift are not as frequent as the previous two. Analysis shows that there is a slightly higher number of shifts in inter-/intra-modal types in the TT1 (nineteen inter-modal and twelve intra-modal shifts), in contrast to the TT2 (where there are thirteen inter-modal and seven intra-modal shifts). A closer look reveals that the majority of these two types of shift relate to the transference of the ST Finite modal operators such as *can*. This is because the ST modal auxiliaries exhibit semantic indeterminacy (Coates 1983: 9), which most probably presents difficult nuances for the two TT translators, as shown in the following example:

Example 7.8 (ST Coetzee 2004: 93)
How **can** I regard myself as a victim of persecution [...]?
Example 7.8a (Al-Ḥājj Ḥusayn 2004: 121)

الاضطهاد [...] ؟	ضحية	نفسي	أعد	أن	لي	كيف
al-ʔiḍṭihādi	ḍaḥyyta	nafsī	ʔuʕidda	ʔan	li	kyyfa
the-persecution	a victim	self-my	regard-(I)	that	for-me	how
Complement	a victim	Complement	Predicator-	-	modal	Adjunct
			(Subject)		Adjunct	

'How was I permitted to consider myself a victim of persecution [...]?'

TT Example 7.8a involves an inter-modal shift, showing misinterpretations of its ST counterpart. The ST instance is presented as a proposal, a state of affairs. The ST Finite modal operator *can* that holds a sense of probability is altered in translation since its TT equivalent modal Adjunct *li* (for-me [I was permitted to]) is subsumed under the obligation system. There are three other occasions in TT1 where the ST interrogative clauses, starting with the how-element and involving different modal auxiliaries of probability (*must* and *could*) are consistently rendered as interrogative clauses expressing obligation meanings and using the same TL modal Adjunct *li* (for-me [I was permitted to]).

In these two types of shift, it is also found that the ST modal expressions of the probability system are altered the most in the TTs. There are eleven occurrences in TT1 and eight occurrences in TT2, where ST modal expressions subsumed under the probability system are rendered as expressions belonging to the other modality systems, most notably the obligation system. By contrast, the opposite trend, rendering the ST modal expressions from other modality systems into the probability system, occurs infrequently in the two TTs. There are also three occasions where the ST modal auxiliaries *can* and *could* in their probability senses are translated as ability expressions in TT2; there is one occurrence in TT1. Similarly, the intra-modal shifts in TT2 alter the degree of the ST modal expressions in the scale of the probability system, except for one occasion, in which the ST willingness expression *would* is transferred as a TL ability one *yumkin* ((be)-possible-it [be able to]). Moreover, TT2 exhibits slightly more shifts of the ST high-value modal expression into low values. Likewise, the majority of intra-modal shifts (eight out of twelve occurrences) in TT1 affect ST probability expressions. As for the remaining occurrences, three are identified in the ST obligation expressions of low value rendered as expressions of high command; and on one occasion, the ST ability expression *can* is translated as a TL *sa* operator (will/would), expressing willingness.

6 Psychological point of view in translation

In this section, I will consider the effects of modality shifts on altering the ST psychological point of view in translation. The discussion will concern three representative examples that contribute to setting the ST fictional world distinctly apart from that of the TTs:

Example 7.9 (ST Coetzee 2004: 92)

I think about him a great deal in the solitude of my cell [...] Vain, hungry for praise, [Carrier + Process + Attribute: interpersonal metaphor:] I **am sure** [...] Who dreams that one of these days he [Finite: probability:] **will** put his foot on my throat and press. And I? I find it hard to hate him in return. The road to the top [Finite: probability] **must** be hard for young men without money, without patronage, with the barest of schooling, men who [Finite: probability:] **might** as easily go into lives of crime as into the service of the Empire (but what better branch of service [Finite: probability:] **could** they choose than the Bureau!).

Example 7.9a (Al-Ḥājj Ḥusayn 2004: 121–2)

translation	فكرت/ فيه/ مطولا/ عبر/ عزلتي/ في/ الزنزانة [...].[...]، || مغرور/، متعطش/للمديح || أنا/ واثق/ من/ ذلك [...] / || وهو/ || / [...] || أنا/ وأنا؟|| /واو/ || [Operator: probability:] /يحلم/ || أنه سيضع/ قدمه/ على/ حلقي || و/ يضغط/ || . /واو/ || فالطريق/ إلى/ القمة/ صعبة/للشباب/ المفلسين/ || ومن/ الصعب/ أن/ أبادله/ الكراهية/ || . /وجدت/ دون شك/،/ [[[الذين/ لا/ أحد/ يتبناهم/، || و/ الذين/ لا/ رصيد/ لهم/ [modal Adjunct: probability:] إلى/ عري/ المدرسة/]]]. ||| إنهم/ الرجال/[[[الذين/ يدخلون/ في/ عالم/ الجريمة || كما/ يدخلون/ في/ خدمة/ الإمبراطورية/]]]. ||| (و/ لكن/ أي/ خدمة/ أفضل/ من/ خدمة/ المكتب/ الثالث/). ||
transliteration	|| fakkrtu/ fīhi/ muṭwaln/ ʕabra/ ʕuzlaty/ fī/ al-zinzānti [...]. || || maġrūrn/ mutaʕṭṭšn li-lmadīḥi. || || **ʔanā/ wāṯqn/** min/ ḏalika [...]. || || ||| wa/ huwa/ yaḥlumu/ || ʔannhu **sayadaʕu/** qadamahu/ ʕala/ ḥallqy/ || wa/ yad̲g̲ṭu/. ||| || wa/ ʔanā/ʔ || ||| wajadtu/ || min/ al-ṣaʕbi/ ʔan/ ʔubadilahu/ al-karāhyyta/. ||| ||| fa-al-ṭarīqu/ ʔila/ al-qimmti/ ṣaʕbatn/ li-al-šabābi/ al-muflisīni/ **dūna šak/**, [[[alldīna/ la/ ʔahda/ yatabanāhum/, || wa/ alldīna/ la /raṣīda/ lahum/ ʔila/ ʕurray/ al-madrasti/]]]. ||| ||| ʔannahum/ al-rrijalu/ [[[alldīna yadḫulūna/ fī/ ʕālami/ al-jarīmati/ || kamā/ yadḫulūna/ fī/ ḫidmmti/ al-ʔimbrāṭūryyati/]]]. ||| || (wa/ lākin/ ʔaay/ ḫidmmt/ ʔafḍala/ min/ ḫidmmti/ al-maktabi/ al-ṯṯālaṯi/). ||

gloss	|| thought-(I)/ in-him/ long/ through/ solitude-my/ in/ the-cell/ […]. || || conceited/, thirsty/ for/ praise/. || || **I/ sure**/ from/ that/ […]. || || and/ dreamt-(he) || that-(he)/ [modal-Particle-Predicator-Subject] **would-put-(he)**/ foot-his/ on/ throat-my/, || and/ press-(he) ||||. || and/ I? || |||| found-(I)/ || from/ the-difficulty/ that/ shared-(I)/ the-hatred/. |||| || and-the-way/ to/ the-top/ difficult/ for-the-young/ broken-(they)/ [modal Adjunct:] without doubt/, || who/ *la* = negative particle/ body/ adopt-them-(they)/]], || who/ *la* = negative particle/ balance/ to-them/ to/ nakedness/ the-school/]]. |||| || Indeed-they/ the-men/ [[[who/ entered-they/ in/ world/ the-crime/ || as/ entered-they/ in/ service/ the-empire]]]. || (and/ which/ service/ better/ from/ service/ office/ the-third). ||
back-translation	I thought of him for long through my solitude in the cell […] conceited, thirsty for praise. **I was sure** of that […] And he was dreaming that he **would put** his foot on my throat and press. And I? I found it hard to reciprocate hatred. The way to the top was difficult for broke people without doubt, whom no body patronized and who were without money to the nakedness of the school. Indeed, they are men who entered the world of crime and they entered the service of the empire. (And but which service was better than the service of the Third Bureau).

The ST excerpt clearly illustrates A–ve form, as there is a proliferation of probability meanings realized non-congruently by a projecting relational clause (*I am sure*) and congruently by modal auxiliaries (*will, must, might* and *could*), which reflect various scalar points along the continuum of the probability system. The presence of the likelihood markers in this passage, moving from strong to lesser conviction, undermine the factuality of the description proffered by the narrator-character in relation to the narrative existents. In other words, the I-narrator's report is perceived as less real. It is characterized by his predicated knowledge about the officer's traits (e.g. *hungry for praise*), and about the young people of Empire who descend into a world of criminality by electing to serve the Third Bureau. The ST nuance, however, is obviously under-represented in translation. Its TT counterpart yields a slightly different depiction of the ST excerpt. A few epistemic choices are offered through the relational projecting clause *ʔanā wāṯqn min ḏalika* (I sure from it [I am sure of it]), the operator *sa* (will/would) and the modal Adjunct *dūna šak* (below doubt [without a doubt]). The translator opts for the omission of the ST modal auxiliaries *might* and *could* towards the end of the TT passage, which presents the narrator-character's full confidence in his propositions. That is, the ST narrative clauses relating the young people of the Empire are given as categorical assertions in the TT. Accordingly, this choice helps lessen the uncertainty of the I-narrator, as he is enabled to relate unquestionable facts. The negative shading of the original is therefore reduced in translation.

The creation of a different picture of the narrator-character's involvement can also be recognized in the following examples:

Example 7.10 (ST Coetzee 2004: 104)
I walked into that cell a sane man […] however incompetent I continue to find myself to describe what that cause [Finite: probability:] **may** be.

Example 7.10a (Sabdullāh 2004: 137)

translation	||| سرت/ إلى/ داخل/ الزنزانة/ رجلاً/ سليم/ العقل/ [...]. ||| ||| مهما/ كنت/ غير/ كفء،/ || فإنني/ أواصل/ الحكم/ على/ نفسي/[[[لوصف/ || ماذا/ [:Predicator: obligation] **يجب**/ أن/ تكون/ تلك/ القضية [[[.|||
transliteration	||| surtu/ ʔila/ dāḫli al-zinzānti/ || rajulan/ salīma al-ʕaqli/ [...]. ||| mahmā/ kuntu/ ġayra/ kufʔin/ || fa-ʔinnany/ ʔuwāṣilu/ al-hukma/ ʔala/ nafsī/ [[li-waṣf/ māḏa/ **yajib**/ ʔan/ takūna/ tilka/ al-qaḏyyata/]]. |||
gloss	||| walked-I/ to/ inside/ the-cell/ || a man/ sound/ the-mind/ [...]. ||| ||| whatsoever/ to-be-I/ not/ competent/ || indeed-I/ continue-(I)/ the-judgment/ on/ self-my/ [[[for-description/ || what/ [Predicator: obligation] **must-(it)**/ that/ to-be/ that/ the-case/]]]. |||
back-translation	I walked into the cell a man of a sound mind, [...] regardless if I was incompetent, I am continuing judging myself for describing what the cause **must** be.

Example 7.11 (ST Coetzee 2004: 81)

Let them enjoy their feast. [quasi-modal operator:] **Let** me not hinder them from imagining it is my throat they cut.
Example 7.11a (Sabdullāh 2004: 108)

translation	||| [:particle: permission] **فـل**/يستمتعوا/ بوليمتهم/، || [:Predicator: obligation] **يجب**/ ألا/ يشعروا/ || أنني/ منعتهم/[[من/ التخيل/ [[أن/ ما/ قطعوه/ هو/ حلقي**/** [[. |||
transliteration	||| [particle: permission:] fa-**li**-yastamtiʕū bi-walīmatihim/, || [Predicator: obligation:] **yajib**/ ʔanla/ yašʕirū || ʔannany/ manʕtuhum/ [[min/ al-taḫayyuli/ [[ʔann/ mā/ qaṭaʕūhu/ huwa/ ḫallqy/]]. |||
gloss	||| and-let-enjoy-they/ feast-their/ || **must-they**/ that-not/ felt-they/ that-I/ prevented-them/ [[from/ the-imagining/ [[that/ what/ cut-they/ he/ throat-my/]]. |||
back-translation	And let them enjoy their feast. They **must** not feel that I prevented them from imagining that what they cut was my throat.

The ST Example 7.10 is presented as a proposal, a state of affairs in translation. Showing a misinterpretation of the ST modalized utterance, TT Example 7.10a, involves an inter-modal shift. A TL obligation expression of high-value *yajib* (must-(it)/(be) necessary for [must]) is selected as a translation of the ST modal auxiliary *may* in its probability sense; an alternative would be the TL modal Adjunct *rubbma* (perhaps) that expresses probability, and would then be equivalent to the ST modal expression. Here the deviation into a model of obligation in the TT proffers a different reading. Whilst the ST example foregrounds the consciousness of the narrator-character, conveying a negative feeling in respect of the narrative existents, its TT counterpart bestows positive prominence to his. Put differently, in the ST the indeterminacy of the narrator-character, shown in his slight doubtfulness as to the cause, is the very opposite of the TT, which projects the explicit commitment to bring about certain courses of action.

The other TT example exhibits an intra-modal shift. The ST modal expression in Example 7.11 that occupies one pole of necessity is shifted in translation towards the other pole. The interpersonal meaning of permission realized by the quasi-modal auxiliary *let* is rendered as a modal expression of high value *yajib* (must-(it)/(be) necessary for [must]), conveying an inescapable duty, apparently because the translator aims to avoid repeating the MSA particle *la* that conveys permission and thus monotony. Interestingly, the translator not only shifts the intensity of the ST modal expression but also ascribes the obligation to the other characters, his companions, rather than to the narrator-character. The overall effect of the intra-modal shift does not radically transform the shading of the ST in translation. The TT Example 7.10a shows A+ve as approximate as that of the ST, manifested through the use of modal expressions of obligation *yajib* (must-(it)/(be) necessary for [must]), *li-yastamtiʕū* (let-enjoy-they [let them enjoy]) and *verba sentiendi yaʃʕirū* (they felt), However, the shift represents varying degrees of the narrator-character's involvement in his fictional universe, as a stronger form of modal expressions is adopted in translation. This, in turn, affects the ST point of view on the psychological plane, leading to a blurring of the ST fictional world in translation.

7 Conclusion

This study has sought to explore the rendition of ST modal expressions realizing the psychological viewpoint. It has shown a deviation in translation from the ST modal patterns. The overwhelming majority of shifts are located in the translation of the ST modal auxiliaries, especially those expressing probability meanings. There is also a tendency towards the omission of the ST modal auxiliary *can* in its ability and probability senses, especially if followed by mental processes of perception and recognition or behavioural processes. Much more work still needs to be done to investigate whether these kinds of omission are the norm in MSA, and whether the MSA users employ fewer modal expressions of ability or any other modality systems in the mental and behavioural clauses than the English language users. The close lexicogrammatical analysis of the original narrative and its translations is of paramount value in foregrounding the inherent ST narrative features. These include the employment of the epistemic elements closely related to the choice of the ST narrative tense. The linguistic analysis reveals the translator's treatment of these narrative features which are subtle but important nuances that present a challenge to be mirrored in translation.

The established modal grammar of point of view links translation shifts at the lexicogrammatical level to that of the global, narrative point of view. The modality shifts identified lead to alteration of the foregrounding in the ST narrative episodes, which in turn affects the immediate experience of the narrator-character and then the ST world of imagination. Useful as it is, it should be acknowledged that the present model chiefly focuses on the linguistic properties in the texts, while other contextual and cognitive properties around the texts remain to be accounted for. In this regard, Simpson (2010: 308) highlights the usefulness of possible integration between stylistic approaches to narrative viewpoint and experimental psychology within the domain of reader response; such a route may lead to a more inclusive model of narrative viewpoint to be applied in future studies.

Notes

1. Coetzee (2004: 112).
2. Coetzee (2004: 121).
3. *ʿal-yurū yattaih ṣawba al-ḥad al-ʔadnā liniṭāqhi hāḏā al-ʕām* ['The Euro Is Heading towards the Minimum Level This Year'] (2019), *Alarabiya.net*, 17 July.
4. Coetzee (2004: 62).

References

ʿal-yurū yattaih ṣawba al-ḥad al-ʔadnā liniṭāqhi hāḏā al-ʕām' ['The Euro Is Heading towards the Minimum Level This Year'] (2019), *Alarabiya.net*, 17 July. Available online: https://www.alarabiya.net/ar/aswaq/financial-markets/2019/07/17/%D8%A7%D9%84%D9%8A%D9%88%D8%B1%D9%88- (accessed 20 July 2019).

ʕabdullāh, ʔ., trans. (2004), *fī ʔintiẓār al-barābira* [*Waiting for the Barbarians*]. By J.M. Coetzee, Casablanca: Al-Markaz Al-Ṯaqafī Al-ʕarbī.

Abdel-Fattah, M. M. (2005), 'On the Translation of Modals from English into Arabic and Vice Versa: The Case of Deontic Modality', *Babel* 51 (1): 31–48.

Abu-Chacra, F. (2007), *Arabic: An Essential Grammar*, London: Routledge.

Al-Ḥājj Ḥusayn, Ṣ., trans. (2004), *fī ʔintiẓār al-barābira* [*Waiting for the Barbarians*]. By J.M. Coetzee, Syria: Dārd Ward li-Ṯibāʕah wa Al-Nnašr.

Anghelescu, N. (1999), 'Modalities and Grammaticalization in Arabic', in Y. Suleiman (ed.), *Arabic Grammar and Linguistics*, 130–42, Richmond: Curzon.

Badran, D. (2001), 'Modality and Ideology in Translated Political Texts', *Nottingham Linguistic Circular* 16 (1): 47–62.

Bahloul, M. (2008), *Structure and Function of the Arabic Verb*, London: Routledge.

Bakker, M., Koster, C. and van Leuven-Zwart, K. (2008), 'Shift', in M. Baker and G. Saldanha (eds), *Routledge Encyclopaedia of Translation Studies*, 2nd edn, 269–73, London: Routledge.

Bardi, M. A. (2008), *A Systemic Functional Description of the Grammar of Arabic*, PhD Thesis, Sydney: Macquarie University.

Bernaerts, L., De Bleeker, L. and De Wilde, J. (2014), 'Narration and Translation', *Language and Literature* 23 (3): 203–12.

Bosseaux, C. (2007), *How Does It Feel?: Point of View in Translation: The Case of Virginia Wolf into French*, Amsterdam: Rodopi.

Coates, J. (1983), *The Semantics of the Modal Auxiliaries*, London: Croom Helm.

Coetzee, J. M. ([1980] 2004), *Waiting for the Barbarians*, London: Vintage.

Dickins, J., Hervey, S. and Higgins, I. (2002), *Thinking Arabic Translation: A Course in Translation Method: Arabic to English*, London: Routledge.

Halliday, M. A. K., and Matthiessen, C. M. I. M. (2014), *Halliday's Introduction to Functional Grammar*, 4th edn, London: Routledge.

Hatim, B., and Munday, J. (2019), *Translation: An Advanced Resource Book*, 2nd edn, London: Routledge.

Hermans, T. ([1996] 2009), 'The Translator's Voice in Translated Narrative', in M. Baker (ed.), *Critical Readings in Translation Studies*, 193–212, London: Routledge.

Hewson, L. (2011), *An Approach to Translation Criticism*, Amsterdam: John Benjamins.

Lyons, J. (1977), *Semantics*, vol. 2, Cambridge: Cambridge University Press.

Margolin, U. (1999), 'Story Modalized, or the Grammar of Virtuality', *GRAAT* 21: 49–61.

Matthiessen, C. M. I. M. (2009), 'Ideas and New Directions', in M. A. K. Halliday and J. Webster (eds), *A Companion to Systemic Functional Linguistics*, 12–58, London: Continuum.

Munday, J. (2008), *Style and Ideology in Translation: Latin American Writing in English*, New York: Routledge.

Palmer, F. R. (2001), *Mood and Modality*, Cambridge: Cambridge University Press.

Perkins, M. R. (1983), *Modal Expression in English*, Norwood, NJ: Ablex Pub. Corp.

Simpson, P. (1993), *Language, Ideology and Point of View*, London: Routledge.

Simpson, P. (2004), *Stylistics: A Resource Book for Students*, London: Routledge.

Simpson, P. (2007), 'Introduction to McIntyre, D., Deixis, Cognitive and the Construction of Viewpoint', in M. Lambrou and P. Stockwell (eds), *Contemporary Stylistics*, 118, London: Continuum.

Simpson, P. (2010), 'Point of View', in D. McIntyre and B. Busse (eds), *Language and Style*, 293–310, New York: Palgrave Macmillan.

Thompson, G. (2004), *Introducing Functional Grammar*, New York: Arnold.

Uspensky, B. (1973), *A Poetics of Composition*, trans. Z. Zavarin and S. Wittig, Berkeley: University of California Press.

van Leuven-Zwart, K. (1989), 'Translation and Original: Similarities and Dissimilarities I', *Target* 1 (2): 151–81.

van Leuven-Zwart, K. (1990), 'Translation and Original: Similarities and Dissimilarities II', *Target* 2 (1): 69–95.

Winter, M. (2013), 'German Modal Particles – from Lice in the Fur of Our Language to Manifestations of Translators' Styles', *Perspective: Studies in Translatology* 21 (3): 427–45.

8

SFL at the heart of translator training: An experimental case study within applied translation studies

Sami Jameel Althumali
Taif University

1 Introduction and background

The absence of an independent SFL module in many Arab universities, and the shortage of experimental research on using SFL as a serviceable tool for translator training and assessment between English and Arabic, calls for a rigorous empirical study. In specific terms, the present experiment situates the concept of a linguistically theoretical background in the context of an applied domain of education and training. For that purpose, four research questions are addressed in this study:

1. To what extent does an awareness of the metafunctional analysis of short English extracts of fiction help the students in the study locate and identify the 'unmotivated' shifts in their own English–Arabic translations?
2. Does knowledge of SFL raise the students' self-awareness as translators and enhance their capabilities to produce more accurate metafunction-based Arabic translations of English fiction?
3. In the SFL-based translator training course, what is the relationship between the two skills of assessing short Arabic translated extracts of English fiction and translating short English extracts of fiction into Arabic?
4. How effective overall is the SFL training model for the students in the study?

The current SFL model dates back to the 1960s and before. Halliday and his followers, influenced by Malinowski, Saussure, Hjelmslev and Firth, used the concept of language function for pedagogic purposes and curriculum design in the field of education, English in particular: 'learning language, learning through language and learning about language', or 'teaching language in use and for use' (Christie 2004: 17–18). Halliday's followers used this (English focused) linguistic model to contribute copiously to many related fields, such as child language development, language education, text and discourse analysis, cohesion, register analysis, corpus and computational linguistics.

In translation, many theoretical perspectives and empirical studies have been inspired by the SFL model. Examples of areas permeated by this linguistic model include, for example, translation quality assessment (House [1977] 1997, 2015), discourse analysis, registers and variations (Hatim and Mason 1990, 1997), thematic system and cohesion in translation (Baker [1992] 2011), interlingual shifts in translation, how metafunctions work in texts, appraisal and mediation in the process of translation (Munday 2002, 2012), the environments of translation, metafunctional considerations in translation (Matthiessen 2001, 2014), textual meaning, translation assessment, translator education, translation error analysis (Kim 2007a, 2007b, 2009, 2010), thematic progression in translation and target readers' reactions to Theme choices (Kim and Huang 2012).

Training, in its broadest sense, is a specific, oriented process that aims at 'preparing people to cope with problems anticipated in advance and amenable to solution by the application of formulae' (Widdowson 1984: 207). Translator training as an applied field of study brings together features from Translation Studies (TS) and education. The key concern raised in the current study is whether the SFL model is a useful tool to improve the accuracy and quality of translation performance in English-to-Arabic translation of fiction. Over forty years ago, Halliday argued that 'my interest in linguistic questions is ultimately an "applied" one, a concern with language in relation to the process and experience of education' (1978: 5). Baker holds a similar view on translation, considering that modern linguistic theory can provide the field of translator training with a guide to decision-making (2011: 4). Support for this opinion is found in Wilss' (2004) claim that, in order to eliminate the danger of subjectivity in TS, researchers should focus on establishing results on which the next generation of researchers and students can build. Conducting this experiment in a university environment is therefore perfectly logical. Malmkjær, to this effect, points out that 'the position of translation programmes in universities implies a strong emphasis on education as well as on training and on research application as well as professional practice' (2004: 2).

2 Approaches to translator training

Research on English–Arabic translator training is rather sparse. However, the three studies discussed below address the field of translator training empirically, the common thread running throughout being the examination of the effectiveness of well-established strategic models. Bnini (2007) examined the general approach of text linguistics in teaching translation. More specifically, he designed his experiment to explore the viability of incorporating context, discourse, register and genre insights into translator training. The study came to the conclusion that text and discourse analyses were useful in understanding the ST more deeply, and thus reducing the presence of unjustifiable literal translations.

Motivated by principles and tools drawn from critical linguistics and discourse analysis, Najjar (2008: ii) set out to design and examine a curriculum for training Arab translators. The overall hypothesis was simply that TS-based theoretical translator training programmes yield better results than do the classical, non-theory-based programmes. The study concluded that 'the more the translator is aware of the grammatical, linguistic, stylistic, situational, and cultural backgrounds the better the performance' (2008: 137). Finally, Mannaa (2011) conducted her experiment on two groups (control and experimental) in two countries (Syria and Jordan) to test the effectiveness of a composite translator training model: Dickins, Hervey and Higgins' (2002) textual matrices and Bolaños' (2002) dynamic translation model, with the aim of measuring the improvement of the performance of English-to-Arabic translation of journalistic texts. Mannaa concluded that the performance of the experimental group improved significantly in English-to-Arabic translation as compared with the control group.

The training approaches adopted in this experiment are somewhat different, centring on the SFL-based knowledge along with its application in translation. Baker clearly points out that theoretical knowledge should not be sought per se unless it is plausibly applied in a practice-motivated environment ([1992] 2011: 2). In the most general terms, theory in training is not a desired outcome by itself, but it is taken as 'a starting point for the adoption of the methods required to ensure continuous learning' (Bartrina 2005: 177). So this experiment merits the use of SFL-based knowledge as a standpoint from which a better understanding of the English text (in this case fiction) can be gained and a better Arabic translation can then be produced.

Two general concepts of translator training work collaboratively in this experimental study: self-awareness and responsibility. These refer to 'the development of students' attitudes towards other translations and, accordingly, to their own translations as well' (Orel 1996: 131). This can be achieved psychologically and textually, argues Orel (1996), using existing translations into the students' L1 (especially literary translations) to stimulate discussion, that is, (i) **psychologically**. In moving from known (the existing translations) to unknown (the production of new translations), students will not be pressurized by existing knowledge, that is, (ii) **textually**. Such discussion will create an empathetic response with the translator's choices as well as the target language readers. In conformity to this view, Hönig states that 'translator training must sharpen self-awareness while at the same time building up students' self-confidence' (1998: 8). Pym (2012) asserts that students should learn how to evaluate information for themselves. In this experiment, this is mirrored through engaging the students in assessment tasks of ascending difficulty in the initial and final exams on the basis of SFL knowledge.

The viewpoint in the current chapter is that an SFL-based training course given to an experimental group, preceded by an initial exam and followed by a final exam, can effectively measure how far the acquaintance of the final-year Arab university students with new linguistic knowledge makes them aspire towards a more effective understanding of the English STs, a more effective assessment ability and more accurate metafunction-based Arabic translations. The approach here is inspired by Matthiessen's (2001: 99) hypothesis that languages are metafunctionally congruent, and that 'there is a high degree of "equivalence" or congruence between languages as far as metafunctions are concerned'. As a consequence, he claims that 'in translation, metafunction tends to be preserved'.

3 Design and methods

The experiment was carried out on two groups: a control group and an experimental group (forty participants in each). The control group did not receive any SFL training, while an experimental group received a 20-hour metafunction analysis and SFL-based translator training. In particular, it should be noted that SFL-based translator training is the only dependent variable of the study. The independent variables are equal: both groups belonged to the same academic level (the final year of undergraduate studies), both studied the same linguistic and translation courses, both were taking an English-to-Arabic translation module at the time of the experiment and neither had been exposed to SFL either in linguistics or translation courses in their BA programme. The variable was the training programme, which the experimental group undertook. There were three main reasons for not designing a 'placement' test in this experiment: the students were already divided into two groups because of their high number; re-dividing the students into two new groups would create too much disturbance to their normal timetable and finally, the effectiveness of the SFL framework at BA level was meant to be explored without paying too much attention to the students' individual differences.

The SFL-based translator training course was designed to achieve several course learning outcomes (CLOs) at three levels: knowledge, skill and competence. Table 8.1 summarizes these CLOs, along with their associated levels, teaching strategies and assessment methods. These CLOs cover the notional, conceptual and practical framework of the course and are closely aligned with the experiment research questions stated above.

The SFL-based translator training programme was ethically approved by the Research and Innovation Service at the University of Leeds, UK (reference PVAR 14-008). The course was taught by the researcher and the content was carefully selected from key references in the field: Halliday and Matthiessen (2014); Eggins (2004); Matthiessen (2001); Kim (2010) and Bardi (2008). Even though there is a paucity of such works in Arabic, Bardi provided an adequate SFL-based description of Arabic grammar.

The initial and final exams involved three types of questions addressing the questions of the experiment and assessing the CLOs at the skill and competence levels. Question 1 was a closed-ended, three-exercise question. It involved two parts: locating and labelling an 'unmotivated' metafunctional translation shift (as argued by Matthiessen 2014) in actual English-to-Arabic translations of fiction. To illustrate, this is an example from the initial exam:

QI) In your opinion, which part of the source text has a major translation mismatch or shift in the target text? Choose from the list below the number identifying the label or type of your choice.

Table 8.1 The CLOs of the translator training course

Level	CLO	Teaching strategies	Assessment methods
Knowledge	1. Defining the basic notions of SFL model (stratification, instantiation, etc).	Lectures (aided by PowerPoint presentations), class discussion, group work, individual work	Assignments and peer evaluation
	2. Describing the various SFL-based ways in which the English STs can be analysed (top-down and bottom-up analyses and the rank scale for the SFG labels).		Assignments and peer evaluation
Skill	3. Dividing short fictional texts into their constituent clause complexes and then into different clause types.		Peer evaluation, teacher's feedback, initial and final exams
	4. Analysing the metafunctions of short English fictional STs.		Peer evaluation, teacher's feedback, initial and final exams
	5. Sketching out the conceptual and organizational resemblance and discrepancy between the description of systems of English and Arabic.		Peer evaluation, teacher's feedback, initial and final exams
	6. Producing more accurate metafunction-based Arabic translations of short English extracts of fiction.		Peer evaluation, teacher's feedback, initial and final exams
Competence	7. Making informed judgements about short selected Arabic translations of English fiction in terms of locating and identifying the translation shifts.		Peer evaluation, teacher's feedback, initial and final exams

The list of labels

1. Participant	2.	Process	3.	Circumstance	
4. Attribute	5.	Tense	6.	Logical Relation (between clauses)	

Here is an illustrative example:

He drove his car fast in the evening.
A B   C   D

هو قاد سيارته بسرعة في المساء.

The part is: [A] *The label is:* [1]

1. The old man was thin and gaunt with deep wrinkles in the back of his neck.
        A   B   C   D

كان الرجل العجوز نحيلًا تنتشر التجاعيد العميقة في أنحاء وجهه.

The part is: [D] *The label is:* [3]

Question 2 marked a further step in the ascending difficulty scale of the exam. Again, it included three exercises. It was a mixture of closed- and open-ended question, involving two parts: choosing the most accurate metafunction-based translation of actual English-to-Arabic translations of fiction and justifying the choice. Here is an example from the final exam:

QII) Circle the most accurate translation in your view. Then briefly justify your choice:

1. *You're with a lucky boat. Stay with them.*
   a. أنت تعمل في مركب ابتسم الحظ لأصحابه. امكث معهم.
   b. ها أنت تعمل في مركب حسن الطالع، فابق مع أصحابك ودعك مني.
   c. أنت مع زورق محظوظ. ابق معهم.
   d. أنت في مركب محظوظ، وأريدك أن تبقى حيث أنت.
      a. You/ work/ in a boat / the luck/ is smiling/ to its owners. / Stay/ with them.
      b. Here/ you/ work/ in a boat / with good fortune/ so/ stay/ with your friends/ and/ be away/ from me.
      c. You/ are/ with a lucky boat. / Stay/ with them.
      d. You/ are/ in a lucky boat/ and/ I/ want/ you/ to stay/ where/ you/ are.

Reason: _____
_____

Question 3 is an open-ended question in the form of translating an English extract of fiction (a short paragraph) into Arabic. An example of this question will be given in Section 6.

4 The procedural framework

A pilot test was carried out on two volunteer Arab students studying for the Translation MA Programme in the School of Languages, Cultures and Societies, the University of Leeds, UK. One student was given a copy of the initial exam and the other a copy of the final exam. The pilot test study was conducted to achieve three purposes related to the test validity and reliability, as suggested by Angelelli (2009: 18):

1. To check the test setting and the physical conditions under which the experimental exams were to be administrated. This was intended to help eliminate problems in reliability and neutralize possible variations in performance related to environmental factors.
2. To check the efficiency of the exam presentation guidelines and instructions given to the participants. The two students were able to understand these instructions. The questions were presented logically, moving from the easiest to the most challenging. This helped to avoid 'unanticipated difficulty for candidates' (2009: 20). Further, the participants were provided with appropriate bilingual dictionaries.
3. To observe the time devoted by each participant to each question as well as checking the adequacy of the time allotted for completing the entire exam. The 75 minutes assigned was found to be adequate; one participant finished in an hour and the other took about 65 minutes.

At the Saudi University, the training study objectives and methodology were introduced to both groups separately. An information sheet described the purpose of the training course, the methodology, benefits and possible risks. After a week, the students' signatures were taken on individual consent forms. Both groups sat a 75-minute initial exam in different sessions. They were free to use dictionaries. The students were not asked to write their names on the exam papers. The papers, however, were coded to track the individual performance at the stages of assessment and analysis. The training course, carried out on the experimental group, covered 20 hours, comprising one hour twice a week. At the end of the academic semester (about 13 weeks), the two groups sat a 75-minute final exam in different sessions. Again, the students were free to use dictionaries.

An L1 Arabic-speaker colleague in the Department of English helped to provide the Arabic translations to be used as models to compare against the students' translations. It is a common belief that translating into L1 gives the TT a higher quality of linguistic command and cultural background. Dickins, Hervey and Higgins note that 'translator training normally focuses on translation into the mother tongue, because higher quality is achieved in that direction than in translating into a foreign language' (2002: 2). The scripts were first evaluated by the researcher. To ensure inter-rater reliability, an assistant professor of translation in the same department helped to evaluate the papers and double-check the scores as guided by the scoring rubric (see Section 5). Finally, the participants' scores from both groups were analysed and compared using different statistical tools, schematic diagrams and illustrative charts.

5 The scoring rubric

As opposed to a *norm-referenced* exam, which is used to assess professional translators or those who have graduated from translation programmes, this exam is *criterion-referenced*. It thus produces information describing how far the participants meet the skills and behaviours determined in advance (Angelelli 2009: 15–16). This exam is neither certification-based nor comparison-oriented. It is rather a training-governed exam, for which there is a need to define the criteria that form the sub-competences investigated in this experiment. This was accomplished through a rubric (Reddy and Andrade 2010: 435) specially designed to define the framework of the operational assessment construct, capturing and measuring the different levels of the SFL-based translation knowledge, abilities and skills involved in the experiment: the test itself entails assessing short translated fiction extracts and translating a longer extract of English fiction into Arabic.

The rubric was divided into four sub-competences corresponding to the different SFL-based assessment and translation abilities covered by the three questions of the exam:

1. The metafunction-based interpretation of the ST. This involved analysing and understanding the metafunctional components of the ST, identifying the different lexicogrammatical resources used by the ST author to create the 'meaning in context through choice' (Matthiessen 2014: 272) and dividing the ST into its constituent clause complexes and clauses in order to assign the unit of translation and define the logical relations between clauses. This sub-competence was present in all three questions, particularly Question 1 – part 2, as well as Questions 2 and 3.
2. The SFL-based assessment of translation. This mainly involved finding out the recreation of meaning through choices of the lexicogrammatical resources of both texts, taking into account the way these resources were recreated in the TL system. This sub-competence was reflected by Questions 1 and 2 (part 1).
3. An SFL-oriented justification for choosing the most accurate metafunction-based translation. This involved using specific functional analysis and terms, in non-technical wording, to justify the choice. This sub-competence was particularly prominent in Question 2 (part 2).
4. The production of a metafunction-based target text (TT) in the appropriate TL systems. This sub-competence, which carried the highest burden of the assessment construct, was exclusively covered by Question 3. In SFL terms, emphasis was placed on analysing and interpreting the meaning realized by the lexicogrammatical resources construing the different metafunctions of the ST and the recreation of these choices in the TL systems.

The other step was the definition and description of the operational scoring construct in the most accurate manner possible. A continuum on a 4-to-0-point scale was employed. The zero point was used to cover the possibility that some questions were left unanswered. This scale grid measured the extent of mastery of each sub-competence. The proportional weight for each sub-competence was approximately determined according to three factors: the pervasiveness of the sub-competence in the exam, estimated time for coverage as observed in the pilot test study and importance placed on each sub-competence in the training course. Figure 8.1 represents the detailed scoring rubric. It is worth mentioning here that there is no substantial correlation between the total score and total percentage: the scores are distributed evenly between the four sub-competences, but what matters is the proportional weight given for each sub-competence which is reflected in the cumulative percentage.

Assessment Element (Sub-competence)	Scale Point/Statement of Measurement					Initial		Final	
	4	3	2	1	0	Score	%	Score	%
I) Metafunction-based interpretation of the ST	To demonstrate in all 3 questions a masterful ability to analyse and understand the metafunctional constituents and configuration of the ST.	To demonstrate in all 3 questions a proficient ability to analyse and understand the metafunctional constituents and configuration of the ST.	To demonstrate in all 3 questions a good ability to analyse and understand the metafunctional constituents and configuration of the ST.	To demonstrate in all 3 questions a weak ability to analyse and understand the metafunctional constituents and configuration of the ST.	To demonstrate in all 3 questions an inability to analyse and understand the metafunctional constituents and configuration of the ST.	4	25%	4	25%
II) SFL–based assessment of translation	To demonstrate in Questions 1 and 2 (part 1) a masterful ability to find out the re-creation of meaning through the choices of the lexicogrammatical resources of both texts (getting 6 correct answers)	To demonstrate in Questions 1 and 2 (part 1) a proficient ability to find out the re-creation of meaning through the choices of the lexicogrammatical resources of both texts (getting 4 or 5 correct answers)	To demonstrate in Questions 1 and 2 (part 1) an average ability to find out the re-creation of meaning through the choices of the lexicogrammatical resources of both texts (getting 3 correct answers)	To demonstrate in Questions 1 and 2 (part 1) a weak ability to find out the re-creation of meaning through the choices of the lexicogrammatical resources of both texts (getting 1 or 2 correct answers)	To demonstrate in Questions 1 and 2 (part 1) an inability to find out the re-creation of meaning through the choices of the lexicogrammatical resources of both texts (getting 0 correct answer)	4	15%	4	15%
III) SFL–oriented justification for choosing the most accurate metafunction-based translation	To provide a strong, specific SFL–oriented justification for Questions 2, part 2.	To provide a good, mostly specific SFL–oriented justification.	To provide a satisfactory, SFL–oriented justification.	To provide a weak, SFL–oriented justification.	To provide an invalid, SFL–oriented justification or when it is left unanswered.	4	10%	4	10%
IV) Production of a metafunction-based translation in the TL systems	To produce a complete, metafunction-based equivalent TT in the correct TL system.	To produce a good metafunction-based equivalent TT in the acceptable TL system.	To produce a satisfactory metafunction-based equivalent TT with some mistakes in the TL system.	To produce an almost incomplete, incorrect metafunction-based equivalent TT with many mistakes in the TL system.	To produce an incomplete, invalid metafunction-based equivalent TT with very many mistakes in the TL system or when it is left unanswered.	4	50%	4	50%
Total						16	100%	16	100%

Figure 8.1 The rubric and the scoring grid of the study.

6 Discussion of examples of participants' responses

Although the study has as a quantitative approach to this experiment, it is important to discuss participants' responses qualitatively. Representative examples will be discussed, noting that they may understandably contain grammatical and spelling errors. The participant's code is supplied with each example. English 'functional-based' literal translations for the Arabic scripts are provided for Examples 1 to 4 in the Appendix.

In Question 2, the participants were asked to give the reason why they chose a certain translation as the most accurate or successful one. In fact, most responses in the initial exams of both groups were unsuccessful or just left unanswered. However, very few papers included good understanding and justification. Example 1 (see Figure 8.2) shows two students giving a relatively good reason for not choosing choices (c) and (d) in Question 2, part 2.

But a new factor (the SFL-based translator training course) changed the picture completely, and more relevant, successful and SFL-oriented responses were given by some experimental group participants. The responses ranged between simple and more specific or even highly detailed. A few participants used underlining or circling techniques to highlight the mismatched parts or unmotivated shifts in the unsuccessful choices. Here are Examples 2 and 3 (see Figures 8.3 and 8.4).

Question 3 in the final exam saw a fundamental improvement in the performance of the experimental group participants. The clearest example was found in the enormous difference between the initial and final exam translations of the same participant

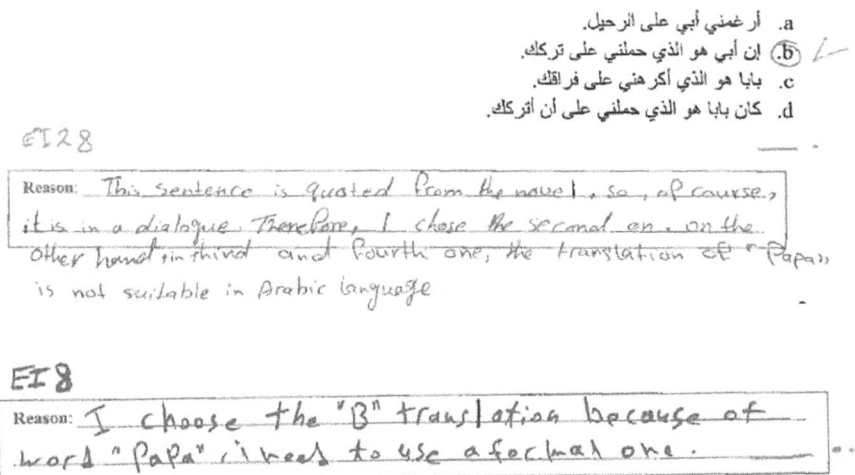

It was papa made me leave.

a. أرغمني أبي على الرحيل.
b. إن أبي هو الذي حملني على تركك.
c. بابا هو الذي أكرهني على فراقك.
d. كان بابا هو الذي حملني على أن أتركك.

EI28

Reason: This sentence is quoted from the novel, so, of course, it is in a dialogue. Therefore, I chose the second en. on the other hand, in third and fourth one, the translation of "Papa" is not suitable in Arabic language

EI8

Reason: I choose the "B" translation because of word "Papa", I need to use a formal one.

Figure 8.2 (Example 1) Photocopied responses of Question 2, part 2 in the initial exam, the experimental group.

2. The brown blotches of the benevolent skin cancer the sun brings from its reflection on the tropic sea were on his cheeks

a. علت خديه القروح السمراء الناشئة عن سرطان الجلد غير المؤذي الذي هو ثمرة انعكاس الشمس على صفحة المياه في المناطق الاستوائية.

b. ظهرت على وجنتيه بثور سمراء من سرطان الجلد الحميد الناشىء من انعكاس الشمس على مياه البحر في هذه المنطقة الاستوائية.

c. وعلى خديه بقع بنية هي نوع من سرطان الجلد الذي سببته الشمس من جراء انعكاسها على البحر في تلك المنطقة الاستوائية.

d. انتشرت على خديه البقع البنية لسرطان الجلد الحميد الذي تسببه الشمس من انعكاسها على البحر المداري.

ملاحظة: سرطان الجلد الحميد: the benevolent skin cancer

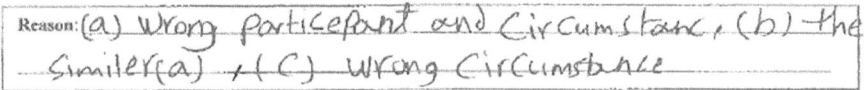

EF34

Reason: (a) Wrong participant and Circumstance, (b) the Similer(a) + (c) wrong Circumstance

Figure 8.3 (Example 2) A photocopied response of Question 2, part 2 in the final exam, the experimental group.

EF25

3. It made the boy sad to see the old man come in each day with his skiff empty.

a. ولقد أحزن الغلام أن يرى الشيخ يرجع كل يوم خالي القارب.

b. في نهاية كل يوم, يحزن الطفل وهو يرى معلمه يعود خاوي الوفاض.

c. مست كبد الصبي لوعة حزن وهو يرى العجوز يجيء كل يوم بمركبه خاويا.

d. كان الحزن يجتاح قلب الفتى, حين يرى العجوز عائداً إلى الشاطىء كل يوم صفر اليدين.

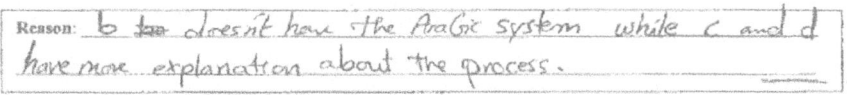

Reason: b doesn't have the Arabic system while c and d have more explanation about the process.

Figure 8.4 (Example 3) A photocopied response of Question 2, part 2 in the final exam, the experimental group.

(E7). As shown in the scanned Example 4 (see Figures 8.5 and 8.6), the initial exam translation was extremely poor and decontextualized. It was just an accumulation of unrelated words. Further, the clause boundaries as well as the logical relations were completely overlooked so that the entire translation consisted of one paragraph with one full stop. The final exam translation, by contrast, demonstrated important progress in preserving most metafunctions of the ST in a TT that basically complied with the Arabic systems. As a practical example, when the participant learned during the course the significance of clause division before translating, the quality and accuracy of the final exam translation vastly changed.

QIII) Translate the following short extract from a novel into Arabic:

They walked up the road together to the old man's shack and went in through its open door. The old man leaned the mast with its wrapped sail against the wall and the boy put the box and the other gear beside it. The mast was nearly as long as the one room of the shack. The shack was made of the tough bud shields of the royal palm which are called *guano* and in it there was a bed, a table, one chair, and a place on the dirt floor to cook with charcoal.

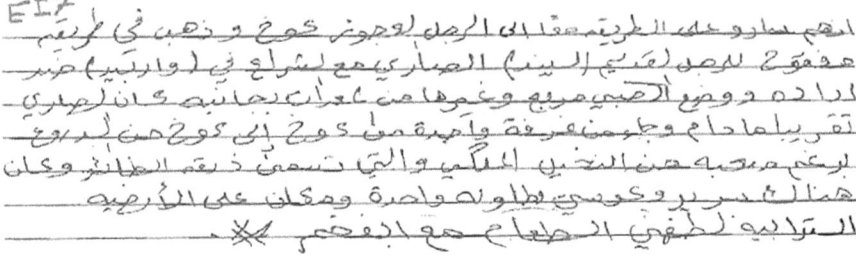

Figure 8.5 (Example 4) A photocopied response of Question 3 in the initial exam for an experimental group participant.

QIII) Translate the following short extract from a novel into Arabic:

The old man and the boy sat on the Terrace/and many of the fishermen made fun of the old man/and he was not angry./Others, of the older fishermen, looked at him/and were sad./But they did not show it/and they spoke politely about the current and the depths/they had drifted their lines at/and the steady good weather/and of what they had seen./The successful fishermen of that day were already in/and had butchered their marlin out/and carried them laid full length across two planks/with two men staggering at the end of each plank, to the fish house where they waited for the ice truck to carry them to the market in Havana.

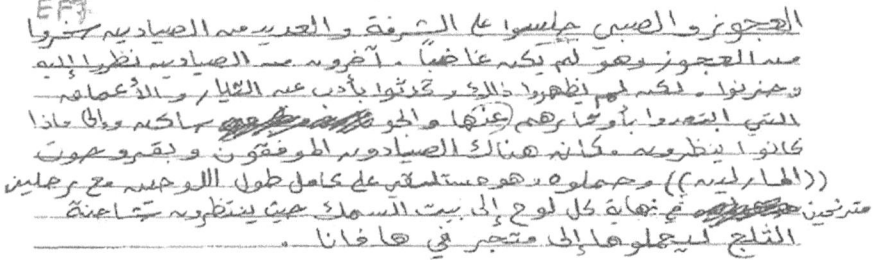

Figure 8.6 (Example 4) A photocopied response of Question 3 in the final exam for an experimental group participant.

7 The initial and the final exam results

The papers of both exams were rated first by the researcher according to the rubric and the guidelines of the scoring grid. The two exams were rated and double-checked another time by an assistant professor of translation in the Department of English at the same Saudi University to ensure sufficient inter-reliability. In fact, there were no significant differences between the two ratings because the scoring grid was detailed enough to make valid assessments. Using Excel, the mean scores for each sub-competence were calculated in a 0-to-4-point continuum scale for each group in both exams. The results of both exams are presented in Figures 8.7 to 8.10.

Figure 8.7 The mean sub-competences scores of the initial and final exams for the control group.

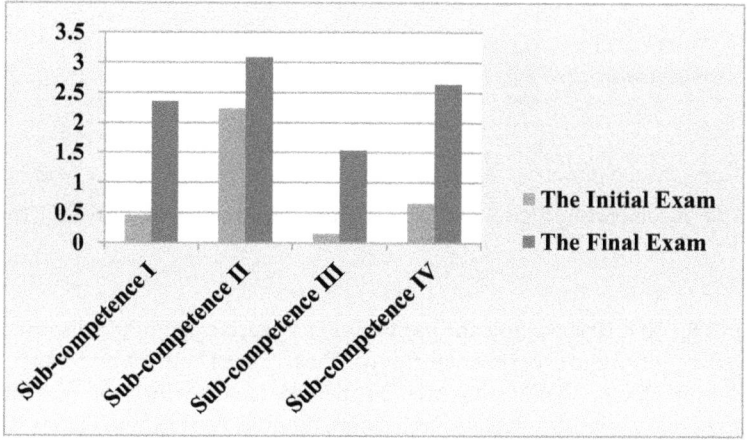

Figure 8.8 The mean sub-competences scores of the initial and final exams for the experimental group.

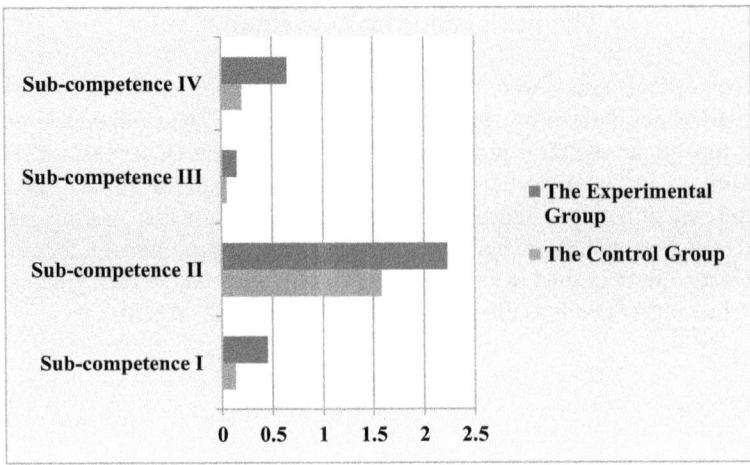

Figure 8.9 A comparison between the results of the two groups in the initial exam (in mean scores).

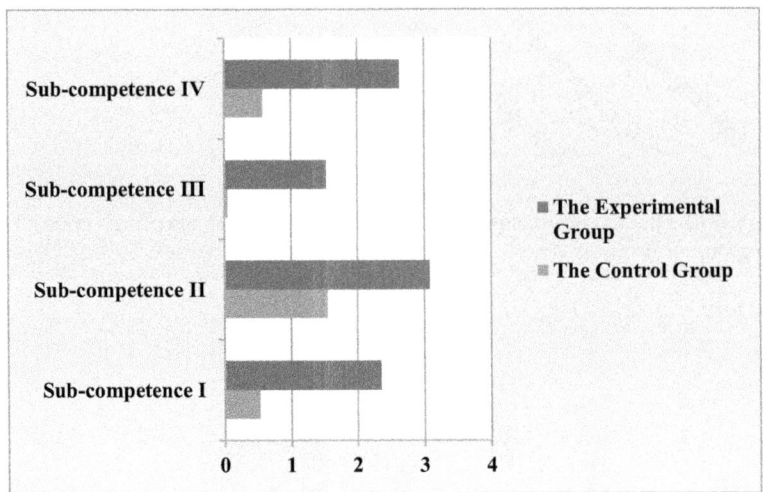

Figure 8.10 A comparison between the results of the two groups in the final exam (in mean scores).

Figures 8.7 to 8.10 show how the performance in each exam differed substantially between the control and experimental groups. The results of both exams for the control group did not change significantly over this period, during which the students only took the ordinary English-to-Arabic translation module. As shown in Figure 8.7, sub-competences II and III (the SFL-based assessment of translation and the provision of an SFL-oriented justification for choosing the most accurate metafunction-based translation) remained almost the same, and the other two (the metafunction-based interpretation of the ST and the production of a metafunction-based target TT in the TL system) increased by a score of approximately 0.4. In contrast, when comparing the results of the initial and final exams for the experimental group (see Figure 8.8), a substantial increase in all sub-competences can be perceived. The sub-competences increased, respectively, by scores of 1.9, 0.85, 1.38 and 1.98 after attending the SFL-based training course. The sub-competence recording the lowest increase was the second (the SFL-based assessment of translation), which carried 15 per cent of the total exam percentage and which involved, for the most part, multiple-choice exercises (Questions 1 and 2). The low increase could be ascribed to the relatively high result obtained in the initial exam and to the luck factor, which could not be totally excluded. The fourth sub-competence (translating an English fiction extract into Arabic), which was so fundamental to the experiment, had a statistically significant result (an increase of 1.98). This value could not possibly occur by chance; it was therefore attributed to a specific cause or factor (the SFL-translator training course). This result answers the *second question* of the study, that the SFL-based translator training course exerted a strong positive influence on the participants' accuracy and quality of translation.

When comparing the performance of the two groups in each exam, the picture becomes much clearer. Although the experimental group had higher scores, on the whole, than the control group in the initial exam (see Figure 8.9), the differences between them were insignificant. The increase ranged only between a score of 0.1 and 0.65 in the four sub-competences. By comparison with the initial exam, the differences between the two groups in the final exam was another story, told with many contrasts: as illustrated in Figure 8.10, the experimental group comfortably surpassed the control group in all sub-competences; the sub-competences of the experimental group beat those of the control group, respectively, by scores of 1.82, 1.53, 1.48 and 2.05. The fourth sub-competence, in particular, made an enormous difference to the validity of attending the SFL-based translator training course.

Calculating the percentages is another way of presenting the results of the two exams for the two groups. This is particularly useful when looking at whether the value in the initial exam increases, decreases or remains the same in the final exam. The 0-to-4 mean scores were represented in percentage according to the proportional weight for each sub-competence. The percentages are presented in Figures 8.11 to 8.14.

Measuring the percentage change of the participants, sub-competences and total percentage is an efficient tool to find out how much each component of the experiment gained, lost or just remained unchanged. The difference between the initial and final exams in the total percentage for the control group was 7.1 per cent, while the experimental group did vastly better in the final exam, achieving a performance increase of 43.1 per cent in the total percentage. Half the participants of the control group had a positive total percentage change (with an average percentage of +366.38%), seven participants had a negative change (with an average percentage of −64.39%). Twelve participants remained unchanged. Participants C5 and C36 had, respectively, the lowest negative and highest positive percentage change. On the other hand, the experimental group had only one participant with a negative percentage

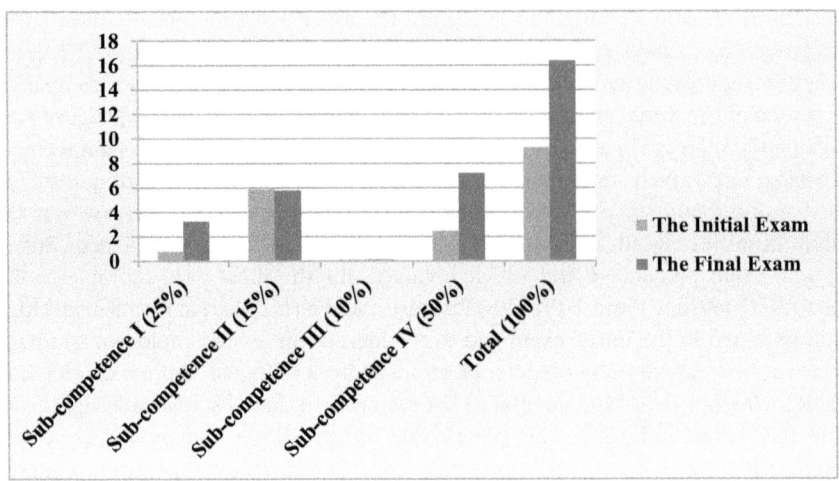

Figure 8.11 The results of the initial and final exams for the control group (in percentages).

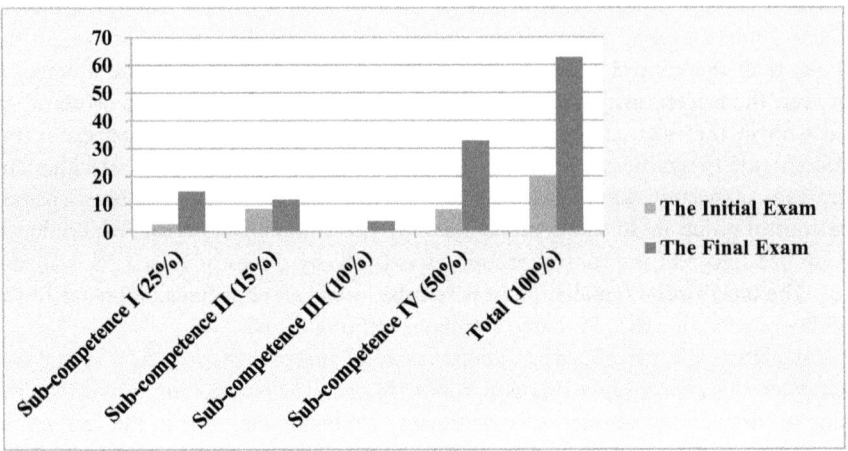

Figure 8.12 The results of the initial and final exams for the experimental group (in percentages).

change (–12.5%) and three participants with zero change. The other 36 participants had a mean change of +491.3 per cent. Participant E22 had an enormous positive percentage change (+1533.3%).

The change in sub-competences of the control group varied considerably. Sub-competences I and IV (the metafunction-based interpretation of the ST and the production of a metafunction-based target TT in the TL system) changed positively, sub-competence II (the SFL-based assessment of translation) recorded a slightly negative change and sub-competence III (the provision of an SFL-oriented justification for choosing the most accurate metafunction-based translation) remained unchanged.

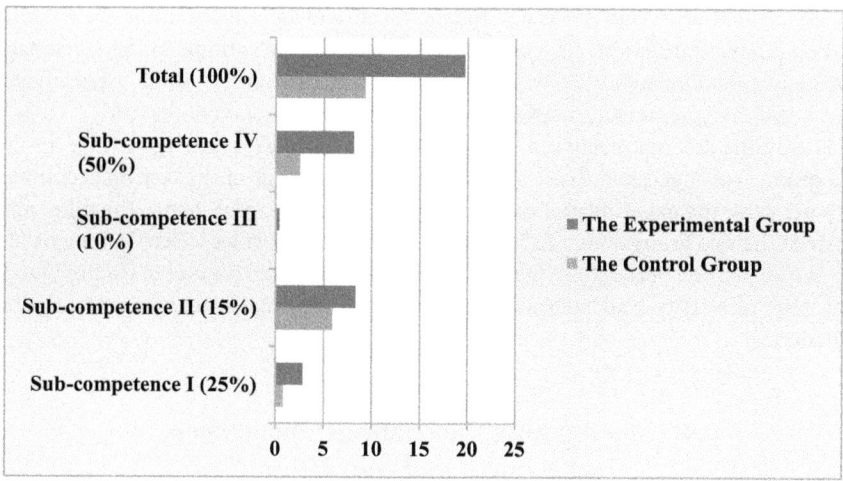

Figure 8.13 A comparison between the results of the two groups in the initial exam (in percentages).

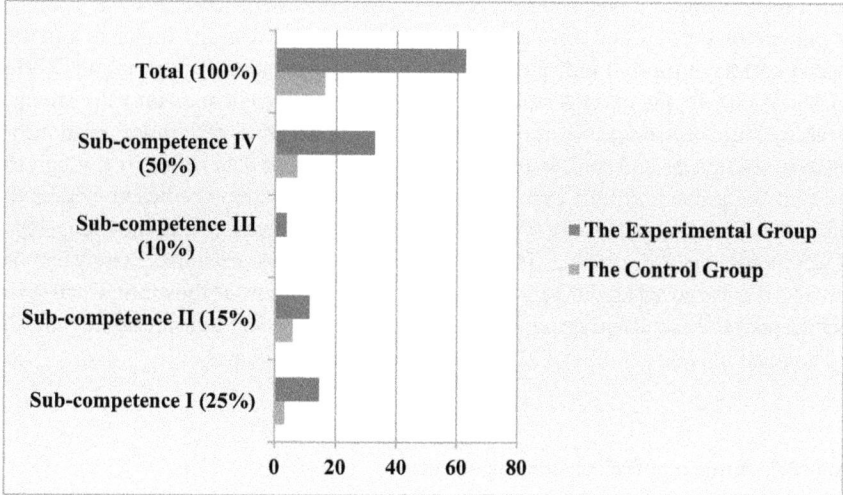

Figure 8.14 A comparison between the results of the two groups in final exam (in percentages).

In contrast, all the sub-competences of the experimental group had a significant positive change between the two exams. For example, sub-competence III had the highest positive change (900%). This showed the direct effect of the SFL knowledge gained by the participants on their interpretation, assessment and justification (as shown in Example 3). This result provides a sufficient answer to the *first question* of the study, that the awareness of the metafunction analysis of short English extracts of fiction effectively helped the final-year Arab university students locate and identify the unmotivated shifts in their Arabic translations. The difference between the two groups in the percentage change of sub-competence IV was 115.8 per cent in the interest of the experimental group, and this gives an affirmative answer to the *second question* of the study.

Finally, the difference between the two groups in the total percentage change for the two exams was suggestive. The overall improvement change of the control group was 76.3 per cent; the experimental group improved 218.8 per cent, hence the difference between the two groups was 142.5 per cent. This figure provides a clear-cut answer to the *fourth question* of the study that the SFL model is an effective tool in training final-year Arab university students (majoring in English) in English-to-Arabic translation of fiction.

8 Investigating the relationship between assessment and translation

The last important issue to be raised in this study is the investigation of the nature of relationship between the two main skills or competences in this study: assessment and translation (the *third question* of the study). The most valid way to find out the nature of this relationship is to generate Pearson's Correlation Coefficient. This is a 'test used for parametric data ... and can have a value of between -1 and 1: 1 indicates a perfect positive correlation and -1 indicates a perfect negative correlation' (Saldanha and O'Brien 2013: 159–60). In the current study, the correlation coefficient measures the strength (weak, medium or strong) and the direction (positive or negative) of the linear relationship between assessment and translation for a particular pool of data collected through the scores of the initial and final exams. Calculating the correlation coefficient evinces the behaviour of sub-competence IV when the score of sub-competence II or sub-competence III was increasing or decreasing. The first sub-competence was excluded, mainly because it involved areas covering different parts of the three questions of the exam. Correlation coefficients were calculated using Excel. They are presented and interpreted in Table 8.2 and graphed in Figures 8.15 to 8.22. A detailed explanation follows.

Table 8.2 Summary of correlation coefficients

Variables/exam/interpretation		The control group	The experimental group
Sub-comp. II and IV	**Initial exam**	0.278	−0.173
	Interpretation	Weak positive correlation	Weak negative correlation
	Final exam	0.442	0.548
	Interpretation	Medium positive correlation	Strong positive correlation
Sub-comp. III and IV	**Initial exam**	0.150	−0.065
	Interpretation	Weak positive correlation	Weak negative correlation
	Final exam	0.166	0.571
	Interpretation	Weak positive correlation	Strong positive correlation

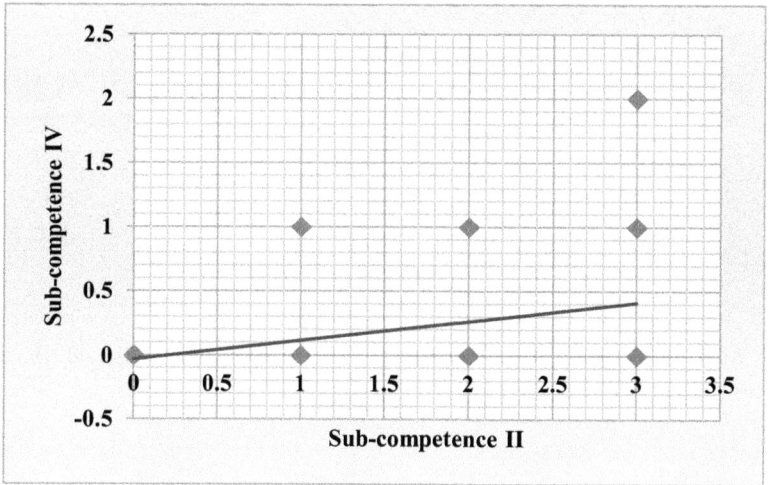

Figure 8.15 Scatter plot correlation (0.278) of sub-competences II and IV in the control group initial exam.

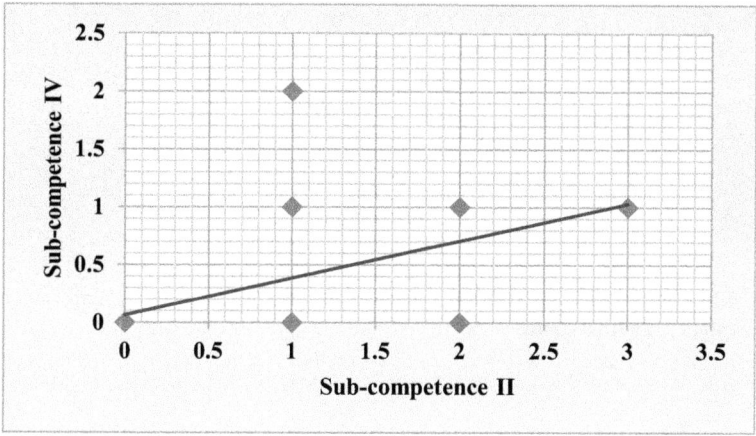

Figure 8.16 Scatter plot correlation (0.442) of sub-competences II and IV in the control group final exam.

Table 8.2 and Figures 8.15 to 8.22 draw a detailed comparison of the correlation coefficient values between the two competences of assessment and translation of both groups in both exams. The correlation coefficients of the control group did not increase significantly between the initial and final exams; they only increased by 0.164 and 0.016, respectively. In contrast, the correlation coefficients of the experimental group for the same elements increased substantially by 0.721 and 0.636, respectively.

In response to the *third question* of the study, these results provide empirical evidence for the existence of a positive relationship between the assessment of

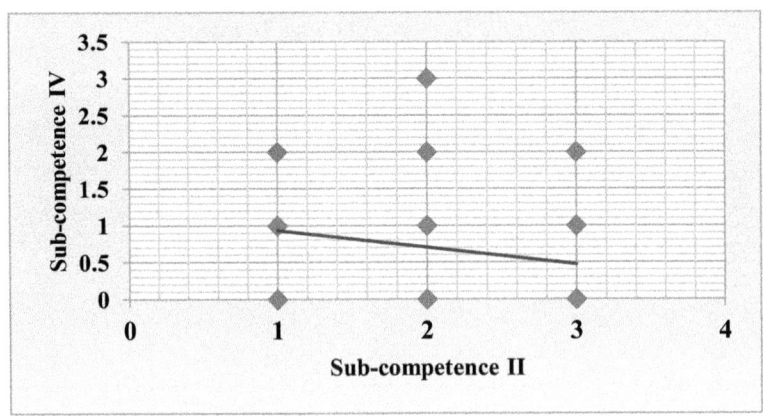

Figure 8.17 Scatter plot correlation (−0.173) of sub-competences II and IV in the experimental group initial exam.

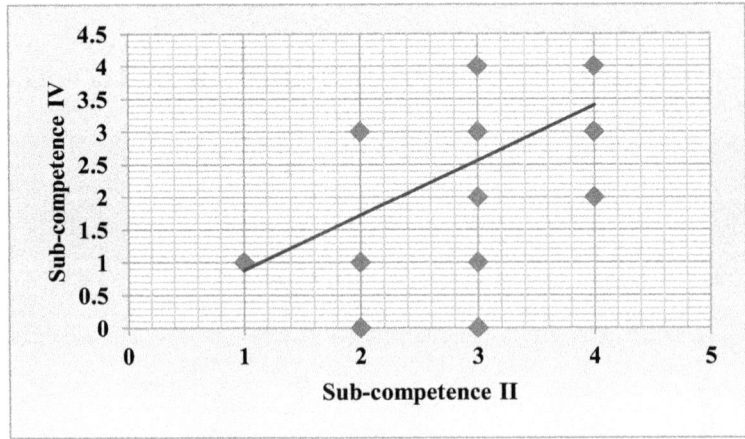

Figure 8.18 Scatter plot correlation (0.548) of sub-competences II and IV in the experimental group final exam.

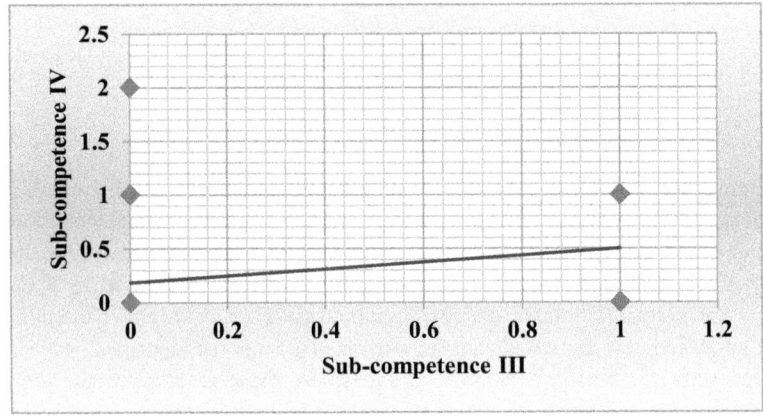

Figure 8.19 Scatter plot correlation (0.150) of sub-competences III and IV in the control group initial exam.

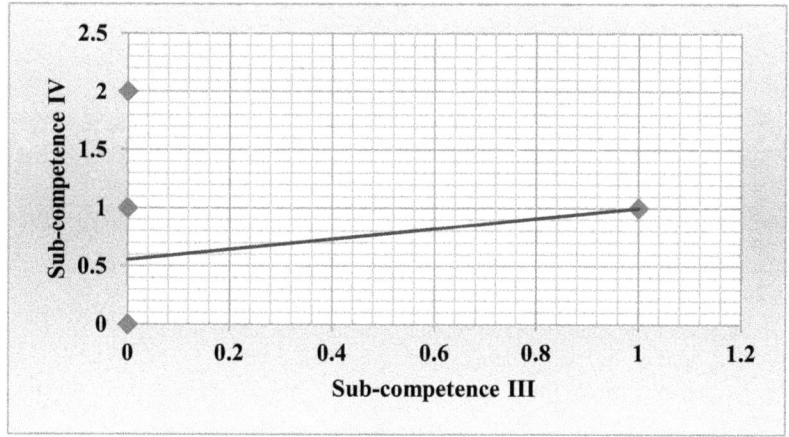

Figure 8.20 Scatter plot correlation (0.166) of sub-competences III and IV in the control group final exam.

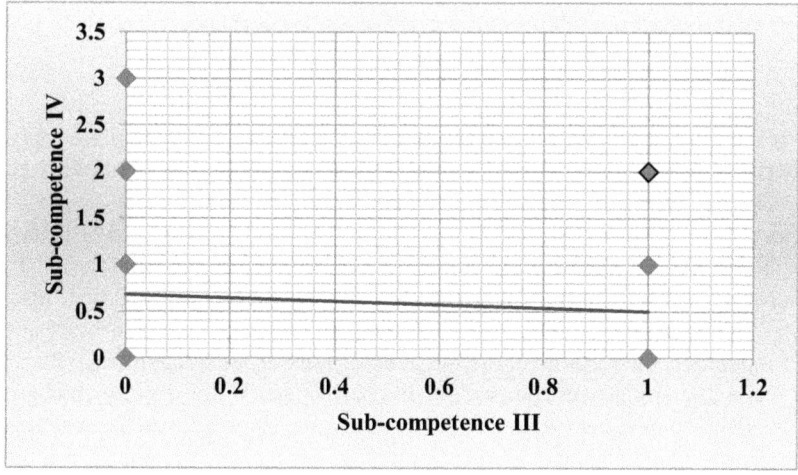

Figure 8.21 Scatter plot correlation (–0.065) of sub-competences III and IV in the experimental group initial exam.

short English-to-Arabic translated extracts of fiction and the production of better metafunction-based Arabic translations once the SFL-based translator training has been delivered. It can be convincingly argued that the experimental group was armed with a linguistic theory that made it possible for the students to interpret precisely the metafunctional choices of English STs and how effectively they can be recreated in Arabic TTs.

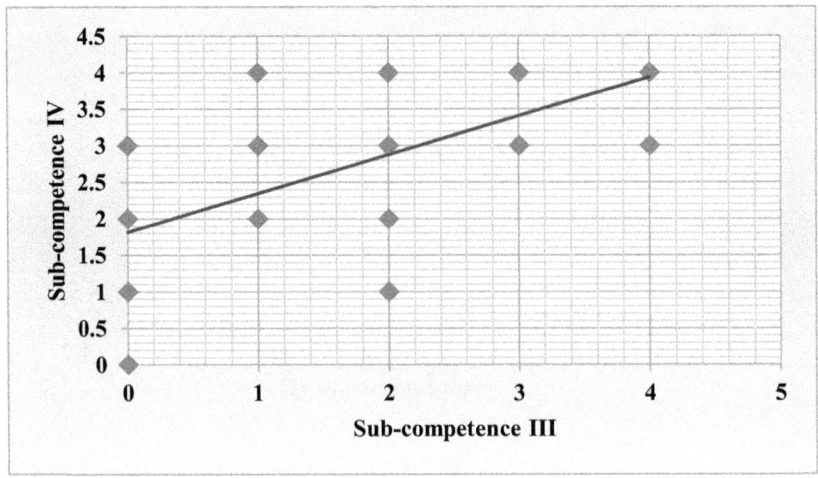

Figure 8.22 Scatter plot correlation (0.571) of sub-competences III and IV in the experimental group final exam.

9 Conclusion

Despite the emergence of significant results in this empirical study, complacency is not appropriate. There were two main inherent limitations to this experiment. First, there was no questionnaire to collect the experimental group's views and opinions on the training course. This was because (i) the time available for completing the study was not sufficient to add another tool; (ii) there would have been doubts about the reliability of the responses as many students were likely to be complimentary to their teacher, especially if he was familiar to them; (iii) although the participants of the control group were cooperative, their results in the initial exam were lower (though insignificantly) in all four sub-competences compared to the participants of the experimental group. This was likely to have contributed to the experimental group's anticipation generated by the prospective advantage of attending the training course. However, it must be admitted that controlling this variable of motivation precisely and consistently would have been extremely difficult.

The empirical data obtained from this translator training experiment have responded to *questions one, two* and *four* of the study. The results have shown that the difference between the control group and the experimental group scores in the initial and final exams has been significant. This difference can be seen in the significant variation in the mean score for each sub-competence as well as in the percentage change and total percentage. It should not be a surprise that the decisive factor in this difference was the application of the SFL-based translator training course through which the inevitability of progress in the experimental group became real. For example, the scores of the four sub-competences of the initial exam increased considerably in the final exam for the experimental group as compared to the control group. The four sub-competences of the control group showed an increase/decrease of 10 per cent, –0.75 per cent, 0.0 per cent and 9.5 per cent, respectively, whereas in the experimental group they showed an increase of 47.5 per cent, 21.25 per cent, 34.5 per cent and 49.5 per cent, respectively.

Question 3 of the study addressed a task that could prove quite challenging. It investigated whether or not the SFL knowledge helped to increase the two skills of assessment and translation correspondingly. A calculation was made of the correlation coefficients to characterize the behaviour of the scores of sub-competence IV when the scores of sub-competence II or sub-competence III increased or decreased. The results provided clear indications about the existence of a strong positive relationship (0.548 and 0.571) between assessing short English-to-Arabic translated extracts of fiction and producing better metafunction-based Arabic translations after giving the experimental group the SFL-based translator training course.

The central investigation underlying the entire study is that translation starts from a source text, and that, when the starting point is an English source text, the SFL framework is found to be a particularly useful choice. SFL is efficient at analysing the functions and thus understanding the meanings given in the English text. What remains to be done after that is to consider the functions and produce a TT in which the meanings of the ST are reconstrued using the Arabic network of systems. If this has been empirically proved applicable to translating English fiction into Arabic, then it is likely to be adaptable to a wide range of genres and for other language pairs.

The results of this experimental study yield the general conclusion that SFL is effective in training prospective English/Arabic translators in academic institutions. Though this work has provided significant accounts of the emergence of SFL applications in TS, further developments are likely to take place. For example, long-term, genre-based research can provide more valid results that would help to support the inclusion of SFL and its applications in the academic programmes in Arab universities. Another example can be seen in the nature of investigation. The current study focused on *how far* the participant was able to provide good interpretation of the ST and provide metafunction-based translations. However, further research can address more of *why* questions. In this case, a rigorous qualitative analysis can yield valuable insights into other variables, such as ideology, gender or education level.

References

Angelelli, C. V. (2009), 'Using a Rubric to Assess Translation Ability: Defining the Construct', in C. V. Angelelli and H. E. Jacobson (eds), *Testing and Assessment in Translation and Interpreting Studies*, 13–47, Amsterdam: John Benjamins.

Baker, M. ([1992] 2011), *In Other Words: A Coursebook on Translation*, 2nd edn, London: Routledge.

Bardi, M. A. (2008), *A Systemic Functional Description of the Grammar of Arabic*, PhD Thesis, Department of Linguistics, Macquarie University.

Bartrina, F. (2005), 'Theory and Translator Training', in M. Tennent (ed.), *Training for the New Millennium: Pedagogies for Translation and Interpreting*, 177–89, Amsterdam: John Benjamins.

Bnini, C. (2007), *The Empirical Status of Text, Discourse and Genre in the Training of English/Arabic Translators*, PhD Thesis, School of Languages, Heriot-Watt University.

Bolaños, S. (2002). 'Equivalence Revisited: A Key Concept in Modern Translation Theory'. *Forma y Función* (15): 60–88.

Christie, F. (2004), 'Systemic Functional Linguistics and a Theory of Language in Education', *Ilha do Desterro*, nº 46: 13–40. Available online: http://www.periodicos. ufsc.br/index.php/desterro/article/view/7390 (accessed 12 February 2013).

Dickins, J., Hervey, S., and Higgins, I. (2002), *Thinking Arabic Translation: A Course in Translation Method: Arabic to English*, London: Routledge.

Eggins, S. (2004), *An Introduction to Systemic Functional Linguistics*, 2nd edn, London: Continuum.

Halliday, M. A. K. (1978), *Language as Social Semiotic: The Social Interpretation of Language and Meaning*, London: Edward Arnold.

Halliday, M. A. K., and Matthiessen, C. (2014), *Halliday's Introduction to Functional Grammar*, 4th edn, London: Routledge.

Hatim, B., and Mason, I. (1990), *Discourse and the Translator*, London: Longman.

Hatim, B., and Mason, I. (1997), *The Translator as Communicator*, London: Routledge.

Hönig, H. G. (1998) 'Complexity, Contrastive Linguistics and Translator Training: Comments on Responses'. In C. Schäffner (ed.), *Translation and Quality*, 83–9, Clevedon: Multilingual Matters.

House, J. ([1977] 1997), *Translation Quality Assessment: A Model Revisited*, Tübengen: Gunter Narr.

House, J. (2015), *Translation Quality Assessment: Past and Present*, London: Routledge.

Kelly, D. (2005), *A Handbook for Translator Trainers: A Guide to Reflective Practice*, Manchester: St. Jerome.

Kim, M. (2007a), *A Discourse Based Study on Theme in Korean and Textual Meaning in Translation*, PhD Thesis, Department of Linguistics, Macquarie University.

Kim, M. (2007b), 'Using Systemic Functional Text Analysis for Translator Education', *Interpreter and Translator Trainer* 1 (2): 223–46.

Kim, M. (2009), 'Meaning-Oriented Assessment of Translations: SFL and Its Application to Formative Assessment', in C. V. Angelelli and H. E. Jacobson (eds), *Testing and Assessment in Translation and Interpreting Studies*, 123–58, Amsterdam: John Benjamins.

Kim, M. (2010), 'Translation Error Analysis: A Systemic Functional Grammar Approach', in C. Coffin, T. Lillis and K. O'Halloran (eds), *Applied Linguistics Methods: A Reader*, 84–94, London: Routledge.

Kim, M., and Huang, Z. (2012), 'Theme Choices in Translation and Target Readers' Reactions to Different Theme Choices', *T & I Review* 2: 79–112.

Malmkjær, K. (2004), 'Introduction: Translation as an Academic Discipline', in K. Malmkjær (ed.), *Translation in Undergraduate Degree Programmes*, 1–7, Amsterdam: John Benjamins.

Mannaa, M. (2011), *The Effectiveness of a Composite Translator Training Model for Syrian Translation Masters Students*, PhD Thesis, The Department of Languages, Faculty of Arts, University of Salford.

Matthiessen, C. (2001), 'The Environments of Translation', in:E. Steiner and C. Yallop (eds), *Exploring Translation and Multilingual Text Production: Beyond Content*, 41–124, Berlin: Mouton de Gruyter.

Matthiessen, C. (2014), 'Choice in Translation: Metafunctional Considerations', in K. Kunz, E. Teich, S. Hansen-Schirra, S. Neumann and P. Daut (eds), *Caught in the*

Middle – Language Use and Translation: A Festschrift for Erich Steiner on the Occasion of His 60th Birthday, 271–333, Saarbrücken: Saarland University Press.

Munday, J. (2002), 'Systems in Translation: A Systemic Model for Descriptive Translation Studies', in T. Hermans (ed.), *Crosscultural Transgressions: Research Models in Translation Studies II: Historical and Ideological Issues*, 76–92, Manchester: St. Jerome.

Munday, J. (2012), *Evaluation in Translation: Critical Points of Translator Decision-Making*, Abingdon: Routledge.

Najjar, O. (2008), *Discourse Analysis Models in the Training of Translators: An Empirical Approach*, PhD Thesis, School of Management and Languages, Heriot-Watt University.

Orel, S. (1996), 'Teaching Literary Translation: "The Translation Happens When You Read It"', in C. Dollerup and V. Appel (eds), *Teaching Translation and Interpreting 3: New Horizons: Papers from the Third Language International Conference, Elsinore, Denmark 9–11 June 1995*, 129–36, Amsterdam: John Benjamins.

Pym, A. (2012), 'Training Translators', in K. Malmkjær and K. Windle (eds), *The Oxford Handbook of Translation Studies*, 313–21, Oxford: Oxford University Press.

Reddy, Y., and Andrade, H. (2010), 'A Review of Rubric Use in Higher Education', *Assessment and Evaluation in Higher Education* 35 (4): 435–48.

Saldanha, G., and O'Brien, S. (2013), *Research Methodologies in Translation Studies*, Manchester: St. Jerome.

Widdowson, H. G. (1984), *Explorations in Applied Linguistics 2*, Oxford: Oxford University Press.

Wilss, W. (2004), 'Translation Studies: A Didactic Approach', in K. Malmkjær (ed.), *Translation in Undergraduate Degree Programmes*, 9–15, Amsterdam: John Benjamins.

9

A translated volume and its many covers: A diachronic, social-semiotic approach to the study of translated book covers

Long Li

University of New South Wales

1 Introduction

Although translation as a form of communication has always had to deal with multimodal elements, whether it be font, size or images, and the physical presentation of the final translation product or facial expressions and body language in interpreting, the importance of non-verbal elements has only recently been recognized within Translation Studies (TS) since the 2000s (cf. Harvey 2003; Gambier 2006; Alvstad 2008; Littau 2011; Chueasuai 2013; Fu 2013; Lee 2013; Borodo 2015; Taylor 2016; Yu and Song 2016; Batchelor 2018; Summers 2018; Li, Li and Miao 2019). However, to date, translated book covers have received relatively little scholarly attention, even though virtually all translated publications contain a textually prominent front cover. As Sonzogni (2011) points out, considering book cover design as a form of intersemiotic translation has been a virtually uncharted territory of research. This gap in studying translated book covers may be attributed to the general conceptualization of translation as the rendering of written text as written text (O'Sullivan 2013), echoing Matthiessen's (2001) criticism of a neglect of other semiotic systems in TS – despite Jakobson's ([1959] 2004: 138–43) longstanding proposal for intersemiotic translation in his often-cited tripartite taxonomy of translation.

As most translation scholars are probably not systematically trained to read non-linguistic resources for meaning-making, it becomes necessary to look to relevant theories and methodologies in multimodal studies. The field of social semiotics, especially the seminal work of Kress and van Leeuwen ([1996] 2006), is now a major school in multimodal discourse analysis (Bateman, Wildfeuer and Hiippala 2017). This work has been strongly influenced by the notion of 'language as social semiotic' in Halliday's (1978) Systemic Functional Linguistics (SFL). Nonetheless, few researchers have adopted a social semiotics perspective to study translated book covers – with the exception of Yu and Song (2016) and Li, Li and Miao (2019).

This study sets out to bridge this gap in the study of translated book covers by offering an empirical case study of verbal–visual interactions on translated front covers from a social-semiotic approach. To do this, six covers of the highly successful but politically volatile family chronicle, *Wild Swans* (Chang 1991, 2003, 2016; Chang 1992, 2006, 2015, translated by Zhang), have been analysed – including three English-language source text (ST) covers and three Chinese target text (TT) covers. The main objectives are to investigate the text–image relations within a cover, the ensemble of shifts in meaning between source and target covers and potential contextual reasons for diachronic changes across translated covers. This study will hopefully serve as a useful point of reference in systematizing dimensions of multimodal choice-making in translated book covers. This study also calls for multimodal social semiotics as an empowering tool for translation scholars, in much the same way that translation scholars have advocated the usefulness of SFL in reducing the subjectivity of translation evaluation (cf. Munday 1998; House 2013; Kim and Matthiessen 2015).

2 Social semiotic approaches to multimodality and translation

Extending as it does the concept of text to other semiotic systems, social-semiotic approaches to multimodality have incorporated key concepts from Systemic Functional Linguistics (SFL) such as function and system. The underlying principle that language is a system of choices available to its users within a given context is well suited to the study of other meaning-making semiotic resources (Jewitt, Bezemer and O'Halloran 2016: 45). Just as SFL offers a common theoretical framework to describe both the source and target languages, social-semiotic multimodal studies establish some common ground, albeit with differences, between language and other modes (Bateman, Wildfeuer and Hiippala 2017: 50). This commonality enables translation scholars to explore the ensemble of meaning-making choices across modes in translation.

O'Toole (1994) and Kress and van Leeuwen ([1996] 2006) have been seminal in multimodal discourse analysis and both drew on SFL in their frameworks for analysing and interpreting images. In their adaptation of Halliday's concept of metafunction to visual texts, both the above frameworks adopt a trinocular perspective on resources 1) to engage our attention and interest, 2) to convey some information about reality and 3) to structure these into a coherent textual form. Some terminological divergence should be noted. The three metafunctions have been re-labelled by O'Toole (1994: 5) as 'modal' (interpersonal function in SFL), 'representational' (ideational function in SFL) and 'compositional' (textual function in SFL) for art. Kress and van Leeuwen ([1996] 2006) use the terms ideational, interpersonal and textual to generalize across semiotic modes, but propose 'representational', 'interactive' and 'compositional', respectively, in their discussion of the grammar of images. Despite some differences, the frameworks presupposed both by O'Toole (mainly the systems for describing paintings) and Kress and van Leeuwen have inspired the present study because of the appliability of their systems to translated book covers.

This study undertakes manual analyses of a small corpus in modelling a social-semiotic approach to multimodal TS. It adopts the overall framework of the visual grammar of Kress and van Leeuwen ([1996] 2006) as the basis for the proposed analytical framework for book covers due to the relevance of their focus on visual artefacts combining image and writing. In addition, this study supplements visual grammar analysis with three additional theoretical considerations: 1) Genette's (1997) theoretical work on paratext; 2) the notion of unit or rank (O'Toole 1994; Bateman, Wildfeuer and Hiippala 2017) and 3) a critical consideration of visual typology of the Western and the Chinese[1] conventions. First, the notion of 'paratext' as proposed by Genette (1997: 5) includes 'peritext' – those elements around the text proper such as cover and footnotes – and 'epitext' – those distant elements outside the text, such as related interviews and websites. This study of book cover is essentially a study of the translation of paratext, however, the intertextual relation between the cover and the text proper will be explored. Second, the notion of unit (O'Toole 1994: 24) in displayed art, deriving from 'rank' in SFL (Matthiessen 1995; Halliday and Matthiessen 1999; Halliday and Matthiessen 2014: 21), refers to the compositional hierarchy from the highest Work to the lowest Member. Work refers to the overall narrative themes and interplay of episodes; Episode refers to actions and events; Figure refers to specific characters, objects and acts; Member refers to parts of a Figure. This study will borrow O'Toole's notion of rank to identify and analyse systems at the ranks of Work, Episode and Figure within a book cover, but does not explicitly include the more delicate Member. As a proposal for an analytical framework that may potentially suit other translated covers, this study elaborates the framework presented in Li, Li and Miao (2019: 4–5) as in Table 9.1, which makes an original contribution in aligning visual and verbal systems functionally and at the same rank.

Within the ideational function, the key visual elements at Work rank are the overall setting, background, colour and the bringing-together of different episodes. The key verbal element is the translation of the book title and, where applicable, its subtitle. While a title potentially realizes all three metafunctions, its function is considered to be primarily ideational; as Grivel points out (in Genette 1997: 76), the functions of the title are mainly to identify the work and to designate the work's subject matter that may attract interest. In the case where there is a secondary title or subtitle, Genette (1997: 85) usefully explains that 'the subtitle nowadays often gives a more literal indication of the theme that the title evokes symbolically or cryptically'. This division between title and subtitle applies to the chosen corpus.

Within Episode and Figure, this study focuses on visual and verbal agency and dynamism. 'Agency' and 'agent' have been used inconsistently in multimodal studies, with meanings ranging from an external cause in a narrative process, to the level of energy and motion and to the stakeholders in text production such as the editor (cf. O'Toole 1994; Machin and Thornborrow 2003; Kress and Van Leeuwen [1996] 2006; Liu 2011; O'Sullivan 2013). We will use the term 'agent' to specifically refer to a represented participant who functions as an initiator in a narrative process; for example, a police officer who is visually represented as instigating the arresting of somebody. However, a lack of represented agency of a character does not mean the character does not have any quality of being able to affect the world around him/

Table 9.1 Analysis of verbal and visual elements in translated book covers

Rank	Ideational function		Interpersonal function		Textual function	
	Visual	Verbal	Visual	Verbal	Visual	Verbal
Work	interplay of episodes; the overall background setting and colour	title and subtitle; overall representation	modality; intensity; aesthetic appeal	author's and translator's names; marker of translation status; emblem of publisher; publisher blurb and press quotation appraisal	typicality of book size; salience; framing	textual markedness; information structure
Episode	actor-goal; agency and dynamism; a group of people/ objects	transitivity; ergativity; agency and dynamism;	shot of frame; perspective	mood; modality; appraisal	regional salience; sub-framing	Theme; information structure
Figure	a character/ object; act/gesture		contact; angle; contrast in colour and light	modality; appraisal	local salience; size and font of the blurb and quotation	

her: one who does not instigate a narrative process can nevertheless be considered to affect the world around him/her through dynamic vibrant behaviours and actions such as athletic moves, dance and confidence smile – we shall refer to this as 'dynamism' borrowing Hasan's (1985: 45) concept to visual text.

Within the interpersonal function, key visual elements for the unit Work include modality, intensity, aesthetic appeal and appraisal. Modality is the level of commitment to certainty and reality and can be adjusted either linguitically or through visual devices such as colour, representational and background detail and brightness. Modality will be discussed in this study alongside the linguistic concept of the degree of intensity (Halliday and Matthiessen 2014: 189). This can be applied to visual grammar in terms of gradable, intensifying dimensions such as brightness and colour saturation (conceptualized by Painter, Martin and Unsworth [2013: 45] as 'visual graduation' based on the appraisal framework). Aesthetic appeal refers to the potential of certain images and design to be considered 'beautiful' by certain cultural groups (Bednarek and Caple 2017: 66). In spite of the impossibility of a completely objective measurement of beauty, one may use less subjective variables such as skin condition and the balance of a facial profile to help evaluate beauty in human images. Aesthetic appeal is closely linked to the linguistic resources of appraisal to inscribe or invoke positive appreciation, which may be crucial for a cover in terms of marketabilty.

Verbal elements in Work include the writer's and translator's names (or pseudonyms) and publisher's emblem, which are considered to be interpersonally more significant because they reveal the identity of the de factor text producers to the readers. The author's name may reveal, conceal or even manipulate important information about the author, such as gender, race, ancestry and nationality – all of which can have crucial thematic relevance (Genette 1997: 40) and powerfully impact on readers' perceptions. In addition, any observed adherence to or deviation from an established naming convention may reveal an author's level of solidarity with an institution of a particular norm. For example, a choice from numerous conventions of Romanisation of Chinese characters may reveal whether a Chinese author originates from the Mainland or Taiwan. We also consider whether there are considerable differences in the naming conventions between the ST and the TT languages, choices in the author's name may reflect strategies of domestication or foreignization (Venuti 2008). A publisher's emblem can also have thematic relevance as a publisher is often associated with a particular genre or even ideological stance.

Within the units Episode and Figure, key visual interpersonal systems include size of frame, contact and angle (Kress and van Leeuwen [1996] 2006: 116–43), which are particularly meaningful when a cover features human figures. Size of frame is the choice amongst long shot, medium shot and close-up, which respectively suggest impersonal, social, and personal/intimate social distance between represented participants and readers. Contact refers to either a function of 'demand' through gaze and certain gestures/postures of the represented participant or of 'offer' through an absence of gaze. Angle can be manipulated either horizontally or vertically to fine-tone the intended relations of power and solidarity between represented participants and viewers – a frontal angle invites viewers' involvement, whereas an oblique angle detaches viewers from the represented participants; at the same time a high angle assigns more symbolic power to viewers, whereas a low angle allocates more power to the represented participants and an eye level angle suggests equal power relations. In addition to involvement, relationships amongst represented participants have been conceptualized as 'orientation' (Painter, Martin and Unsworth 2013: 17) in relation to the bodily orientation of the participants towards each other. Similar relationships will be discussed in the present study but only in relation to framing within the textual function.

Within the textual function, key elements in Work include overall salience and the typicality of the size of the book. Information value has not been included, since it refers to specific informational value attached to various zones within a book cover (left/right: interpreted as Given information/New information, top/bottom interpreted as Ideal/Real, centre/margin interpreted as information nucleus/subservient information. This was deemed unsuitable for the present study because of the different orthographic conventions between the STs and the TTs. While a left–right orthographic convention has become the norm in books published in Mainland China and Hong Kong, a mixture of traditional[2] Chinese orthographic convention (top to bottom; right to left) and the Western left–right convention is often found on Taiwanese book covers. This renders the intended information structure of the covers indeterminate. Hence, for this study in the textual function we have placed emphasis on salience and framing.

Visual salience in a narrow sense refers to the relative foregrounding and back-staging of certain verbal and visual elements within a cover through graphic devices such as graphic position, colour, size, font and style and focus. More broadly speaking, foregrounding can be achieved through any unexpected visual regularities or unexpected irregularities (McIntyre 2003). Likewise, a verbal element can be linguistically foregrounded when it deviates from the expected regularities or irregularities; what is considered regular or irregular clearly varies across cultures and situations. Another textual system is framing, which is a common device in cover design. Framing uses actual frame lines or other elements to signify individuality, differentiation or disconnection.

3 Data selection

The function-based systems above have been analysed on the front covers of *Wild Swans* (Chang 1991, 2003, 2016), a successful but politically sensitive Chinese family chronicle written in English by a Chinese female migrant writer, and of its Chinese translation published in Taiwan (Chang 1992, 2006, 2015, translated by Zhang). Reinterpreting Chinese history in the twentieth century through the stories of the author's maternal grandmother, her mother and herself, this book has become the most well-known English work written by a contemporary Chinese writer, having sold over 15 million copies and been translated into forty languages (Chang 2020). Despite the phenomenal success in the West, it is virtually unknown in Mainland China due to censorship. The Chinese translation published in Taiwan presents two interesting translation peculiarities: the directionality of the translation into the source author's first language (Chinese) and the contribution of the source author to the translation.

Although Chang is quoted as the sole author, she acknowledged important inputs of knowledge, clarification and copyediting in shaping the ST from L1 speakers of English, including a bestselling biographer, a historian and editors/publishers (Chang 1991, 2003, xi–xii). Chang also directly translated the Introduction into Chinese (Chang 1992: 12–14, translated by Chang), even though the overall credit of the Chinese translation is attributed solely to Pu Zhang (張樸 Zhāng Pǔ), the brother of Chang and a London-based Chinese-language writer. However, whether Chang has made more contributions to the Chinese translation remains unclear, and to date neither the ST author nor the translator has responded to the request for an interview to provide additional information about the translation process, including choices taken by ST author/translator/editor/publisher/design professionals in designing the translated covers. The present study therefore limits its contributions to a study of translated covers as a product by drawing its conclusions based on the shifts of meaning in the verbal and visual elements.

One can find around forty different covers of *Wild Swans* on Chang's personal website[3] across languages and editions. These covers greatly differ even in the ideational domain: for example, the French cover omits the subtitle, and the Portuguese cover omits the images of the three Chinese women. Such striking differences suggest liberal choice-making in translating the paratext (Genette 1997), which may be beyond the translator's responsibility or control but is nevertheless a meaningful issue when considering translation as a product.

To compare changes on the front covers over time, the first (1991 and 1992) and the most recent (2016 and 2015) versions of the English ST and Taiwanese Chinese TT have been singled out as two pairs of parallel texts. In addition, two other covers that can be considered mid-way versions are added – the 2003 Touchstone cover is taken from the initial U.S. edition and is distinctively different from the British cover in the background colour and the interplay of episodes. Subsequently, the 2006 Taiwanese version was chosen because it was the first Chinese translation published after the 2003 U.S. version. The six covers form the main data in the present study, as shown in Table 9.2.

In particular, any press blurbs on the front covers has been extracted in Table 9.3.

In addition, covers in other languages listed on Chang's personal websites will serve as references within the perspective of the present study.

4 Results and discussions

4.1 Overall similarities between the source covers and the target covers

The six covers show similarities in key systems in the ideational function, which suggest strong source cover influence on the target covers. All English and Chinese covers contain a title and a subtitle that remain consistent across time within the same language, not unexpected for a bestseller. However, the inclusion of both a title and a subtitle in Chinese contrasts with the covers in some other languages that omit the subtitle, such as the French cover. In addition, all English and Chinese covers

Table 9.2 Covers in scope

English covers	Chinese covers
Wild Swans – Three Daughters of China (Chang 1991, 2003, 2016) Author: Jung Chang	鴻-三代中國女人的故事 (Traditional Chinese) *Hóng-Sāndài Zhōngguó Nǚrén de Gùshì* *Hong – The Story of Three Generations of Chinese Women* Author: 張戎 (Jung Chang) Translator: 張樸 (Pu Zhang)

ST1:
1991
Publisher: Harper Collin (London)
Image reproduced with the kind permission of Harper Collin (London)

TT1:
1992
Publisher: Chung Hwa Book Company (台灣中華書局) (Taipei)
Image reproduced with the kind permission of Chung Hwa Book Company

ST2:
2003
Publisher: Touchstone (New York)
Image reproduced with the kind permission of Jung Chang

TT2:
2006
Publisher: Heliopolis/Clio Culture (日月文化) (Taipei)
Image reproduced with the kind permission of Jung Chang

English covers	Chinese covers

ST3: 2016 Publisher: Harper Collins UK (London) Image reproduced with the kind permission of Harper Collin (London)	TT3: 2015 Publisher: Rye Field Publishing Co (麥田) (Taipei) Image reproduced with the kind permission of Rye Field Publishing Co

Table 9.3 Press blurbs on the covers

Blurbs on the English covers	Blurbs on the Chinese covers (translated into English by the present author)
ST1: 'It is impossible to exaggerate the importance of this book' – Mary Wesley	TT1: N/A
ST2: 'This real-life saga of a Chinese family over three generations contains more violence than any film noir, more heartrending tragedy than *Little Dorrit* … There has never been a book like this.' – Edward Behr, Los Angeles Times With a new introduction by the author	TT2: 本書已譯成三十餘種文字，全球銷售量達一千兩百萬冊 [This book has been translated into over 30 languages; the global sales figure has reached 12 million.] TT3: 走過纏足的時代、封建體制的婚姻、抗日戰爭、國共內亂……直至文化大革命的劫難，她們經歷了人間的悲歡離合，也創造了不平凡的一生。三代中國女性 一部感人家史 理解二十世紀中國的重量級磅礡史詩
ST3: 'Riveting; an extraordinary epic' *Mail on Sunday*	[Having gone through the era of foot-binding, marriage under the feudal system, the Anti-Japanese War, the civil strife between the Kuomintang and the Communists … all the way to the catastrophic Cultural Revolution, they experienced joy and sadness and the ebbs and flows of the world, and created extraordinary lives. Three generations of Chinese female. A touching family chronicle. A significant, epic saga to understand China in the 20th century.]

have incorporated the same photos of the three Chinese women despite differences in photo size, colour and resolution. Furthermore, there is a degree of resemblance in the background colour and the overall style in each pair of English and Chinese covers – the 1991 British cover and 1992 Chinese cover both choose dark title colours and muted background colours such as light green and light blue; and the 2003 English cover and the 2006 Chinese cover have both chosen white colour for title and bright red and orange as the background, creating high intensity. These clearly show the influence of English source cover design on the contemporary Chinese target cover. On the other hand, although the 2016 English version was published after the 2015 Chinese translation, the covers share a style with the background in plain colours, which may be indicative of a global shift in aesthetics over time, a hypothesis to be further studied.

Although the Chinese covers follow the contemporary English-language covers in preserving the structure of one title and one subtitle, and in using the same three images, some considerable shifts have been found across ideational interpersonal and textual metafunctions.

4.2 Ideational function

Halliday (2001: 16–17) assigns the highest value to the ideational equivalence in translation, without which in his opinion a translation would generally not qualify as translation. The Chinese covers show visual resemblance to the English source covers in a key visual component – the images of the three Chinese female participants, who are represented as being beautiful, as partially evidenced through the airbrushed quality of their skin and balanced facial profile. However, all images are static conceptual images (i.e. not performing any social action, verbal or mental activities or behaviour such as laughing or smiling confidently as often seen on the covers of the autobiographies of female leaders such as Michelle Obama and Hillary Clinton). In our case these images display a low level of dynamism in terms of affecting their surrounding environment and do not display any agency. While low visual dynamism and agency of a protagonist on the front covers of biographies do not absolutely equate with low agency in the main verbal text of a book, in this case it is congruent with the overall theme of tragedy and the linguistic representation of the three characters in the book – the women all bear the brunt of Chinese history in the twentieth century rather than being drivers of that history (Li 2018). Overall, the translated covers are compliant with the source covers in visually representing the women with no agency and low dynamism.

A main visual difference in the ideational function between all the source and all the target covers is the inclusion of a pictorial Chinese character on the English covers: 鴻 (*hóng*), in an artistic style that arguably calls to mind a long-necked bird with flapping wings. Although this character also appears as the title on the Chinese cover, it is not represented in a pictorial, bird shape. Therefore, the same character should be considered a different sign on the translated covers. On the English covers, it is mainly a visual signifier serving three purposes: 1) to reaffirm the nationality of the Asian women with an exotic symbol from the Chinese writing system; 2) to visually elaborate the aesthetic, feminine and romantic bird 'swan' in the title with its pictographic imagery; 3) to signify China and communism through the red colour. Taken together, the red pictorial character conveys cultural exoticism and femininity to English readers. In comparison, the same character is mainly a verbal signifier on the Chinese covers, with its linguistic meaning to be directly deciphered by the readers; the character is also not in red, suggesting a reduction of cultural exoticism – even though both the 2006 and 2015 TT covers nevertheless use a red background to signify communism to Taiwanese readers.

The uses of the same character as different symbols also bring attention to the shifts in translating the title, which are ideationally more significant than the visual shifts. *Wild Swans* eulogizes the three Chinese women as swans, because both the mother's name and Chang's nickname contain the character 鴻(*hóng*), which was said to mean 'wild swans' (Chang 1991, 2003, 44). Subsequently, the original character 鴻 (*hóng*) mentioned in the English ST became the Chinese title as a back translation of 'Wild Swans'. However, 鴻 (*hóng*), being a vague morpheme on its own, means swan goose when referring to a bird; and swans and swan geese are different birds (the latter does not carry the positive attributes of romance and femininity in the Western context [Li, Li and Miao 2019]). Therefore, the English title *Wild Swans* is not a direct translation as Chang has claimed, but rather, an artistic creation – perhaps intended to evoke positive associations for marketability (van Leeuwen 2015). This discrepancy in meaning may be a reason that the Chinese covers, targeting readers who understand what 鴻 (*hóng*) signifies, retain the vague morpheme 鴻 (*hóng*) instead of a more literal 野天鵝 (*yě tiān'é*: wild swan), and do not recreate the imagery of a long-necked bird.

Visual and verbal elements on the covers of translations in some other languages also confirm a correction of this artistic interpretation on the source covers. Thus, a pictorial character and a literal translation of 'swan' have been avoided on the translated Korean and Japanese covers, both of which are situated within the sphere of Chinese characters: the Korean title is 대륙의 딸 (*daelyug-ui ttal*), which literally translates as 'Daughter of the Continent'; the Japanese title is ワイルドスワン (*wairudo suwan*), which is a transliteration of the English title, even though the option of '野の白鳥' (*no no hakuchō*: wild swans) was available in the way Andersen's *The Wild Swans* was translated. It is unclear whether the ideational inaccuracy of translating 鴻 (*hóng*) into 'wild swans' in the ST was carefully manipulated or simply a fortunate error. That said, necessary shifts have been introduced in Chinese, Korean and Japanese to avoid such inaccuracy.

Another major ideational shift in the verbal text can be found in the translation of the subtitle, *Three Daughters of China*, into 三代中國女人的故事 (the story of three generations of Chinese women). The English subtitle appears more personal by focusing on the people, whereas the Chinese subtitle appears more detached by focusing on the genre. In addition, the lexical choice of 'daughter' in the English subtitle carries a sense of dependence, youth and lower status within the family hierarchy, in comparison to 女人 (woman) used in the Chinese subtitle. Lastly, the Chinese translation emphasizes the generation gaps amongst the women, whereas the English subtitle represents the women as an undifferentiated group of daughters; this difference in the subtitle has further implications on the textual function, which will be explored in Section 4.4.

In sum, while the visual designs of the source covers have clearly influenced subsequent Chinese translated covers ideationally, greater shifts have been found in the translation of verbal text, especially in the title and the subtitle.

4.3 Interpersonal function

The interpersonal function concerns the symbolic relationship between the author and the readers and between the represented participants and the readers. The front cover shows no clear indicators to a first-time reader that the book is a family chronicle or that the three represented women are the author–narrator, her mother and her maternal grandmother; this only becomes apparent in the photo captions within the book. Key interpersonal systems under analysis include shot of frame, angle, contact, modality and intensity, the author's name, the translator's name and the publisher's and press blurb.

While certain aspects in the visual elements may create distance for English readers (such as the pictorial Chinese character, the Asian ethnicity of the women and the black-and-white/faded colour of the photographs), the English covers overall have represented the three Chinese women as intimate (through choices of photos with a close-up shot), contactable and demanding reader attention (through direct gaze), having equal power with readers (through eye-level angle), and being part of or being close to the readers' world (through a frontal angle shot of the grandmother and the mother, and a slightly oblique angle of the author). Because the same images are adopted on the Chinese covers, there is no significant visual shifts in the interpersonal meaning – except that the Chinese ethnicity would not produce foreign unfamiliarity for the Taiwanese readers.

The Taiwanese TTs do, however, show higher visual modality and intensity than the contemporary English covers through contextualizing the photos, higher photo resolutions, brighter and more saturated colours. For instance, both the 2006 and 2015 TT covers not only show higher modality though black-and-white photos with higher resolution but also display high intensity through a saturated red background colour. This is congruent with the higher degrees of linguistic modality and intensity found in the Chinese TT than in the ST (Li 2017; Li and Wu 2019).

Some key verbal systems within these covers are the author's and the translator's names, and other markers of a translation status. The author's English name is a marked choice, as it does not follow the official Romanisation system of Pinyin in Mainland China, where the author grew up; instead, the foregrounded adoption of the Wade-Giles system, Romanizing the name 張戎 (*ZHĀNG Róng*) into 'Jung Chang', suggests that Chang distances herself from the Chinese government. In addition, the name suggests an East Asian ancestry, which, in combination with the pictorial character and the images, delivers a clear message that this book is written by a Chinese woman about Chinese women. Perceptive English-language readers would unlikely be oblivious to such clear markers of ethnicity, nationality and gender. Hence, it may be a worthwhile future undertaking to explore whether the design of covers in Western European languages has been influenced by an Orientalist ideology (Said 1978), which views the East–West relations as a gendered dichotomy and a power imbalance. On the other hand, the markedness in the choice of the Romanisation system is lost in the Chinese translation: the author's name in traditional characters suggests neither the author's origin nor her attitudes towards Mainland China.

All translated covers include at least a marker of translation status: the 1992 cover shows the translator's name and role, and the 2006 cover shows two additional markers, including the author's Romanized name and the English source title, clearly presenting the text as a translation of an English book. The consistent inclusion of the translator's name, which contrasts with translations in other languages such as French (Chang 2020), exemplifies the translator's visibility (Venuti 2008) in the Chinese translations, perhaps as a marketing strategy to foreground the unusual success of a book by a Chinese writer in the Western market. International success for people of Chinese heritage is generally highly regarded in the Sinophone sphere. The translator being the brother of the ST author may also have contributed to the recognition of his name on the TT cover. In addition, the inclusion of the ST title and the ST author's Romanized name may help interested Chinese readers identify the work and the author in English sources.

As for the press endorsements, applying the appraisal framework (Martin and White 2005) to the key lexical items has found positive appreciation of the valuation of the work in all cases. However, while the blurbs on all the English covers show explicit (inscribed) positive appreciation such as the high importance (i.e. 'impossible to exaggerate the importance of this book' in ST1) and outstanding quality (i.e. 'There has never been a book like this' in ST2; 'riveting; an extraordinary epic' in ST1, the Chinese blurbs show less explicitly positive appreciation. While only the 2015 Chinese cover has explicit, positive appreciation (i.e. 重磅級磅礡史詩 [a significant, epic saga]), the 2006 Chinese cover has implicit (afforded) appreciation, through mentioning sale figures (i.e. 全球銷售量達一千兩百萬冊 [the global sales figure has reached 12 millions]), and the 1992 Chinese cover does not contain any press endorsements. In addition, words of negative appreciation of the book such as 'heartrending' and 'violence' are used on the 2003 English cover to positively appraise the ST as a great tragedy. The Chinese covers show no items of negative appreciation of the book; instead, only the 2015 cover shows negative appreciation of the historical events that the women lived through (i.e. the catastrophic Cultural Revolution). Considering that blurbs for bestsellers may be highly formulated within a given context, the preference of the TT covers for more implicitly positive appreciations suggests a potential difference in the convention of blurb between the Anglophone sphere and the Taiwanese context. Positive appreciation is more implicit in the Chinese blurbs, and the Chinese translations are marketed as a touching family story, rather than a tragedy.

The interpersonal analyses have found that, while the Chinese women are represented as being exotic but close to the English readers at the same time, cultural exoticism has been reduced on the TT covers. Nevertheless, the Chinese covers consistently mark the status of the books as a translation of a foreign work; the Chinese blurbs not only provide a more implicitly positive appreciation of the book but also suggests a genre shift in translation away from tragedy.

4.4 Textual function

The textual function shows the most significant visual shifts. Key systems under analysis include salience, book dimension and framing. Images can be made salient through devices such as larger size and stronger contrast. While no consistent patterns have been observed in image size, the three photos appear more salient on the Taiwanese covers due to a stronger contrast between the grey photos and the bright background colours. The contrasts are weaker on all source covers either due to the ink brush underneath the photos or to the faded effect.

A key difference can be observed in the textual salience of the author's name on the cover. On the 1991 and 2016 covers, the size of the author's name matches that of the title, both being the verbal element with the largest size. On the 2003 cover, although the size of the author's name is slightly smaller than that of the title, the strong framing, bold black font, and strong contrast with the background colours render the name highly salient. All these suggest the elite star-pulling power of Jung Chang in the ST culture. On the Chinese covers, by contrast, the size of the author's name is consistently smaller than that of the title: on the 1992 and the 2006 covers, the author's name is smaller even than the subtitles; on the 2015 cover, the author's name is also printed with low salience due to the low contrast between black words and grey background, even though the author's name is slightly larger size than the subtitle. The smaller sizes may suggest Chang's lesser fame in the Chinese-speaking world, as books written by authors with celebrity status often feature the author's names in extra-large characters on the front covers in both the Taiwanese and Mainland Chinese book markets. This echoes the sharp contrast between a status of the ST as a contemporary Western classic, symbolized by a convenient pocket size, and the unmarked book size of the Taiwanese TT (Li, Li and Miao 2019).

Another interesting finding from the translated covers is the trend of reduced visibility of the translator's name over time. While the 1992 cover prints the author's and the translator's names in equal size and font, the 2006 cover uses a considerably smaller size for the translator's name and the most recent 2015 cover prints the translator's name in a barely legible typeface size. In conjunction with the larger image sizes, this suggests a more deliberate attempt in the latest TT to obscure the translation status and to reduce the distance between the ST author and the Chinese-language readers.

Lastly, there are noticeable differences between the source covers and the target covers in framing devices, which may signify individuality and differentiation amongst the three represented participants. The images on the 2003 English cover are so weakly framed that the women can be seen as an undifferentiated group of the daughters of China. In comparison, all images on the Chinese covers are strongly framed. In addition, the three images are more disconnected on the Chinese covers: while they are linked via connected frames on the 2015 cover, the same images are only partially linked via the red ink brush on the 2006 cover, and are disconnected on the 1992 cover. This strongly contrasts with the English covers, on which the images are always linked. This heightened individuality on the translated covers may have been influenced by the family hierarchy and stronger generational differentiation in Chinese culture, which is further confirmed verbally by the explicit addition of the Chinese classifier 代 (*dài*: generation) in the Chinese subtitle.

In short, the textual function shows greater shifts in visual elements in the Chinese covers than do the other two functions. While the English covers highlight the status of the author through foregrounded sizes of the author's name, the sizes are unmarked on the Chinese covers. In addition, the Chinese covers emphasizes the generational hierarchy amongst the three women, in comparison to an emphasis on their oneness and connectedness on the English covers. Furthermore, the Chinese covers show decreasing visibility of the translator through time, perhaps suggestive of changing trends.

4.5 An ensemble of similarities and differences

This study has explored the verbal–visual interactions on four levels: within a given book cover, between a book cover and the text proper of the book, between a comparable English cover and a Chinese cover and diachronic changes across selected translated covers. Within a book cover, this study has found a high degree of verbal–visual complementarity: for example, the images visually complement the title and subtitle by pointing to the same referents in a different mode. In between a cover and its text proper, there is congruency between the linguistic representations of the women as bearers of history in the book and the front-cover visual representation of the women as being non-agentive with low dynamism.

Between a comparable English cover and Chinese cover, especially in the first two pairs where the English can be considered the source cover for the Chinese target, strong ST influences have been identified. However, there are also considerable overall translation shifts from English to Chinese. The English covers include a more sensational and personal title and subtitle, which evoke aesthetic and feminine associations; this is perhaps influenced by the associated likeability of Asia with its female members within the prevalent Orientalist worldview. In comparison, the Chinese titles are more impersonal, with reduced aesthetic and feminine associations. While the English covers present the women as being both exotic and close to English readers, the Chinese covers remove such exoticism but highlight the translation status. The English covers contain more explicitly positive evaluation of the work in the blurbs and endorsements and a more explicit indication of the book's genre as a tragedy, whereas on the Chinese covers positive evaluation of the work is more implicit and the genre of book as a tragedy is obscured. Furthermore, the English covers deploy textual devices of salience to deliver a strong message about the stardom of both the work and the author. In stark contrast, the translation covers show considerably less textual markedness. This shows that foregrounding devices are overall used less intensively in these Chinese translations, except for the higher visual modality and intensity, showing more detachment in the pursuits of marketability and ideological interests.

Lastly, despite some significant differences between the English and Chinese covers, the diachronic comparisons suggest that certain differences have reduced over time. While the Chinese translations shed considerably less light on the author than do the English covers, there is an increasing trend to place visual emphasis on the author's name at the expense of the visibility of the translator. This all suggests that the Chinese versions may have moved closer to the English convention of foregrounding the author on a cover.

5 Conclusion

This study has used the common SFL language of a metafunctional approach to analyse both the verbal and visual elements on three source covers and three Chinese target covers and has found more visual similarities in the ideational and interpersonal functions but more differences in the textual function. The similarities in the first two functions reaffirm strong ST influences in the cover design of the translations even when they are not formal 'translations' like the verbal texts. However, there are clear shifts which distance the target texts from certain ideational inaccuracy, highly sensational elements and overt compliments in the source covers. Shifts in the textual function, especially in the visual, are the most prominent, removing foregrounding devices that symbolize the stardom of the book and the author. For this and other reasons, this study calls for empirical research into the commensurability of visual information structure between the Western and Chinese conventions.

The ensemble of the similarities and differences has resulted in the translated covers being plainer and more detached, perhaps less ideologically invested, despite being reasonably faithful to the source covers. On the other hand, differences between a source and a target cover are highly fluid, as evidenced by a trend of the Chinese covers in moving towards certain ST conventions such as the visual spotlight on the author. This is an area that requires further work.

Limitations of the present study are the lack of interviews, the need to develop the visual typology of information structure and some subjectivity involved in the selection of data from the many covers available. Nevertheless, it is hoped that this study will serve as a point of reference for analysing multimodal meaning-making in translated book covers from a social-semiotic perspective. In addition, it highlights the importance of typological considerations from both a linguistic and visual perspective. Third, the diachronic shifts across various translated covers highlight the importance of the context of culture; the trend towards increased visibility of the ST author suggests that certain cultural differences are being flattened in an increasingly globalized world.

Notes

1. The word 'Chinese' in this study applies to the entire Sinophone sphere, including Mainland China. Taiwan, Hong Kong and Macao.
2. This convention is separate from the choice of simplified versus traditional characters: both scripts can be written or printed either horizontally or vertically, although vertical orthography is more common in Taiwan where traditional characters are officially used.
3. http://www.jungchang.net/wild-swans

References

Alvstad, C. (2008), 'Illustrations and Ambiguity in Eighteen Illustrated Translations of Hans Christian Andersen's "The Steadfast Tin Soldier"', *Meta: Translators' Journal* 53 (1): 90–103.

Batchelor, K. (2018), *Translation and Paratexts: Paratexts and Translation Theory*, London: Routledge.

Bateman, J., Wildfeuer, J. and Hiippala, T. (2017), *Multimodality: Foundations, Research and Analysis–A Problem-Oriented Introduction*, Berlin: Walter de Gruyter GmbH.

Bednarek, M., and Caple, H. (2017), *The Discourse of News Values: How News Organizations Create Newsworthiness*, New York: Oxford University Press.

Borodo, M. (2015), 'Multimodality, Translation and Comics', *Perspectives* 23 (1): 22–41.

Chueasuai, P. (2013), 'Translation Shifts in Multimodal Text: A Case of the Thai Version of Cosmopolitan', *Journal of Specialised Translation* (20): 107–21.

Fu, L. (2013), 'Indigenizing Visualized Knowledge: Translating Western Science Illustrations in China, 1870–1910', *Translation Studies* 6 (1): 78–102.

Gambier, Y. (2006), 'Moves towards Multimodality and Language Representation in Movies', *Readings in Intersemiosis and Multimedia. Proceedings of the 3rd TICOM, Pavia*: 1–10.

Genette, G. (1997), *Paratexts: Thresholds of Interpretation*, trans. J. Lewin, Cambridge: Cambridge University Press.

Halliday, M. A. K. (1978), *Language as Social Semiotic*, London: Arnold.

Halliday, M. A. K. (2001), 'Towards a Theory of Good Translation', in E. Steiner and C. Yallop (eds), *Exploring Translation and Multilingual Text Production: Beyond Content*, 13–18, Berlin: Mouton de Gruyter.

Halliday, M. A. K., and Matthiessen, C. M. I. M. (1999), *Construing Experience through Meaning: A Language-based Approach to Cognition*, London: Cassel.

Halliday, M. A. K., and Matthiessen, C. M. I. M. (2014), *Halliday's Introduction to Functional Grammar*, London: Routledge.

Harvey, K. (2003), ' "Events" and "Horizons": Reading Ideology in the "Bindings" of Translations', in M. C. Pérez (ed.), *Apropos of Ideology: Translation Studies on Ideology – Ideologies in Translation Studies*, 43–70, Manchester: St. Jerome.

Hasan, R. (1985), *Linguistics, Language, and Verbal Art*, Victoria: Deakin University.

House, J. (2013), 'Towards a New Linguistic-Cognitive Orientation in Translation Studies', *Target. International Journal of Translation Studies* 25 (1): 46–60.

Jakobson, R. ([1959] 2004), 'On Linguistic Aspects of Translation', in L. Venuti (ed.), *The Translation Studies Reader*, 2nd edn, 138–43, London: Routledge.

Jewitt, C., Bezemer, J. and O'Halloran, K. (2016), *Introducing Multimodality*, London: Routledge.

Kim, M., and Matthiessen, C. M. I. M. (2015), 'Ways to Move Forward in Translation Studies: A Textual Perspective', *Target. International Journal of Translation Studies* 27 (3): 335–50.

Kress, G., and van Leeuwen, T. ([1996] 2006), *Reading Images: The Grammar of Visual Design*, Oxon: Routledge.

Lee, T. (2013), 'Performing Multimodality: Literary Translation, Intersemioticity and Technology', *Perspectives* 21 (2): 241–56.

Li, L. (2017), 'An Examination of Ideology in Translation via Modality: Wild Swans and Mao's Last Dancer', *Journal of World Languages*, 4 (2): 118–44. doi:10.1080/21698252.2 017.1417689.

Li, L. (2018), 'The Influence of Political Ideology in the Chinese Translations of English Works by Chinese Migrant Writers', PhD diss., Department of Linguistics, Macquarie University, Sydney.

Li, L., Li, X. and Miao, J. (2019), 'A Translated Volume and Its Many Covers – a Multimodal Analysis of the Influence of Ideology', *Social Semiotics* 29 (2): 261–78. doi: 10.1080/10350330.2018.1464248.

Li, L., and Wu, C. (2019), 'Degree of Intensity in English-Chinese Translation: A Corpus-based Approach', *Functional Linguistics* 6 (3). doi:https://doi.org/10.1186/s40554-019-0068-1.

Liu, F. (2011), 'On Collaboration: Adaptive and Multimodal Translation in Bilingual Inflight Magazines', *Meta: Translators' Journal* 56 (1): 200–15.

Littau, K. (2011). 'First Steps Towards a Media History of Translation', *Translation Studies* 4 (3): 261–81.

Machin, D., and Thornborrow, J. (2003), 'Branding and Discourse: The Case of Cosmopolitan', *Discourse & Society* 14 (4): 453–71.

Martin, J. R., and White, P. R. R. (2005), *The Language of Evaluation: Appraisal in English*, New York: Palgrave Macmillan.

McIntyre, D. (2003), 'Using Foregrounding Theory as a Teaching Methodology in a Stylistics Course', *Style* 37 (1): 1–13.

Matthiessen, C. M. I. M. (1995), *Lexicogrammatical Cartography: English Systems*, Tokyo: International Language Sciences Publishers.

Matthiessen, C. M. I. M. (2001), 'The Environment of Translation', in E. Steiner and C. Yallop (eds), *Exploring Translation and Multilingual Text Production: Beyond Content*, 41–126, Berlin: Mouton de Gruyter.

Munday, J. (1998), 'Problems of Applying Thematic Analysis to Translation between Spanish and English', *Cadernos de Tradução* 1 (3): 183–213.

O'Sullivan, C. (2013), 'Introduction: Multimodality as Challenge and Resource for Translation', *Journal of Specialised Translation* 20: 2–14.

O'Toole, M. (1994), *The Language of Displayed Art*, Rutherford: Fairleigh Dickinson University Press.

Painter, C., Martin, J. and Unsworth, L. (2013), *Reading Visual Narratives: Image Analysis of Children's Picture Books*, Sheffield: Equinox.

Said, E. (1978), *Orientalism: Western Conceptions of the Orient*, New York: Random House,.

Sonzogni, M. (2011), *Re-Covered Rose: A Case Study in Book Cover Design as Intersemiotic Translation*, Amsderdam: John Benjamins.

Summers, C. (2018), 'The Institutional Reframing of Authorship in Translated Peritexts', in V. Pellatt (eds), *Text, Extratext, Metatext and Paratext in Translation*, 9–32, Newcastle upon Tyne: Cambridge Scholars.

Taylor, C. (2016), 'The Multimodal Approach in Audiovisual Translation', *Target. International Journal of Translation Studies* 28 (2): 222–36.

van Leeuwen, T. (2015), 'Looking Good: Aesthetics, Multimodality and Literacy Studies'. In J. Rowsell and K. Pahl (eds), *The Routledge Handbook of Literacy Studies*, 426–39, London: Routledge.

Venuti, L. (2008), *The Translator's Invisibility: A History of Translation*, London: Routledge.

Yu, H., and Song, Z. (2016), 'Picture–Text Congruence in Translation: Images of the Zen Master on Book Covers and in Verbal Texts', *Social Semiotics*: 1–20, doi:10.1080/10350330.2016.1251104.

References for the corpora

English corpora

Chang, J. (1991), *Wild Swans – Three Daughters of China*, London: HarperCollin.
Chang, J. (2003), *Wild Swans – Three Daughters of China*, New York: Touchstone.
Chang, J. (2016), *Wild Swans – Three Daughters of China*, London: HarperCollins.

Chinese corpora

Chang, J. (1992), *Hong: San Dai Zhong Guo Nu Ren De Gu Shi [orig. Wild Swans]*, trans. P. Zhang, Taipei: Chung Hwa Book.
Chang, J. (2006), *Hong: San Dai Zhong Guo Nu Ren De Gu Shi [orig. Wild Swans]*, trans. P. Zhang, Taipei: Heliopolis/Clio Culture.
Chang, J. (2015), *Hong: San Dai Zhong Guo Nu Ren De Gu Shi [orig. Wild Swans]*, trans. P. Zhang, Taipei: Rye Field.

Corpora in other languages

Chang, J. (2020), 'Wild Swans – Three Daughters of China', *Jung Chang – Official Website*. Assessed on 15 August 2020, http://www.jungchang.net/wild-swans.

10

Shifting the gaze to the paradigm: Translation as a tool for multilingual studies

Giacomo Figueredo

Federal University of Ouro Preto – (UFOP)

1 Systemic similarity in language comparison and translation

In this chapter we depart from translation operations – equivalence, shift and formal correspondence (Catford 1965) – and explore them further from a Systemic Functional perspective (Matthiessen 2001). More specifically, we focus on the systemic relationship between languages in a translation environment established according to Systemic Functional Linguistics (henceforth SFL). An SFL approach to translation (Steiner and Yallop 2001; Teich 2003) within the Multilingual Studies framework (Matthiessen, Teruya and Wu 2008) is adopted to explore linguistic relations between source and target languages.

Our main goal in this chapter is to show how explicit translation operations – equivalence, correspondence and shift – as described in previous studies (Catford 1965; Matthiessen 2001; Teich 1999, 2003; Munday 2004; Hatim and Munday 2019) can be used as a tool in the investigation of language relations.

We follow a Multilingual Studies perspective (Matthiessen, Teruya and Wu 2008) to interpret the phenomenon of translation. In Multilingual Studies, language comparison (including typology) is not divorced from translation rather it is an important step towards understanding linguistic aspects of translation as a phenomenon. Our point is that in order to compare languages one must, first and foremost, translate. By revisiting the operations of translation equivalence, shift and formal correspondence through the SFL lens we will show how these operations can depict different multilingual relations, including typology and comparison.

1.1 The *tertium comparationis* and translation

The *tertium comparationis* can be defined as the comparable characteristic shared by two different items. It is the common point from which a comparison can be carried out. Accordingly, comparison involves finding both sameness and difference in the behaviour of a feature in different languages. If only sameness is found, then it is impossible to obtain a comparison because all language items must be exactly the same. Conversely, if language items are absolutely different, then it is impossible to compare them at all. As a result, only partially identical/different items can be compared. The term we use to refer to items that are partially identical/different is 'similarity'. Technically, similarity is always established in language comparison and translation by three considerations: (i) the relevant category in Language A/Source; (ii) the relevant category in Language B/Target and (iii) the third part of the comparison, or the criteria for establishing similarity.

Language comparison based on SFL recognizes the role of theory in defining platforms of comparison. Caffarel, Martin and Matthiessen (2004) – a seminal work on functional typology – uses the metafunctional profile of different languages as the main criterion to establish similarity among languages. In addition, description has also been important for comparison (Matthiessen 2004). As a result, categories are compared and their similarity across languages is pointed out. SFL-based studies tend to rely both on theoretical and descriptive categories. Both have been used as *tertiae*. For instance, Munday (2015) analyses translations of English and Spanish and resorts to strata and metafunction (theoretical categories) as well as to appraisal (descriptive categories).

Because translation is a complex phenomenon that involves not only different language strata, but also context, the *tertium comparationis* is expected to be complex as well. Hatim (2009), for example, suggests the text as a translation unit. Once the text is established as minimal unit of translation, it opens up a number of possible comparisons between source and target languages; and many language functions can be used as the *tertium*, such as categories from discourse, register and genre. Steiner (2000) goes on to deploy more than one *tertium comparationis* to investigate the translation when exploring the notion of 'discipline' relating Translation Studies, evaluation and criticism to discourse analysis, anthropology and history. It is in this sense that the *tertium comparationis* lies at the core of comparative studies (cf. Ellis 1966). It forms the basis for formal and non-formal comparisons.

1.2 Range and confidence

The fact that languages and translations cannot be directly compared poses issues for comparison (Krzeszowski 1990). For the purpose of this chapter, issues in direct comparison will be described in terms of two problems: the *tertium*'s range and level of confidence.

The problem with range – or the extent to which a category is found similar through languages – is that the *tertium* must be theory-bound or at least based on the limiting restraint of observable overt phenomena. Not all languages have the same categories because languages are organized differently. In this sense, some categories of a language might never find a similar item in other languages to which they could be compared.

For example, descriptions of languages such as French, German and English (Steiner and Teich 2004; Caffarel 2006; Halliday and Matthiessen 2014) have identified and described the function of Finite, which arguably does not exist in Tibetan, Tagalog or Japanese (Teruya 2007; Martin and Cruz 2018; Wang 2020). Similarly, Behavioral Process has been described in English and French (Caffarel 2006; Halliday and Matthiessen 2014), but it does not exist in Japanese or German as a type of its own (Steiner and Teich 2004; Teruya 2007).

The problem with level of confidence – or how far a description can be trusted – is that currently there is not a method of measuring to which extent language descriptions draw on theory and argumentation in the same way. This means that different descriptions may involve different interpretations of theory and argumentation when addressing language phenomena. As a result, we cannot, unfortunately, be sure that all descriptions of different languages are truly comparable.

Even if we could make sure that descriptions followed exactly the same principles, we would still face the fact that languages are different by their very nature (Barros 2020). When language categories are given the same labels, it is difficult to determine with absolute confidence that descriptions are talking about the same categories and that descriptions of different languages are capturing the same phenomenon (cf. Halliday 1984).

For example, the SFL description of French (Caffarel 2006) uses the label 'Negotiator' to refer to the function-structure potentially consisting of Subject, Finite and Predicator, which Caffarel describes as 'functionally analogous to the Mood element of English' (2006: 81). The description of Japanese also has the label 'Negotiator' but uses it differently to refer to choices of certain types of MOOD and evaluation, that is, 'the negotiatory or attitudinal value of the clause such as question, insistence or assertion' (Teruya 2004: 191). As we can see, the label 'Negotiator' in two grammars informed by SFL refers to two very different categories. In French, it is a mandatory function which comprises the joint grammatical work of Subject, Finite and Predicator. In Japanese, it is an optional function unaligned with Subject and Predicator.

In this chapter we deploy a *tertium* derived from theory but acknowledge the problems of range and level of confidence that ensue.

In order to address these problems

1. We first reduce the range of the *tertium* to a minimal unit of meaning, understanding that all languages are meaning-making resources organized as a system. Thus, our *tertium comparationis* will be derived from the dimension of axis.
2. Then, we subsequently increase confidence by using the translation of minimal units of meaning to establish comparisons between Source and Target Languages.
3. We use translations between Source and Target categories as a basis for language comparison.

Translation, as any semiotic phenomenon, occurs naturally and independently of any theory. Whatever item is translated becomes a unit of comparison answering the confidence problem, since the TL unit is the translation of the SL unit. Moreover, translation as a tool can be managed by a systemic approach in that translation can be established by the commutation of features in SL and TL systems (see Section 2).

Admittedly, if we compare the negotiator in French and Japanese, we are perhaps comparing only labels. But through translation we can compare negotiator in French to predicator in Japanese and negotiator in Japanese to adjuncts or tags in French, or maybe yet more options. It all depends on the translation, that is, on the units of translation created by the relationship between a source language unit and a target language unit.

2 Valeur as the minimal *tertium comparationis*

In this section, we will suggest 'valeur' in systems as our basic unit of comparison between languages and our basic unit for comparing translations. We will show how to find the valeur in system networks and how to measure it.

The meaning-making relationship between two signs in a semiotic system is called 'valeur' (Saussure 1966). In a system, signs have a relative valeur in relation to one another because (i) they are very similar, since they are more detailed versions of their entry condition, yet (ii) they are mostly different at some specific point (ibid). In this respect, system rationale is mapped onto comparison since it captures similarity. Thus, language phenomena can be represented paradigmatically as features in systems (Halliday 2002; Martin 2013). Their structural manifestation can be described as the realization of features (see Figure 10.1).

Valeur is a fundamental property of all semiotic systems – a basic, minimal unit of meaning-making. For the purpose of this chapter, it can consequently be used as our *tertium comparationis* for the following reasons. First, it is a minimal unit; it does neither require much theoretical formulation to be understood nor have so many categories to, in Krzeszowski's words (1990), 'haze comparison out'. Secondly, it is fully derived from the dimension of system, which makes valeur a suitable category to explore language relations within the SFL framework. Finally, valeur is an objectively explicit property which does not need an implicit agreement as a universal category. In addition, valeur can also be used as a measure of how much meaning a system makes in comparison to other systems, which in turn can lead to a measurable method of comparing features across languages.

In SFL, language is modelled paradigmatically as a network of systems (Martin 2013), and the valeur of a feature involves two factors: agnation and delicacy. Agnation (Gleason 1965) is the factor of valeur that operates contrast. Delicacy (Halliday, McIntosh and Strevens 1964) handles the specificity of a feature in a given system. Every system has an entry condition and at least two contrasting features which, in turn, become entry conditions to subsystems at further levels of delicacy. For example, the system of NUMBER of English is described as shown in Figure 10.1.

The class of word 'nominal' is referred to as the entry condition – or the phenomenon being classified according to the criterion 'NUMBER' in English. The features in this system are realized in structure by selecting some noun function as element. There are two features in this system, [singular] and [plural], meaning this is the paradigm from which a choice is to be made. The feature [plural] is realized in structure by the root

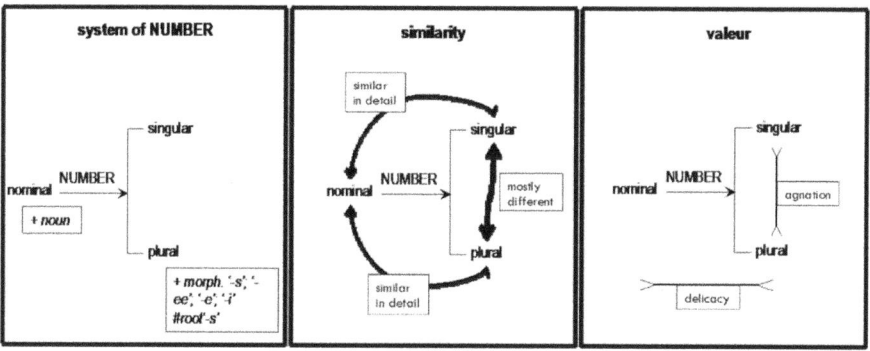

Figure 10.1 The system of NUMBER in English, similarity and valeur.

of a noun with a suffix of plurality, phonologically expressed as /s/ in the regular case (books), or /i:/ (teeth), /i/ (women) or /ai/ (mice) in the irregular case.

2.1 Quantifying valeur and its factors

The amount of valeur in a system can be found by counting the number of agnations and multiplying them by the number of delicacy levels in a system network. Agnation and delicacy also have factors of their own and these must also be taken into account. For all examples in this section, we will use the system of MODALITY: VALUE in English.

Agnation is determined by two factors: the number of features (represented by *fe*) and the number of contrasts (represented by *c*) between these features. Agnation is calculated as a product of its factors since they are proportional. The formula in (1) describes the relationship between agnation and its factors.

$$a = fe \times c \qquad (1)$$

When systems are joined together in a system network, agnation is calculated via the summation of each system in the network. The formula in (2) is very similar to that in (1). It shows the adding when a system has more agnations (i.e. $a_1 + a_2 + a_3 \ldots + a_n$), or

$$a = \sum_{i=1}^{n} fe_i \times c_i \qquad (2)$$

For example, MODALITY: VALUE in English has four features, in two systems forming a network. The system of VALUE has the features [median] and [outer]. The system of OUTER TYPE has the features [high] and [low]. There is a contrast between [median] and [outer]. There is also a contrast between [high] and [low] (see Figure 10.2).

By plugging these numbers into equation (2) we find that for the system of VALUE, agnation equals two features (median and outer) multiplied by one contrast (contrast between median and outer) or $2fe \times 1c$. For the system of OUTER TYPE, agnation equals

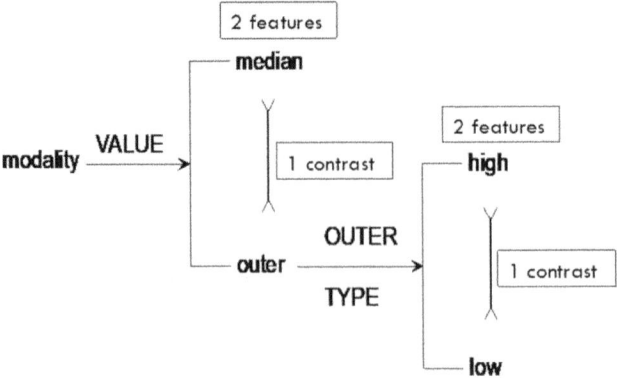

Figure 10.2 Agnation in the system of MODALITY: VALUE in English.

2 features (high and low) multiplied by one contrast (contrast between high and low); again $2fe \times 1c$. Agnations for VALUE and OUTER TYPE are added together, so $(2fe \times 1c)_{\text{VALUE}} + (2fe \times 1c)_{\text{OUTER TYPE}} = 4$.

$$a = \sum_{i=1}^{n} fe_i \times c_i = (2 \times 1) + (2 \times 1) = 4 \tag{3}$$

Delicacy is also determined by two factors: level (represented by l) and the number of choices that can be made (represented by e). The formula in (4) describes it is the product of these factors:

$$d = l \times e \tag{4}$$

In a system network, delicacy is totalled for each subsystem. Because choices are made at each level, then l will always equal 1.

$$d = \sum_{i=1}^{n} 1 \times e_i \tag{5}$$

For example, MODALITY: VALUE in English has two levels of delicacy. The first starts at the entry condition [modality] and goes up to the level of [median] and [outer]. The second level of delicacy starts at the now entry condition [outer] and goes up to the level of [high] and [low]. At the first level, only one choice can be made: either [median] or [outer]. At the second level, again there is only one choice, between [high] and [low] (see Figure 10.3).

By plugging these numbers into equation (5) we find that: for the system of VALUE, delicacy equals one level of delicacy multiplied by one choice, or $1l \times 1e$. For the system of OUTER TYPE, delicacy equals one level multiplied by one choice; which again is $1l \times 1e$. The delicacies for VALUE and OUTER TYPE are added together, so $(1l \times 1e)_{\text{VALUE}} + (1l \times 1e)_{\text{OUTER TYPE}} = 2$ delicacy.

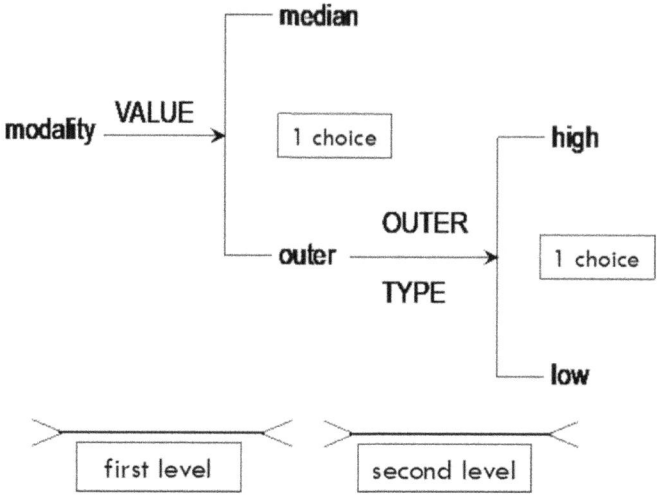

Figure 10.3 Delicacy in the system of MODALITY: VALUE in English.

$$d = \sum_{i=1}^{n} 1 \times e_i = (1 \times 1) + (1 \times 1) = 2 \tag{6}$$

Now we are in the position to calculate valeur. Valeur (represented by v) is a product of agnation (a) and delicacy (d) ($v = a \times d$). For a network of size n, valeur can be described as in formula (7) – which defines valeur as the total agnations multiplied by the total delicacies.

$$v = \sum_{i=1}^{n} a_i \times \sum_{i=1}^{n} d_i \tag{7}$$

The formula for valeur is important for translation because it tells us how much meaning a system can make. For example, in the system of MODALITY: VALUE in English agnation equals 4 and delicacy equals 2. By plugging the numbers into equation 7 we find that valeur is 8. Thus, v = 8 is the amount of meaning that MODALITY: VALUE can make in English. We can then examine how this feature is translated into other languages and compare the amount of meaning made in a translation.

$$v = \left[(2 \times 1) + (2 \times 1) \right]_{agnation} \times \left[(1 \times 1) + (1 \times 1) \right]_{delicacy} = 8 \tag{8}$$

We know that valeur is valuable because all systems can be compared in terms of the amount of valeur they make. From the calculations shown above, we can use meaning-making resources as our basic unit of language relations – both in comparison and translation. Since it is the fundamental property of meaning-making systems, valeur may be considered to be our minimal *tertium comparationis*.

3 Language relations: Variation, comparison, correspondence, equivalence and shift

In this section we use the calculations of valeur presented above and apply them to multilingual phenomena, focusing particularly on translation. If we consider systems as language organization, then comparisons may happen in different parts of the system: between features in a single system, between comparable systems in the two languages or even between different systems altogether. We will explore these relations and quantify them in terms of valeur (i.e. similar by this much ..., comparable by this much ..., equivalent by this much ...).

We treat language relations as forms of comparing meaning-making measured in valeurs. Because we are interested in language comparison and translation, we will describe variation, comparison, correspondence, shift and equivalence. For this section, as our examples, we will use the systems of MOOD: IMPERATIVE in French (Caffarel 2006) and MOOD: IMPERATIVE in Chilean Spanish (Quiroz 2013).

3.1 Variation

Variation is the language relation that captures behaviour of single systems in different environments. As a technique in controlled situations, it is used to compare features of the same system. Thus, it is an intra-system comparison.

The *tertium comparationis* for variation is valeur. The variation of features belonging to the same system is the amount of valeur that each feature has. We can calculate variation (represented by ω) between two features in a system by subtracting the valeur of one feature (v_0) from the valeur of the other (v_1). The formula in (9) describes the difference in valeur between two features; it is an important formula because it describes how we can use a common unit of meaning (v) to compare features.

$$\omega = v_1 - v_0 \tag{9}$$

The system of MOOD: IMPERATIVE in French may be used as an example (Figure 10.4).

If we need to compare, for instance, the feature [exclusive] to [singular] and [informal], we can do so by establishing their variation. The first step is to calculate their valeur.

$$v_{exclusive} = a_{exclusive} \times d_{exclusive} = (2 \times 1) \times (1 \times 1) = 2 \tag{10}$$

$$v_{singular} = a_{singular} \times d_{singular} = \big[(2 \times 1) + (2 \times 1)\big] \times \big[(1 \times 1) + (1 \times 1)\big] = 8 \tag{11}$$

$$v_{informal} = a_{inf} \times d_{inf} = \big[(2 \times 1) + (2 \times 1) + (2 \times 1)\big] \times \big[(1 \times 1) + (1 \times 1) + (1 \times 1)\big] = 18 \tag{12}$$

Then, we need to find the difference in valeur between features. This tells us the variation ω.

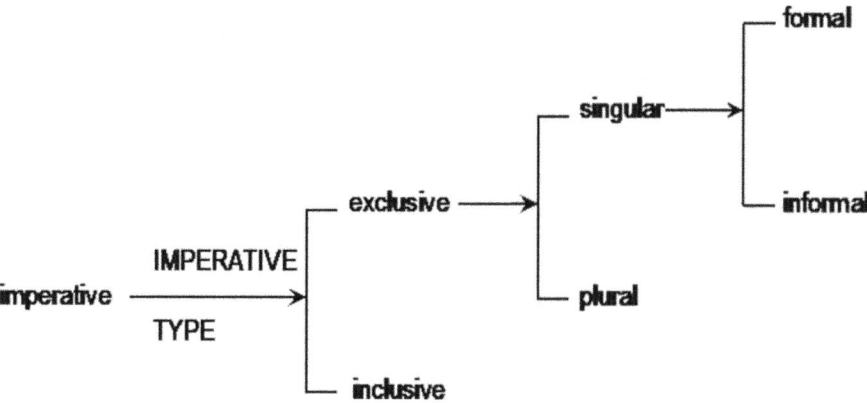

Figure 10.4 The system of MOOD: IMPERATIVE in French (Caffarel 2004: 93).

$$\omega = v_{singular} - v_{exclusive} = 8 - 2 = 6v \tag{13}$$

$$\omega = v_{informal} - v_{exclusive} = 18 - 2 = 16v \tag{14}$$

The comparison between features [exclusive] and [singular] means that the system of MOOD: IMPERATIVE deploys more systemic resources in the process of meaning-making for [singular] and this amounts to a variation of 6 valeurs for imperative. By the same token, the variation between [exclusive] and [informal] is 16.

Variation allows us to understand how each feature of a system is related to the entry condition, and how each feature is compared to others in the system. It is useful because it reveals the potential of meaning-making of each feature and how a system behaves (i.e. causes variation). Knowing this variation is important for translation because it can be motivated by the relationship between SL and TL.

3.2 Comparison

Comparison captures the behaviour of more than one system in different environments. As a technique, it is used for features which do not belong to the same system. It can be described as the difference in variation of different systems.

Valeur is a system-dependent measure and can be used as a *tertium comparationis* only if features have the same entry condition. It does not work directly as the *tertium* for comparison because a feature of a system cannot be directly compared with features in other systems when their valeur is given by agnation and delicacy relations which are particular to each individual system.

The minimal unit of meaning-making between different systems is precisely the potential systems have to make meaning. This potential can be measured by variation – or the amount of valeur between the entry condition and the features we are interested in comparing. Consequently, when features have different entry conditions, the *tertium comparationis* measure used is the variation between each of these features and their specific entry condition.

Comparison (represented by the small letter ψ) is calculated by finding the difference in variation of valeur between comparatives or features in a system (ω_0) and the variation in valeur between features in another system (ω_1). The formula in (15) describes how to compare features in different systems by finding the difference between the valeur of feature 1 in relation to its entry condition and the valeur of feature 2 in relation to its entry condition.

$$\psi = \omega_1 - \omega_0 \tag{15}$$

Consider the systems of MOOD: IMPERATIVE in French (see Figure 10.4) and Chilean Spanish (Figure 10.5) and compare, for example, the feature [informal] in French to [informal] in Chilean Spanish.

In order to compare, we need to take the following steps. First, we need to find the valeur for the features we want to compare. The valeur for [informal] in French is 18 (equation 12), and in Chilean Spanish is 39:

$$v_{inf} = a_{inf} \times d_{inf} = \left[(3 \times 3) + (2 \times 1) + (2 \times 1) \right] \times \left[(1 \times 1) + (1 \times 1) + (1 \times 1) \right] = 39 \tag{16}$$

Second, we need to find the variation between the comparatives and their entry condition – or how much variation in meaning-making there is for each MOOD: IMPERATIVE TYPE system in relation to the comparatives we want to compare.

$$\omega_{French} = v_{informal} - v_{imperative} = 8 - 0 = 18v \tag{17}$$

$$\omega_{Chilean} = v_{informal} = v_{imperative} = 39 - 0 = 39v \tag{18}$$

Finally, we can carry out their comparison through the difference in variation.

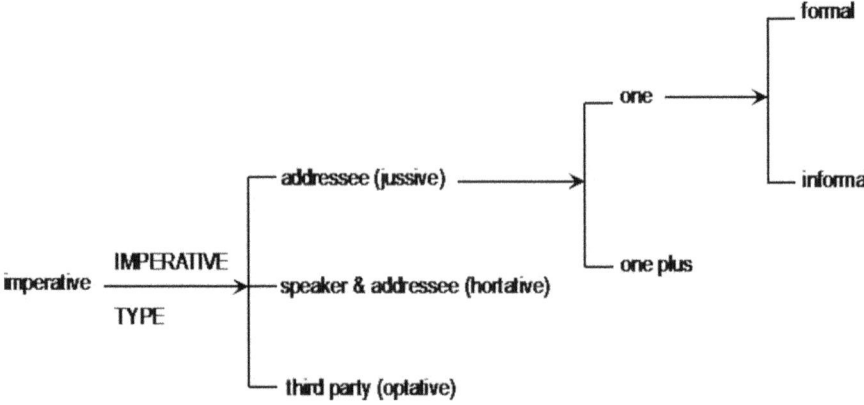

Figure 10.5 The system of MOOD: IMPERATIVE TYPE in Chilean Spanish (Quiroz 2013: 132).

$$\psi = \omega_{Chilean} - \omega_{French} = 39 - 18 = 21\nu \qquad (19)$$

Through these steps, any two systems may be compared. All systems again share the same property – namely, variation in valeur – which in turn is the *tertium*.

It is worth noting that comparison can potentially be carried out between any two systems.

However, in order to be of interest, comparisons need to be 'contextualized'. They have to go beyond the meaning-making process of individual systems to include their co-variation with other systems.

3.3 Correspondence: Correspondents and shifts

Correspondence is the relation describing contextualized comparisons. By 'contextualized' we mean comparing systems and their co-variations with other systems (i.e. the way systems pattern co-selections). We have established above that the comparison between features is based on similarity, meaning that features cannot be identical. Correspondence is only partial. Features, in turn, can sustain 'more correspondence' or 'less correspondence', depending on the amount of valeur of their comparison (ω). The comparison of features with more correspondence – that is, the amount of ω is relatively small – causes them to be correspondents. The comparison with less correspondence – that is, the amount of ω is relatively large – causes features to become shifts.

First described by Catford (1965), correspondents are defined as 'any [L2] category which can be said to occupy, as nearly as possible, the "same" place in the "economy" of the [L2] as the given [L1] category occupies in the [L1]' (p. 27). The 'economy of a language', in turn, is defined as the relationship between a system and its co-variance with respect to other systems.

Shifts are derived from the same language relation as correspondents, being also related to contextualized comparisons and encompassing both variation and comparison. Catford (1965) defined shifts as 'departures from formal correspondence in the process of going from the SL to the TL' (p. 73). Shifts,[1] consequently, happen when categories begin to gradually occupy more different places in the economy of a language.

The 'economy of a language' involves all systems of the language, which would be completely understood only through the language's full description. For practical purposes – since full descriptions are still not feasible – we can identify the semiotic address (Butt 2007) of our feature of interest and place it into a Whorf table of reactances (see Figure 10.6) to find systems that directly co-vary with the system of our feature.

3.3.1 *Whorf Table of Reactances*

The degree of interaction between systems in a network (reactances, Whorf 1987) can be used to map out the 'economy of a language' in relation to a particular feature. For each interaction (i.e. every time a feature of a system reacts to a feature from another system) a weight of $w = 1$ is added to the valeur of that feature. Correspondence (represented by'Φ') is described as

$$\Phi = \psi + w \qquad (20)$$

The formula in (18) is important because it describes the relationship between comparison (ψ) and the relevance (w) of this comparison to a translation investigation. A list of reactances assigned to each feature in a network is given by comparing them to a reactance table. Reactance tables were first developed by Whorf (1987) on co-variation in language description.

Table 10.1 is an example of a reactance table. The left-hand column 'locates' a feature in the system's architecture in terms of language dimensions, for example, axis. The mid-column details aspects of each dimension involved in the comparison of features, for example, in axis, the place of the feature in the system as well as its realizing structure. Finally, the right-hand column scores fe_1 in relation to their commonality to fe_0. Each commonality is scored zero and each difference is scored one. The total score tells us how apart features are. A score close to zero means similar features; conversely a score distancing from 'zero' means features are more different.

For example, if we compare fe_0 [imperative: inclusive] and fe_1 [imperative: exclusive] in the system of IMPERATIVE MOOD in French (see Figure 10.4) and use axis/system as our table of reactances we have (Table 10.2):

They have the same entry condition, but different levels of delicacy (exclusive has three levels). They are agnate. Reactances are different and can be probed for person, formality and so on. They co-select differently and the distribution is skewed towards exclusive. The difference in score is 4.

It is expected that no two features fe_0 and fe_1 will score exactly the same. Accordingly, correspondence between features is a matter of degree and can be placed in a cline. It depends first and foremost on the degree of similarity between the systems being related.

Features are correspondents (represented by the lower caseϕ) when the correspondence (represented by the upper case Φ) between features in different contextualized systems tends towards zero.

$$\phi\left(fe_0; fe_1\right) = \lim_{\Phi \to 0} \Phi \qquad (21)$$

Accordingly, features are shifts (represented by the lower case χ) when the limit of correspondence between them tends to move away from zero.

$$\chi\left(fe_0; fe_1\right) = \lim_{\Phi \to \infty} \Phi \qquad (22)$$

The formula in (19) states that the difference between the valeur, between two features, tends to zero when they are compared. This means that the features are very similar, because they make similar amounts of valeur. The formula in (20), however, shows that the difference in the amount of valeur between two features tends to increase.

Table 10.1 A table of reactances

Location			Commonality in features between fe_0 and fe_1	Score per system	
				yes	no
Stratification-instantiation matrix			global semiotic address	0	1
Function-rank matrix			local semiotic address	0	1
local	axis	System	entry condition	0	1
			level of delicacy	0	1
			agnations	0	1
			co-selections	0	1
			skewedness	0	1
		structure	structural function	0	1
			realization (inter-axial)	0	1
	Rank		Rank	0	1
			class	0	1
			pre-selection	0	1
global	Stratification		context	0	1
			semantics	0	1
			grammar	0	1
			phonology	0	1
	Instantiation		relative frequency	0	1
			register/genre generalization	0	1
			multilingual set	0	1
	Metafunction		interpersonal	0	1
			ideational	0	1
			textual	0	1
			conflation	0	1

Table 10.2 A table of reactances of 'axis/system' in French for [inclusive/exclusive]

Location			Commonality between fe_0 and fe_1	Score		
				Yes	No	
local	axis	system	entry condition	0	1	yes
			level of delicacy	0	1	no
			agnation	0	1	yes
			reactance	0	1	no
			co-selection	0	1	no
			skewedness	0	1	no
						Total 4

3.4 Equivalence

Equivalence is the language relation resulting from translation. Translation is a spontaneous phenomenon and can be mapped onto any formal language relation. This means that equivalence is not a controlled language relation and it can happen between comparatives, correspondents and shifts.

Single-language descriptions operate more directly with variation and comparison, since they are developed from the intra-systemic relations between any two systems. Typology and comparative linguistics operate more directly with correspondence, since they are interested in contextualized variation and comparison of systems within different languages. Translation as an object of study, differently, operates with all relations since all have the potential to establish equivalents.

Equivalence is established through the procedure of commutation as developed by Catford (1965). Commutables (represented by the lower case κ) are features which systematically replace one another. As a technique, commutation (represented by the upper case K) may be carried out between any two features irrespective of the number of languages involved. From the point of view of meaning-making, it is measured in valeurs made by commutables. If only one language is involved, commutation may be described as taking out a feature κ_0 and replacing it by its commutable κ_1:

$$K_{(0;1)} = -\kappa_0 + \kappa_1 \tag{23}$$

If we use the system of MOOD: IMPERATIVE in French as an example, by commuting [inclusive; v=2] and [informal; v=18] we have

$$K_{(inclusive, informal)} = -2 + 18 = 16 \tag{24}$$

Equation (24) is important because it describes what happens when a feature is replaced by another and how this replacement affects meaning. It shows that replacing [inclusive] by [informal] adds 16v to the meaning-making output of the operation. This provides important information to translation (especially Machine Translation) because such replacements happen all the time in translated texts.

Moreover, the intra-system commutation maps onto variation. This is expected, since variation is precisely the commutation between features in the same system. For translation, this may be relevant because it can track different choices in translation and how they affect the overall meaning-making process. Accordingly, commutation between different systems maps onto correspondence.

In any language comparison or typology, a commutable is a feature in L2 which systematically replaces a feature from the L1. Because it is closely related to correspondence Φ, the operation is carried out by commuting correspondences. Formula (25) shows that commutation is necessarily 'taking out' one correspondence and 'adding in' a different correspondence.

$$K_{(L1;L2)} = -\Phi_{L1} + \Phi_{L2} \tag{25}$$

For example, consider the parallel pair of clauses in BP and English *Vá pra casa, Olivia/Go home, Olivia* when it is replaced by *Dá pra vc ir pra casa, Olivia?/Could you go home, Olivia?* In terms of MOOD options, the [imperative] 'go' is commutable with the [interrogative/modality] 'could you go?' When these are compared, the correspondence of [imperative] needs to be 'taken out' in order for the correspondence of [interrogative/modality] to be 'added in'.

In translation, if the balance between 'taking out' and 'adding in' tends to zero, then it may reveal a closer relation between source and target languages in terms of the meanings they are making. However, a bigger difference may show organizational differences between languages.

Since correspondence is contextualized comparison 'ψ' between different systems, commutation brings all language relations together. The relations of comparison can be substituted in equation (23), and be described as

$$K_{(L1;L2)} = \left[\psi + w\right]_{L1} + \left[\psi + w\right]_{L2} = -\left[\omega_1 - \omega_0 + w\right]_{L1} + \left[\omega_1 - \omega_0 + w\right]_{L2} \qquad (26)$$

Equation (26) is plugging the variables of (14) into (23). It shows that commutation involves correspondence, comparison and variation, and that all these multilingual phenomena are related. This is what we mean when we say *translation is fundamental to any language comparison – it involves all language relations.*

If we use the systems of MOOD: IMPERATIVE in French and Spanish as an example, by commuting [informal French; v=18] and [informal Spanish; v=39 + w= 1] we have:

$$K_{(French;Spanish)} = -\left[18\right] + \left[39 + 1\right] = -\left[18 - 0 + 0\right] + \left[39 - 0 + 1\right] = 22v \qquad (27)$$

Equation (26) enables us to establish a definition of commutation when derived from systemic relations: commutation is the process of replacing the variation of corresponding systems in the L1 by the variation in corresponding systems in the L2.

In translation, commutation is an operation of equivalence observed between SL and TL and between ST and TT; accordingly 'commutables' are called 'equivalents'. An equivalent is a feature in the TT which replaces a feature from the ST. Equivalents can be related to one another as correspondents or shifts, since both are different aspects of correspondence.

As described above (equations 21 and 22; cf. Catford 1965) correspondents are features which conserve similar semiotic addresses and are formally related. Shifts are differently departures from formal correspondence. In broad terms, correspondents are 'expected correspondents' (i.e. limit to zero) and shifts are 'non-correspondents which break expectation' (i.e. limit away from zero).

When equivalence in translation (ε) is mapped onto correspondents, then an SL feature is translated by its correspondent TL feature, similar to the description in equation (25).

$$\varepsilon_{(SL;TL)} = -\Phi_{SL} + \Phi_{TL} \qquad (28)$$

Again using MOOD: IMPERATIVE in French and Spanish as an example, let's say the commuting [informal French; v=18] and [informal Spanish; v=39 + w= 1] are actually a translation. Then we'd have:

Table 10.3 Equivalents as correspondents and shifts

	SL	Equivalence	TL
Correspondents	feature x	$\Leftrightarrow$	feature x
Shifts	feature x	$\Leftrightarrow$	Ø
	Ø	$\Leftrightarrow$	feature y

$$\varepsilon = K_{(French;Spanish)} = -\left[18\right] + \left[39+1\right] = -\left[18-0+0\right] + \left[39-0+1\right] = 22v \qquad (29)$$

When equivalence is mapped onto shifts, an SL feature is translated by some 'non-correspondent'. In this case, we have an SL feature correspondent to Φ in the TL, and a TL feature correspondent to Φ in the SL.

Table 10.3 shows that equivalents as shifts cause the inclusion in the equation of these two empty correspondents – for SL, the feature x being translated and its empty correspondent; and for TL, the feature empty being translated and its correspondent translation y. In addition, equivalents as shifts work as a comparison between commutations of correspondents (x to Φ and Φ to y). For the description, both the empty correspondents and the comparison of commutations need to be included.

$$\varepsilon_{(x,y)} = K_{(x;\varnothing)} - K_{(\varnothing;y)} \qquad (28)$$

As a consequence, equivalence includes all language relations, including the operation of commutation as well.

$$\varepsilon_{(x;y)} = K_{(x;\varnothing)} - K_{(\varnothing;y)} = \left[-\Phi_{SL} + \Phi_{TL}\right]_x - \left[-\Phi_{SL} + \Phi_{TL}\right]_y \qquad (30)$$

For example, the translation of MOOD: IMPERATIVE in French and Spanish as [informal French; v=18] and [formal Spanish; v=39 + w= 1] we have:

$$\varepsilon_{(x;y)} = K_{(x;\varnothing)} - K_{(\varnothing;y)} = \left[-18_{SL} + 0_{TL}\right]_x - \left[-0_{SL} + 40_{TL}\right]_y = -58v \qquad (31)$$

Equation (31) shows that a negative valeur is found when a feature from SL is translated through shift, and a shift equivalent has a modular value always greater than any correspondent equivalent value.

Figure 10.6 presents a taxonomy of the language relations discussed above.

4 Case study: Interpersonal language relations in Brazilian Portuguese and English

The aim of this section is to show how we can operationalize variation, comparison, correspondence/shift and equivalence in a translation study. Here, we use quantities (calculations of valeur) to establish 'by how much' source and target language features can be related. Our focus will be the interpersonal grammar systems of MOOD, MODALITY, POLARITY and MODAL ASSESSMENT in Brazilian Portuguese (BP) [henceforth L1] and English [henceforth L2] and follow the systemic derivations presented above.

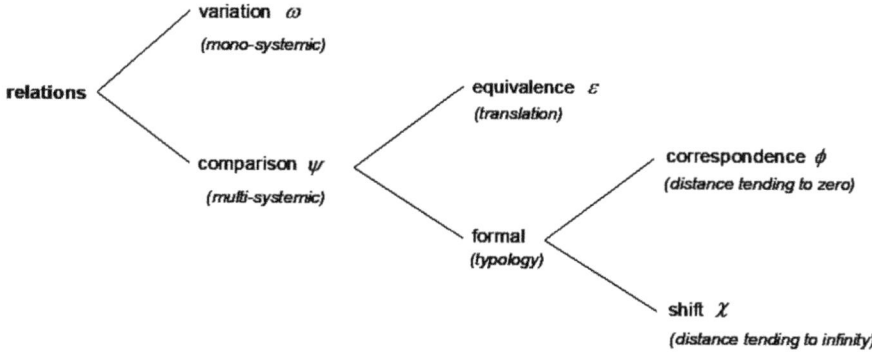

Figure 10.6 Taxonomy of language relations.

Table 10.4 The corpus

Subcorpora	Description	Tokens
1 L1	Audio transcription BP	290
2 L2	Audio transcription English	220
3 L1	Subtitles English	179
4 L2	Subtitles BP	197
5 bilingual parallel	Parallel L1-L2	460
6 bilingual parallel	Parallel L2-L1	417
7 comparable monolingual	A – BP	487
8 comparable monolingual	B – English	339

4.1 Methodology

(1) Corpus compilation

The corpus was compiled from texts that (a) established a representative translation relation in both directions and (b) demanded grammar work from interpersonal systems. Spoken dialogic texts with open negotiation (cf. Martin 1992) were collected. They are the transcriptions of an excerpt from the movie 'Os Normais' (excerpt 01:11:48 -> 01:13:04) and the TV Show 'The Middle' Season 1, Episode 4, excerpt 00:12:52 -> 00:13:53), including their translated subtitles. Spoken texts were STs and their subtitles were TTs. The texts were grouped into four monolingual subcorpora: two comparable monolingual subcorpora and two bilingual parallel subcorpora – STs and their translations (cf. Kenning 2010) (Table 10.4).

(2) Determining grammatical resources for analysis

2.1) MOOD, MODALITY, POLARITY and MODAL EVALUATION systems were selected as units of analysis. These were chosen according to existing descriptions of

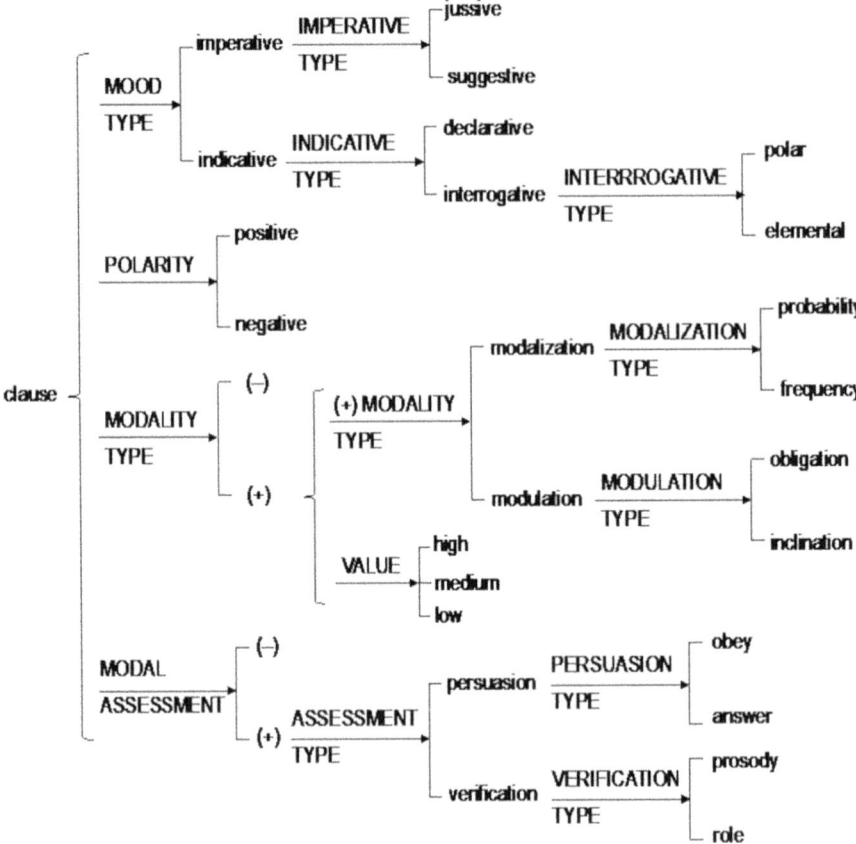

Figure 10.7 Interpersonal grammar systems for L1 and L2.

interpersonal grammar for English and BP (Halliday and Matthiessen 2014; Figueredo 2011).

2.2) We carried out a comparison between all features of BP and English – using equation (13) $\psi = \omega_1 - \omega_0$. This comparison formed the basis of a generalized correspondence between systems – using equation (20) $\Phi = \psi + w$. A generalized system network for corresponding BP and English was drawn (Figure 10.7).

2.3) We used a Whorf Table to establish correspondence between features and contextualize them in L1 and L2 (Table 10.5).

2.4) This correspondence was then redefined for our study through the mapping of equivalence on correspondence – using equations (28) $\varepsilon_{(SL;TL)} = -\Phi_{SL} + \Phi_{TL}$ and (30) $\varepsilon_{(x;y)} = K_{(x;\varnothing)} - K_{(\varnothing;y)}$. Grammar analysis was carried out and features were identified in the corpus.

Table 10.5 Levels of analysis

				Valeur in BP	Valeur in English	ϕ (fe$_{BP}$; fe$_{ENG}$)
mood	indicative	declarative		4	4	0
		interrogative	polar	6	6	0
			wh-	6	6	0
	imperative	jussive		4	4	0
		suggestive		4	4	0
modality	minus modality			2	2	0
	modalization	frequency / value		13	13	0
		probability / value		13	13	0
	modulation	obligation / value		13	13	0
		inclination / value		13	13	0
polarity	positive			2	2	0
	negative			2	2	0
modal assessment	minus assess.			2	2	0
	persuasion	obedience		6	6	0
		answer		6	6	0
	verification	prosody		6	6	0
		speaker role		6	6	0

4.3 Equivalence and correspondence in the multilingual environment

Each language was analysed separately. The number of occurrences is shown in Table 10.6.

Table 10.6 shows that L1 deploys MOOD, MODALITY, POLARITY and EVALUATION. MOOD selected all features of [indicative] in the corpus, but [imperative] has only one level of delicacy for [jussive]. In MODALITY, [probability] and [obligation] were deployed. VALUE selected [medium] and [high]. POLARITY was [positive] and [negative]. In MODAL ASSESSMENT, [verification] was selected. The variation ω between 'potential' BP (found in the description of BP language) and L1 data (found in the corpus) can be seen in Figure 10.8.

The amount of valeur made by variants is seen in Table 10.7.

In L2, MOOD displays [indicative] and only [jussive] for [imperative]. MODALITY is restricted to [obligation]. VALUE deploys [medium] and [high]. POLARITY is [positive] and [negative]. The variation ω between L2 and 'potential English' is shown in Figure 10.9.

The amount of valeur made by variants is seen in Table 10.8.

By comparing the findings shown in Tables 10.7 and 10.8, we can establish comparison ψ between L1 and L2 (Table 10.9).

The correspondence is made by the intersection between L1 and L2 – that is, when the variation in valeur of features in L1 and L2 tend to zero. The mapping of equivalents onto correspondents was found in the corpus (49 occurrences); they were established through the calculations of commutation of correspondence (equation 28).

Table 10.6 L1 and L2 features in the corpus

Features			L_1	L_2	Examples
Mood	indicative	declarative	50	41	– Já nos casamos. – We are already married.
		interrogative	15	16	– Como é que eu vou saber? – How would I know?
	imperative	Jussive	2	2	– Vá pra casa, Olivia. – Go home, Olivia.
		suggestive	---	---	---
Modality	modalization	Frequency	---	---	---
		probability	1	---	– Não, claro que não.
	modulation	Obligation	9	8	– Bem, eu acho que terá de deixar. - Wow, I think you have to.
		inclination	---	---	---
	value	Low	---	---	---
		Medium	7	7	– O Brick pode sair para brincar? – Can Brick come out and play?
		High	3	1	– Bem, eu acho que terá de deixar. – Wow, I think you have to.
Polarity	positive		47	45	– Já nos casamos. – We are already married.
	negative		20	14	– Eu não sei nem do que que eu tô sendo acusado. – I don't even know what I'm being accused of.
Modal assessment	persuasion	Obedience	---	---	---
		answer	---	---	---
	verification	prosody	1	---	– Ué, as pessoas fazem coisas loucas
		speaker role	6	---	– as pessoas fazem coisas loucas, né?

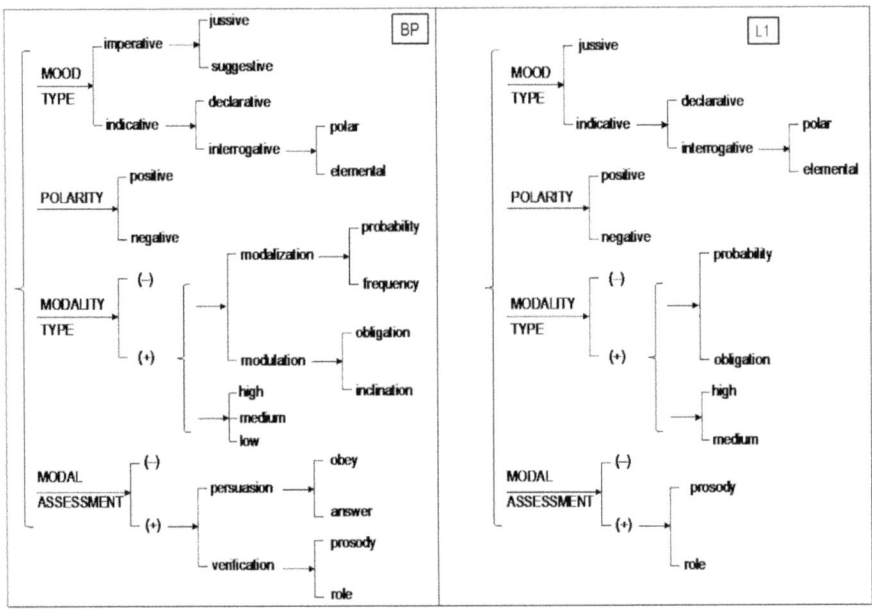

Figure 10.8 Variation (ω) BP and L1.

Table 10.7 Amount of valeur in variation (ω) BP and L1

				BP	L1	$\omega = v_{L1} - v_{BP}$
mood	indicative	declarative		4	4	0
		interrogative	polar	6	6	0
			wh-	6	6	0
	imperative	jussive		4	2	-2
		suggestive		4	0	-4
modality	minus modality			2	2	0
	modalization	frequency / value		13	0	-13
		probability / value		13	4	-9
	modulation	obligation / value		13	4	-9
		inclination / value		13	0	-13
polarity	positive			2	2	0
	negative			2	2	0
modal assessment	minus assess.			2	2	0
	persuasion	obedience		6	0	-6
		answer		6	0	-6
	verification	prosody		6	4	-2
		speaker role		6	4	-2

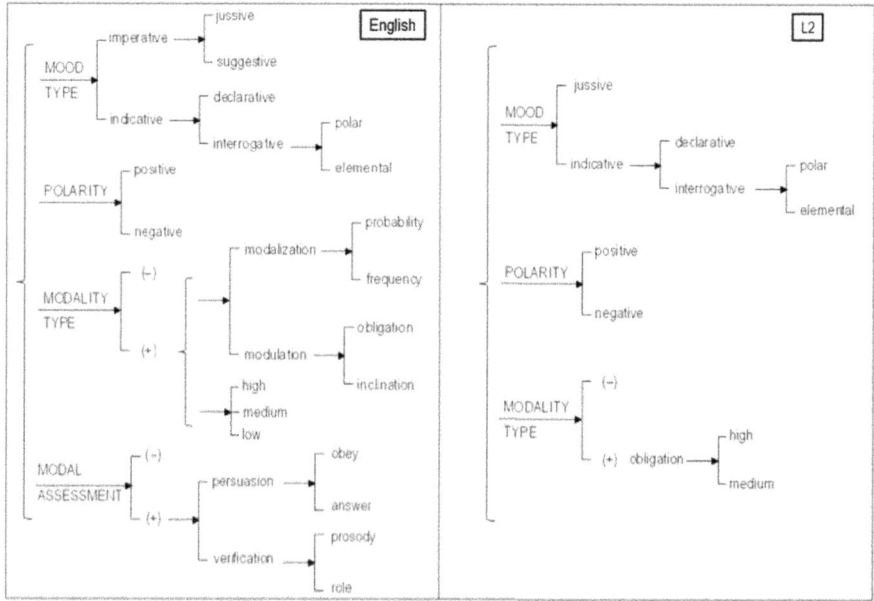

Figure 10.9 Variation (ω) English and L2.

Table 10.8 Amount of valeur in variation (ω) English and L2

				English	L2	$\omega = v_{L2} - v_{ENG}$
Mood	indicative	declarative		4	4	0
		interrogative	polar	6	6	0
			wh-	6	6	0
	imperative	jussive		4	2	−2
		suggestive		4	0	−4
Modality	minus modality			2	2	0
	modalization	frequency / value		13	0	−13
		probability / value		13	0	−13
	modulation	obligation / value		13	4	−9
		inclination / value		13	0	−13
Polarity	positive			2	2	0
	negative			2	2	0
Modal assessment	minus assess.			2	2	0
	persuasion	Obedience		6	0	−6
		Answer		6	0	−6
	verification	Prosody		6	0	−6
		speaker role		6	0	−6

Table 10.9 Amount of valeur in comparison (ψ) L1 and L2

				L1	L2	$\psi = \omega_{L1} - \omega_{L2}$
Mood	indicative	Declarative		4	4	0
		interrogative	polar	6	6	0
			wh-	6	6	0
	imperative	Jussive		2	2	0
		Suggestive		0	0	0
Modality	minus modal.			2	2	0
	modalization	frequency / value		0	0	0
		probability / value		4	0	4
	modulation	obligation / value		4	4	0
		inclination / value		0	0	0
Polarity	positive			2	2	0
	negative			2	2	0
Modal assessment	minus assess.			2	2	0
	persuasion	Obedience		0	0	0
		Answer		0	0	0
	verification	Prosody		4	0	4
		speaker role		4	0	4
Total Variation in Valeur				42	30	12

Table 10.10 Equivalence and correspondence between L1 and L2 relative to BP and English

Equivalence	Correspondence		Occurrences
Yes	correspondent	$\varepsilon_{(SL;TL)} = -\Phi_{SL} + \Phi_{TL}$	49
Yes	shift	$\varepsilon_{(x;y)} = K_{(x;\varnothing)} - K_{(\varnothing;y)}$	11
No	yes		0
No	no		5

Table 10.11 Examples of equivalents and shifts

Shift	L_1	L_2
(L_1) *role* $\Leftrightarrow \varnothing$ (L_2)	Ah, sei lá, Vani. Como é que eu vou saber?	How would I know?
(L_1) *jussiv.* $\Leftrightarrow$ *polar* (L_2)	Veja bem o nível de paranoia ...	You see the level of paranoia?
(L_1) *decl.* $\Leftrightarrow$ *polar* (L_2)	Cê trouxe aquela mulher aqui, Sérgio?	You brought that girl in here!
(L_1) *prosody* $\Leftrightarrow \varnothing$ (L_2)	Ah, não trouxe no seu quarto, ela ficou o tempo todo na sala.	Was she in the living room the whole time?
(L_1) *verification* $\Leftrightarrow \varnothing$ (L_2)	Ué, as pessoas fazem coisas loucas, né?	People do crazy stuff.

Some equivalents were mapped onto shifts (11 occurrences); these were calculated through the commutation of 'non-correspondents' (equation 30).

We can also investigate the equivalence between L1 and L2 relatively to the possibilities of correspondence between 'potential' BP and 'potential' English, having equivalence as a tool to identify the resources shared by the languages (Tables 10.10 and 10.11 for examples).

5 Final remarks

We have chosen here to privilege the systemic organization of languages, and thus derive the relations between them from the dimension of system. As a result, the systemic property of valeur was used. The calculation of valeur made the relationship between intra- or inter-systemic options possible.

We then established the relations of

- variation – difference in valeur between features of the same system; comparison – difference in variation of valeur between features of different systems;
- and correspondence (correspondents and shifts) – the comparison of features contextualized through the reactances.
- equivalence in translation – the difference in valeur of commutation between correspondents – allows us to observe how these relations happen in a multilingual environment.

The multilingual environment modelled here focused on the interpersonal grammatical resources of the clause. It established which features are common or distinct in each system. It also described the subsets relating both to the languages and the features common to them. The grammatical behaviour of the linguistic relations, in turn, was described as a variation of language use because it can only be investigated when the multilingual environment is compared to the language as a whole.

Translation was used as a tool for comparing languages: it focuses on the variation generated in each multilingual environment – or the role each language plays in creating the meanings of a single text – as opposed to the assumption that languages as a whole can be compared through universal categories.

Note

1. It is worth noting that Catford (1965) uses the term 'correspondence' for the phenomenon and 'correspondent' for the category. But Catford uses 'shifts' for the phenomenon and possibly the category. In this chapter, we are using the terminology somewhat differently in order to capture the rationale we have been developing so far. 'Correspondence' is the phenomenon. 'Correspondent' and 'shift' are categories and express a high or low degree of correspondence, respectively. The degree of correspondence is calculated from the variation in the amount of valeur in the comparison.

References

Barros, A. (2020), *Influência Linguística Cruzada na Perspectiva da Produção Multilíngue* [*Cross-linguistic Influence in the Perspective of Multilingual Acquisition*] Programa de Pós-Graduação em Letras, Universidade Federal de Ouro Preto, Mariana, Departamento de Letras.

Butt, D. (2007), 'Method and Imagination in Halliday's Science of Linguistics', in R. Hasan, C. M. I. M. Matthiessen and J. Webster (eds), *Continuing Discourse on Language, Volume 1*, 81–116, London: Equinox.

Caffarel, A. (2006), *A Systemic Functional Approach to Grammar of French: From Grammar to Discourse*, London: Continuum.

Caffarel, A., Martin, J. and Matthiessen, C. (eds) (2004), *Language Typology: A Functional Perspective*, Amsterdam: John Benjamins.

Catford, J. (1965), *A Linguistic Theory of Translation: An Essay in Applied Linguistics*, Oxford: Oxford University Press.

Dąbrowska, E. (2015), 'What Exactly Is Universal Grammar, and Has Anyone Seen It?' *Frontiers in Psychology* 6.

Ellis, J. (1966), *Towards a General Comparative Linguistics*, The Hague: Mouton.

Figueredo, G. (2011), *Introdução ao Perfil Metafuncional do Português Brasileiro: Contribuições para os Estudos Multilíngues*, Tese – Programa de Pós-Graduação em Estudos Linguísticos, Faculdade de Letras, Universidade Federal de Minas Gerais, Belo Horizonte.

Gleason, H. (1965), *Linguistics and English Grammar*, New York: Holt, Rinehart & Winston.

Halliday, M. A. K. (1984), On the Ineffability of Grammatical Categories', in A. Manning, P. Martin and K. McCalla (eds), *The Tenth LACUS Forum 5 1983*, 3–18, Columbia: Hornbeam Press.

Halliday, M. A. K. (2002), *On Grammar*, London: Continuum.

Halliday, M. A. K., and Matthiessen, C. M. I. M. (2014), *An Introduction to Functional Grammar*, 4th edn, London: Routledge.

Halliday, M. A. K, McIntosh, A. and Strevens, P. (1964), *The Linguist Sciences and Language Teaching*. London: Longmans.

Hatim, B. (2009), 'Translating Text in Context', in J. Munday (ed.), *The Routledge Companion to Translation Studies*, 36–53, London: Routledge.

Hatim, B., and Mason, I. (1990), *Discourse and the Translator*, London: Longman.

Hatim, B., and Munday, J. (2019), *Translation: An Advanced Resource Book*, London: Routledge.

Kenning, M. (2010), 'What Are Parallel and Comparable Corpora and How Can We Use Them?' in A. Keene and M. Mccarthy (eds), *The Routledge Handbook of Corpus Linguistics*, 487–500, Madison: Routledge.

Krzeszowski, T. (1990), *Contrasting Languages: The Scope of Contrastive Linguistics*, Berlin: Mouton de Gruyter.

Martin, J. R. and Cruz, P. (2018). 'Interpersonal Grammar of Tagalog: A Systemic Functional Perspective', *Functions of Language* 25(1): 54–96.

Martin, J. R., Zhu, Y. S. and Wang, P. (2013), *Systemic Functional Grammar: A Next Step into the Theory – Axial Relations*, Beijing: Higher Education Press.

Matthiessen, C. M. I. M. (2001), 'The Environments of Translation', in E. Steiner and C. Yallop (eds), *Exploring Translation and Multilingual Text Production: Beyond Content*, 41–124, Berlin: Mouton de Gruyter.

Matthiessen, C. M. I. M. (2004), 'Descriptive Motifs and Generalizations', in A. Caffarel, J. R. Martin and C. M. I. M. Matthiessen (eds), *Language Typology: A Functional Perspective*, 41–123, Amsterdam: John Benjamins.

Matthiessen, C. M. I. M., Teruya, K. and Wu, C. (2008), 'Multilingual Studies as a Multi-dimensional Space of Interconnected Language Studies', in J. Webster (ed.), *Meaning in Context: Implementing Intelligent Applications of Language Studies*, 146–220, London: Continuum.

Munday, J. (2004), 'A Comparative Analysis of Evaluation in Spanish and English World Cup Reports', *Revista Canaria de Estudios Ingleses* 49: 117–33.

Munday, J. (2015), 'Engagement and Graduation Resources as Markers of Translator/ interpreter Positioning', *Target* 27 (3): 406–12.

Quiroz, B. (2013), 'The Interpersonal and Experiential Grammar of Chilean Spanish: Towards a Principled Systemic-functional Description Based on Axial Argumentation', PhD Dissertation, University of Sydney, Sydney, Australia.

Saussure, F. (1966), *Course in General Linguistics*, New York: McGraw-Hill.

Steiner, E. (2000), 'Translation Evaluation – Some Methodological Questions Arising from the German Translation of Goldhagen's 'Hitler's Willing Executioners', in E. Ventola (ed.), *Discourse and Community. Doing Functional Linguistics*, 291–307, Tubingen: Günter Narr Verlag.

Steiner, E., and Teich, E. (2004), 'Metafunctional profile of German'. In A. Caffarel, J. Martin, C. Matthiessen (eds), *Language Typology: A Functional Perspective*. Amsterdam: John Benjamins.

Steiner, E., and Yallop, C. (eds) (2001), *Exploring Translation and Multilingual Text Production: Beyond Content*, Berlin: Mouton de Gruyter.

Teich, E. (1999), 'Contrastive Linguistics and Translation Studies Revisited', in A. Gil (ed.), *Modelle der Translation: Grundlagen fur Methodik, Bewertung, Computermodellierung*, 187–210, Frankfurt am Main: Lang.

Teich, E. (2003), *Cross-linguistic Variation in System and Text: A Methodology for the Investigation of Translations and Comparable Texts*, Berlin: Mouton de Gruyter.

Teruya, K. (2004), 'Metafunctional Profile of the Grammar of Japanese', in A. Caffarel, J. R. Martin and C. M. I. M. Matthiessen (eds), *Language Typology: A Functional Perspective*, 185–254, Amsterdam: John Benjamins.

Teruya, K. *A Systemic Functional Grammar of Japanese*, London: Continuum, 2007.

Wang, P. (2020) Axial Argumentation and Cryptogrammar in Interpersonal Grammar: A Case Study of Classical Tibetan MOOD', in J. R. Martin, Y. J. Doran and G. Figueredo (eds), *Systemic Functional Language Description: making meaning matter*, 73–101, New York: Routledge.

Whorf, B. (1987), *Language, Thought, and Reality*, Cambridge, MA: MIT Press.

Appendix

English Translation for the Arabic Scripts

Example 1

a. My father/ forced/ me/ to depart.
b. It/ was/ my father/ who/ made/ me/ leave/ you.
c. Papa/ was/ the one/ who/ forced/ me/ to desert/ you.
d. My papa/ was/ the one/ who/ made/ me/ to leave/ you.

Example 2

a. His cheeks/ were covered/ by the dark ulcers/ caused by/ the harmless skin cancer/ which/ is/ the fruit/ of the reflection of the sun/ on the page of water/ in the tropic areas.
b. Dark pimples/ appeared/ on his cheeks/ from the benevolent skin cancer/ caused from/ the reflection of the sun/ on the sea water/ in this tropic area.
c. And/ on his cheeks/ brown blotches/ that/ are/ a kind of skin cancer/ which/ the sun/ brought/ because of/ its reflection/ on the sea/ in that tropic area.
d. The brown blotches/ of the benevolent skin cancer/ spread/ on his cheeks/ which/ the sun/ brings/ from its reflection/ on the tropic sea.

Example 3

a. And/ it/ made/ the boy/ sad/ to see/ the old man/ come/ each day/ with a skiff/ empty.
b. In the end of each day/ the boy/ feels/ sad/ when/ he/ sees/ his educator/ come/ empty-handed.
c. The agony of sadness/ touched/ the liver of the boy/ when/ he/ sees/ the old man/ come/ each day/ with his skiff/ empty.
d. The sadness/ was/ overrunning/ the heart of the boy/ when/ he/ sees/ the old man/ coming/ to the shore/ each day/ zero-handed.

Example 4

The initial exam

They/ walked/ on the road/ together/ to the old man/ shack/ and/ went/ in an open road/ to the ancient man (the mister)/ the mast with the sail/ in (wrapped) against his hands/ and/ put/ the boy/ the square and other equipment/ beside it/ the mast/ was not/ nearly/ as long as/ it/ came/ from one room/ from shack to shack/ from shields/ although/ difficult/ from royal palms/ which/ are called/ blueness of the bird/ and/ there/ was/ a bed/ a chair for one table/ a place/ on the sandy floor/ to cook/ the food/ with charcoal.

The final exam

The old man and the boy/ sat/ on the terrace. Many of the fishermen/ made fun/ of the old man/ and/ he/ was not/ angry. Others of the fishermen/ looked/ at him/ and/ felt/ sad. But/ they/ did not show/ that/ and/ spoke/ politely/ about the current and the depths/ which/ they/ drifted/ their lines to/ and/ the weather/ was/ steady/ and/ at what/ they/ were looking. There/ were/ the successful fishermen/ and/ they/ butchered/ their marline fish/ and/ carried/ it/ laid full length/ across two planks/ with two men staggering/ at the end of each plank/ to the fish house/ where/ they/ wait for/ the ice truck/ to carry/ it/ to a shop/ in Havana.

Index

Lightning Source UK Ltd.
Milton Keynes UK
UKHW022152180521
383950UK00003B/162